BRITI
MURDER

A Compendium
1901–2000

William Wright

AMBERLEY

Journalist William Wright is the former chairman of the Victorian Military History Society. He has had many articles published in journals such as *Soldiers of the Queen*. He is the author of five books, amongst them *Fighting Generals of the Victorian Age* and for Amberley, *A British Lion in Zululand: Sir Garnet Wolseley in South Africa* and *Manipur Mischief: Rebellion, Scandal and the Dark Side of the Raj, 1891*.

Praise for William Wright's *A British Lion in Zululand*:

'Excellent... Wright's description of battles is masterly. The detail never gets in the way of the excitement and a feeling of "being there".' (*Pennant*)

First published 2019

Amberley Publishing
The Hill, Stroud
Gloucestershire, GL5 4EP

www.amberley-books.com

British Library Cataloguing in Publication Data.
A catalogue record for this book is available from the British Library.

ISBN 978 1 4456 8724 7 (paperback)
ISBN 978 1 4456 8725 4 (ebook)

Typeset in 10.5pt on 13pt Sabon.
Typesetting and Origination by Amberley Publishing.
Printed in the UK.

Contents

Introduction

In the winter of 2015/16 the Museum of London, in conjunction with Scotland Yard, staged an exhibition of some of the Metropolitan Police's notorious exhibits from its justly famous 'Black Museum'. Like many curious private citizens wanting a once-in-a-lifetime chance to see some of these things close up, I went along one bleak December morning. It was a weekday but even at opening time there was a queue of people of all ages. Within an hour the exhibition rooms were filling up and by the time I left the place was buzzing.

Two things struck me; first, the very ordinariness of the visitors who seemed to range from well-dressed pensioners to office workers, all of them seemingly fascinated by murder. The second thing was the ordinariness of some exhibits which, over the years, have developed almost a legendary status. The trunk, for instance, in which John Robinson had disposed of Minnie Bonati and which he had deposited at Charing Cross left luggage office seemed, on inspection, to be so delicate a thing that it was hard to believe it once held a corpse. Neville Heath's notorious whip with the diamond pattern turns out to be a remarkably short and shoddy-looking little item. Did it really inflict so much pain and leave its marks on a dead woman's skin? Worst of all, perhaps the ultimate horror on show, was a small and insignificant-looking tin opener, slightly rusted. So small, so ordinary, and yet the instrument used by the Blackout Ripper, Gordon Cummins, to gut some of his victims.

Preparing this book for publication, I debated with a friend the photographs of murderers. She was of the opinion that there was something in their eyes that spoke of dark deeds and unstable minds. While some killers, such as John Straffen or Patrick Mackay, certainly seem to betray those psychological traits, others such as Patrick Mahon,

Norman Thorne, and Ruth Ellis smile out from their photographs as seemingly normal people. Do murderers fascinate and repel us because they are different from the rest of society – or is it that in most cases we and they are horribly similar? Take Peter Allen, for example, one of the last two men to hang in Britain. He was poor, a weak man, but not inherently evil. Wanting to give his wife and child a better life he agreed to go on a robbery to try to steal enough money to lay a deposit on a house. This pathetic act led him to the scaffold.

Odd facts abound, one of which is that killers seem to like their pets, especially dogs, far more than the human race: John Christie's last act on leaving the charnel house at 10 Rillington Place was to have his beloved old dog humanely put to sleep; Haigh worshipped an animal he had acquired from one of the men he had dissolved in acid; Dennis Nilsen killed and dismembered at least 13 young men while his beloved mongrel, 'Bleep', watched and stayed true to its master; even that Essex rogue Samuel Dougal gave a home to his fiancée's spaniel, 'Jacko', after having neatly shot its mistress and stuffed her body in a drainage ditch.

George Orwell wrote a famous essay, 'Decline of the English Murder', which appeared in the Socialist weekly *Tribune* on 15 February 1946. He described how a typical family might enjoy a Sunday lunch of roast pork, apple sauce and suet pudding before father sat in his armchair, opened the *News of the World,* and relaxed with the details of the latest murder trial. Orwell viewed the 1944 Karl Hulten 'Cleft Chin Murder' case in which a young American and his British girlfriend had committed a 'thrill killing' as banal; he lamented the great 'classics' such as Seddon, Crippen, Smith and Armstrong (all in this book). He thought such crimes revealed intense hatreds and loves, murders worthy of a novel. Modern murder, by 1946, Orwell felt was 'meaningless'. In my opinion Orwell missed a major point or two; there is no such thing as a 'meaningless' murder since every crime reveals something about the culprit and the victim. Any real study of Neville Heath, John Haigh or John Christie – three of the most notorious psychopaths of the post-war years – reveals fascinating and, in Heath's case especially, tragic stories. These men and their crimes have over the years become legendary. Even the Cleft Chin Murder story derided by Orwell has been turned into a motion picture.

This book features 119 killers and some 500 victims. Its aim is to retell the story of 20th-century British murder by examining one case per year. The cases have been chosen quite arbitrarily and any other writer might turn up another 100 different stories. Notorious murderers such as Crippen or Haigh find equal space with much lesser known but also fascinating killers such as Rhoda Willis, last of the baby farmers, or Albert Walker, who almost got away with the 'perfect murder'. There are stories of those – dubbed killers – who may have been innocent (Armstrong, Thorne) and those who most decidedly were not (Smith, Rose West). The century began without even fingerprinting skills but in the past 40 years it seems every year some new advance is made in forensic science so that it becomes harder and harder to get away with murder – and yet people still think they can outwit the law. The last entry is in some ways the worst: Dr Harold Shipman, a bearded egotist who would have been a great companion for Drs Palmer, Pritchard and Lamson in the 19th century, is believed to have murdered as many as 284 persons in his medical career. Shipman used poison, the ancient tool of his guild, and he also ended his life by hanging, a supreme irony given that judicial executions stopped on 13 August 1964.

A list of sources is given at the end of the book. These include suggestions for further reading on many of these cases. In dealing with so many facts and dates a book can incorporate errors. Sometimes sources disagree on a certain point of information. I have tried to be as accurate as possible but apologise for any errors that may accidentally be in the text. Generally, I have tried to adopt the approach of Gordon Honeycombe and treat each case impartially and without hyperbole. Thanks go to my editor, Shaun Barrington, for his support, to my assistant, Krisztina Elias, and Dean Barker, who carefully photographed the rogues' gallery. The book had a long gestation; I conceived it back in the 1980s and began work on it several years ago. My simple hope is that real-crime enthusiasts enjoy it. A companion volume, *The Gallows Brood*, is now in preparation on British murder 1801–1900.

William Wright
Budapest

1901–1910

It was the long hot summer of the Edwardian age, although for the first 22 days it belonged to the fast-failing Queen Victoria. Britons were proud of their achievements and also of their Empire, though lads were fighting and dying in a war in South Africa when the decade started. Britain was a land of huge contrasts between rich and poor, countryman and town dweller.

*The Criminal Law Evidence Act of 1898 now allowed any person on a criminal charge to give evidence in his or her behalf. Several of those on trial for their lives at the start of the century, such as Bennett (**1901**), still chose not to go into the dock. The doctor and the chaplain were beginning to be established prison officials. Britain in 1901 had 46,800 policemen and 243 constabularies. When Newgate Prison was demolished and the new Old Bailey built on its site a red flag was no longer used to denote a hanging. Instead, a bell was tolled. In 1903 there were 27 people hanged, the highest figure in 70 years. During the decade some 3,031 persons stood trial for murder, attempted murder or manslaughter. Forensic science had barely begun to play a role but a major step took place when the Stratton Brothers were executed as a result of fingerprint evidence (**1905**). A humane advance occurred in 1908 when the Criminal Justice Amendment Act banned the execution of persons younger than 16 years of age.*

1901 Murder on the Sands: Herbert John Bennett

Great Yarmouth has long been noted for its bracing Norfolk air, fine promenades and expansive sands. Charles Dickens visited in 1841, staying at the Royal Hotel overlooking South Beach, an area of dunes and marram grass much favoured by families during the day and courting couples at night.

It was here, about 6am, on the morning of Sunday, 23 September 1900, that 14-year-old John Norton, a lad whose job it was to take care of bathing machines in which people dressed and undressed on the beach, was on his way to work when in a sandy hollow he discovered the body of a young woman lying on her back, legs apart, stiffened hands clutching the sands. Her skirts were pulled up to the knees, slightly bloodstained bloomers were around her ankles, sand churned about and over the clothes suggesting a desperate struggle. The woman's purple face showed cause of death – a mohair bootlace was wound tightly round her throat, tied in first a reef knot and then a granny knot.

Police Surgeon Thomas Lettis concluded that the woman had been dead about six hours. The bootlace, it was discovered, was not new and had been mended with a second reef knot at the back of the woman's neck. Reef knots were uncommon in those pre-scouting days; they were mainly used by fishermen. Some of the dead woman's clothes bore the laundry mark '599'.

It was soon discovered that the victim was a 'Mrs Hood' who had been staying for a week at a lodging house in the town. She claimed to have come from York, but had received a letter, recalled her landlady, marked Woolwich. Despite extensive press coverage, the trail seemed to go cold. After several adjournments, an inquest concluded on 29 October with a verdict that a woman unknown had been murdered by a man unknown.

Chief Inspector Alfred Leach of Scotland Yard had by now taken over the investigation from Norfolk constabulary. Described as 'austere, taciturn, painstaking', Leach was a resourceful detective who usually got his man; he believed the key to cracking the murder lay with the '599' laundry mark. At the same time he decided to check on all 'Mr and Mrs Hoods' who had taken passage to South Africa in the past year since the landlady recalled her lodger saying she had recently made such a trip. These careful investigations gradually wove a net around 21-year-old Herbert Bennett who, it transpired, was the husband of the murdered woman – his wife, Mary Jane Bennett.

Handsome in his way, with a thin moustache waxed at the ends (being an attempt to make him look older than he was), Bennett, the son of a cement works foreman from Gravesend, had tried various occupations yet he never seemed short of money. He lived, it seemed, on the edge of the law, scamming people for fake violins, carrying out insurance frauds, was perhaps involved in some shady blackmail plots and, in view of his visit to Cape Town that had lasted barely five days followed by a new job at Woolwich Arsenal on his return, there was the possibility that he had been spying for the Boers (the farmers of Dutch extraction, then engaged in a bitter war against the British in South Africa). Mary Bennett, it turned out, was no shrinking violet either, but had been complicit in several of her husband's schemes.

Relations between the couple had turned cold after their return from South Africa. The pair had moved apart, Mary taking with her their two-year-old daughter. Herbert now wooed and apparently fell in love with a young parlour-maid named Alice Meadows. He told her nothing about his family and even gave Alice an engagement ring. During the fine summer of 1900 he took his new fiancée on holiday to Great Yarmouth, staying in a good hotel, though, as propriety demanded in those days, they had separate rooms.

When police visited Bennett's lodgings they found a mass of highly damaging circumstantial evidence – collars with the '599' laundry mark, wigs, a false moustache, love letters and a gold chain with a silver watch. This last item, in police eyes, was the same one that Mary had been photographed wearing in Great Yarmouth just a few days before her murder. Unfortunately, the links on the chain were fuzzy in the photograph and it was known that Mrs Bennett had owned another that was very similar.

Herbert denied being at Great Yarmouth on the night of the murder, though witnesses soon came forward and testified that a man resembling his appearance had been seen waiting for the London train early on the morning of 23 September. Lies were always Bennett's first line of defence and he could not explain his whereabouts that weekend – but was he lying because of his guilt in his wife's death, or because of some other secret, or even as a result of a web of deceit formed by years of dishonesty? On the surface, then, the Bennett case seems open and shut; he killed his wife for another woman. But then the doubts and red herrings take over; why would such a clever young criminal, who had all the time in the world to plan a murder (with a new love in his life, and a lot to live for), bungle it all so dreadfully? Why choose Great Yarmouth where he might be recognised? Why the sexual struggle before death? Mary had been seen kissing someone that week, so was an unknown lover of hers the killer? One witness recalled seeing a strange man and woman acting nervously near the murder spot on the day after the body was found and had even tried to shadow their movements, but lost them in the holiday crowds. Could this pair have been the killers? Then, just before the trial, a member of the public, a respectable gentleman no less, Mr Douglas Sholto Douglas, came forward to say that he had met

Bennett while out for a walk during the late afternoon of 22 September at Eltham, Surrey. He had even had a drink with the accused. If Douglas was telling the truth, and he was convincingly adamant that the stranger he met was Bennett, then it would have been impossible for him to be in Great Yarmouth that night.

Bennett had got very negative press coverage and it was decided that Norfolk might not be the best venue for a fair trial, so the case was moved to the Old Bailey in London. It thus became the first murder trial of the 20th century to be held in the Central Criminal Court. Herbert's hard-working solicitor, Elvey Robb, was able to get the services of Edward Marshall Hall, fast rising as the greatest defence counsel of his generation. Hall thought his client was a rogue but no murderer. Oddly enough, the entire defence team, many of whom were tough old criminal lawyers who had met more than their fair share of killers, all came to the same conclusion.

It seemed for a time that the trial, which began on 25 February 1901, before the Lord Chief Justice, Baron Alverstone, would go in Bennett's favour. The young man, who chose not to give evidence, remained cool in the dock, watching intently as Marshall Hall laid on his famous display of histrionic talents, but the weight of circumstantial evidence was skilfully built up by Charles Gill Q.C., prosecuting counsel, whose slow and methodical courtroom style was in direct contrast to his opponent. It took the jury just 35 minutes to find Herbert Bennett guilty of murder.

In prison before his execution Bennett wrote no letters and received only one – from Marshall Hall, who had tried hard, but failed, to win his client a reprieve. Herbert made no last-minute confession, though one newspaper reported that he commented 'It is just,' before he died (though this is not exactly an admittance of guilt). He was also overheard to say while in the condemned cell, 'Well, it seems they are going to hang another innocent man.' Writers on the case have speculated that Herbert and Mary had been up to some scam in Great Yarmouth – perhaps a blackmail or major con trick – and that this piece of skulduggery went woefully awry. Living for years amidst a web of lies made Bennett decide that it was best to go to his grave with those secrets intact. We will never know why he refused to be frank with the police or his defence team.

Curiously, at the moment of his execution at Norwich Prison, just as the black flag was hoisted, a great gust of wind suddenly snapped the staff. The crowd murmured in horror as it came clattering down the roof. This event led many to think that an innocent man had been hanged. Even more curious perhaps, just short of 12 years later, on 14 July 1912, an

18-year-old girl named Dora Gray, fair-haired like Mary Bennett, was found strangled on almost the same part of South Beach, Great Yarmouth. Both murders took place on the first night of a new moon. Dora's murderer was never found. She had been strangled with a reef knot.

1902 The Tottenham Horror: George Woolfe

Assisting Charles Gill in the Bennett case had been a silver-haired barrister who was soon to be one of the most formidable prosecutors of all time – Richard Muir. This dour workaholic lowland Scot, tenacious in court, had a victory of his own that year.

The Great Eastern railway line, the same track used by Bennett to visit East Anglia, entered London via an unsavoury stretch of grim marshland near Tottenham in the north-east of the metropolis. It was here on the bitterly cold morning of 26 January 1902 that a boy tried to retrieve his football from a ditch and discovered the broken and battered body of a young woman. Police were called, and by the time a doctor arrived rigor mortis had just set in. Dried blood caked the girl's face and hands, her nose was broken and more blood with ice was matted in her long hair. It looked, on examination, as if she had been slowly beaten to death.

It did not take the police long to find out who the girl was or capture her likely killer. Her name was Charlotte Cheesman and along with hundreds of other girls she worked at a cigar factory in Hoxton. The police arrested her boyfriend, George Woolfe, and charged him with the murder.

There seems to have been a masochistic streak in Charlotte for she had chosen a violent, extremely macho male as her lover. People came forward to say that they had seen Woolfe beat Charlotte on several occasions. The young man may also have been mentally unstable; not only was he a sadistic thug, but out of jealousy he had written anonymous letters to Charlotte's employers saying she was a thief and a drunkard. These statements were in sharp contrast with Miss Cheesman's work record, which was exemplary. For a time a soldier tried to date Charlotte, but George Woolfe made a point of meeting him and, with a smirk, showed him one of her letters which read in part, 'Will you go out with me again, as you know what you have done to me. I think it is a shame how you have treated me, but I will forget that and think of you all the more. You don't know how much I love you.' Having read this letter the soldier agreed not to see Charlotte again.

Despite their on-off relationship George and Charlotte were seen in a public house together on the night of her murder. Two days later, as hue and cry erupted, Woolfe tried to hurriedly enlist in the army under an assumed name. The police, however, soon tracked him down and he was arrested on 6 February.

Woolfe's defence was that he had seen Charlotte briefly on 25 January but she left him early on that evening and never returned. He claimed that scratches on his face were the result of a fight with his father and their landlord, though his lies were uncorroborated. In court Richard Muir got Woolfe to admit that he had written anonymous letters to blacken Charlotte's character. The famous prosecutor later admitted that he found men who beat up women to be especially obnoxious and in a relentless cross-examination made Woolfe seem a pathetic creature. It seemed likely that a drunken Woolfe had once again used his fists on his girlfriend but with homicidal results. The jury were also not impressed with his lies and speedily found against the defendant. On leaving court Muir was heard to remark, 'He will know what it is to suffer before the hangman comes for him.' George Woolfe was executed on 12 May 1902 at grim old Newgate Prison, one of the last persons executed there as the gaol closed that year and was demolished two years later.

1903 The Body in the Moat: Samuel Herbert Dougal

Murder often results from an unpremeditated and colossal outburst of emotional and physical energy, such as the way George Woolfe had pummelled his lover to death. At the other end of the crime spectrum are those individuals who plan their murders weeks, months and sometimes even years ahead. In this unsavoury batch the coldest of killers must surely be the ones who view murder as a business – those who kill for profit. Their number includes Smith, the 'Brides in the Bath Murderer', Haigh, the 'Acid Bath Murderer' – and less well known but no less fascinating, Samuel Herbert Dougal.

Engaging might be the wrong term to use about someone who possibly was (though it was never proved) a serial killer, but Dougal was one of those scoundrels whose beaming face and cheery disposition fooled almost everyone he met. A cockney, born in Bow in 1846, Dougal wore a perpetual smile in public. Behind closed doors his wives and lovers saw a different fellow – coarse, sometimes drunk, and occasionally violent. There is little doubt that the man himself wanted the world to see a genial rough diamond, an old soldier who had served his 21 years before the colours, retiring with the rank of quartermaster-sergeant and a good conduct medal to prove it.

Only at his trial was it announced that Dougal's first and second wives had died in Canada during his army service there. Both women had suddenly developed stomach pains and vomiting and both died in the same year – 1885. Cause of death was listed in both cases as a result of eating oysters. One of these fatalities might have been true but the similarities lead one to the conclusion that Dougal most probably disposed of these unfortunate women. Deaths in military quarters did not have to be registered with the civilian authorities, and the grieving husband had made sure both wives were safely in their graves within a day of their demise.

Fornication was Samuel's chief hobby; he returned to the United Kingdom with a young Halifax girl in tow and a baby (he had already fathered four others but, needless to say, did not let his paternal instincts, or any responsibilities whatsoever, stand in his way of having a good time). In 1887 Dougal discharged himself from the Royal Engineers and began on the slippery slope that led to his downfall. The next 11 years saw him charged with a range of offences including arson, theft and cheque fraud (not one to think small, he even tried to forge the signature of Lord Wolseley, commanding the British Army in Ireland). When he ended up with 12 months' hard labour, Dougal shrewdly made a mock attempt at suicide in Pentonville and got moved as a patient to the London County Lunatics Asylum where, it was noted, he was a model prisoner.

On his release Dougal's third wife, an Irish girl, left him (with another infant in tow). Samuel had forfeited his army pension and was now heavily down on his luck. So it was, using his smile, glib tongue and hearty manner, that he chanced upon a lonely spinster, Miss Camille Holland, at the Earl's Court Exhibition in September 1898. Using all his charm, 'Captain' Dougal, as he introduced himself, soon had the little lady all in a whirl. Prim but far from poor, with an invested legacy worth several thousand pounds, Miss Holland was a good Catholic, an affectionate aunt to her nephews and nieces, a painter of romantic watercolours and writer of maudlin ballads. Her sole companion was an old black and white spaniel called 'Jacko'.

It seems Dougal began the affair by being too pushy; Miss Holland told a friend after only a few weeks of meeting the captain that, 'We've parted. I've found out he doesn't want me, only my money.' Poor Camille. If only she had trusted those first instincts. Persuasive and contrite, Dougal reappeared, Miss Holland relented, and even went so far as to rent a house near Brighton so that the pair could be together. Here they celebrated Christmas and saw in the New Year for 1899.

During all this time Dougal was formulating a plan. Camille Holland was encouraged to buy him a farm for £1,550 (in January 1899 he destroyed the deed and had it made out in her name). Dougal had chosen a remote moated property called Coldhams Farm at Quendon in Essex. This he renamed 'Moat House Farm'. For three months the couple stayed in lodgings at Saffron Waldon while the farm was made ready. Witnesses later spoke of how Dougal seemed to spend a good deal of time away from the area but always returned from the station ringing his bicycle bell as a sign for an extravagant kiss with Camille at the front door. Finally workmen left the farm, furniture had been moved in and, on 27 April 1899, the happy couple set off in a pony and trap for their new abode. She did not know it but Camille Holland had less than three weeks to live.

The first two maids employed at Moat House Farm left very quickly, victims of Dougal's wandering hands. One of them, Florence Havies, aged 19 years, later explained how he 'came up unawares and kissed me. I objected very much, and as soon as I saw Miss Holland I made a complaint to her.' Dougal's behaviour understandably reduced the 56-year-old spinster to tears. A few nights later Samuel tried to get into Florrie's bedroom. The maid was terrified and had hysterics, Miss Holland heard the commotion and a farce ensued as Dougal hid under the sheets in his bedroom and pretended to be asleep while Camille stormed in and admonished him. When Florrie gave in her notice a tearful Camille, who was clearly starting to see the real Dougal at last, begged her to stay. The unhappy maid agreed to do so. On 19 May 1899 Camille set off with the ever-cheerful Samuel in their pony and cart to do some shopping. 'Goodbye Florrie,' she called out, 'I won't be long.' She was never seen alive again.

When Dougal returned about 8.30pm without his fiancée he insisted that she had been summoned away to London. Next morning he told an anxious Florrie that Miss Holland had sent a letter saying she had gone on holiday. The maid did not know what to think but was sure of one thing – Dougal could not be trusted an inch; she left that day and Samuel paid her wages in full. Then he quickly installed his third wife at the farm, telling the local vicar that she was his widowed daughter. As the days passed into weeks, then months and years, rumours about Miss Holland's disappearance proliferated in the small community. Dougal, meantime, had been playing the gentleman farmer up to the hilt. Not that he bothered much with farming; he was soon driving around in the first motor car ever seen in that isolated corner of rural Essex, fornicated to his heart's content with a string of young servant girls (at one time he was sleeping with three teenage sisters and also their mother). Oddest of all, it was said at his trial that he gave one woman bicycle lessons – in the nude!

It is possible that if he had acted more coyly, or been less greedy, Samuel Dougal might have got away with murder. But coyness and parsimony had never been Samuel's forte. The banks kept receiving cheques written out by Miss Holland but with no apparent sign of the lady herself. They began enquiries and concluded, none too soon, that cheque fraud had occurred. Dougal had in fact illegally amassed £2,912 15s of Miss Holland's money. Then, on 18 March 1903, at the Bank of England itself, Samuel pushed his luck by trying to change fourteen £10 notes. A suspicious clerk asked him to step into a detective's office and Dougal made a run for it. His luck was out and he bolted into a dead-end alley. Arrested, he was found to have among his pockets the huge sum of £563 in gold and coins (more than £40,000 today) along with jewellery and watches belonging to Camille Holland. He was charged with forging a cheque and held at Saffron Walden Police Station while the search for the missing woman began.

After five weeks, with no sign of Miss Holland, the police were getting desperate. They had dug all over the farm, even drained the moat, but without success. It was almost by accident that they looked in an old drainage ditch that ran from the pond to the moat. It was full of 'black liquid filth', according to the officer in charge, but then a lady's boot appeared – with a small foot inside. Close to this culvert, in an area shielded by blackthorn bushes, amidst the mud and raw sewage, Miss Holland's clothed body was found face down in the dirt. She had been shot through the head. The murderer had cunningly dug a small trench at the side of the moat and shoved in the body, covering it up with blackthorn bushes. It was 27 April, four years to the very day, by an odd coincidence, since poor Camille had arrived at Moat Farm.

Dougal's trial in the Shire Hall, Chelmsford, was brief. It began on 22 June before Mr Justice Wright and closed the next day. No witnesses were called in Dougal's defence; in a statement the prisoner claimed that Miss Holland had accidentally shot herself. 'Demented', he had laid her in the ditch, 'knelt down and kissed her', before covering up the body. Hanged at Chelmsford Prison on 8 July, Dougal was coerced into an admission of guilt on the scaffold by a zealous chaplain.

Both Miss Holland and her dog went on display in later years: Augustus Pepper, the forensic expert on the case, retained Camille's skull and sometimes used it to show medical students, eventually keeping it in a glass case; Miss Holland's little spaniel went to live with her former landlady at Saffron Walden and, after its death, a wistful-looking 'Jacko' was stuffed and mounted in her parlour where, in happier days, its mistress had used to listen for the tinkling tone of Dougal's bicycle bell.

1904 The Stepney Murder: Rotten & Wade

Shopkeepers have for centuries been the victims of physical assault and wilful murder. Such a one was Miss Emily Farmer, described by a detective as 'a dumpy, fat, little old woman', who owned a newsagent's and tobacconist's shop in the neighbourhood of Commercial Road, Stepney, in London's East End. On one occasion Emily had fended off an attack with some loud screams and told a policeman that she could take care of herself. She lived alone but was up each morning by 5.45am to take in the daily papers from the wholesaler. Forty-five minutes later, Miss Farmer normally had everything ready for her young delivery assistant to start his newspaper round. It was said that on a quiet afternoon the old lady liked to deck herself out in all her jewellery. This collection included several rings, a couple of bracelets, 'a long gold chain round her neck, attached to a watch tucked in at her waistband, and a pair of gold pince-nez, also secured by a hanging gold chain'.

In a working-class neighbourhood like Stepney such an ostentatious display did not go unnoticed. Perhaps it was not so surprising that when the errand boy arrived for work at 6.30am on 12 October he found the shop door open. Lying inside was a bundle of newspapers tied up with string just as they had been delivered. He called out the old lady's name but there was no reply. Peering around the shop he saw the odd sight of her false teeth, along with one of her shoes, lying on the floor in front of the counter. The boy wisely fetched the police. Upstairs they found Miss Farmer; she was lying face down on the bed, hands tied behind her back and a piece of rag stuffed in her mouth. A police pathologist quickly assessed that she had choked to death. Around the bedroom, which had been ransacked in apparent haste, were strewn clothes, books and the contents of several drawers. The old lady's jewellery had vanished along with every penny she possessed. Everything pointed to an unexpected and hasty attack by a person or persons she knew. The back door and all windows remained fastened. Whoever killed Emily Farmer had entered and left from the front of the shop. It seemed likely to have been a gang, or at least two persons, because the state of things suggested that she had struggled and been carried upstairs.

For the first two days the police investigation seemed to lead nowhere. False trails and a clear lack of support from the local community stifled the inquiry. Police skills now turned on those local known criminals with predilection towards violence. Three had been seen idling in Commercial Road that night and they were brought in for questioning (two were quickly released and the third was on the run from a provincial police force who now got their man), but then a member of the public made a statement that a fellow employee of his – a fish curer who worked nights – had seen two men whom he could describe leave Miss Farmer's shop very early on the morning of the murder. Detective Inspector Divall quickly interviewed this witness, a frightened youth called Rae, and the lad admitted that he had indeed seen two men leave the shop. Fear had kept him from saying anything as he recognised the men as members of a local gang. Even the police could not get him to provide any names, but luckily his descriptions were detailed enough for arrests to be made. The criminals were two half-brothers with long records – 34-year-old Conrad Donovan (real name Conrad Rotten) and 22-year-old Charles Wade. After investigation it turned out that Wade was the same man who had attempted to rob Miss Farmer once before, an attack interrupted by her screaming and the presence of a quick-acting copper on his beat.

With police protection young Rae now formally identified the two toughs as the men he had seen leaving the shop about five minutes before the delivery boy had arrived. Wade's landlord also came forward to declare that on the morning of the murder he had woken him by special request at 5am. Normally he was a late riser so why had Wade wanted such an early morning call? The case was nevertheless based on circumstantial evidence and flimsy at best. Their Old Bailey trial lasted three days. Afterwards it was felt that the jury might have shown them more sympathy if they had testified, but both men decided not to go into the witness box. Both Rotten and Wade were found guilty of murder and condemned to death.

Even on the eve of their execution the police were on tenterhooks that more evidence to disturb the case might turn up. It did not. Shortly before he was hanged Rotten confessed that he had never intended to kill Miss Farmer. This seems more than likely. It was a bungled robbery. He and Wade, who was very much under the influence of his elder stepbrother, had intended to gag the old lady just to stifle her screams. Unfortunately for them and more so for her, the violence of their assault led to her death – and took them both to the scaffold.

1905 Foiled by a Fingerprint: Albert & Alfred Stratton

Scotland Yard had set up its Central Fingerprint Branch in July 1901 under a remarkable Assistant Commissioner, Edward Henry, who quickly got to work building up files on known criminals. It was clear that before long the use of fingerprints would send a killer to the gallows.

The man who earned this dubious distinction was 22-year-old Alfred Stratton, an athletic, clean-shaven burglar with an eye for the ladies who, with his younger brother, Albert, had managed until then to avoid police records. Not that the two brothers were unknown to the local constabulary in South London. Alfred, very much the leader of the duo, lived off the proceeds of gambling and burglary. Albert, two years his junior, was a burly youth who had spent a short time in the Royal Navy before being discharged for insubordination. At that time he was living with (and two-timing) a Mrs Kate Wade. Her later decision to assist the police may have been due to Albert's philandering ways.

New Cross and Deptford, then as now, was a tough part of south-east London. Both Strattons were members of the Mufflers, a street gang of young rowdies with an unsavoury reputation for violence, gambling and racketeering. On the night of Sunday 26 March young Hannah Cromarty, Alfred's latest paramour, could not afford an evening meal. Casual prostitution was an accepted way of life for many unfortunate working-class girls and Hannah, without Alfred to scrounge off, went onto the streets and soon found a willing customer. She brought him back to the dingy ground-floor room she shared with Alfred. Sex was agreed for a small fee. Right in the middle of this tawdry bargain Alfred turned up and went berserk. He threw the client out into the street with his trousers round his ankles, then proceeded to punch Hannah, knocking the semi-clad girl onto the floor. Throwing in a few well-aimed kicks for good measure, he grabbed the one shilling she had earned and stormed out again. It was almost midnight when he returned and managed, perhaps because alcohol had softened his anger, to patch up his differences with Hannah. The pair settled down to sleep.

Around 1.30am they were awakened by a loud tapping at their window. It was younger brother Albert who had been spending a few hours with a lady friend, a servant girl called Rose Wood. The two brothers then had a conversation in hushed tones, but Hannah heard Alfred ask the question, 'Shall we do it tonight, or leave it for another night?' Desperately short of money, Albert gave his brother an affirmative for that night and the pair went off together.

It seems that the first thing the Stratton Brothers did was fortify their nerves with some alcohol, and cups of coffee, chatting with Muffler Gang pals and some of the prostitutes near the Broadway Music Hall. After a game or two of cards the boys were ready for a spot of burglary. Previously they had cased likely premises to rob. This was an oil and paint supplies shop at 34 Deptford High Street. Living on the premises was the shop's manager, elderly Thomas Farrow and his 63-year-old wife, Ann. The Strattons planned to steal the shop cashbox and Mr and Mrs Farrow's life savings, which they wrongly believed to be on the premises.

Most mornings Mr Farrow opened the shop about 7am and sat on a step to enjoy his pipe. Monday 27 March was rainy and windy. His neighbour saw no sign of old Thomas until about 7.25am, some 10 minutes after two men had been seen exiting the shop. Mr Farrow was staggering with blood streaming down his face. He appeared to look out of the door before disappearing back inside his shop. At 8am shop assistant William Jones arrived for work but found the door locked. Unable to raise anybody he set off for Greenwich, where the owner of the building lived, to get a key. Back in Deptford young William gained entry through the rear of the shop where he soon saw the dead and battered body of Mr Farrow. Upstairs on her bed lay Mrs Farrow. She had been savagely hit over the head with what seemed to be a jemmy and was unconscious (three days later she died in hospital). Nearby on the floor was a cash box emptied of the week's takings. The thieves, as it later turned out, were richer by a paltry £9.

That evening the London newspapers were full of the crime while in Deptford and New Cross the murder was on everyone's lips. Alfred had returned to his lodgings at 9am. To Hannah's surprise he seemed flush with money, but she noted that his clothes stank of paraffin. Reading a news report later that day she realised with what must have been mounting horror that the descriptions of two men seen leaving the murder scene matched exactly the clothes worn by Alfred and Albert on the previous night.

Hannah now questioned her boyfriend and was not satisfied with his evasive replies. She was not alone; Rose Wood, Albert's bit on the side, lived in the same building as Alfred and Hannah; she was surprised to come across her boyfriend's brother busily polishing the brown boots he had worn on the night of the murder. Albert's nervous answers to some of the questions Rose posed made her exclaim, 'I know exactly who those two men are.'

Yet it was not Hannah, or Rose, or even Kate who finally reported the Strattons to the police, but a respectable fourth lady called Ellen Stanton. She had been on her way to work when the brothers Stratton came running down Deptford High Street. She recognised only Alfred but on reading of the murder she thought it best to report the incident to the police. Warrants were issued for both men, who tried to hide but were soon discovered. Both denied any wrongdoing. Indeed, at their first court appearance in Greenwich the brothers spent much of their time waving and joking with Muffler pals in the public gallery. It was the following week when the smiles left their faces; a thumb print had been taken by police off the cash box. Detective Inspector Charles Collins and his team at Scotland Yard had also taken prints of the Farrows and anyone else who might have touched the object. The thumb print matched none of the 85,000 sets already held by the police but it had 11 points of similarity with one of Albert Stratton's – and four were considered sufficient for prosecution purposes.

News of this print made Albert extremely jittery. In the lunchtime recess at Tower Bridge police court he confided to a gaoler that he thought Alfred would be 'swung up' while he might end up with 10 years. Talking too much, Albert went on, 'I shan't say anything until I can see he has got no chance and then...' Albert suddenly stopped talking as if realising how such loose talk could take him to the gallows.

The Stratton Brothers went on trial at the Old Bailey in May before Mr Justice Channell. One of the finest defence barristers of the Edwardian age, Henry Curtis Bennett, represented Alfred. The Crown team was led by the coldly efficient Richard Muir who described the crime as the most brutal he had ever prosecuted. Aided by Collins, using giant enlargements of fingerprints, Muir led the jury through the vagaries of this new forensic science. The defence tried to show that despite some minor successes fingerprinting lacked reliability. Curtis Bennett argued that there were several differences between Alfred Stratton's thumb print and the bloody one found on the cash box. In the witness box Detective Inspector Collins was not fazed; it was perfectly natural, he countered, because different pressures cause different variations. He then proved his point beyond any doubt by taking the prints of the jurors several times over and showing how the same differences occurred. The defence also called experts; one of these, Dr J. G. Garson, claimed that the police had no idea how to use fingerprinting. Richard Muir was able to produce two letters, both written by Garson on the same day, offering his services to both the defence and prosecution. From the bench Mr Justice Channell lambasted the doctor as 'an absolutely untrustworthy witness'.

In his summing-up the judge pointed out very sensibly to the jury that the thumb print on the cash box 'was made only with perspiration and was not so satisfactory as it would have been if the material with which it was made had been of a kind that would give a better impression'. He advised the jury not 'to act upon it alone...' They did not need to do so; Kate Wade's testimony of finding burglars' masks hidden under her mattress, with the statements of Hannah Cromarty, Rose Wood and Ellen Stanton, all helped bring in a verdict of guilty and the sentence of death.

In prison before his execution Albert found solace in religion and told his sister, 'I hope you pray for me, I am praying for all of you, and especially for Alfred.' The elder brother did not find God and being the more practical of the two complained to his mother that she could have done more in his defence. He was, however, not troubled 'in the least' by the turn of events and declared that 'the time passed very quickly at the trial, as it was the first one I had ever seen, I was rather interested'. Unfortunately Alfred Stratton had very little time to meditate on his new-found interest in the British legal system; he was hanged alongside his brother at Wandsworth Prison on 23 May.

1906 The Old Soldier Case: Walter Marsh

An ex-sergeant of the North Staffordshire Regiment, Marsh had been honourably discharged in 1901. A series of business ventures subsequently failed and matters were not helped when the 39-year-old decided to woo and wed a woman 16 years younger than himself.

Soon the couple were seen to be arguing a great deal; Walter accused his wife of being lazy and drunk half the time, while she said he was violent towards her. On 9 August Eliza Marsh stormed out after a row and went to see some friends. Later that afternoon she agreed to return after Walter promised to behave decently towards her. The goodwill was short-lived; about 5pm he walked out of their home at 6 Goyt Terrace, Brampton, near Chesterfield, waving a bloody razor and shouting, 'I've done for her this time.'

Soon the police were on the scene and found Mrs Marsh lying on the bed. Her throat had been so viciously slit that the head was almost severed from the body. At his trial at the Derby Assize, the old soldier claimed that his wife had attacked him and he had used the razor in self-defence. The prosecution took a different view and argued that Marsh had attacked his wife as she lay sleeping. The severity of Eliza

Marsh's injuries clearly distressed the jury and they found Walter guilty after a short deliberation. Mr Justice Ridley donned the black cap and condemned the ex-soldier to death, a fate he met with great courage on 27 December 1906.

1907 Last of the Baby Farmers: Rhoda Willis

Baby farming, the fostering of young children, agreed and undertaken with little care and no supervision, was one of the least savoury aspects of Victorian society. It led to many court cases and also the trial for murder of some its most notorious practitioners. It has been estimated that Amelia Dyer, hanged in June 1896, may have been England's greatest serial killer, possibly responsible for the deaths of upwards of 1,000 infants in a career spanning more than three decades. Another three women, Ada Williams in 1900, and Annie Wallace and Amelia Sachs in 1903, were executed for the same loathsome offence. By now the furore caused by the Dyer Scandal had led to a second Infant Life Protection Act that provided authorities with powers to identify and supervise the nursing and adoption of infants under their jurisdiction. Inspectors could now search any premise they suspected was a baby farm and remove any children found to be abused. Newspaper advertising 'relating to establishments for taking in infants' now had to be vetted in advance by the authorities.

On the morning of 4 June a landlady called Mrs Wilson of Portmanmoor Road, Cardiff, heard a loud thump in the bedroom of one of her lodgers, Mrs Leslie James. Knowing her tenant to be a drunkard Mrs Wilson and another lodger hurried to the room. On entering they found, as they guessed, Mrs James comatose on the floor and smelling heavily of alcohol. The pair tried to lift her back on the bed but it was impossible. Straightening the bedclothes Mrs Wilson then made a curious discovery. Between the mattresses was a bundle wrapped in a towel. She prodded Mrs James and asked what it was. 'Hush, don't say anything, I'll get rid of it tonight,' mumbled the 39-year-old long-haired inebriate. Inquisitive Mrs Wilson opened up the bundle and was horrified to find the corpse of a baby girl barely one day old.

Police were then quickly called and Leslie James was arrested for murder. It turned out much later that her real name was Rhoda Willis. She had been born Rhoda Lascelles into a respectable upper-middle-class family in Sunderland and been educated at a boarding school for young ladies in London. Her future in the middle-class marriage market looked secure. Sure enough, Rhoda was married while still a teenager to a Sunderland engineer with good prospects, but it was then that things started to go awry. She left her husband and their baby daughter at their Grangetown, Cardiff, home and became the mistress of another marine engineer named Macpherson. She had two more daughters by this man but once again the relationship fell apart. By now Rhoda was drinking heavily and this slide into full-blown alcoholism was not helped when she went to live with her brother, who was a pub landlord in Birmingham, for two years.

By the time she returned to Grangetown, Rhoda was calling herself 'Leslie James' and Macpherson and her daughters were living in Liverpool. For Leslie/Rhoda life had become one of basic survival; she spent much of her time dossing in the workhouse or in various Salvation Army homes when she wasn't trying to make ends meet as a prostitute. Early in 1907 a seemingly lucky break occurred when David Evans, a Pontypool carpenter, agreed to give her a job as his housekeeper. To help both their incomes 'Mrs James' suggested they try their hands at baby farming. Their one attempt at this occupation ended in a fiasco; the pair conned a Mrs Stroud of Abertillery into parting with her three-week-old son. The adoption fee of £7 was paid, but much of this was spent on booze, while the baby wrapped in a rug and, suffering from acute diarrhoea, was left on the doorstep of a convenient Salvation Army hostel. The infant died one week later and its demise was attributed to natural causes, especially so since a note was found on the child which read: 'Do take my baby in. I ham [*sic*] one of your girls gone wrong. I will come back if you forgive me, and will bring money.'

The baby found in Mrs Wilson's boarding house turned out to be the illegitimate daughter of Maud Treasure, a single girl from Pengram. Three months earlier, her sister, a Mrs English, had replied to a newspaper advertisement offering adoption of a new-born child. 'Leslie James' was interviewed by the women and agreed to adopt the baby. Duly, within an hour of the unfortunate and unwanted little girl's birth, she had been presented to 'Mrs James' by Maud's mother, a certified nurse, who had been the midwife. 'Leslie James' even wrote out a receipt for £6 paid that day 'for taking baby entirely as my own for life'.

There seems little doubt that murder, cold and heartless, was on the killer's mind throughout this entire business. The deed was done on the train back to Cardiff. Rhoda later claimed that 'a sudden temptation came over me and I couldn't resist it'. This does not tally with her confession to a fellow prisoner that she had 'thought of drowning it in a bath, but afterwards decided to smother it. I squeezed it hard and some white stuff oozed from its mouth. I then wrapped it up and hid it.'

In the dock at her trial Leslie James/Rhoda Willis was described as a heavy-jawed woman with a fine crop of golden hair atop of which perched a black sailor hat. She did not give evidence on her behalf and the jury were seemingly not impressed by defence attempts to suggest that she had suffocated the infant by accident. They took just 10 minutes to find her guilty of murder. On the day before her execution Rhoda confessed to her solicitor that 'I wilfully killed the child ... I particularly want those who tried me, and especially the judge, to know that I was quite guilty, as I shouldn't like to die with any possible chance of them thinking I was innocent. It has been a great comfort to me to tell you this, as I can now die with a clear conscience.'

Whatever her failings and the horrendous crime, the last of the baby farmers went courageously to the scaffold, the first – and only – woman executed in Wales since 1843.

1908 Quick to the Gallows: James Phipps

The murder of children is always an ugly business and an emotive one. So intense were local feelings against 21-year-old Phipps, an unemployed decorator, that he was hastily brought to trial at Chester Assizes just eight days after the crime was committed.

At about 7.30pm on 12 October the accused had been seen on a footpath leading 10-year-old Eliza Warburton by the hand towards some wasteland near Station Road, Winsford, Cheshire. Earlier that day Phipps, who had lost an eye in a schoolyard accident many years before and wore a white scarf tied at the back of his head to hide the dead socket, had asked a gang of kids if they could fetch him some cigarettes from a nearby shop. Eliza had volunteered and Phipps had promised her tuppence as a reward. When she failed to return home her distraught father led a posse of locals in a wide search. They soon found Phipps, whose immediate reaction was to run away. He was quickly apprehended by the local police.

In prison that week Phipps said the children had teased him about his missing eye and thrown stones at him. He had chased them, caught hold of Eliza and in a rage drowned her in a muddy pool. When Phipps story of chasing the children was disproved, his defence counsel then tried to argue that this tale only confirmed his client's insanity. The prosecution argued that Phipps had deliberately lured Eliza into a field for sex, then assaulted her, thrown her into a ditch and drowned her. The jury came back with a verdict of guilty in just seven minutes, one of the shortest deliberations on record. Mr Justice Lawrence donned the dreaded black cap and sentenced Phipps to death, an execution carried out by Henry and Thomas Pierrepoint at Knutsford Gaol on 12 November, exactly one month from the date of the crime.

1909 Foul Deeds in Room 13: Mark & Morris Reubens

It had been 21 years since the infamous Jack the Ripper slayings, but human blood was still regularly spilt on the pavements of Whitechapel, one of the toughest districts in London's grimy East End. Those two decades had seen some modest improvements in slum clearance but the Ripper would have felt very much at home in the slum streets and dark alleys of Edwardian London.

Not that its plentiful supply of pubs and prostitutes did not make it an exciting place for a real cockney night out on the town. With about £5 each in their pockets, two sailors, freshly docked that day after a long voyage from Australia, set off from nearby Victoria Docks on the night of 16 March to have a spree. After visiting several pubs and downing a goodly quantity of best bitter they fell in with two accommodating ladies of the night, Ellen Stevens and Emily Allen. The girls eventually got the men back to their lodgings at 3 Rupert Street, Whitechapel, and a room with a sinister '13' on the door.

A party was in full swing when suddenly from an adjoining room two men entered and one of them started clubbing second engineer William Sproull with a heavy hippopotamus-hide stick. Sproull, who was a 'powerfully built man of about thirty-five', tried to defend himself against the blows rained down with such force that they broke the weapon. His friend, second mate McEachern, was, in his own words, 'hopelessly drunk'. Nevertheless, he staggered to his feet and tried to give Sproull some assistance. The girls had rushed out of the room as soon as the fighting erupted. McEachern, who only vaguely remembered events afterwards, somehow blundered into the street. A short time later he was found leaning against a wall in the Whitechapel Road by a police constable on his beat. Worse for wear, the sailor was trying to explain things to the copper when up rushed a distraught night watchman with the news that a bloody body was lying on the pavement in Rupert Street.

Just around the corner from Rupert Street is Leman Street, which was home to one of the toughest police stations in the country (now made world famous by the TV series, *Ripper Street*). Word was sent there and Detective Inspector Frederick Wensley, fast rising as one of the sharpest detectives in 'H' division, was soon hot-footing it to the scene of the crime. Sproull lay in the street, clearly dead. A thick frost and bright moonlight allowed the detectives to follow a trail of gleaming patches of blood and silvery threepenny bits that had fallen out of the dead man's pockets. This crimson and silver track led to 3 Rupert Street where, as a clear sign of foul play, one of the front door panels gleamed with the bloodstained imprint of a man's hand. The drops of blood continued as far as Room 13 wherein the police could see all the signs of a heavy affray.

It was not very difficult for a good local detective such as Wensley to track down and arrest the two prostitutes along with a pair of brothers who, like the Strattons, lived off burglary and pimping; Mark Reubens tried to get rid of a bloodstained handkerchief on the way to the police station, while his brother, Morris, unwisely startled gabbling, 'I don't mind telling you I robbed the fellow who was lying on the ground over there. I hope he is not dead? There was only me and my brother there.' On arrival at Leman Street a now very nervous Morris went even further, volunteering that 'I did not stab him. If he was stabbed, my brother must have stabbed him.' Up to that time the police had said nothing of how Mr Sproull had died.

Fred Wensley, known as 'the Weasel' by the criminal underworld, was a tenacious copper who came from a tough school. He now put the screws on Ellen Stevens and Emily Allen so that murder charges were dropped against the prostitutes in return for turning King's evidence assisting the prosecution. Considering their involvement the women were extremely lucky, some might say too lucky, in view of what happened to their pimps. Clearly, in one of the oldest scams in the book, the two sailors had been set up for a robbery. It seems likely that the thuggish Reubens brothers did not expect Sproull to put up such a stiff fight. It was Morris who had used the heavy stick and brother Mark who had finished the unfortunate sailor off with a knife. A week after the murder, Wensley made a second and more thorough search of Room 13 and found the knife hidden behind a gas stove where one of the girls had placed it.

During their trial at the Old Bailey both brothers frequently interrupted the proceedings with tears, groans and other signs of hysteria. The defence argued that their attack was provoked by the two sailors. Morris's counsel claimed his client did not know that Marks was carrying a knife. The judge, Mr Justice Jeff, trying his first murder case, was a stickler for the letter of the law and pointed out to the jury that under British jurisprudence if two persons take part in a violent crime, each one must take responsibility for the actions of the other. He would not allow a verdict of manslaughter – both brothers were thus entirely innocent of murder or guilty as charged. It took the jury only 12 minutes to reach a decision: Morris was pronounced guilty first and with a shriek he fainted before, recovering a little, histrionically opening his arms and begging for mercy; Mark went completely berserk, screaming at the top of his voice while, as an eye witness wrote, 'the voice of Morris ceaselessly whining "Mercy! Mercy!" made a sort of dreadful obligato'.

The brothers Reubens were both executed on 20 May. Their case had some similarities insofar as their appeal was concerned with the far more famous case in the 1950s of Craig & Bentley. Just a few months before the Sproull Murder, a gang of East European agitators had killed a policeman and wounded two others during a spectacular getaway that became known as 'the Tottenham Outrage'. The killers, Paul Helfeld and Jacob Lepidus, Jewish Latvian immigrants, committed suicide at the end of the pursuit. It was felt by the Home Secretary and the Lord Chief Justice, Baron Alverstone, that after such dreadful acts of violence in the East End it was necessary to get tough with criminals who carried guns or knives. It was said by Wensley that after the Reubens brothers were executed, the crime of scamming a prostitute's 'john' went out of fashion. Murder by orthodox Jews was also rare and the Reubens Brothers were the first to go to the scaffold in London for several decades.

1910 The Mildest Murderer: Hawley Harvey Crippen

It is one of the supremely classic cases, a murder monolith that sums up a vanished age. It is, besides Jack the Ripper, the most famous of all British murder stories. If the gloomy, fogbound streets of old London town seem time-warped in the image of the gaslit ghoul of Whitechapel, most notorious of all serial killers, then the passions running deep beneath the outwardly respectable, damask-curtained confines of turn-of-the-century middle-class society are forever etched in the sad little tale of Hawley Harvey Crippen, poisoner. The cunning way he appears to have planned his crime and almost got away with it, the flight to Canada with a young mistress in disguise, the brilliant way Scotland Yard detectives outwitted him – these are the stuff of legend. In the dock Crippen behaved as he had done all his life – with calmness and politeness. Yet after his conviction, determined that his mistress should not be blamed for his misdeeds, he went to the gallows a courageous man. Indeed, he demonstrated such a deep and pure love that it raised his sordid story to undreamt heights until it became one of the great tragic romances of all time.

In this most famous of Edwardian murder cases (though Crippen's trial was one of the first in the new reign of King George V), the accused was an American citizen. So was his victim. Crippen had been born in Michigan in 1862. Thirty years later, he met and married a vivacious 18-year-old from New Jersey who called herself 'Cora Turner' (in fact she was the daughter of a Polish immigrant called Mackamotzki). Hawley Crippen, who always liked to be called 'Peter', had lost his first wife earlier that same year. She had died of apoplexy in the ninth month of her pregnancy. Oddly enough, apoplexy is a symptom of hyoscine poisoning, but no scandal attached to Mrs Crippen's passing (and women often died during pregnancy). A young son, also called Hawley, was sent to California to live with his grandparents. There is no record that the boy ever saw his father again.

Crippen was a genuine doctor, but spent much of his career in the field of homeopathic medicine promoting quack tonics. In 1898 the Crippens moved to London where 'Peter' continued this line of work, occasionally jobbing as an ear and eye specialist, or doing dentistry. Cora, who had originally dreamed of being an opera singer, had by now put on a lot of weight. As the years rolled by she became a flabby and faded bottom-of-the-bill music hall artiste (though she and her kindly, well-mannered husband had a large circle of theatrical friends). She liked to call herself 'Belle Elmore', which was her stage name. By 1910, the couple were living at 39 Hilldrop Crescent, Camden Town, an unassuming semi-detached middle-class villa (rent £50 a year) with occasional lodgers and a daily maid. All but one of the lodgers later described the Crippens as devoted to one another; there were no signs of quarrelling.

At his trial Crippen claimed that he was henpecked but we only have his word for it. He clearly was attracted to strong-willed, assertive women who would take charge of things. Boisterous Belle was probably bossy, but 'Peter' Crippen, at least so far as his neighbours and friends could see, did not seem to mind. He was earning good money and showered his wife with gifts of jewellery and expensive clothes. Dinner parties attended by Belle's showbusiness acquaintances were frequent and these folk later recalled the Crippens as being on the best of terms, joking and often arm-in-arm together. Many of these visitors thought Crippen a little pathetic or unmanly because he looked like the perfect dormouse.

Slightly built, with a drooping moustache, thinning hair and bulging eyes magnified by thick spectacles, he was, as one wit later recalled, something like a bream or a mullet. Soft-spoken, always polite, the good doctor did not smoke, never touched wine or spirits and allowed his wife to choose his suits and ties. He was the complete 'insignificant-looking man' destined to be on the side-lines of any social event.

Quiet types often hide dark secrets and deeper passions. So it was with Crippen, who fell hopelessly in love in 1902 with a new young typist at his workplace called Ethel Le Neve. This petite and very cute 18-year-old brunette was also slowly drawn to her employer until an affair, with illicit sex in hotel rooms, led to a miscarriage in 1908. A cooling-off period followed this dramatic incident but, a year later, the affair was on the boil again. Ethel, naturally enough, badgered Crippen to get a divorce. There is a possibility that she suffered a second miscarriage. Cora Crippen could never be a parent – her ovaries had been removed years earlier – and divorce does not seem to have been on the cards (she was also a strict Catholic).

So what prevented the little doctor and his birdlike lady friend from simply running away together? Crippen clearly gave the matter much thought and decided against it; most of the money he possessed – £600 – was tied up in a joint bank account with his wife, a divorce might ruin him financially and there were the social niceties to be observed. No, the stumbling block to a good life with Ethel was his wife. She would have to go.

In the middle of January 1910 Dr Crippen purchased five grains of hyoscine, a relatively uncommon drug, better known today as scopolamine, a derivative from the leaves and seeds of the henbane plant. In tiny hundredths of a gram the drug acts as a depressant on the central nervous system (it is still used in many travel sickness remedies). But hyoscine has an unsteady metabolism. It can affect different individuals in different ways. More than a quarter of a grain is likely to be fatal if ingested, proceeded by dementia, convulsions and violent behaviour.

A little knowledge can be a dangerous thing. On the night of 31 January the Crippens hosted a supper party at home for theatrical friends. All seemed normal and the guests left Hilldrop Crescent in seemingly good spirits at 1.30am on 1 February 1910. Some neighbours later told the police that they heard two gunshots around 7am. This leaves the question of what happened in the house. Only the Crippens were in residence and it is highly probable that the doctor thought the drug would softly take his wife into the arms of Morpheus, but if she turned violent or acted erratically, perhaps it was necessary to finish her off with a revolver (he owned one but it was never tested by the police).

Next day, perhaps not coincidentally, Dr Crippen started a new job. He acted normally but quickly began telling anyone who would listen that Cora had returned to America. The lies soon got bigger; he wrote to his son informing him that his stepmother had died in California (the young man tried but could find no trace of her passing away). Within two days, Ethel was sleeping at Hilldrop Crescent and soon seen wearing Cora's jewellery which, oddly enough, Mrs Crippen had not taken with her to the United States. To what extent Miss Le Neve knew what the doctor was up to is anyone's guess but it is fair to conjecture that it was far more than came out at the trials.

For four months the lovers kept up this charade while a number of Cora's friends got more and more irritated by 'Peter's' evasive answers to their questions. It was as if he didn't care, going around flaunting a girl half his age who was clearly his mistress and wearing Mrs Crippen's best diamond brooch and rings. It was too much. Finally a complaint was made to Scotland Yard. Women went missing all the time and the London police were used to busybodies. Crippen seemed respectable enough and a few simple inquiries might settle the matter. A detective of over 20 years' experience, Chief Inspector Walter Dew, was requested to visit the little doctor and check out the facts. Crippen was surprised by Dew's visit on 8 July yet was courtesy personified. He confessed that he had been telling a few white lies; his wife was not dead but had left him for another man. He had lost contact with her and had no idea where she was living in America. Would it help if he placed advertisements in several American newspapers? Dew thought this sounded an excellent idea. After taking a statement he helped the doctor prepare a missing persons notice.

After Dew's departure Crippen and Ethel, according to the maid, went into a long and whispered conversation. Clearly the detective's visit had alarmed them both. Ethel was heard to say, 'For mercy's sake, tell me whether you know where Belle Elmore is. I have a right to know.' Crippen replied, 'I tell you truthfully that I don't know...' We must ask ourselves, if they had nothing to hide then why did they run away? For that was their next step. On the very next day, with Ethel disguised as a boy, the pair took the train to Brussels.

Inspector Dew had been fairly satisfied with Crippen's demeanour and the answers he gave to questions but decided he needed clarification on a few points in the statement. He returned to the house on Monday 11 July only to discover that Crippen had gone away, having removed all the money in his bank account and closed down his business. Dew speedily got a warrant to search the house. Nothing seemed amiss. It was on the afternoon of the second day of searching that a few loose bricks in the coal cellar (beneath the front door steps) were prised away to reveal some body parts. A post-mortem examination showed a mix of filleted (no bones whatsoever) human remains without a head, genitals or limbs, apart from a piece of thigh and a smaller part of the lower abdomen. Intact and fairly well preserved were the heart, lungs, kidneys, spleen, stomach (which was empty) and the pancreas. The small abdominal section had a mark that the pathologists concluded was a scar of an old operation such as an ovariotomy (implying it might belong to Cora Crippen). All the pathologists agreed that it would have taken someone with real medical skills to have removed the body parts and filleted the remains.

Crippen and Ethel were overnight the most wanted couple in Europe. He was described, not very flatteringly, as having 'a rather slovenly appearance, throws his feet out when walking, speaks with an American accent, wears hat back of head, very plausible and quiet-spoken, speaks French, carries firearms, shows his teeth much when talking', while Ethel was 'good-looking, medium build, pleasant appearance, quiet, subdued manner'. On 20 July the couple boarded the *Montrose* at Antwerp bound for Canada. With almost no luggage the game was up just three hours into the voyage when the sharp-eyed captain, Henry Kendall, saw 16-year-old 'Master John Robinson' tightly squeezing the hand of his 'father'. The ship was equipped with the Marconi telegraph for transmitting messages, a recent wonder of science. Two days into the voyage, convinced that the Robinsons were Crippen and his mistress, Commander Kendall wired Scotland Yard. The news was also reported to the press. For the next few days only Hawley and Ethel, stuck out in the Atlantic, did not know what the rest of the world knew – that they were being pursued. Chief Inspector Dew caught a faster ship, the *Laurentic*, and arrived in Quebec one day ahead of the *Montrose*. As its passengers disembarked Dew was there to say, 'Good morning, Dr Crippen.' The little doctor replied politely, 'Good morning', as calm as ever.

Both Hawley and Ethel were taken into custody and were tried separately (Miss Le Neve only as an accessory). Crippen's prosecution was in the hands of the brilliant, dour, workaholic Richard Muir, assisted by a team of forensic experts that included Bernard Spilsbury and the famous chemist William Wilcox, who had discovered half a grain of hyoscine in the remains, an amount which suggested that probably two grains had been in the whole body (more than eight times the amount needed to kill a person). Only since 1898 had defendants been allowed to speak in their defence. Crippen agreed to be cross-examined but he did absolutely nothing to help his case and made a poor show. He rather feebly suggested that the hyoscine had been purchased to use in homeopathic concoctions but was vague on the subject. Richard Muir's opening exchange with the prisoner was brilliant and devastating as Crippen agreed in question after question that he had done nothing to search for his missing wife. The little man had no explanation for the body parts in his cellar and Muir was able to show that a pyjama jacket of his, apparently buried with some of the remains, had been purchased by Cora in January 1909. This raises a fundamental question – if the remains were buried in his cellar during the last 18 months of his occupancy at Hilldrop Crescent, then why did Crippen know nothing about their disposal?

It took the jury less than half an hour to find Crippen guilty of murder. It is true that his defence team were far from brilliant, led by Alfred Tobin, a mediocre advocate. Ethel at her trial was more fortunate; she had the services of Mr F. E. Smith, one of the rising new talents at the Bar, and his passionate defence got her quickly acquitted. Before, after and during his trial Crippen's only concern was for Ethel, to restate his love and confirm her innocence, though he continued to deny that he knew anything about the body in his cellar. He declared that his love for Ethel was 'not of a debased and degraded character. It was... a good love... Her mind was beautiful to me... Whatever sin there was – and we broke the law – it was my sin not hers... As I face eternity, I say that Ethel Le Neve has loved me as few women love men, and that her innocence of any crime... is absolute.' Crippen awaiting execution broke down finally when he read her last telegram, sent a few hours before his execution at 9am on 23 November 1910. 'My living thoughts and prayers are with you,' wrote Ethel, 'God bless you darling.' Crippen kissed her photo and begged that it be buried with him. He left Ethel all his possessions. After his execution there was an outpouring of sympathy for 'good old Crippen', as F. E. Smith called him, 'a brave man and a true lover'. Even one of the prosecution team, Travers Humphreys, a formidable barrister who later got a reputation as a 'hanging judge', felt that on the Continent the 'extenuating circumstances' of the case would have at least saved Crippen's neck from the rope.

Great crime stories have a way of re-inventing themselves; so it was that in 2007 the world was shocked to learn that after careful study of the slide of the abdominal scar kept by pathologist Sir Bernard Spilsbury, new DNA testing techniques proved that it belonged to a man! Mitochondrial DNA samples had also been taken from known relatives of Cora and the slide did not match them. Two weeks before he was hanged Crippen had written, 'I am innocent and some day evidence will be found to prove it.' His family in America have asked for – and to date been refused – a posthumous royal pardon.

Other researchers have pointed out that Spilsbury's slide could have been mislabelled or was contaminated. This is quite possible. There is a likelihood that the police fiddled the evidence to convict the doctor. Yet disturbing aspects of Crippen's behaviour remain unanswered too; why run away using elaborate disguises after a first visit from the police unless he had something to hide? Why no explanation from him on what was found in his cellar? And no one disputes the fact that those filleted remains required clever medical skills. Even if one ignores the fact of the pyjama jacket remnants (which the police could have planted to strengthen their case), why, oh why, was nothing more ever heard or seen of Cora Crippen? The case was a world-wide sensation and front-page news on every newspaper in America. It is one thing to leave your husband but quite another thing to stand idly by and let him swing on a gibbet just for having an affair. Crippen clearly took some secrets to the grave with him.

Ethel had to go to court to win her lover's belongings but the judge found in her favour. She kept his watch all her life but changed her name and duly got married. She never spoke a word about her past. Ethel Smith, as she became, died in Dulwich Hospital on 9 August 1967 at the ripe age of 84 years. Dr Crippen still lies in Plot 16 (now cemented over) in that awful little annexe between the wings of Pentonville Prison. During the Second World War the Madame Tussauds waxworks museum received a direct hit. The Chamber of Horrors was decimated, smashed wax statues lying everywhere, save one totally undamaged figure. A slightly dusty Crippen was found smiling enigmatically but otherwise unblemished among the debris.

1911–1920

This was a decade dominated, of course, by the 'war to end all wars'. Because so many men were away fighting and dying in the trenches and battlefields, the murder rate dropped to its lowest in the century – just 2,685 persons were tried for murder, attempted murder or manslaughter. The 1914 Special Constables Act had allowed for the appointment of citizens as 'specials' and the war also led to policemen being unionised. In 1919 this resulted in a strike and the union being criminalised. It was replaced by the Police Federation of England and Wales. The 1919 Police Act also guaranteed officers a pension. A constable was earning a basic wage of 43 shillings a week.

In 1916 the chief executioner, Henry Pierrepoint, retired. He had been in office for 10 years. He was succeeded by his brother, Thomas Pierrepoint, whom he had trained. Another man called John Ellis, a barber, became his 'Number One' assistant and in due course acted without Pierrepoint. Wages for the executioners were 10 guineas for the head hangman and just 2 guineas for his assistant.

1911 The Steamship *China* Murder: Francisco Godinho

Alice Brewster was a first-class saloon stewardess on the P&O steamship *China*. A bossy, small, rotund, 54-year-old woman, Alice took an instant dislike to Francisco Godinho, a 40-year-old bathroom attendant. On a voyage from Sydney to London they were seen to have several arguments; he called her names and on one occasion she even slapped his face. Miss Brewster called Godinho a thief, which he hotly denied, while she, in turn, was the recipient of several mysterious cards accusing her of impropriety with a male steward.

On the night of 10 June, while crossing the Indian Ocean in a monsoon, Miss Brewster left her shared cabin to try to sleep in an empty one across the gangway. At 5.30am Godinho woke Annie Crutchley, the stewardess who shared Alice's cabin, with a tray of morning coffee and tea. He asked, 'Where is Miss Brewster sleeping?' Annie told him and he offered to wake her friend. A short time later it was Godinho who reported that something was amiss; the porthole was open, seawater was slopping across the floor, and beneath a mattress lay the bloodied and nude body of Miss Brewster. Her skull had been smashed, possibly by a heavy porthole key, or a hammer.

At Godinho's trial at the Old Bailey before the implacable Mr Justice Avory it was ascertained that the trail of fresh bloodstains and brain matter seemed consistent with an attempt to push the murdered woman through the porthole (which also seemed to explain the absence of her clothes). Miss Brewster's bulk and the heavy gale had made this method of disposal too daunting. Witnesses, as well as medical evidence, put the time of her death at within three hours prior to the discovery of the body. Godinho did not help matters in the days before his trial by making several incriminating statements. His defence counsel argued that Francisco and Miss Brewster had gotten into a fight but the jury were not impressed by this line of argument. Horace Avory once again donned the black cap and the little Goanese steward was executed at Pentonville Prison on 17 October 1911.

1912 Arsenic and Old Lace: Frederick Henry Seddon

The murder of spinster Eliza Barrow by arsenic remains one of the great poisoning cases. It sent her landlord, Frederick Seddon, to the gallows, hanged by a chain of circumstantial evidence. The most likely killer, though Mr Seddon may have planned the deed, was his wife, Margaret Ann Seddon, who was set free. Lawyers connected with the case all condemned the man as 'a fiend', 'a poisonous snake' and a 'mad dog', while Seddon's barrister, the great Sir Edward Marshall Hall, thought it 'the blackest case I've ever been in'.

It is true to say that Seddon was not hanged by any of the evidence but by his manner in the dock during his long cross-examination by the Attorney-General. 'If the evidence does not convict this man, his conceit will,' said Marshall Hall truthfully. Seddon answered the tough questions clearly and forthrightly, but in a manner of appalling smugness, revealing himself to be a penny-pinching miser. Money – from the counting of coins in his parlour, to the reading of each day's wills in the newspapers, to acquiring as much lucre as he could – this was Seddon's obsession.

For 21 years he had worked for the London & Manchester Industrial Insurance Co., and was the proud superintendent of collectors and canvassers for north London. He speculated in property and in 1910 he moved into 63 Tollington Park, Holloway, London N4. It was a corner block linked to the house next door, yet substantial enough, with 14 rooms, for its owner to keep a ground-floor office (rent naturally charged to his employers, at five shillings a week), and space for his wife, five children, elderly father and one live-in servant. The two sons, both youths, were expected to contribute six shillings each a week towards expenses and the second floor was let out as a separate apartment for 12 shillings a week.

Frederick clearly thought himself a pillar of respectable middle-class society; he was the proud owner of a motor car, and he was a Freemason, a chapel goer and occasional preacher. In appearance, with his waxed moustache and high forehead he looked every inch a gentleman, a sight confirmed by his frockcoat and top hat, which he habitually wore out of the house. In the evenings he sometimes went to the music halls but was known to haggle over the prices. At home he enjoyed reading wills in the newspapers and was heard to remark when someone died intestate, 'All that money thrown into the gutter. It's criminal!'

In 1910 there arrived as lodger 49-year-old Miss Barrow – 'sour, argumentative, sluttish, deaf, partial to alcohol and Seddon's perfect match in meanness'. She was also comfortably well off, with investments and property worth some £4,000. Eliza arrived with an odd retinue of friends acting as her servants but, within a few weeks, after several arguments, they left. Clearly Miss Barrow was not an easy person to get along with. She had previously been lodging just a few streets away with a cousin, Frank Vonderahe, but had spat at his wife. Now she was the paying guest of the Seddons. Her sole companion was 10-year-old Ernest Grant, an orphan whose alcoholic parents had been old friends of Eliza's.

It was not long before Frederick and Eliza started talking about money and those conversations became pretty intense; over the next 12 months he skilfully milked her of just about everything she owned so that by October 1910 she had transferred £1,600 of India Stock into his name, in return for a small annuity and remission of rent, while in January 1911 her Camden properties were likewise transferred. Seddon astutely sold the India Stock and bought 14 houses with the money. Worry that the banks might crash, according to the Seddons, led Miss Barrow to change her remaining assets into notes and gold coins and place the money in a cash box in her bedroom. Mr and Mrs Sneddon offered no explanation why all the money had vanished by the time of their trial.

Gradually Miss Barrow's health started to fail her. August 1911 saw London sweltering in a heatwave. It was too much for Mr Seddon who took his whole family off to the seaside including the lodgers. Back in Holloway, Miss Barrow complained of sickness and abdominal pains. 'I had seen her like this before,' said Mrs Seddon. 'Off and on, with those sick bilious attacks every month.' The family doctor was called and did what he could but Eliza refused to take the chalky bismuth he prescribed. She also refused to spend money on a nurse. Mrs Seddon, with a young baby in tow, along with servant girl, Mary Chater, prepared her non-solid diet of soda water, milk, gruel, milk puddings and meat juice extract.

The smell of vomit and faeces in the continuing heat brought swarms of flies to the open windows. On 4 September, according to Mrs Seddon, Eliza asked her to buy some flypapers. These were put in saucers of milk. Each flypaper contained enough arsenic to kill any number of flies – and more than one human being.

By 11 September Miss Barrow was much weaker, though Dr Sworn thought matters were not critical. Early that evening Eliza asked Seddon to write out her will, declaring him as sole executor, though he later said she had refused to have a solicitor present. She also signed the document leaving her personal belongings, furniture, clothing and jewellery to young Ernest and her sister. Curiously, Mr Seddon, the consummate man of business, found no time to take this will to a solicitor for confirmation and he somehow forgot to raise the matter of the money in the cash box.

That night, seemingly in a good mood, Frederick took his wife, father and some visiting relatives to the Finsbury Park Empire music hall. Two nights later he went out again, this time to the Marlborough Theatre, returning home just after midnight and extremely annoyed that the cashier had tried to short-change him. Mrs Seddon told him that Eliza Barrow was complaining she was dying. 'Is she?' he asked. 'No,' said his wife. It was to be a long night; several times Ernest came down to say Miss Barrow was out of bed and several times Margaret Seddon had to climb the stairs and help the smelly and sick woman on and off the commode and into bed. Finally Frederick got dressed and sat with his pipe reading a newspaper outside his lodger's rooms while Margaret sat dozing in a chair. They later claimed that Miss Barrow drifted off to sleep, snoring heavily, before she stopped breathing around 6.15am. What happened next is astonishing: within 45 minutes Seddon was at the doctor's office and got a certificate certifying cause of death as 'epidemic diarrhoea'; by 9.30am young Ernest (who did not know Miss Barrow was dead) was packed off to Southend with the Seddon girls; by noon a cheap and quick £4 funeral was arranged. Never one to miss a financial opportunity, Frederick Seddon even demanded and pocketed a commission of 12s 6d from the undertaker for the business.

The Seddons now made their first mistake; they forgot to inform Frank Vonderahe of his cousin's death. Later they claimed a letter had been sent to him but this never arrived. It is worth bearing in mind that he lived only a few streets away. By the time he got the news Eliza had been four days in a cheap public grave. Vonderahe was appalled and said Miss Barrow could and should have been interred in a family vault (though even after the Seddon trial he did not move her body). What really interested Cousin Frank and the rest of the family was Eliza's money and property. When they found out the ramifications of Seddon's financial dealings with Miss Barrow their anxieties led them to report the matter to the police. Frederick Seddon was mortified; he felt that he could explain everything apart from the missing cash box money. It was true, he said, that only £10 had been found in Miss Barrow's room and he was therefore keen to point out that what with the funeral costs and young Ernie's upkeep he was, in fact, one pound, one shilling and ten pence halfpenny out of pocket!

Exhumed and examined by the country's leading pathologists, Drs Spilsbury and Wilcox, analysis showed Eliza Barrow's body to be 'saturated' with arsenic. The police learned quickly that following her death the Seddons had been busy counting mysterious bags of gold, making alterations to some of Miss Barrow's jewellery and buying shares. On 4 December 1911 Mr Seddon was arrested outside his home. It was all too much for his self-respect. 'What a terrible charge – wilful murder,' he cried, 'It is the first of our family that has ever been accused of such a crime...'

It must have been a black Christmas for him and the rest of the family. On 15 January 1912 Margaret Seddon was also arrested and their joint trial began at the Old Bailey on 4 March before the elderly Mr Justice Bicknell, a judge with a reputation for mildness. In poisoning cases it is traditional that a senior law officer leads for the Crown. This was the Attorney-General, Sir Rufus Isaacs, 'a great advocate with a formidable intellect', assisted by two other top barristers, Richard Muir and fast-rising Travers Humphreys. The Seddons' defence was led by the legendary Sir Edward Marshall Hall, assisted by Gervais Rentoul and others. It was to be a 10-day trial, one of the longest capital cases on record up to that time.

In the dock Mrs Seddon came across as a weak woman very much in the shadow of her husband. Mr Seddon answered Marshall Hall's questions adroitly but was heavily grilled by Isaacs. Asked about four bags of gold he had been seen counting after Eliza's death, Seddon answered, 'That I should bring it down from the top of the house to the bottom, into the office, in the presence of my assistants and count it up – is it feasible ... I am not a degenerate. That would make it out that I was a greedy inhuman monster ... The suggestion is scandalous.' Then, over-reaching himself in smugness, he added with a sarcastic smile, 'I would have all day to count the money.' It was later said that this remark, more than any other thing, hanged Frederick Seddon.

The prosecution could find no direct link between Seddon and the purchase of the arsenic. It was also agreed that he had not fed or nursed the deceased woman. Seddon maintained his hurt pride throughout the trial; in a note to his counsel he declared that he had given his lodger quite a 'decent' funeral. Yet the jury took only one hour to find him guilty. Then, to the surprise of many, they found Margaret Seddon to be innocent. Before being taken away Frederick made an expansive gesture and said, 'I declare before the Great Architect of the Universe, I am not guilty.' This outburst clearly unnerved the judge, whom Seddon must have known was a fellow Mason, and with barely suppressed anger he replied, 'You and I know we both belong to one brotherhood... But our brotherhood does not encourage crime.' In prison before his execution Frederick wrote, 'There is no question of my confessing. If you hear it, do not believe it.' He went to the gallows bravely and Marshall Hall, despite his dislike of Seddon, called him, 'the ablest man I ever defended on the capital charge'.

In hindsight there are several uncomfortable aspects of the case. Seddon was well off with a good job. He hardly needed Miss Barrow's money – unless greed of a really nasty kind got the better of him. Perhaps he advised his wife to help Eliza to meet her Maker by impregnating her tea with arsenic from dipped flypapers? One odd aspect of the case usually overlooked is the role of the maid, Mary Chater. She was mentally unstable, with a brother and cousins in lunatic asylums. She was also known to be dishonest. Did she, in fact, play some role in Miss Barrow's death?

Within a few months Margaret Seddon remarried. Then she admitted in a popular newspaper that she had seen her ex-husband poison the lodger. He had threatened to kill her with a revolver if she told anyone. This story sounded good until Margaret recanted her confession. More than 250,000 people petitioned for Seddon's release, showing the groundswell slowly yet steadily building a half-century before the abolition of capital punishment, but he was executed on 18 April. In his last days Frederick refused to see his family. He remained stoic but became quite emotional when his possessions were auctioned and his beloved car fetched less than he had paid for it. 'That's finished it!' he exclaimed. He might have been cheered to know that more than a century later his Holloway house still stands externally much the same as he left it in Tollington Park.

1913 The Body in the Wood: William Walter Burton

Love, the purest of emotions, might seem a long way from murder, the basest of human acts, yet it is astonishing how many times in these pages the two become intertwined. All too often when love affairs go wrong, it seems as if the only way out is to settle the matter by killing someone.

Gossage St Michael is a lonely, peaceful little village in the green folds of beautiful Dorset. This is classic Thomas Hardy country and the sad little tale of what happened there that spring is worthy of one of Hardy's short stories. An upstanding labourer in the village was handsome 29-year-old William Burton, a bell ringer at the local church, member of the choir and husband to the local postmistress. On the surface this veil of upper-working-class respectability was perfect, but beneath things were not as plain as they seemed. Mrs Burton was several years older than her husband and though he had never given her reason to doubt his spousal affections, Bill Burton's hobbies ran from playing the melodeon in the parlour to dallying, when away from his wife's eyes, with the affections of several local young ladies.

Bill was a rabbit catcher at nearby Manor Farm. It was here in October 1912 that he met an irresistible, attractive new cook, 23-year-old Winifred Mitchell. Spoken words led to letters of seduction, then kisses, and soon the couple were lovers. Six months later, during spring 1913, Winnie told Bill that she was pregnant. During their affair, Bill had tried to stretch his small income as far as he could, buying his lady friend a few small gifts. Now she talked of babies and the pair discussed eloping to Canada or a big city like London. Then Burton, who was clearly starting to feel like a frightened rabbit in one of his own traps, changed his mind. Conversation turned to bitter arguments. Winnie threatened to make the affair very public and also tell Bill's wife of the other girls he had dallied with. Shame and disgrace stared Bill Burton in the face.

Dressed in her best clothes, Winifred Mitchell set off from the village by bicycle at 2.55pm on Monday 31 March. Accidentally she came across Mrs Lily Burton, her lover's wife, who was unaware of the affair. The two women exchanged pleasantries. Near the edge of the village she met Bill Burton. The pair were seen in earnest conversation by passers-by. It was the last time Winnie was ever seen alive. After she had vanished friends of Burton asked questions, as people are inclined to do. 'She may be up to London with somebody with more money than thou and I have,' Bill told one acquaintance. Later he told someone else that Winnie was definitely in the metropolis but 'I shouldn't be surprised to see her back here before long'.

It was a month after Winnie had departed that the local rector, the Reverend Wright, visited one of his parishioners, a dairyman called George Gillingham, and was told how he had found a pair of false teeth in Sorel Wood. It seemed an odd find and the vicar, who may have had his own suspicions, reported the matter to the local police. The Dorset constabulary began some enquiries and discovered that Bill Burton had borrowed a shotgun on the same afternoon that Winnie disappeared. Furthermore, he had asked someone, 'Do you think if I get up close to anybody with this gun, it would kill them?' Another villager reported that on the same evening he had seen Bill pushing a woman's bicycle and Burton had angrily said that 'it'll be a bad job for you' if the man told anybody, a threat he repeated several more times that month. Finally, two boys said they had come across an unusual sight – a freshly dug grave – in Sorel Wood on the day before Winnie had vanished.

On 2 May one of the boys, Henry Palmer, led police to the spot where the poor girl's body was found, face down, partially nude, but with a veil over her face, lying just 18 inches below the surface. Burton was speedily arrested but denied the murder. 'This is a bad job,' he said, 'the only one I worry about is my wife, who's as good a woman as any man can have. It's a pity I ever saw the girl. I know I've been a fool to write letters to her.'

In the dock at the Dorset Assizes the accused man tried to suggest that Winifred Mitchell had another lover at Poole, evidence he had not previously shared with his defence team. The jury took 19 minutes to find him guilty of murder. Before his execution Burton made a full confession. He said that he was too poor to take Winnie to Canada and his attempts to borrow money had failed. 'She nearly drove me wild,' he wrote, 'this is why I done it... The poor girl did not suffer anything. She fell dead in an instant and did not speak.'

Burton was hanged on Midsummer Day 1913, the first execution at Dorchester Prison in 26 years. He had bidden his wife a tearful farewell and taken Holy Communion during his time in gaol. Like any good Thomas Hardy story, the case has a tragic irony; after a post-mortem examination it was found that Winnie Mitchell had not, in fact, been pregnant. She had lied to her lover in order to get him to run away with her. Winnie's lie and her determination to force the issue had led inexorably to her own death.

1914 An Unlucky Killer: George Frembd

With Britain in the grip of war hysteria, spies being executed and already one soldier shot for desertion, it was fairly certain that a jury would not look kindly on a German grocer who slit the throat of his wife at 44 Harrow Road, Leytonstone, on 28 August 1914. To make matters worse 71-year-old Herr Frembd had only been living in England for a few years. It mattered little if Louisa Frembd was a heartless shrew, as George tried to claim. A maid had found the couple in bed, both covered in blood, both with cuts to the throat, though George Frembd's were hastily self-inflicted. He had left a suicide note on the bedside table that read: 'Her first husband made off with himself. I cannot stand it any longer. God forgive me. Her temper done it.'

It was rotten luck for Herr Frembd to be a German in England that autumn, bad luck that his pathetic suicide attempt had failed, bad luck that a jury was in no mood for clemency or the manslaughter charge that might have been preferred in a later age. It was his dubious distinction to be the oldest man executed in Britain during the 20th century. Even his execution was ill-timed; Frembd's head hit the trapdoor as he fell, bruising his eye, a last mischance in a sad case.

1915 Brides in the Bath: George Joseph Smith

The Great War held Britain in a bloody vice; losses on the Western Front steadily mounted while on the home front German Zeppelins even tried to bomb the king at Sandringham. It took a unique series of murders and a cunning killer to drive the war reports off the front pages, but then George Joseph Smith was no ordinary villain. He was a sociopath before the term had even been coined and an amazing rogue – amoral, selfish, manipulative, superficially charming and astonishingly attractive to women, a man who knew neither remorse nor guilt and a liar on a grandiose scale.

It was on a January morning in 1915 that Inspector Arthur Neil – a zealous detective who had found temporary fame in the newspapers

13 years earlier when he had apprehended George Chapman (alias Severin Klosowski), a Whitechapel poisoner who killed three women (and was rumoured to have been Jack the Ripper) – noted in a 'suspicious deaths' memo that a newlywed, Mrs Margaret Lloyd, had been found dead in her bath in Highgate, north London, on 18 December 1914, a sad fact that somehow seemed odd alongside the recorded passing of another bride, Mrs Alice Smith, in Blackpool, one year earlier. Neil pondered the matter and wondered if Mr Lloyd and Mr Smith could, by a freak coincidence, be the same man? He decided to make what the police liked to call a few 'discreet inquiries'.

Neil would have been interested to know that other people were also alarmed by brides dying in their baths. Alice Smith's father, for one, had written to his local constabulary to complain that in his opinion 'foul play had taken place'. Another bright-eyed reader who had seen reports of Mrs Smith's demise, a Joseph Crossley of Blackpool, was sharp enough to write to his Chief Constable that Mr Smith had insured his bride with several insurance companies shortly before her death and buried his wife hurriedly in a common grave and a plain deal coffin.

To begin his investigation Inspector Neil called on the landlady of the Lloyds, Miss Louisa Blatch. She thought the husband would not have had much time to kill his wife. She had heard splashing in the bathroom, then the sound for 10 minutes of Mr Lloyd playing 'Nearer My God to Thee' on the harmonium in the sitting room, before the front door slammed. A short time later the bell rang and Mr Lloyd was on the step saying, 'I forgot I had a key. I have been for some tomatoes for Mrs Lloyd's supper.' Together she and Mr Lloyd had found his 38-year-old bride dead in the bath. The post-mortem cause of death had been listed as 'syncope' or suffocation from drowning, the coroner concluding that 'if she had influenza that, together with a hot bath, might tend her to have a fainting attack'. Inspector Neil was intrigued that the description of Mr John Lloyd, 'a man about 40, height five feet and a half, complexion and build medium, full dark moustache', aptly fitted Mr George Smith (actually, Smith was 5 feet 10 inches tall with very muscular arms). He noted too how both Margaret and Alice had been insured by their husbands shortly before their deaths and how in both cases the husbands had moved quickly to cash in their claims and acquire any money in their wives' bank accounts.

Good detective work led Arthur Neil to discover 'John Lloyd' in Kentish Town on 1 February. Their conversation was worthy of a comedy film; asked if he was George Smith the suspect said, 'I'm not Smith. I don't know what you are talking about.' When told by Neil that Alice

Smith's father would be called to identify him, the man then said, 'In that case I may as well say that my proper name is Smith and my wife died in Blackpool,' adding, 'The two deaths were a phenomenal coincidence.'

With Smith in custody Neil now determined to learn all he could about the man and, if he was a murderer, his methods. Both inquests had listed the deaths as accidental, they had taken place in houses where other people were present, and police officers and doctors who came to the scenes observed no signs of a struggle. So how could someone be drowned quickly and without any apparent marks on the body? Forensic examinations told the Home Office pathologist, Dr Spilsbury, very little and he saw no signs of heart disease or evidence of poisoning. Two days after Margaret's exhumation Inspector Neil was told there might be a third victim – Bessie Mundy – who had married a 'Henry Williams' in Weymouth, Dorset, in 1910. Less than 24 hours before her death Bessie had changed her will leaving an inheritance of £2,500 (about £150,000 today) to her new husband. Cause of death – drowning due to an epileptic fit. 'Williams' was quickly identified as none other than George Joseph Smith.

After more than 120 witness statements were taken, the real facts about Williams/Lloyd/Smith began to emerge. The man was a serial bigamist with no less than seven wives in total of whom three – Bessie Munday, Alice Burnham and Margaret Lofty – had died in their baths. George Smith had only been faithful, it appeared, and that in a very loose way, to one woman named Edith Pegler. She had replied to an advertisement for a housekeeper and subsequently married Smith in 1908. Rather amusingly, Edith later said that she saw Smith take only one bath in the seven years she knew him. Between his other marriages Smith had returned to Edith and duped her into thinking his long absences were due to business trips.

Smith had been born in Bow, East London, in 1872. The son of an insurance salesman, like Seddon, young George, at nine years of age, was sentenced by a hard judge to eight years in a reformatory. One can well imagine the misery and abuse he suffered there, an awful experience that clearly hardened him and set him on a career of crime; in 1896 he was sentenced to one year in gaol for receiving stolen goods but by then his modus operandi was established. Twelve months after being released from prison George married Caroline Thornhill, an 18-year-old who worked in the bakery business he had started in Leicester. Soon he had turned his young wife into a criminal and had her thieving for him. Even after serving a short prison sentence Caroline returned to her abusive husband with the magnetic eyes. It took a thrashing from two of her brothers to finally drive Smith away. In the meantime he was in and out of prison and, when free, his scams of women continued; in 1909 he had married a Sarah Falkner in Southampton, got his new bride to empty her Post Office account of £290 – her entire savings – and duly absconded with everything 'except a few pence' including all her jewellery, worth a further £110.

Murdering his wives must have seemed just another small step to Smith since it is clear that by 1910 bigamy had become his main business. Yet the question remained for the police and pathologists – how had Smith drowned his brides? Spilsbury devised various tests using the three murder baths with allowances made for body weights of the victims in kneeling, sitting and lying positions and the water at different levels. He was assisted by an athletic young lady swimmer. The tests proceeded normally until Spilsbury tried hoisting the girl up by her ankles. Her head quickly went under the water. 'Suddenly I gripped her arm, it was limp,' he later wrote, 'she was unconscious.' It took him and some detectives a nervous 30 minutes to revive the lady. She told them how the water had rushed up her nostrils and then she had blacked out. This theory of death, not from asphyxia, but shock, medically termed 'inhibition', had been referred to by a police surgeon who had to regularly deal with drownings in the Thames in a talk given to the Medico-Legal Society in 1909. Death in such circumstances was, he noted, mechanical and due to excitation of the nervous system.

Smith's trial lasted 10 days, a very long one indeed by 1915 standards, and each morning saw bevies of women queuing to see the man. His judge was white-bearded Mr Justice Scrutton. From the dock George vilified the judge, the barristers and his trial – 'It's a disgrace to a Christian country, this is. I'm not a murderer, though I may be a bit peculiar.' Defending Smith was Sir Edward Marshall Hall, but he had doubts about his client, whom he thought guilty, and thought he had hypnotised his victims. This theory of hypnotism has been noted by several commentators alongside Smith's commanding manner and magnetic eyes. His ability during almost two decades to charm and con so many gullible women does make the possibility of a skill like hypnotism seem all the more likely.

The jury were out for just 22 minutes on 1 July before finding Smith guilty. The forensic evidence had been carefully presented by Spilsbury but it is likely that George's cold-hearted display of greed did more to hang him. Not content with simply ransacking his victims' bank accounts or claiming insurance money, after Bessie's funeral Smith had demanded the bath money back from the ironmonger; Alice had been rushed into a pauper's grave, without even a wreath from him; he told the undertaker at Margaret's internment to 'get it over with as quick as you can'; demanded one-third off his usual fee; and left Miss Blatch's lodgings owing 10s in rent. Families and loved ones of the victims, perhaps needless to say, had not been informed of their demise and had been kept at a distance.

Forty-six seconds after leaving his cell on the morning of 13 August 1915, the 'Brides in the Bath Murderer' was hanged at Maidstone Prison by executioner John Ellis. Smith remained unrepentant to the end, though he found solace in talks with the prison chaplain. He was mourned by only one person, Edith Pegler, and to her Smith had written from his condemned cell that she had been his 'true love'. Using the kind of blarney he must have lavished on his victims, George wrote: 'May an old age, serene and bright, and as lovely as a Lapland night, lead thee to thy grave... good night until we meet again.' On a brighter note, Caroline Thornhill, the girl Smith had abused and then forced into crime, got married on the day after his execution to a Canadian soldier serving with the Royal Engineers. History does not record, but one hopes they had a happy marriage.

1916 The Murder of Big Dan's Wife: Daniel Sullivan

South Wales early in the last century was a land of scarred valleys, slagheaps, smoking furnaces and black coal pits. Dowlais, near Merthyr Tydfil, was a typical village dominated by its sprawling iron and steel foundry. One of the cokers there was a heavyset man called Daniel Sullivan, known to the locals as 'Big Dan'. It was best to steer clear of Dan when he drank, which was often, because he usually turned violent under the influence of alcohol.

On the hot summer night of Saturday 18 July Big Dan had spent his week's pay in the bar of the Antelope Inn, bought a bottle of rum after hours and staggered towards his home. Once there he dragged his poor wife, Catherine, from her bed, demanded some supper and threw her into the kitchen. There in a blinding alcohol-induced frenzy he literally kicked her to death wearing his heavy nailed coker's boots.

At his trial before Mr Justice Ridley at Swansea Assizes Dan's stepdaughter, Bridget, aged nine, told how he frequently used to beat her mother. That terrible night he had asked the girl where Catherine was and on being told she was asleep roared, 'There'll be a corpse leaving the house tonight!' During his attack the 38-year-old man had literally stamped all over Catherine, who seemed to put up no resistance.

Her body had been pummelled all over and was covered in bloodstains. Young Bridget ran screaming in fear from the house and the police found drunken Dan hiding in a chicken coop. The jury deliberations took just 30 minutes. 'Big Dan' went to meet his Maker at 9am on 6 September at Swansea Prison. He had earlier taken the last ministrations of the Roman Catholic faith. A postscript to the case is that the landlord of the Antelope Inn found himself in hot water for selling Dan Sullivan the bottle of rum after hours. The magistrates reflected on how Mrs Sullivan might just have been alive without that fiery spirit inside the killer; they sentenced the publican to 28 days in gaol and a fine of £20.

1917 The Sadistic Coward: Thomas McGuiness

The kind of people who can murder a child, especially those who torture or beat up youngsters, are in a special league shunned even by most hardened criminals. Just such a man was Thomas McGuiness, a 25-year-old unemployed, pint-sized bully who romanced a servant girl in Aberdeen and proposed marriage. When he discovered the girl had a five-year-old son called Alexander he withdrew the marriage offer but persuaded the girl to leave her job and join him on the road. This kind of life soon lost its appeal and the couple split up, the girl moving to Edinburgh, but eventually McGuiness turned up like a bad penny and they all set up a home in Glasgow.

Ill and confined to bed, young Alexander's mother was at the mercy of McGuiness. He, in turn, soon showed his sadistic nature, beating up the five-year-old, pushing him violently around and stubbing cigarettes out on the boy's arms. Eventually he went too far, throwing Alexander down some stairs and then proceeding to kick and punch the little chap's head. McGuiness told the child's mother that the boy had suffered a fit. Then he repeated the story to a nosy neighbour but she had her own suspicions and, realising the kind of man he was, went for the police. McGuiness had fled but was arrested when he returned to the house on the next day.

At his trial the jury quickly found him guilty. In gaol as the days passed towards his execution the man who could beat a little boy to death was in a fearful state. Offered some brandy shortly before he went to the scaffold, McGuiness replied that 'I've been a teetotaller all my days and I'll manage without it now', yet this bravado left him as the executioner, John Ellis, placed the noose around his neck and he swooned into a faint. Shouting a warning to his assistant to jump clear, Ellis dashed to pull the lever and the trap doors crashed open, swinging McGuinness into eternity.

1918 The Bloody Butcher: Louis Marie Joseph Voisin

By the autumn of 1917 the violence of the Great War had reached London. On the night of 31 October the capital experienced its worst Zeppelin raid thus far; sirens screamed as people ran for cover, bombs rained down, lives were lost and fires raged. The sheer terror of the night led a French woman to seek the arms of her lover and a surprise visit ended in her brutal death.

Early on the morning of 2 November a young man, a male nurse by profession, found a large sacking-covered parcel just inside the railings of Regent Square, Bloomsbury. On opening the package he got the shock of his life – it contained the torso, minus the head, legs and hands, of a woman. The gruesome find was wrapped in a sheet and dressed in delicate lace and blue-ribboned underwear. A piece of torn brown paper was also found with the handwritten words given in most accounts as 'Blodie Belgium' (Andrew Rose says 'Bladie' not 'Blodie' and since he has seen the case file he is probably correct) hastily scrawled. Police were soon on the scene and found nearby a second parcel that contained a pair of mutilated legs.

The state of dried blood on the torso revealed to the police surgeons that the woman had been killed within 36 hours of her discovery; the mutilations had taken place after death and been done by someone with a knowledge of dissection. Detective Inspector John Ashley quickly saw a clue in a laundry mark, 'IIH', on a corner of the sheet. By the next day inquiries among laundries led police to 50 Munster Square, Regents Park, where 32-year-old Madame Emillienne Gerard had been absent from her rooms since the night of the air raid. She was the wife of a French chef serving in the trenches. A search of Mme Gerard's rooms revealed a handwritten £50 IOU signed by a Louis Voisin (a 'very ignorant, illiterate French butcher' as his defence counsel called him), and a framed photograph of the chubby-faced, burly ox of a man with a dark moustache. Mme Gerard had been acting as his housekeeper, but it was rumoured that she and Voisin were lovers. The police were especially interested to learn that Voisin traded as a butcher.

Led by Superintendent McCarthy of Scotland Yard, a large number of officers descended on Voisin's basement apartment at 101 Charlotte Street, Soho. Here they found the 42-year-old Frenchman sitting in his bloodstained kitchen talking with another Gallic émigré named Berthe Roche. Her husband had been killed on the Somme in 1916 but the pair had managed a hotel for expatriates in Lisle Street since 1910. Voisin and

Roche were taken to Bow Street Police Station where Voisin, who spoke no English, was interviewed via an interpreter by Chief Inspector Frederick Wensley (whom we had last encountered in these pages in 1909). The suspect described himself as Mme Gerard's brother-in-law. He said that he had last seen her alive on 31 October when he thought she was going to Southampton to see a friend off to France. He admitted visiting her apartment on 2 and 3 November to feed her cat.

Police meanwhile searching the Charlotte Street address had made a horrible discovery; in Voisin's cellar, within a wooden cask covered in powdered alum, were the head and hands of Emillienne Gerard. Voisin had already tried to explain the bloodstains in his kitchen by saying that he had recently butchered a calf's head. On a hunch, Wensley asked him to write down the words 'Bloody Belgium'. He asked him to do it five times. Each time the suspect wrote 'Blodie Belgium'. Immediately Wensley charged Voisin and Roche with Mme Gerard's death. Furiously Berthe Roche screamed at Voisin, 'You nasty man. You have deceived me.' He simply shrugged his shoulders and with Gallic sang-froid replied, 'It is unfortunate.'

In January 1918 the two French citizens faced tiny dilettante Mr Justice Darling at the Old Bailey. By then the prosecution team had received substantial forensic help from Sir Bernard Spilsbury. Voisin's defence was that he found Emillienne Gerard's severed head and hands in a flannel jacket at her apartment. He then lost his nerve and instead of telling the police he tried to clean up some of the bloodstains (though leaving a bloody water pail and bedspread). He suggested that Mme Gerard knew some unsavoury people. 'The crime was committed at Mme Gerard's place,' he said, adding gallantly, 'Madame Roche is not concerned in this crime at all.'

The amount and distribution of blood at Munster Square convinced Spilsbury that it was not the murder site. He was able to show that the killing took place at Charlotte Street. Fourteen stains on the kitchen door were all shown to be human blood. He found more samples on the floor, in the sink, on the draining board, gas stove, ceiling, a wall leading to the back yard and a hearth rug in the stable. There were sinister objects too: a stained butcher's knife and chopping board, along with a man's shirt, woollen jacket, a towel and three pieces of cloth all found in the cellar.

The jury quickly found Voisin guilty, but Mr Justice Darling directed them that there was insufficient evidence to convict Berthe Roche of wilful murder. Darling delivered the death sentence in French and the burly butcher was executed at Pentonville on 2 March. It is highly likely that the roles of Voisin and Roche should have been reversed and that she was the killer of Emillienne Gerard. In court it was explained by Spilsbury that 'in all possibility Madame Gerard was done to death between 11.25pm on the night of October 31st and 8 o'clock of the following morning... Her head had been battered by a great number of successive blows with a blunt instrument, which would account for the splashes of blood all around the door. Apparently the dead woman had tried to defend herself to some extent because on her right hand were marks showing that she had tried to ward off the blows.' Spilsbury also found clots on Gerard's heart indicative of partial strangulation and the blood-soaked towel, with an earring attached, suggested it had been wrapped around her head to stifle the screams. Together, Spilsbury and Richard Muir, the famous Crown counsel, concluded that Emillienne Gerard, perhaps terrified by the Zeppelin raid, had fled to the home of her lover only to find him in the arms of another mistress, Berthe Roche. The two women had never met before. With bombs falling and nerves frayed, harsh words led to violence. The tough butcher could have felled Mme Gerard with a single blow, so it seems likely that Mme Roche attacked her rival and bludgeoned her repeatedly. Perhaps Voisin, fearful that the noise might alert his neighbours, had used the towel to strangle Emillienne. Panicking, he then dismembered the body, took part of it to Munster Square hoping to lay a false trail, then began the grisly task of disposing of the rest of her body as he passed by Regent Square in his pony and trap.

The press were unhappy with the outcome of the trial and the *Daily Express* ran the headline 'Innocent Man Hanged'. There are several oddities in the case and one of the defence team thought Voisin was trying to shield a third person. Emillienne seemed to have several lovers and she may have been a British government agent with enemies in the foreign émigré community in London.

Berthe Roche reappeared at the Old Bailey on 28 February 1918 before Mr Justice Avory who sentenced her to seven years' penal servitude. Her violent and unstable nature manifested itself while in prison. Most accounts say that she died insane but historian Andrew Rose was able to discover that she was released from prison on licence with terminal cervical cancer in September 1919 and died in a Hackney hospice three months later. Buried in the Home Office files is information that Voisin had been charged with the robbery and murder of a farmer in Angers in 1901, but there is no record of a trial.

1919 The Lethal Lodger: Henry Perry

Soldiers and demobbed men returning to civilian life were suspects or killers in 42 of the 127 murder cases reported in the press in this year. In the case of Henry Perry, his prosecutor said at the trial: 'The war has done great good for some persons, it has taught them discipline and made honest and honourable men of people who started badly. But the brutalities of war may have made more vicious a person who was vicious before.'

Perry was an habitual criminal with 17 convictions and three terms of penal servitude before he joined the colours. As a soldier it must be said that he fought gallantly in the Dardanelles, was wounded in action (with shrapnel splinters embedded in his brain), was taken prisoner by the Turks and tortured with the bastinado. Returning from the Middle East the 37-year-old Perry found lodgings in the home of his stepfather's sister, 43-year-old Alice Cornish at Forest Gate, north London. There were arguments. One can imagine after his terrible experiences and the headaches brought on by the brain injuries that Perry was not the easiest of men to get along with. Alice Cornish thought he was rude and morose and she told her lodger to leave.

A few weeks later, on 28 April, Perry was seen by Mrs Cornish as he passed the house and she invited him in. This was a huge mistake because the pair were soon arguing again. Something then exploded in Henry Perry's brain, perhaps the result of stress and mental breakdown; he hit Alice Cornish with the kitchen poker, carried her to an outhouse and whacked the unconscious woman with a pickaxe before fetching a carving knife and sticking it into her throat. Having thrown the body in some rubbish, Perry went on slaughtering the rest of the family in a very gruesome manner: five-year-old Marie was next, the little schoolgirl being hit over the head with a hammer and thrown in the cellar; 14-year-old Alice was next to arrive and she was also hit by a hammer before having her head severed by an axe. Last came Mr Walter Cornish who fatally turned his back on Perry, a bad mistake, as the killer drove the axe into his back. Perry made off but Mr Cornish staggered into the street and managed to blurt out, 'That soldier...' before collapsing. He died in hospital two days later. Perry had escaped the bloody crime scene after grabbing some money and other valuables.

At his trial before Mr Justice Darling, the defendant claimed he had heard voices telling him to murder someone. In view of his sufferings in the war and gallant service record this line of defence might have saved Perry from the gallows, but the jury were not impressed by his long criminal record, while the enormity of slaughtering an entire family of four persons with an axe, including a five-year-old child, almost certainly decided his fate. Passing sentence, Darling said it was the most horrible case he had ever tried. Perry was hanged for his quadruple killings at Pentonville on 10 July 1919.

1920 The Murder of Irene Munro: Field & Gray

The terrible war was truly over. The Jazz Age had begun. A new mood and changing morality were reflected in the novels of F. Scott Fitzgerald, Elinor Glyn and other writers. Modern youth partied to the Charleston and office girls dreamed of making love to Rudy Valentino, John Barrymore and other matinee idols, or guzzling champagne at wild parties hosted by the likes of Joan Crawford and other dancing flapper girls.

Just such a teenager was 17-year-old Irene Munro. She was 'dark and unremarkably pretty with rather prominent front teeth' and worked as a shorthand typist for a West End firm of underwriters. Her pay was £2 3s 1½d a week and she lived with her widowed mother in South Kensington. After Irene's death it was found that she was not a virgin. Some of the press labelled her a harlot. They were wrong. She had been out with the boys but Irene was not a goodtime girl. Like many young women, then and now, she was no rambling rose, nor a shrinking violet, but something in between.

When it came to her annual fortnight's holiday in August, Irene's mother wanted her company on a trip to see relatives at Portobello near Edinburgh. The daughter, despite being only 17, was adamant that she didn't want to stay with stuffy relations, but needed a real holiday with sea air, fun and adventure. So despite Mrs Munro's misgivings Irene saw her Mum off to Scotland, then headed alone for the breezy delights of Eastbourne. Three days later she wrote to her mother that 'the weather is simply gorgeous ... and I feel much better already. I had the most awful job to get a room... It is a pity in a way that you are not here as my room is large enough for two people... Yesterday I went to Pevensey Bay – walked there and back. I have two pounds fifteen left... so please do send me down as much as you can to reach me by Saturday...' The letter ended: 'Goodbye for the present. Please give my love to Grannie, Aunt Jean and everyone. Your affectionate Rene.'

Not long after posting this letter the young woman was murdered. Her fully clothed body was found next day by a boy playing on the shingle along the lonely stretch of beach known as the Crumbles. Her face had been smashed by a large ironstone brick that lay nearby.

Scotland Yard were called in and it did not take Detective Chief Inspector Mercer long to track down two men who had been seen on the Crumbles with Irene on the afternoon she was killed. They were Jack Field, a 19-year-old unemployed youth with a criminal record, who had recently been discharged from the Royal Navy, and 28-year-old William Gray, an illiterate South African-born ex-serviceman who had married an Eastbourne girl. Like Field Gray was unemployed, and though he had no criminal convictions his several brushes with the law included accusations of rape and robbery.

The trial of the two men began on 13 December before Mr Justice Avory at Lewes Assizes and despite the best efforts of Sir Edward Marshall Hall, defending Gray, and Mr J. D. Cassels, appearing for Field, the outlook was bleak. In gaol prior to his trial Gray had made matters worse by saying to a fellow prisoner, 'I was with the girl almost till the hour it happened,' adding, 'but that does not mean to say I done it.' The other lag had asked him how the murder happened. 'By dropping a stone on her head,' replied Gray garrulously. 'How do you know that?' asked the other prisoner. Gray replied, 'I have seen the stone.' Young, lonely, friendly Irene had been seen by several people on the afternoon of her murder. They described her talking to the two men and seeming 'quite jolly' as she offered them sweets and fruit from a paper bag. Just before she was last seen alive, Irene had picked up a stray kitten and was seen stroking it. One of her companions handed it over to some navvies working on the railway line as the two men and the girl strolled away in the sunshine. Her body was found just 300 yards from this spot further along the Crumbles.

The jury delivered a verdict of guilty on both men, with a recommendation of mercy since they felt 'the crime was not premeditated'. Horace Avory, with his famously thin lips, stern countenance and creaky voice, was not the judge to show much mercy to convicted killers who had heinously attacked a young and defenceless woman. Marshall Hall had tried to confuse the jury by suggesting the two men had no motive to kill Miss Munro but Avory pointed out that it was not something the jury need worry itself about. In the Court of Criminal Appeal the case was virtually retried, only this time both men had to be separated as they blamed each other for the killing. Both appeals failed and the two men were executed at Wandsworth Prison on the morning of 4 February 1921.

The exact reason for Irene Munro's death will never be known. She had not been raped so it seems likely that Field and Gray, who had both been drinking, thought the chirpy girl might be an easy seduction. When she resisted, one of them, in fury, crushed her head with the brick.

1921–1930

The cosy, disciplined pre-war world was at an end, though it might linger on in the countryside to some extent; in big cities such as London and Manchester, society was in a state of flux. Sexual morality was changing. The Great War returned many veterans with shocking physical and mental injuries. There were plenty of illegal weapons for the members of the underworld to lay their hands on.

It was a classic decade for murder – the cases of Armstrong (1922), Mahon (1924), Thorne (1925), Robinson (1927) and Browne & Kennedy (1928) being among the most famous British cases of the century. In 1922 a new charge of infanticide replaced that of murder for mothers killing their children in the first year of life. In 1930 a forward-thinking Parliamentary committee even suggested that capital punishment be suspended for a trial period of five years, but no action was taken. John Ellis, the hangman, retired in 1923. He was a neurotic person who drank a lot and in August 1924 he tried to commit suicide by shooting himself but failed; however, he succeeded in 1931 by cutting his throat. In the years 1921–1930 a total of 2,731 persons were put on trial charged with murder, attempted murder or manslaughter. In 1921 and again in 1930 only five persons were hanged.

1921 The Musical Milkman Murder: George Arthur Bailey

On 17 September 1920 a seemingly cheerful 32-year-old milkman named George Bailey, with his heavily pregnant wife – 10 years his junior – and their two-year-old daughter, Hollie, moved into Barn Cottage, Church Road, Little Marlow, Buckinghamshire, after paying in advance a £6 rent. Kate was found dead by police barely a fortnight later, on 2 October, clad only in her nightdress and woollen undergarments. Her husband and child had vanished.

Five months earlier Bailey had taken a position as a milkman for Mr Edwin Hall who ran a dairy in Bourne End, about 1½ miles from Little Marlow. In his application George had described himself as 'abstemious, steady, energetic, of decent appearance...' While he may have looked decent, George's past, if he had owned up to it, told a different story. Yet within a few days it was clear that Mr Hall's customers liked their new milkman. He was a short, thickset man who always had a cheery smile for everybody. So successful was he in boosting egg and cheese sales as well as selling milk that soon his employer offered him an extra five shillings a week. Always whistling or humming a tune, Bailey was nicknamed by locals as 'The Musical Milkman' or 'The Whistling Milkman'.

George started his new job by leaving his pregnant wife and infant with relatives in Wiltshire while he rented a semi-detached house called 'Millbank' in Bourne End. There is no question that George loved music and he had been working for some time on a musical notation system that would simplify the playing and teaching of music. On 25 June he advertised in the *Bucks Free Press* for a 'refined' young lady to help 'copy manuscript proof sheets' and help him market his ideas. Two months later George placed another advert which gave some indication of what was really on his mind; he specified he needed 'Young ladies, not under 16, must be 5ft 6in, well-built, full figure or slim build...' He offered an outrageously high salary of five guineas (£5 5s) per week. So many young ladies applied that the local constable, John Gray, was told to watch Bailey's house. Later P.C. Gray claimed to have seen 30 young women come and go, usually between 5pm and 8pm. Naturally in a small place like Little Marlow such comings and goings were noted by neighbours, gossiped about and frowned upon. Hollie and Kate arrived to join George on 22 July. By this time Bailey's landlady was angrily demanding that he leave since George had sub-let part of the house without her permission and the 'wear and tear of two families and three children' was an arrangement 'I strongly disapprove of...'

It was then that Bailey saw the advert for Barn Cottage, which was being rented fully furnished including a piano. It was a handsome gabled property, formerly an old bakery, with a welcoming horseshoe nailed to the front door and a rustic garden filled with mature fruit trees.

No sooner had Bailey taken possession of Barn Cottage than he reported to Mr Hall that he was too sick for work. To be fair to George he had been unwell for much of his life and his absence from work may have been quite genuine. Sometime between 4pm on 29 September and the discovery of her body three days later, Kate Bailey died of prussic acid poisoning. Neighbours thought her a timid little 22-year-old but on the last afternoon she was seen alive she had chatted with some of them and seemed quite happy.

On 30 September Miss Lilian Marks, a 21-year-old grocer's assistant, complained to the local vicar that Bailey had made improper advances to her on the previous evening and she was quite distressed. The local police were also informed of these allegations and on the morning of 1 October Detective Inspector William West turned up at the cottage but found the place all shut, save for a few open windows. Two constables climbed inside and at first nothing seemed amiss. It was in the fourth and last bedroom they searched that Mrs Bailey was found on the floor, covered in a sheet, lying under a camp bed. A preliminary examination by a doctor showed no signs of violence, although the woman's face was a purplish-blue colour and a stain of red mucus covered her right eye. That evening, about 8.30pm, Bailey was apprehended outside Reading Station by a local constable who recognised him. When searched his pockets contained no less than four poisons – prussic acid, chloroform, opium and stramonium. Bailey said very little but told the police his daughter was now with relatives in Swindon and 'I do not want to see her again.' He was speedily and formally charged with his wife's murder.

The great Sir Bernard Spilsbury arrived to conduct a forensic examination of Kate Bailey's body. He noted that she was six months pregnant but there did not appear to be any signs of an attempted abortion. Her death, Spilsbury concluded, was consistent with prussic acid poisoning.

Bailey's trial began at Aylesbury Crown Court on Wednesday 12 January 1921 before Mr Justice McCardie, a stern bachelor judge of strong moral views who suffered from depression (and who would commit suicide within 10 years). The jury was the first ever in Great Britain to include women, three of them, deciding whether a man accused of murder was innocent or guilty. Soon it was revealed to these good citizens that George Bailey was not quite all he seemed. He had been born on 13 March 1888 in West Hampstead to extremely poor parents. At an early age he had left school to work as a clerk in a coal merchant's office. In 1905, when George was 17, his father died in a workhouse of 'religious mania'. This event may have sent him off the rails because in 1908, George was sentenced to 20 months' hard labour for fraud and forgery. Five years later when working at a London dairy as a milkman he vanished with his takings. This crime earned him another six months behind bars. In June 1916 he enlisted in the Devonshire Regiment but deserted two months later. It was while on the run from the army that he married Kate Lowden at Lambeth Registry Office. Marriage did not stop George's criminal ways and he stole £11 10s from a Torquay boarding house, then some cheques and jewellery in London, crime that earned him a three-year stretch in Parkhurst. Kate had helped pass some of the cheques and she was sentenced to six months in Winchelsea Prison, where their daughter was born. George finally left prison on 6 February 1920 on licence (meaning that he would be recalled if he reoffended).

It is worth noting that in addition to the poor health that dogged Bailey all his life, probably starting in a malnourished childhood, he had also had a spell in in a mental asylum and made attempts to commit suicide in 1911 and 1917.

The prosecution argued that Bailey had tired of his wife, whom he had married in her teens. She was heavily pregnant and had lost the bloom of youth. It was suggested that the couple had quarrelled and Kate was depressed by George's obsession with musical notation and the money he wasted on his hobby. One witness said he had seen George put his hands around Kate's throat saying, 'My God, I will put an end to you' (a rather melodramatic incident that the accused hotly denied). He had acquired the prussic acid by lies. His love of music and obsession with a musical notation system were real enough, but the defendant had used his musical sessions as a means to lure young women to the cottage with the hope that some might consent to sex. He had attempted to rape Miss Marks while his wife lay dead upstairs and it was suggested that the poison had been administered early that evening while Lilian Marks was out of the house for a time.

George's chief line of defence was that Kate had committed suicide. In his pockets when he was arrested was a long rambling letter that implied an elaborate suicide pact between him and his 'loving' wife. It ended with the words, 'My darling I am coming.' A letter from Kate to her mother could have been interpreted as a suicide note; in it she complained about her husband's offhand treatment of her and asked the older woman to care for Hollie as 'I can't stand it any longer'. The trial ended on Monday 21 January and Mr Justice McCardie donned the black cap after a guilty verdict from the ladies and gentlemen of jury.

An appeal was launched and duly heard by the famously severe, yet invariably correct, Mr Justice Avory. He dismissed the attempt to save Bailey because the accused's evidence had been a mass of contradictions;

it was clear that Bailey had bought poison and had either administered it or helped his wife commit suicide. Evidence of motive, noted Horace Avory, was admissible because Bailey had invited young women to his home on the day of the crime and tried to assault one of them under the same roof as his dead wife. The jury had also not found Bailey insane, nor had he offered insanity as a defence.

The musical milkman went quietly to the gallows at Oxford Prison at 8am on 2 March 1921. He never made a confession. On the day before his execution he met with his solicitors for the last time and told them 'Don't let my music die', a reference to his musical notation system. Hollie Bailey was brought up by her stern grandmother who told the child that her parents had died in the great influenza epidemic after World War I. It was many years before she got to know the truth. In the 1980s she told an investigator that she felt 'very bitter' towards her father. 'He robbed me of my mother,' said Hollie. 'She didn't deserve to die like that...'

1922 The Hay Poisonings: Herbert Rowse Armstrong

Hay-on-Wye is a perfect example of a small English market town nestled in the soft green hills of the Welsh border. Even today it seems somewhat remote with its ornate little clock tower and partly ruined castle overlooking quaint alleys and streets, the widest of which is imposingly called Broad Street – a medieval avenue of antiquarian bookshops, a florist, a butcher's shop and so on. There is no sign of a modern supermarket. Hay-on-Wye seems time-warped in the 1950s and you might expect to run into Miss Marple or Hercule Poirot on any street corner. Nearby, on the outskirts, is a little place called Cusop Dingle, a name that conjures up in the mind visions of croquet on the lawn, with scones and strawberry jam for tea.

Here was played out one of the greatest poisoning stories in British criminal history – and like all good mysteries it has grown even more arcane with the passage of time. While Seddon and his flypapers is a fascinating case it must be agreed that for sheer quirkiness right out of a Twenties thriller, nothing quite equals the story of little Major Armstrong, the deadly chocolates, buttered scones for tea, and arsenic – lots of arsenic – to kill the dandelions.

Striding up the driveway of 'Mayfield', the big house in Cusop, came Oswald Martin on the late autumn afternoon of Wednesday 26 October 1921. He was one of Hay's two solicitors and he had been invited to afternoon tea by his rival, widower Herbert Armstrong, who lived in the lovely old house with extensive lawns and gardens. There had been a recent legal dispute between the two firms but Martin was making a social call. Much younger than Armstrong, he had got married four months previously and, although not invited to the wedding, his fellow solicitor had sent a pair of silver candlesticks as a gift. At his trial Armstrong claimed to have poured the tea, let Martin help himself from the cake stand, then reached over to get a scone with the words, 'Please excuse me.' Martin ate some currant loaf, saying it was his favourite cake. The prosecution at the trial claimed that Armstrong put a buttered scone on Martin's plate, saying, ''Scuse fingers' or 'Excuse fingers'. The 52-year-old solicitor was adamant that he did not do any such thing. It would have been a social *faux pas* in his eyes. He was solicitor and clerk to the justices in three divisions of magistrates and an ex-army major who had served throughout the Great War from 1914 until demobilisation in 1919. More important, perhaps, he had served the citizens of Hay with a legal practice since 1906 while Martin, who came from a lower social class, took up his practice only in 1918.

Both Armstrong and Martin were brother Freemasons and the conversation that afternoon stayed friendly and off business matters. Both ate heartily from the cake stand. That evening Martin and his wife also had a dinner of hot jugged hare and a coffee cream dessert before retiring to bed. About 9.10pm Oswald was sick and continued to vomit throughout the night. His wife, Constance, an ex-nurse, did not summon the doctor until next day. Dr Hincks concluded that Martin, who was feeling a little better, had been victim to one of the bilious attacks prevalent since August and treated his illness as gastric influenza. While in bed Oswald was visited by his mother-in-law, Mrs Davies, wife of the local chemist. She hinted to her son-in-law that Katherine Armstrong, the major's late wife, had died in somewhat mysterious circumstances and perhaps his sickness was really a poisoning. Next to call by was Fred Davies, who owned Hay's only chemist's shop. Oswald was by now downstairs and feeling much better. Fred warned his son-in-law and daughter to watch out for mysterious gifts in the post such as chocolates. In unison the Martins replied, 'We have already been sent some chocolates anonymously through the post.' Despite first suggesting they throw the gift away, Mr Davies later requested and was given the chocolates to study.

On Sunday 30 October Fred Davies called in on Dr Hincks and told him of his suspicions regarding the tea party and the chocolates. The doctor had a long ride ahead of him to visit a client in the mountains and its seems that during his journey he pondered on many things, not least of which were the curious tale weaved by the chemist and troubled memories of Mrs Armstrong's death. Hincks came to the conclusion, as he soon told the authorities, that the major was a 'homicidal maniac'. He also later admitted that he had no suspicions until that date. The doctor sent the chocolates for analysis along with a sample of Oswald Martin's urine. Then he demanded and got a meeting with the Chief Constable of Herefordshire and a representative of the Director of Public Prosecutions. The result was that on 10 December a Scotland Yard detective, Alfred Crutchett, and his police sergeant, arrived in Hay-on-Wye to begin discreet inquiries. They interviewed the Martin and Davies families and traced the sale of the chocolates (though this line of investigation was not very helpful). Crutchett was especially interested to learn from Fred Davies that Major Armstrong had purchased at the chemist's shop one quarter of a pound of arsenic in 1919 and the same amount again on 11 January 1921. Meanwhile, the analysis of samples had revealed $\frac{1}{33}$rd of a grain of arsenic in Martin's urine and just over 2 grains of arsenic in one of two tampered chocolates in the box. Two grains of arsenic, Crutchett knew, had been known to cause death in an adult.

Adding a small element of farce to the proceedings, and certainly unnerving Oswald Martin, was that Major Armstrong seemed to have enjoyed their tea party so much that he kept bombarding his rival solicitor with further invitations throughout November. He even invited him to pop over from his office, which was opposite his own on Broad Street, and enjoy a cuppa. Crutchett's investigations were done so discreetly that Armstrong was totally surprised when he was arrested in his office on the last day of the year and charged with attempting to murder Oswald Martin with arsenic on 26 October. On Monday 2 January 1922 the major appeared in the dock of his own police court, 'a small, dapper man who stood rigidly to attention'. While his arraignment was going on, the grave of Armstrong's wife was exhumed in Cusop churchyard. She had died 10 months earlier on 22 February 1921. Her remains were examined by Sir Bernard Spilsbury and found to be saturated with arsenic. Herbert Armstrong now found himself on the far more serious charge of murder in the first degree.

The major's arrest shocked Hay-on-Wye's townsfolk to the core and divided the community. Some hinted that Armstrong was a philanderer, a syphilitic even, who had been after his wife's money and wanted to dispose of her because she was a shrew. Others recalled this long-respected pillar of the community with affection, remembering his cheery manner and twinkling intense blue eyes. One of the nurses who saw Armstrong trying to help his wife through a long and difficult illness thought they seemed 'a devoted couple'; others noted how he behaved as a good father to his three children. More than 30 years after his execution, one researcher who was helping to prepare a book on the Armstrong case got a visit from a man who had travelled across England to tell him: 'I was only a lad and I was damn near starving here in Hay at the end of the First World War... Major Armstrong couldn't take me on, but he gave me a hot meal and got me a job. He saved my life. Put that in your book.'

Armstrong's murder trial started on 3 April 1922 at the Hereford Assizes before Mr Justice Darling. While the major seemed composed and even engaged in friendly banter with his K.C., Sir Henry Curtis Bennett (both men were alumni of Cambridge University which had recently won the Boat Race), the case stacking up against him was bleak. Armstrong had kept arsenic all over the place including his study. He even had one small packet on him when arrested. He insisted that the poison was used to keep down the weeds and dandelions in his large garden. His tale of dividing the arsenic into 20 little packets and making a hole next to each dandelion, then tipping in the poison, along with using arsenic in the kitchen to make liquid weed killer, all went down very badly with Lord Darling who pressed the accused on having so many packets, 'each a fatal dose for a human being'. More fatal for the major was Spilsbury's evidence that 'a large dose of arsenic' had been ingested by Katherine Armstrong: 'a fatal dose must have been taken within 24 hours of death... the arsenic given in a number of doses extending over a period certainly of some days, possibly not less than a week.' Spilsbury cemented his fame in this case. He was now pre-eminently the Crown's forensic expert. The importance attached to his every word was shown by Darling who said to him in court with great sycophancy, 'It is not a fact, that you have very large experience of poison cases?' Spilsbury replied: 'A considerable experience, almost weekly, but certainly of monthly occurrence.' This kind of exchange convinced juries that the great man was infallible (and was to have tragic consequences).

To the surprise of many, after only 48 minutes' deliberation, the jury returned on 13 April with a verdict of guilty. Before his execution on 31 May at Gloucester Prison the major retained a remarkable composure and continued to protest his innocence. He gave Curtis Bennett a diamond tie pin, left his earthly belongings to his children and apologised to the two warders who guarded him that he had nothing to give them for their kindnesses – then parted with his spectacles and pipe.

So did he murder his wife? Or even try to murder Oswald Martin? In theory there is much against Armstrong but most of the prosecution case was based on circumstantial evidence. The poisoned chocolates, for instance, could be a classic red herring; anyone with a grudge against Martin might have sent them and it must be said that he was not very well liked and had a much smaller practice than Armstrong. There seems to be very weak grounds for Armstrong to want to kill Martin since he had hardly anything to gain from his death. Martin's sickness does not seem to be so suspicious; a surfeit of cakes followed by a rich meat dish like jugged hare (in those pre-refrigerator days), then by a coffee cream dessert could, it might be argued, be a good recipe for an attack of diarrhoea.

Katherine Armstrong was a sick, hysterical, irritable woman for much of her life. She frequently complained of sores around her mouth, a furred tongue, heart murmurs, dry skin, numbness in her fingers and pains in the right arm and shoulder joint. Her behaviour led to a period in a lunatic asylum in 1920 and she was freed because Herbert fought for her release. The rector of Cusop wrote that she was 'never normal' in all the years he knew her, 'a regular bundle of nerves'. His wife's sister recalled Mrs Armstrong complaining of 'pains like pins and needles' as far back as 1913.

Criticism can be made of Curtis Bennett at Armstrong's trial for not presenting a better defence but in fairness to Sir Henry he was so confident that his client would be released 'that he went out for a walk expecting to come back and either hear the verdict for acquittal or to meet Armstrong himself...' Touts in the town were taking bets at 5/1 for acquittal. During his summing-up Curtis Bennett had made light of Armstrong's use of arsenic saying, 'If you happen to be arrested and you have some in your pocket, it is going to be said you are carrying it about for the purpose of poisoning somebody...' He had been particularly hopeful that the three doctors called as expert witnesses for the defence could confute Spilsbury's evidence but by this point in his career, the handsome, cool Home Office pathologist was considered the fount of all forensic knowledge by jurors.

There the mystery might have stayed but in 1995, 73 years after the trial, a lawyer living in the solicitor's old house at Cusop and working from the same desk in his old office in Broad Street drove a sledgehammer into the prosecution case. Martin Beales argued in a book that Armstrong had been framed by Fred Davies and probably the Martins; as a chemist and the only person in Hay with access to lots of poisons it would have been very easy for Davies to doctor the chocolates – perhaps they were not even sent, since we only have the Martins' word for it. Fred, it is alleged, disliked Armstrong and wanted to advance the career of his son-in-law. Lord Darling was far from impartial and Beales described his summing-up as 'lynch law' and could be condensed as 'Armstrong's wife had died of arsenical poisoning; Armstrong had arsenic; therefore he administered it to her.' But most important of all, Martin Beales, author of *Dead, Not Buried*, put forward a very strong case that Katherine Armstrong died from Addison's Disease, of which she had all the symptoms. This malady would account for her long-drawn-out illness. Just before she died Katherine's tongue went coppery brown. 'This form of pigmentation is not to be expected in arsenical poisoning cases whereas it is a typical sign of Addison's disease,' wrote Beales. Katherine was also a believer in homeopathic medicines, her favourites being *arsenicum album*, ignatia or 'St Ignatius Bean', which contains a large amount of strychnine, and *nux vomica*, commonly called 'poison nut'. Pallid skin, twitching, trembling, headaches, loss of appetite and anxiety disorders are just a few of the symptoms of these poisons if not very carefully regulated. Mrs Armstrong knew where Herbert kept his arsenic so it cannot be ruled out that in her distressed and weakened state she committed suicide. The reasons might be varied; she was terrified of ending up back in the lunatic asylum; agitated, perhaps she wished to end her days at home; arsenic could have been ingested accidentally in her confusion or mistaken for one of her homeopathic remedies.

Or perhaps Armstrong did kill his wife after all? Was he carrying that one packet of arsenic in his pocket with the hope that he could pop off Oswald Martin on an off-chance? We will never know, which is why the story remains such an intriguing mystery. When last I was in Hay-on-Wye, about a year or so ago, I strolled past the major's old office, then ordered some tea and scones at a cafe on the corner of Broad Street. I like to think old Herbert would have appreciated the gesture.

1923 Murder without Motive: Susan Newall

It is not uncommon to hear someone talk of a motiveless crime, but no murder can really be without a motive because some trigger, some inner mental turmoil which we can only hazard a guess at, must set off this most heinous act.

Two housewives staring into a quiet Glasgow street early one June morning were shocked to see a woman, accompanied by a little girl, pushing an old-style handcart. What horrified the women was a foot protruding from a bundle which fell onto the ground and was hastily shoved back on the cart by the stranger. The housewives ran into the street after the woman. She had disappeared down an alley and the women found her sitting on the bundle. When they turned up shouting for her to stop, the unkempt woman heaved the bundle on to her back and ran off, leaving the child and the cart. Police were called and the woman was quickly apprehended; the bundle, dropped in a yard, contained the trussed-up body of a small boy. He had been strangled and had burn marks on the back of his head.

The 'tall, gaunt, shabby' woman was identified as 30-year-old Susan Newall. The child with her, neatly dressed, was her eight-year-old daughter, Janet, offspring of her first marriage. In her statement Mrs Newall openly explained that the boy, 13-year-old Johnny Johnson, had been murdered by her husband on the previous evening. Husband and wife had quarrelled, he had run away and so she had set off to dispose of the body in order to protect her spouse.

The police issued a description of 33-year-old John Newall, who gave himself up on the next day. He stated that he had not been home for 36 hours before the murder and knew nothing about it. With his wife, Newall was sent for trial at the Glasgow Assizes but several witnesses came forward to say that they had seen John in Glasgow on the evening of the murder and he had, in fact, even popped in to Coatbridge Police Station at 10pm to complain that his wife had hit him on the head two days earlier. The judge instructed the jury to acquit him and Mr Newall left the dock 'without a glance' at his wife.

In court Susan Newall's landlady, Mrs Young, said that on the evening of the murder she had given her noisy tenants notice to leave. Was this the trigger that unleashed Susan's rage on a defenceless child? Did her pent-up emotions, stress and resentment explode around young Johnny's head? He was a newspaper boy and had turned up around 6.30pm selling the evening papers. Mrs Newall had invited him in and a few minutes later Mrs Young in her room heard three loud thumps and assumed noisy Susan was packing her things. The jury was not impressed to hear how little Janet had returned home at 7pm to find a dead body on the couch; Johnny's spine had been dislocated during his throttling and the burn on his head had been done while he was still alive. Susan almost immediately set out for a public house to spend 10 pence taken off Johnny on some wine and a pint of beer. Janet told the jury how an hour later she had helped her mother to put the body in a bag and onto the cart. Damningly the little girl said that she had told the police that her father killed the boy, but now admitted, 'Mammy told me to.'

The defence tried to argue that Susan Newall was insane. Certainly her actions seem hardly normal. But the Regius Professor of Forensic Medicine at Glasgow University thought otherwise and the prison doctor had found her 'ready to talk, respectful and well conducted'. The jury returned a majority verdict – lawful under Scottish law – with a unanimous recommendation for mercy. No woman had been executed in Scotland since 1889 but Susan was hanged on 10 October 1923. She went to the gallows without making any confession so her real motive in killing young Johnny will never be known. Her last request was that Janet should be brought up in a convent.

1924 Body Parts: Patrick Herbert Mahon

Mrs Mahon was disturbed. She knew her husband was a philanderer and for two weekends in succession he had been away from home. Then she heard from a friend that he had been seen at the races. After a third absent weekend in a row, her suspicions deepened. Searching through the pockets of his suits in their single-room Richmond flat she found a left luggage label for a bag. She thought Patrick might be hiding a bookmaker's clerk costume and asked a probation officer friend to check the bag. He found a Gladstone bag and inside, once the lock was broken, some bloodstained clothes covered in disinfectant. The friend contacted Scotland Yard and Mr Mahon was arrested the next night as he collected the bag.

D.C.I. Savage asked Mahon to explain the bloodstains. He glibly replied that he liked dogs and the bag had contained meat for them. 'That will do,' said the exasperated detective who had earlier studied the bag's contents, 'these stains are of human blood.' Mahon said little else and sat quietly for 15 minutes, then said, 'I wonder if you can realise how terrible a thing it is for one's body to be active and one's mind fail to act.' He then lapsed into silence for 30 minutes before saying, 'I'm considering my position.' The clock ticked on for another 15 minutes before Mahon said, 'I'll tell you the truth.' Five hours after arriving at Scotland Yard he signed his statement detailing, to the astonishment of detectives, how he had cut up the body of a woman in a bungalow on the Crumbles beach at Pevensey near Eastbourne, Sussex.

What was later found in the 'Officer's House' bungalow horrified not only the investigators but also the great British public. The place was, in fact, not so much a bungalow as a charnel house. A 'rusty and greasy' tenon saw was found in a bedroom surrounded by bloodstained clothing sprinkled with coal dust. The dining room fireplace fender was splashed with human grease. Nearby stood a two-gallon saucepan half full of 'reddish fluid with a thick layer of grease ... a piece of boiled flesh with some skin.' A saucer was full of solid fat. Bloodstains littered the hall carpet. The two reception room fireplaces contained human bones along with the scullery dustpan and coal box. In the scullery stood a gigantic saucepan, a bowl and an iron bath all containing human grease. Inside a smart leather hat box was a silk knitted yellow jumper taking up space with 37 pieces of boiled human flesh. The horrors, all boiled, burnt, chopped and pulverised, culminated in a cabin trunk found in the first bedroom containing 'uncooked and rotting pieces of human trunk'. White silk wrapping enclosed a chest and spinal sections as well as 'two human breasts, each found in a brown paper package, tied with string'. A Huntley & Palmers biscuit tin held a heart, lungs, bowels, liver and kidneys. The victim's head was noticeably absent.

Sorting out all these remains was given over to Sir Bernard Spilsbury who later called it not only his most gruesome case, but also the most interesting, likening it to 'building up a jigsaw puzzle'. In recent years Spilsbury, a much flawed personality, has come under criticism for some of his findings and statements in court. Yet it must be said that his painstaking and difficult work in the Mahon case was remarkable – 'the most detailed pathological exercise carried out to date in England'. Between 900 and 1,000 pieces of bone had to be sifted through, compared and identified along with the various body parts. Sir Bernard concluded that all the remains belonged to 'an adult female of big build and fair hair... probably between three and four months pregnant'. Cause of death was difficult to say.

How the body came to be there and in such a dreadful state was the job of the police to ascertain. Their suspect, who had already confessed to cutting up the body, though not to murder, was a 34-year-old described by detectives as 'teetotal, a non-smoker and very fond of women...' He came from a respectable Liverpool family and had an elder brother who was a vicar in Lancashire. From his youth Patrick Mahon was what an earlier age politely described as a 'wastrel'. Good looking with wavy dark hair, later flecked with grey, a muscular build and blue eyes, he charmed a school friend into marriage in 1910. He was 20 and she was just 18. Within a year he was caught bouncing cheques and bound over. Despite the birth of a baby girl, Mahon was soon arrested again for embezzlement and was sentenced to one year in prison. After a supposed nervous breakdown, one day he attacked a maid with a hammer and got five years' penal servitude, thus missing most of the Great War. His wife, in the meantime, had got a good job with a firm and on his release somehow obtained for Patrick a position with them as a commercial traveller. He did well and by 1922 was their sales manager. Mahon was a stalwart of the Church of England Men's Society and a Sunday school teacher. He also wasted much of his £700 salary (about £35,000 today) on gambling and womanising.

In 1923 the firm went into receivership. The official receiver took on a shorthand typist. Her name was Emily Kaye, 37 years old, described by Andrew Rose as 'a hearty, rather lumpy person of a sort later so brilliantly caricatured by Joyce Grenfell, with a hint of Angela Brazil's ripping school yarns'. She wore false teeth and mackintosh knickers and loved all sports, especially tennis. Her best girlfriend called her 'Peter'. A relation described Emily as 'a cheery, lovable girl', but her 'chum', Miss Edith Warren, described her as 'strong physically and unusually strong mentally'.

Slowly at first, Emily began an affair with the handsome sales manager. He seemed very interested in her £600 savings. There were liaisons in cheap hotels. Emily began selling her investments, buying French francs, spending money on her lover who, it must be said, still dallied with other women and had a wife at home. In March 1924, he bought Emily a diamond and sapphire ring in Southampton and they shared a hotel bedroom. 'Peter' soon told Edith that she was engaged to 'Pat', who was now to be called 'Derek Patterson' and that they would be emigrating to South Africa. She was by now pregnant.

While Emily was telling her friends, 'Don't worry, old sausage,' and talking of being soon in 'Gay old Paris' with 'Pat', Mahon it seems had decided that his pushy girlfriend was just too much trouble. On 4 April he decided to rent a bungalow at Pevensey, which he saw advertised in *The Daily Telegraph* for three and a half guineas a week. On the evening of 12 April, with Easter barely a week away, he met Emily at Eastbourne. That same afternoon Mahon had visited Staines Kitchen Equipment Company in Victoria and purchased a 10-inch cook's knife and a meat saw.

There is no way of telling exactly when Emily Kaye died. She was seen alive by a deliveryman on 13 April and sent a letter to Edith Warren next day, saying that she and Pat were soon setting off for France and Italy en route to Cape Town. Mahon was to tell the court at his trial that he had decided to end his affair but Emily was outraged. 'These letters and actions mean I have burned my boats,' she told him. They argued. 'Disturbed and overwrought', she threw an axe at him. 'We struggled backwards and forwards ... a woman almost mad with anger ... I pushed Miss Kaye off, and we both fell over the easy chair on the left of the fireplace. Miss Kaye's head hit the cauldron and I fell with her – she was underneath... I think I must have fainted... When I did become conscious of what had happened, Miss Kaye was lying by the coal scuttle and blood had flowed from her head.' She was dead. Hours later and in a confused state Mahon claimed to have covered Emily's body with a fur coat. Instead of contacting the authorities, this 'confused' man actually went off to London to see his latest flame, a Miss Emily Duncan. This girl, who must have been either dim or remarkably unobservant, even stayed a night at the bungalow unawares that Emily's corpse was resting in a trunk in the other bedroom.

By Good Friday, and now alone, Mahon was busily dismembering the dead woman. After seeing Miss Duncan over the Easter weekend he returned to the Crumbles and on Tuesday 22 April burned Emily's head. He told police how 'the poker went through the head when I poked it. The next day I broke the skull and put the pieces in the dustbin... It is surprising what a room fire will burn.'

Mahon's trial began at the Lewes Summer Assizes on 17 July before the famously stern Horace Avory. While the frequent rivals Sir Henry Curtis-Bennett (prosecution) and Mr James Cassels (defence) sparred in court the outcome was never much in doubt. Some of what Mahon had said may have been true. But then why buy the knife and saw? More important, perhaps, was the attitude of the jury who followed tradition – British juries never like people who cut up bodies. In his summing-up Avory showed a clear distaste for Mahon. He described Emily Kaye as a 'virtuous and respectable woman' who had been seduced. The jury were reminded by the judge that no less an authority than Sir Bernard Spilsbury was satisfied 'that such a fall could not have caused the immediate death' of the victim. Forty-five minutes after retiring the jury returned with a guilty verdict. Mahon appealed his death sentence, but Lord Chief Justice Hewart called it 'a waste of time', labelling the crime as 'a most cruel, repulsive and carefully planned murder'.

Executed at Wandsworth Prison on 9 September, it is recorded that Mahon 'died twice' in that he struggled so much on the scaffold that he may have been killed when his lower spine struck the sharp edge of the execution platform seconds before his spinal cord was broken by the jerking of the rope.

Police had also learned a valuable lesson from the case. Scotland Yard detectives started carrying a 'murder bag' – a case of forensic and medical items – to the scenes of future murder inquiries.

1925 Under the Chickens: John Norman Holmes Thorne

The Thorne case, sometimes called 'the Murder of Elsie Cameron', is interesting not just as a classic whodunit, but rather as a tragic tale of perverted justice. The prosecution depended to a great extent on the theories of Sir Bernard Spilsbury. Yet other eminent pathologists had quite different explanations for the young woman's death. One is led inexorably to the conclusion that it was the defendant's stupidity in cutting up the body and then telling a web of lies that took him to the gallows.

Twenty-four-year-old Norman Thorne came from a respectable family in Kensal Rise, north London. He trained as an engineer and served briefly in the Royal Naval Air Service in France a month or two before the Armistice, then returned to engineering. The great slump of 1921 saw him out of a job. Undaunted, Norman borrowed £100 from his father, bought a small field at Crowborough, Sussex, and set himself up as the Wesley Poultry Farm. In the middle of the chicken runs he made a home for himself in a 7-by-12-foot wooden hut, formerly a brooding house, which soon became a messy picture of bachelor life – a grubby carpet, a small stove, an untidy bureau, oil lamps and clothes jostling with domestic utensils. A high beam was used to store his hats.

Norman's father was prominent in Wesleyan church activities. The son had also been a Sunday school teacher, a speaker for the anti-alcohol Band of Hope and organiser of a local troop of Boy Scouts and Wolf Cubs. He was generally considered to be 'very reserved... of sober habits'. Despite the slump, with meagre funds, in debt to some local tradesmen, Norman was nevertheless determined to make a success of his modest business.

In 1920 at Kensal Rise the young Thorne met a skinny, birdlike girl called Elsie Cameron. Her family were also prominent in the local Methodist community and the parents had known one another for years. By the end of 1921, the couple were what was called so politely in those days, 'walking out together'. By Christmas 1922 they had become engaged, but Mr Thorne senior was not pleased about it and never really gave his consent. Elsie was two years older than Norman, a girl of poor health who suffered from a multitude of nervous complaints labelled in those days as 'neurasthenia'. She was frequently at the doctors with back problems, sudden tearfulness sometimes, and sickness. She worked as a typist in the City but friends found her strange. On one occasion she had to be led from Broad Street station to her office because of a fright. She told people her head felt funny and she thought she was going mad. Then, one day in September, she could not recall her elementary office duties and two friends had to take her home and put her in the charge of her mother.

In June 1923 Norman and his sickly, neurotic fiancée had intimate relations. He later protested to police that this consisted of 'feeling one another's person and from that it went that I put my person against her, but in my opinion I did not put it into her'. It was not long before Elsie was showing signs of being increasingly sexually aroused and frustrated. She wrote regularly, gushing letters saying, 'Oh, if we only could get married... We can manage in a little hut like yours... Oh, my Darling, how I adore you...' Norman was well aware that his business was under strain and he worked hard on the farm, while trying to keep Elsie, to some extent, at arm's length. In October 1924 he renewed his subscription to the Alliance of Hope, a Christian organisation for promoting chastity before marriage. He even got Elsie to join.

That Whitsun at a local Crowborough dance he met a nice girl called Bessie Coldicott. She was a 'jolly young dressmaker', the opposite of sickly Elsie. In September Bessie had tea at the hut and the couple were soon talking of a future together overseas. Before long they were meeting every night between 8.30pm and 10.30pm. Elsie, of course, had no idea that Norman was two-timing her. She was getting more abusive, depressed, hysterical and lethargic. At the end of October she came down to Crowborough, lodged with some neighbours, had no sex with Norman, but told him she was pregnant. She also told her parents. Elsie's father met with Mr Thorne senior and it was agreed that if she was indeed pregnant, then Norman must do the proper thing and marry her.

Norman was sceptical; he thought Elsie was lying. On 25 November he wrote to her that 'You seem to be taking everything for granted,' then added the cruncher, 'There are one or two things I haven't told you... it concerns someone else... I am afraid I am between two fires.' The next day he spelled it all out: 'What I haven't told you is that on certain occasions a girl has been here late at night... When you gave in to your nerves again and refused to take interest in life I gave up hope in you and let you go... She thinks I am going to marry her, of course, and I have strong feelings for her or I shouldn't have done what I have...' Elsie was understandably upset at this news. She replied on 28 November that Thorne had 'absolutely broken my heart... You have deceived me, and I gave you myself and all my love... Well, Norman, I expect you to marry me and finish with the other girl... My baby must have a name and another thing, I love you...'

Five days later Norman's father turned up at Crowborough and the two men discussed the young man's financial situation and Elsie's supposed pregnancy. Mr Thorne senior wisely counselled his son to delay any marriage commitment until after Christmas. When Elsie heard that her prospective and wary father-in-law had been to the farm she decided it was time to force the issue. She had her hair done and on 5 December put on her best green knitted dress with a new jumper and shoes and set out from Kensal Rise. Her little attaché case contained toiletries, two pairs of shoes and a baby's frock. She walked towards the farm from Crowborough Station with just 'a penny-halfpenny in her purse and an iron resolve'.

Norman was eating his tea when Elsie stepped into the hut. 'I asked her why she had come,' he later told the jury. 'She said nothing except that she wanted some tea, that her head was bad and that she was feeling sick through travelling. She said she wanted to sleep in the hut and would not go to the neighbours, and added that she intended stopping until she was married. She said over and over again that she was pregnant. She seemed to be highly strung.'

Thorne's account thus far has the ring of truth. About 9pm he told Elsie that he had to go down to the station to meet his other girlfriend off a train as he had promised to carry her shopping up the hill. Elsie complained but Norman pointed out 'that if only she had written to me telling she was coming down, I could have made other arrangements'. He set off about 9.45pm leaving his dog with Elsie as she was scared of being left alone.

One can well imagine the neurotic girl's feelings of rejection. Was this the point when it came home to her that she was losing Norman and she decided to commit suicide, or did the couple argue, as the prosecution tried to prove in court, and did he strike her with an Indian club? Or was the scene in the hut as Thorne described it on his return at 11.30pm: 'I saw Elsie Cameron suspended from a beam in the centre of the hut. A cord, like the cord I had been using as a clothes line, had been twisted round and round the beam... The cord was round the middle of her neck and was tied in an ordinary slip knot... at the back of her neck... I cut the cord, holding her with my left arm. The weight fell on me. I twisted her round so that I should not see her face. I struggled to lift her on to the bed ... I thought she was dead and I felt absolutely dazed...'

For an hour he sat in the darkness. Intending to go to neighbours for help, he got up, then decided to hide all trace of the suicide, 'lest I should be accused of being responsible for her death'. In the glow of his fire Thorne laid Elsie on some sacking, dismembering her with a knife and saw. During this macabre operation he noticed 'there was a faint dent of the mark of the cord round the middle of her neck'. Later Thorne washed the floor and at dawn, in a cold sweat, he decided to bury Elsie's remains in a shallow grave in the nearest chicken run. Her attaché case he buried in a potato patch near the gate. The head and neck were treated with a degree of respect and placed before burial in a biscuit tin.

In the following days, quizzed by detectives, the press roaming the farm, Thorne insisted that Elsie had never been there. He even joked with reporters and cheerfully suggested they snap him feeding his chickens. The police were suspicious; witnesses had come forward who insisted they had seen a woman fitting Elsie's description walking towards the farm from Crowborough on 5 December. Finally, on 14 January 1925, Norman Thorne was taken to Crowborough station for more questioning. Searching a tool shed on the farm police found Elsie's wristwatch and some jewellery in an Oxo tin. They decided to dig and at 8.25am on 15 January they found the attaché case. Confronted with this evidence Thorne sat all day in his cell until 8pm when he agreed to make a statement and later showed the police where he had buried the body.

His trial at the Lewes Assizes began on 4 March before Mr Justice Finlay. The duelling pair of James Cassels and Sir Henry Curtis-Bennett, both fresh from the Mahon trial, duly represented the defence and prosecution. For Cassels, an intelligent and witty advocate, this case was very different from the Crumbles Murder since he believed passionately in his client's innocence. Thorne's statement had been very full. The prosecution thus depended to a large extent on their star witness – Sir Bernard Spilsbury. He told the court, much to Thorne's delight, that Elsie was *not* pregnant. Yet Sir Bernard was adamant that she had not hanged herself. There were various external bruises, including a big one on the side of the face, and he thought death resulted from a blow with an Indian club found outside the hut. Defence experts vehemently disagreed with Spilsbury's theories. Thorne also was insistent there had been a mark on Elsie's neck and at his request the body was re-exhumed and examined by all the doctors, though a watery grave made the work difficult. One of the defence team, Dr Hugh Galt, medico-legal examiner for the Crown in Scotland, was very dismissive of the Indian club theory saying, 'I can guarantee... that it would not only make a bruise... but smash the skull at one blow,' like an eggshell. Curtis-Bennett talked of Thorne's need to rid himself of Elsie. He also alluded to newspaper clippings of the Mahon case found at the farm, thus suggesting Thorne meant to improve on that murderer's performance. Police had found no marks on the beam, just dust and cobwebs but then, as Cassels said, it all depended on how Elsie might have hanged herself.

In the dock Thorne was a little too smug and confident. He openly admitted that after finding the body and dismembering it, 'I had gone so far and I could not stop. One lie meant another...' Cassels made a moving and eloquent final speech in his defence but the jury took just half an hour to find Norman Thorne guilty of murder. He remained composed and confident he would be freed on appeal. When that process failed he broke down shouting, 'It isn't fair. I didn't do it!' His father fought valiantly for his son's life and fired off several letters to the newspapers and Home Office. Two days before his hanging Norman Thorne wrote to his parent: 'Never mind, dad, don't worry. I am a martyr to Spilsburyism,' a reference to the infallibility and influence over juries that Sir Bernard now held in courts. Thorne was executed at Wandsworth at 8am on 22 April 1925. In a last letter he told his father, 'By Christ I am free from all sin; all forgiven. I go to Him. All's well.'

1926 When Women Fall Out: Louie Calvert

In 1925 Arthur Calvert, a night watchman living in Hunslet, West Yorkshire, advertised for a housekeeper. The applicant he chose, though heaven knows why, was 33-year-old Louie 'Jackson', a small, ugly and toothless prostitute, petty thief and confidence trickster (she sometimes dressed up in a Salvation Army uniform to work her scams) who told the gullible Arthur that she was a widow. Louie dragged along her four-year-old son, Kenneth, to the job interview but the truth was she had never been married.

After some time Louie told Arthur that she was pregnant and so he honourably married her in August 1925. Several months later Louie was still without a bump and Calvert was starting to ask questions about when the baby might appear. Then, one day, she showed him a pencilled letter from her sister in Dewsbury insisting that she stay with her during the confinement. Leaving little Kenneth in Calvert's care, Louie set off on 8 March 1926. She was back on 1 April with a baby girl and Arthur

Calvert was over the moon with pride. His joy was short-lived, however, because the next thing he knew the police had arrived and wanted to ask his missus some very searching questions.

It turned out that Louie, after a trip to Dewsbury in order to send her husband a telegram saying she had arrived safely, actually stayed the next three weeks just 2 miles from Calvert's home at the house of 40-year-old Lily Waterhouse, another prostitute. Here Louie advertised offering to adopt a new-born child, got a reply on 13 March and picked up an illegitimate baby on 31 March.

Meantime Lily Waterhouse had noticed some of her belongings had been stolen and near the end of the month, searching among Louie's things when she was out of the house, had come across some suspicious pawn tickets. In high dudgeon Lily went to the police station and was told to appear at the magistrate's court on 1 April to take out a summons against her guest. The two women met at the house just after Louie had collected the baby. What happened next is open to conjecture but the police, who called at the house after Mrs Waterhouse failed to appear in court, found bloodstains on the floors and walls and Lily lying dead in the back bedroom, strangled, but with two violent wounds on the back of her head. She had clearly tried to defend herself against a vicious attack. The police noted that her feet were bare and there was no footwear in the house. They also discovered the pencilled note belonging to Louie Calvert, which led them to Arthur Calvert's door. It was Louie who answered the insistently loud knocks of the police. She was wearing Lily Waterhouse's boots, which were several sizes too big for her. She admitted she had been Lily's lodger, even saying, 'Has she done herself in?' A suitcase in the living room supposed to be full of baby clothes actually contained Mrs Waterhouse's cracked china and some stolen linen.

Mrs Calvert's trial took place on 6 and 7 May during the General Strike. This major historical event pushed news of her case off the front pages of the newspapers. Louie was found guilty without much deliberation and sentenced to death. She then pleaded pregnancy but this proved to be another hasty lie. Louie now confessed to an earlier killing; she had acted as housekeeper to an elderly man, John Frobisher, who had been found in a Leeds canal with his head bashed in and his boots missing. This confession was dismissed by many as an attempt at self-publicity, but the truth will never be known. Before her execution at Strangeways Gaol, Manchester, on 26 June Louie confessed her guilt to prison officers and wrote a letter to Arthur Calvert: 'I am keeping up quite well and you will have the joy of meeting me in Heaven.'

1927 The Charing Cross Trunk Murder: John Robinson

The crime that became known as 'the Charing Cross Trunk Murder' was far more than just a grisly dismemberment. This mystery required painstaking detective and forensic work and a cunning criminal owed his downfall very largely to a laundry mark, a cloakroom ticket and a burnt matchstick.

The case began on 6 May when a man who looked like a soldier deposited a large black trunk at Charing Cross railway station left luggage office. Three days later the luggage attendant noticed a nasty smell emanating from the trunk. A policeman was called and the trunk opened; inside were five brown paper parcels roughly tied with string containing a dismembered woman including her head. Putrefaction was well advanced but the Home Office pathologist, Sir Bernard Spilsbury, discerned bruises on the woman's forehead, abdomen, back and limbs that he concluded had been caused before her death. The actual cause he listed as asphyxia 'from pressure over the mouth and nostrils whilst unconscious from head injury and other injuries'. The murder had occurred about one week before the discovery of the body and Spilsbury noted that she was a short, rather stout, woman of between 30 and 40 years of age. Beneath the brown paper the parcelled remains had been wrapped in a few items of clothing, towels and a duster. A pair of black shoes and a handbag were also found in the trunk.

Chief Inspector George Cornish and his team of detectives now set out to discover the identity of the victim – and her murderer. Red herrings galore littered their way; the letter 'A' was painted on both ends of the trunk, a large label was addressed to 'F. Austen to St Lenards', while amongst the bloodstained clothing was an item marked 'P. Holt'. Newspapers were given photographs of the trunk, shops that sold old trunks were contacted, a Mr F. Austen of St Leonards was found – and dismissed – from the inquiry. Yet within 24 hours the marked clothing was traced to a Miss Holt of Chelsea who was alive and well. Her mother was able to identify the body as a former cook, a 'Mrs Rolls' who had been discharged after one week's service, during the previous year. The police search now searched and found Mr Rolls but he said the dead woman was not really his wife. They had parted due to some arguments since she was 'about as strong as two men' and had attacked him on occasions with 'frying pans, saucepans, anything that came to hand'. This might have made him a prime suspect except that his employer was able to prove that he could not possibly have committed the murder. From a friend of the dead woman, the police at last got her real name. She was Mrs Minnie Bonati (maiden name Budd), wife of an Italian waiter. She had been working as a prostitute and was last seen alive in Sydney Street, Chelsea, between 3.45pm and 4pm on 4 May.

Mr Bonati was traced and found to have a good alibi. He had also been separated from his wife for a considerable time. Then a second-hand trunk dealer in the Brixton Road came forward to say he was convinced that he had sold the trunk for 12s 6d to a tanned military type of man who might have served in India. His description was considered 'hazy' by the police and there was uncertainty as to the date of the purchase. More red herrings cropped up; the police were inundated with tales of strange men buying trunks, while an attempt to track down a culprit via Minnie Bonati's clients seemed to lead nowhere. Next came a stroke of luck. A boy shoeblack at Charing Cross Station had picked up a bit of paper blowing around and it turned out to be the cloakroom ticket for the trunk, which enabled detectives to fix the time when it had been deposited and work out that it must have been brought to the station by taxi cab. Further inquiries turned up a taxi driver who recalled picking up a fare at 86 Rochester Row, a man with a large and heavy trunk. 'What have you got in here – money?' the cabman had jocularly asked. 'No – it's books,' the owner had replied.

The police were soon at the Rochester Row building but found it was let out as suites of offices and occupied by several companies. Some of the employees recalled a large trunk blocking a corridor. One office, a seedy set of two rooms on the second floor, had recently been vacated in a hurry on 9 May. This was listed as 'Edwards & Co., Estate & Business Transfer Agents', but the lessee had been a Mr John Robinson. The police traced Robinson to lodgings in Kennington but he had left without leaving a forwarding address. By another stroke of luck, a telegram arrived while the police were there and it was marked 'Robinson, Greyhound Hotel, Hammersmith'. The telegram had been sent to the Hammersmith address but passed on to Kennington marked 'addressee unknown'. At Hammersmith the police found not Mr Robinson but a Mrs Robinson who, it turned out, had married bigamously. The aggrieved second wife agreed to help the police track down her 'husband' so that D.C.I. Cornish and his men were on hand when she caught up with John Robinson at an Elephant and Castle pub on 19 May. According to one of the officers present the smart 36-year-old suspect 'had all his wits about him and told his story with great plausibility'. A Lancashire man, it turned out that Robinson had followed several occupations – soldier, tram conductor, greengrocer, milkman, bookmaker, estate agent – but mainly worked as a public house barman. He had a previous record for theft. Robinson denied seeing a trunk in the corridor of the office building on 6 May and added, 'I have never seen Mrs Bonati or any of her associates.' At an identity parade at Scotland Yard neither the taxi driver, station porter or second-hand trunk dealer recognised him.

John Robinson thus seemed pretty much in the clear and the police were not sure how to proceed. Cornish wisely had the bloodstained duster washed. It revealed the word 'GREYHOUND' in capitals. In the meantime, a further search of the Rochester Row office produced a bloodstained matchstick that had been caught in the wickerwork of a waste paper basket. Robinson was rearrested at his lodgings on 23 May. Perhaps overwhelmed with guilt he volunteered to make a statement saying, 'I done it and cut her up.' His story was that Minnie Bonati had accosted him on 4 May at Victoria Station. He had taken her back to his office where she grew abusive over the price of sex. He had shoved her away, she tripped and fell, hitting her head on a coal scuttle. He had left the body face down all that day, but returned on the morrow with a knife he had purchased (ironically the same place where Patrick Mahon had bought his carving knife and saw). Maybe Robinson recalled the Mahon case, or that of Norman Thorne, because something prompted him to dismember Mrs Bonati's body. He did this grisly task and the job of carefully cleaning his office within sight of Rochester Row Police Station, which was just a stone's throw away. He returned with his newly purchased trunk, stuffed the body parts of Minnie inside, lugged the heavy object to the front of the building and hailed a taxi for Charing Cross. The knife he had buried on Clapham Common, where it was subsequently found by the police.

Robinson's trial began at the Old Bailey on 11 July. He was an unimpressive witness, admitting more or less everything except an intention to kill the victim. He blamed the event on being in 'a blue funk'. Mr Justice Swift asked Robinson why, after Mrs Bonati had fallen to the floor unconscious, he had not summoned help from the police just across the street? He replied: 'I did not look at it in that light.' A doctor called by the defence had argued that Mrs Bonati's demise might have been caused by suffocation within the folds of the carpet or in the crook of her elbow. The judge was not impressed; the carpet was threadbare, Spilsbury and the police surgeon said the bruises were the direct result of blows, while congestion in the woman's lungs showed that Minnie had been on her back for some time. After being out for an hour, the jury returned a verdict of guilty.

In his statement Robinson had been quite detailed – 'She bent down as though to pick up something from the fireplace, and came towards me. I hit her in the face with my right hand. I think I hit the left side of her face, but at this time I was also in a temper and am not certain. She fell backwards: she struck a chair on falling and it fell over. As she fell she sort of set down and rolled over with her head in the fireplace.' A witness for the defence had described how Mrs Bonati had a violent temper. Possibly a row did escalate into violence and Robinson may have been roused to strike the prostitute. It was the grisly act of dismemberment – as in the Mahon and Thorne cases – that saw the jury lose sympathy for Robinson and, as the judge said, he could very easily have called the police. He was hanged at Pentonville Prison on 12 August 1927.

A postscript was provided by Professor Sir Sydney Smith, Scotland's foremost pathologist, who submitted a memo after consultation with colleagues attacking Spilsbury's findings. It was extremely difficult, after putrefaction set in, according to Smith, to diagnose death from asphyxia. The way Minnie Bonati died will never be known.

1928 The Murder of P.C. Gutteridge: Frederic Guy Browne & William Henry Kennedy

The British have always been appalled by the murder of their police officers. When a country constable was found shot in the head on 27 September 1927 the case instantly became a *crime celebre*.

It was close to 6am that Bill Ward, a Post Office employee, was delivering mail near Howe Green along the Ongar–Romford road in Essex when he saw, near a right-hand bend on an incline, a uniformed and caped police constable in a sitting position, legs stuck out into the road, propped up against the opposite bank. The officer's helmet and pocketbook lay near him while a pencil was still clutched in his right hand. The face was covered in blood but Mr Ward recognised the dead man as the local bobby from nearby Stapleford Abbotts: P.C. George Gutteridge.

Detectives were soon on the scene and later that morning, at Romford mortuary, after a post-mortem examination, it was ascertained that the dead policeman had been shot four times, twice through the left cheek near the ear and, very oddly, his eyes had been blasted out by a single shot into each socket at close range. It was surmised that P.C. Gutteridge had been killed between 2.45 and 3.45am.

While the post-mortem was taking place, an abandoned car had been reported by an alert clerk on his way to work in Brixton, south London. The police soon found that that the blue four-seater Morris Cowley car had been reported stolen from the garage of a Dr Edward Lovell at Billericay, Essex. The doctor had last seen his car when he locked his garage about 7.30pm on 26 September. Human bloodstains were found on the running board by the driver's door. Beneath the front nearside seat was an empty cartridge case. A firearms expert destined to be a Crown witness in many subsequent trials involving guns, Mr Robert Churchill, found that the cartridge was a Mark IV type using a flat-nosed bullet and had been scarred by a fault in the breechblock of the Webley revolver that fired it. Externally the vehicle's nearside mudguard was bent inwards, as if in a collision, and tree bark was on the dumb irons.

A determined hunt, aided by extensive newspaper coverage, now followed but the trail went cold. It was, however, decided that a very close watch should be extended to known car thieves and their associates, especially ones in south London. One of the police suspects was Frederick Browne, a 46-year-old 'well-built, dark-complexioned man with a heavy moustache'. An habitual criminal, Browne led a gang of bicycle thieves in Oxford during his late teens, was convicted of carrying firearms in 1910, served 12 months for burglary in 1912, then three more prison terms before a four-year stretch at Dartmoor, reckoned to be one of England's toughest prisons. It was in Dartmoor that Browne, who served his full tariff due to bad behaviour, met William Kennedy, a Scot in his 40s who had served nine years in the army as a young man (including a year fighting the Boers in the South African War), but had a long charge sheet of theft, burglary and indecent exposure crimes stretching back to 1911. The two men struck up a friendship, Kennedy very much under the sway of Browne, who offered a job on release from gaol at his south London garage/repair shop. Kennedy agreed to look after the accounts and general correspondence while Browne, who was a gifted motor engineer, took charge of mechanical things. The pair were also not averse to a little spot of crime if it came their way.

There is every likelihood that Browne and Kennedy would never have been found guilty of Gutteridge's murder had fate not stepped in to bring them to justice. Several months after the killing, Browne drove so recklessly through Sheffield that an indignant van driver, who had to swerve to avoid an accident, took down his number and reported him to the police. It turned out that the car was a stolen Vauxhall from London and Browne had been using false plates and a false licence address. When an old lag revealed to the police the identity of the driver they decided to stake out his Clapham Junction garage. Since he was known as a dangerous criminal who might carry a gun, six officers finally rushed Browne, a wise move since he was supposed to have commented afterwards, 'I shall have to have a machine gun for you bastards next time.' The garage, Browne's home in Lavender Hill, and his clothes, brought forth several firearms including two fully loaded Webley revolvers, 39 loose cartridges, a stockinette mask and another 13 .45 cartridges in the hip pocket of the trousers he had been wearing when arrested.

When Kennedy was arrested a few nights later, he pulled a pistol and tried to fire at Detective-Sergeant Mattinson but the safety catch was down and the bullet jammed without exploding. Mattinson then hit him on the jaw. On the way to the police station Kennedy told the detective, 'I'm sorry. I've no grudge against the police but you should be in Heaven by now, and there was one for me.' At Scotland Yard the detectives allowed Kennedy to see his wife, who was brought from Liverpool. She urged him to make a full confession and after being allowed to kiss her, he promised he would tell the truth. His long statement, later derided by Browne as 'one pack of wilful or imaginative lies', set out plainly how the pair had gone by train to Billericay on 26 September to steal a Riley car. A barking dog so unnerved Browne near the Riley's garage that the two men had ended up stealing Dr Lovell's Morris-Cowley instead. Browne had been driving at top speed towards Ongar sometime after 3.30am when P.C. Gutteridge's torch and shrill whistle had caused them to stop. It was while the constable was jotting down particulars in his notebook that Browne, nervous and annoyed by police harassment, fired the Webley revolver. He is supposed to have said, 'I'll finish the bugger.' Kennedy claimed to have replied, 'For God's sake don't shoot any more – the man's dying.' Browne, addressing Gutteridge, stooped over him and declared, 'What are you looking at me like that for', then blew out his victim's eyes. The two criminals had abandoned the car in Brixton at 5.30am after smashing into a tree on their journey to London in dense fog.

Their trial before Mr Justice Avory started at the Old Bailey on 23 April 1928. Browne simply denied that he was out in the car on the murder night and 'unleashed a torrent of verbosity' in the witness box. He even argued that the oath was nonsense: 'How can I tell the whole truth of something I do not know?' At one point he said: 'How could I shoot a man when I have never fired a revolver in my life?' These kind of remarks won him no friends with the jury or the famously severe judge since Browne had twice been fined in his life for firing a pistol. The case was Horace Avory's last great criminal trial; his career stretched back to Oscar Wilde's 1895 trial where he had been a junior Treasury Counsel; since being raised to silk and ermine in 1910, Avory had presided over some of the most dramatic murder trials of the time and won himself a reputation as a hanging judge (the criminal fraternity had nicknamed him 'Acid Drop').

Four firearms experts were called, but Robert Churchill was able to prove conclusively how one of Browne's Webley revolvers, with its unmistakable gun-print in its breech shield, had been the murder weapon. Kennedy, in contrast to Browne, was contrite and made a statement in which he apologised to Mrs Gutteridge for the death of her husband. In a later age and perhaps with a different judge he might have avoided the death penalty, but Avory was quite right when he explained to the jury that 'if at the time there were two persons in the car, acting with the common purpose of preventing detection or arrest, the person who did not fire the shot was equally guilty with the one who did'. Found guilty, Browne made a short statement in which declared his innocence but paid Avory a compliment (possibly impressed by his no-nonsense fairness), that 'I would not wish to be tried by a better judge'. Kennedy made a little speech and said the whole event had been pre-ordained. 'It was fate,' he said softly, 'and you, my Lord, however fairly you may have tried me, and members of the jury, are mere accessories of that fate.'

Both men were hanged on 31 May – Browne at Pentonville and Kennedy at Wandsworth. While awaiting execution Kennedy converted to Roman Catholicism and on the night before his death wrote to his wife: 'Darling, my last word. I again assert that I had no previous knowledge of what was going to happen that night. I go to my death knowing that, and that my statement is true, and that my own darling believes me. Bxxxx.'

1929 Killing Grandad: William John Holmyard

Holmyard was a 25-year-old ex-army bandsman with an excellent military record. He lived with his parents at 39 Tachbrook Street, Pimlico, next door to his 72-year-old grandfather, a wealthy widower who had his own furniture business and supplemented his earnings as a street bookmaker.

In November 1928 the younger man borrowed £5 from his grandfather, a loan he repaid within one week, but two subsequent amounts of £10 and £7 were still outstanding on 7 December. Trouble started when young Holmyard was confronted about the loans by his father. This argument led William to go next door and take the matter up with grandfather. Temperatures got even more heated as the old man called his grandson a spendthrift and attacked him with a chair. In self-defence young Holmyard hit the old boy with a pair of coal tongs and ran off but thought he had not seriously injured his granddad. The old man, also called William, staggered out into the street where he leaned against some railings as blood poured down his head. An ambulance was called and William Snr died three days later in Westminster Hospital.

Mr Justice Humphreys, appearing on the bench in his first capital murder trial (and soon to take over Avory's mantle as a man the public sometimes referred to as a 'hanging judge'), instructed the jury that a manslaughter verdict was allowable, but they found Holmyard guilty of murder in the first degree with no recommendation for mercy. It was six years after women had been admitted to the Bar and Holmyard's counsel, Miss Venetia Stephenson, was the first woman to lead for the defence in a murder trial. She launched a strong appeal but the judges did not agree with her (the Lord Chief Justice, Lord Hewart, was also a tough judge). Holmyard was executed at Pentonville on 27 February 1929.

1930 Mummy's Boy: Sidney Harry Fox

Sidney Fox was always a mummy's boy. He was Rosaline Fox's fourth, last and favourite child. She was the wife of a signalman at the little station of Great Fransham in Norfolk and about 33 years old when Sidney was born in 1899. There was local gossip that the boy's father was really a railway porter whom Rosaline had moved in with, but no matter, young Sidney was over-mothered from the start.

A cheerful boy with a mass of curly hair, Sidney's charm and vivacity worked miracles on the local girls. Aged 13 he tried to con folks, saying he was collecting for the local hospital. This escapade earned Sydney six strokes of the birch from the local constable, P.C. Wright. Later in his teens he discovered that sexually he could swing both ways and that men and women found him attractive and might pay for his attentions. Sidney was perfectly happy to exploit this bi-sexuality. In the same way, he was also perfectly happy to relieve some clients of cash and personal belongings when their backs were turned in order to supplement his modest income as a hotel page boy. Soon he learned to fake an upper-class accent in order to fool society folk. One aristocrat called him his 'pocket cherub'. The thefts continued and, inevitably, so did spells inside His Majesty's Prisons. Being offered a choice between penal servitude and military service after one crime spree, Sidney opted for the army and had a short and undistinguished career relieved only by another spell in gaol, this time for forgery. The years 1918–27 saw Sidney in and out of prison when his skills as a chequebook fraudster let him down. Always he returned to his mother who by now had morphed into an 'old white-haired woman with the big genial face, and the loose, smiling lips, the shuffling gait and the trembling hands'. Rosaline, sad to say, had advanced Parkinson's disease.

In 1927 Sidney had a romantic fling with a Mrs Morse, who was in the middle of a divorce from her seafaring captain husband. She grew friendly with Mrs Fox and the ladies decided to share an apartment in Southsea. Sidney moved into the apartment too and Mrs Morse, who had fallen for the curly haired crook hook, line and sinker, even changed her will in his favour. Fox might have ended his days in the lap of luxury with a doting lady but he decided to help things along a bit by opening a gas tap in Mrs Morse's bedroom. She spoiled his little plan by waking up, and since the gas tap was hidden behind a heavy chest of drawers, and could not be turned on except by purpose, the lady's suspicions were aroused. An indignant Sidney took his old Mum away, helping himself to some of Mrs Morse's jewellery as he departed. The captain's wife called the police and Sidney ended up in clink again with 15 months to serve.

Rosaline Fox was so poor that during her son's absence she was forced to live in Portsmouth Workhouse. Released from prison in March 1929, Sidney quickly freed Mum from the care of the parish and the couple set off on a duplicitous jaunt, via Canterbury, to the south coast, staying at smart hotels and leaving without paying the bills. Fox's tricks included asking staff to look after a mysterious brown paper parcel that, Sidney hinted, contained great wealth (it was really full of just more brown paper), or saying that their luggage and money was due to be delivered. The pair actually only had the clothes on their backs (Rosaline did not even possess a nightgown), and were living on 18s a week in pensions.

Yet Sidney had a master plan and it involved disposing of Mummy. A month after his release from prison he got Rosaline to make a will, then a week or so later her sole legatee extended her post-mortem value to rather more than £2,000 by taking out the first of two short-term accident policies on the old lady. Of an inquiring mind the dutiful Sidney asked one insurance agent, 'Would this policy cover the case of drowning in the bath? Would it apply supposing a person was poisoned, say, in a restaurant?' Clearly he was concerned deeply for his dear old mother!

Moving always two or three steps ahead of a flurry of unpaid bills, stolen cheques and unredeemed pawn tickets Mrs Fox & Son arrived at the Metropole Hotel, Margate, on 16 October 1929. The manager took an instant dislike to the pair, who were given rooms 68 and 70. Four days later Sidney told the manager that he was worried about his mother's health. She needed to keep warm. The manager agreed to move them to rooms 66 and 67, which were linked by an adjoining door. Room 66, given to Rosaline Fox, had a gas fire.

On 21 October Sidney cashed a cheque in a chemist's shop and used some of the money to buy a rail ticket to London where on the 22nd he saw both insurance companies and extended his mother's policies until midnight on the following day. He then returned to her side in Margate and on Wednesday evening, 23 October he escorted her into the Metropole Hotel dining room where Mrs Fox enjoyed an excellent dinner. Perhaps the repast was part of Sidney's plan or maybe he just wanted to give Mummy a good send-off. After the meal he went out and with cash bought a half bottle of port, which he took up to her room. He was spotted by the manager at 10pm having a lone stiff drink in the bar. When Sidney caught sight of him he stared guiltily, 'as if he had seen a ghost' and quickly went upstairs. The clock was ticking; at 11.40pm, just 20 minutes before Mrs Fox's policies were due to expire, Sidney appeared in the hotel lobby clad only in his shirt. He told surprised guests that there was a fire and led a posse to room 66. The corridor was rapidly filling with dense black fumes. One brave guest groped on his hands and knees into the smoke-filled room and found Mrs Fox semi-naked and unconscious. Another guest pulled a burning armchair into the corridor and dragged out a patch of flaming carpet that had been under the chair. Sidney Fox hopped about in the background, wringing his hands and saying occasionally, 'My Mummy, my Mummy!'

Mrs Fox was buried at Great Fransham on 29 October. Five days later her youngest son was arrested in Norwich and returned to Kent where he was charged with six cases of fraud on hotels. Meanwhile, the insurance companies had called upon Scotland Yard and it was decided to exhume Rosaline Fox's body. Sir Bernard Spilsbury, the great pathologist, insisted that there was no soot in Rosaline's air passages and that she had been strangled before death. Sidney Fox denied it and, whatever his intentions might have been, he had support in the form of the opinion of other eminent pathologists, including Professor Sydney Smith who argued it was impossible to strangle someone without breaking the hyoid bone. Spilsbury said he had seen bruising on the larynx but Smith disagreed and said it could have been a mark of putrefaction.

The forensic arguments hardly mattered since Sidney's actions before his mother's death seemed so suspect. His trial began on 12 March before Mr Justice Rowlatt. Quite apart from the insurance policies on his mother, the jury were told that the strip of carpet in room 66 between the gas fire and chair had not been damaged, a mass of charred newspapers indicated that a fire had been started deliberately and Mrs Fox, incidentally, was a non-smoker. The most dramatic moment took place on the trial's seventh day when Fox was in the witness box. He was asked by the Attorney-General, Sir William Jowitt, who was leading evidence for the Crown, if the atmosphere in his mother's room could suffocate someone. Fox agreed that three or four minutes in there might have killed him if he had stayed inside. Jowitt asked if he had been 'greatly apprehensive' for his mother? Fox again agreed. Then Jowitt hit him with, 'Fox, you closed that door... Can you explain to me why it was that you closed the door, instead of flinging it wide open?' Sidney pondered before replying that he did not want the smoke to get into the hotel. Jowitt returned to the subject of the closed door until Sidney was forced to say, 'You cannot pin me down to details. I cannot remember all that happened that night.' But in the jury's eyes, his answer to Jowitt probably sealed his doom.

Matricide is rare in Britain. In his biography of Spilsbury, Andrew Rose argues that Rosaline Fox died of a heart attack and that Sydney then started the fire. This theory rather ignores his desperate plot to get her insured. Odd that she should die just before her policy expired. On the other hand, there seems ample proof that Spilsbury perjured himself in the witness box and that Sydney Fox did not throttle his mother. The jury were out for 90 minutes before returning with a guilty verdict. Fox did not appeal (the first convicted murderer since 1907 not to do so), or make a final confession. He was hanged at Maidstone Prison on 8 April 1930, the last man to be executed there.

1931–1940

The decade began with Europe and the rest of the world gripped by a depression and it ended with Britain fighting for its very existence against the forces of Nazi Germany. Much of the period, however, saw improvements at home and people seemed almost complacent in their certainty that the League of Nations in Geneva would ensure that world war would never come again.

In 1931 the Sentence of Death (Expectant Mothers) Act decreed that pregnant women should not be hanged (though none had since the 18th century). It was followed in 1933 by a Children and Young Persons Act that raised the age at which convicted murderers could be hanged to 18 years of age. In 1938 a policeman, William Teasdale, became the first and only constable ever to be tried at the Old Bailey for murder. He was convicted and sentenced to death – but reprieved. During the decade 2,839 persons were tried for murder, attempted murder or manslaughter (figures are not available for 1937). A new Criminal Justice Bill in 1938 called for a five-year moratorium on the death penalty, but the outbreak of war in 1939 saw the whole matter shelved. Forensic science took a stride forward with the Ruxton case (**1936**) and there were now so many good tests for most poisons that it was rapidly going out of fashion as a method for murder.

1931 The Blazing Car Murder: Alfred Arthur Rouse

'Remember, remember, the fifth of November' are the words of a children's chant. It refers to Guy Fawkes Night, the traditional British occasion to celebrate a criminal – who tried to blow up Parliament and the king – by letting off fireworks around a blazing bonfire. Usually the bonfires have burned away by midnight. So one can imagine the surprise of two young men who turned into Hardingstone Lane, Northampton, Northamptonshire, about 1.50am on 6 November 1930, when they saw two strange sights almost simultaneously: first, a hatless man carrying a briefcase emerged from a ditch almost facing them, while beyond the hedge and around a slight bend in the lane, they could see a fiery blaze lighting up the sky. It was a bright night with a good moon. As the stranger passed by, one of the men asked what the blaze was. The fellow walked on a further 15 yards before pausing to say, 'It looks as if someone is having a bonfire up there,' before continuing to walk away from the village and towards the main Northampton–London road. Soon he was out of sight.

The youths walked a further 400 yards and found that the blaze was a Morris Minor saloon car, burning fiercely, with flames rising 12–16 feet high and giving off an intense heat. Quickly one of the men fetched a local constable, P.C. Copping, while the other summoned his father, who was also in the constabulary. Back at the blaze, Copping got as close as he could and saw a body in the flames. The four men managed to put out the fire, which had left the car largely destroyed. The charred body was face down on the driver's seat with his trunk lying along the front seats. Among the wreckage was a burst and empty petrol can. There were no marks on the road that might indicate a collision. Later that morning, the police found a mallet in the grass about 14 yards in front of the vehicle. After forensic examination Sir Bernard Spilsbury detected human hair on the mallet, which was also covered in dirt. Luckily for the investigators, the registration plate of the car was undamaged and MU 1468 showed its owner to be an Alfred Rouse, a 36-year-old commercial traveller living in Finchley, north London.

Less than two days later, Rouse was caught by detectives and volunteered to go with them to Hammersmith Police Station. His story, put simply, was that he had picked up a stranger on the Great North Road leaving London. Many miles later he had got out of the car to relieve himself and told the man, 'There is some petrol in the can; you can empty it into the tank while I am gone.' The fellow had asked about smoking a cigarette (Rouse himself was a non-smoker). As he was pulling up his trousers, Rouse saw that the car was in flames: 'I saw the man was inside and I tried to open the door, but I could not, as the car was then a mass of flames... I did not know what to do and ran as hard as I could along the road when I saw the two men... I lost my head and did not know what to do, and really don't know what I have done since.'

An insurance assessor who was an expert in car fires examined the vehicle and was satisfied that a nut on the carburettor had been loosened to spread the blaze. The police were unable to identify the dead man and Rouse was no help in this respect. The matter was clearly serious and he was charged with murder of an unknown person.

His trial took place at the Northampton Winter Assizes before Mr Justice Talbot and started on 26 January 1931. Norman Birkett K.C., one of the most eloquent defence counsel of his day, was, for once, the chief prosecutor. So often a canny defender of those in the dock, Birkett now used his considerable talents in an adversarial role to run rings around Alfred Rouse, who had agreed to give evidence in his own defence. Unfortunately for the defendant, he had told a whole pack of lies to account for his movements after the blaze and up to the time of his arrest. He had been carrying on affairs with several women and had fathered a brood of illegitimate children. Referring to his mistresses as 'my harem' was not the sort of thing to impress the good county folk who made up the Northampton jury. Those same 12 citizens took 75 minutes to find Rouse guilty. Before his execution at Bedford Gaol on 10 March, he made a full confession in a newspaper, explaining how his love life 'was in a tangle'. He needed to start afresh and hit on a plan to dispose of the kind of man 'no one would miss'. Rouse had picked up a traveller in London, got him drunk on whisky, strangled him and set the vehicle on fire hoping that the burned remains would be mistaken for him. He denied clubbing the man with the mallet. The murder was botched from the start; Rouse forgot to put his identity disc on the victim. He planned to get a train from Northampton to Scotland and start a new life but seeing the two men in Hardingstone Lane had so unnerved him that he had walked away in the wrong direction and ended up in South Wales and then London.

Despite the callous deed that resulted in the end of his own life, Alfred Rouse was not entirely bad; he had signed up for King and Country just four days after the declaration of war in 1914 and was severely wounded a year later at Festeubert. After three years he was still suffering, including having nightmares. A quiet young man until his call-up, it has been suggested by some commentators that Rouse's injury affected him sexually; with his brilliantined hair slicked down and shallow features Rouse, like so many Lotharios before and since, did not seem the most handsome of lovers, yet 80 cases of seduction were traced by the police and he was spending every penny he earned on supporting his numerous women and a growing number of illegitimate children. He seemed to be genuinely fond of all his 'harem' and their offspring.

Perhaps the most callous aspect of the murder was Rouse's complete lack of interest in finding out who his victim had been. He gave the police almost no help in this regard. In 2014, more than 80 years since the crime, it was reported in the media that forensic scientists were still hoping to identify the remains using DNA strands. The scientists' work had resulted in a list, which had narrowed down the likely victim to one of ten persons reported missing in 1930.

1932 Jilted Love: Maurice Freedman

Annette Friedson was a 31-year-old Jewish woman whose family disapproved of her latest boyfriend. This was 36-year-old Maurice Freedman, an ex-policeman who claimed to be a commercial traveller but was a debtor who even pawned his clothes to fund a gambling addiction. What incensed the Friedson family was that they discovered Freedman was married. This news came as the final straw for Annette. The couple's 18-month relationship had been stormy, and she had forgiven Maurice several times for various indiscretions, but Annette drew the line at being a married man's mistress. She wrote to Freeman on 23 January 1932 saying the affair was over and she did not want to see him again. So worried was Annette's brother that Freedman might behave irrationally that he escorted her to the legal typist job she had in the City of London.

Three days after Annette sent the letter, Freedman arrived at 103 Fore Street and accosted her on the stairs around 9.20am. A man entering the building at 9.26am saw the couple arguing heatedly. Moments later, Freedman sliced Annette's throat with a razor. A trail of blood ran from where her body lay halfway up the stairs towards the first floor, down past a bloody handbag left on the stairs, to the entrance hall. No murder weapon was left at the scene of the crime.

Freedman was quickly apprehended by detectives the next day at his home in Clapton. He immediately said, 'I am the man you are after. I admit cutting her throat in the City.' However, in court he denied this confession and said he had taken a cutthroat razor to cut his own throat if Annette had spurned him, but she grabbed it and killed herself. He claimed to have thrown the razor into a canal. Maurice's defence was utterly ruined at his Old Bailey trial on 8 March before Mr Justice Hawke by the prosecution, who showed the court a bloodstained safety razor found in its holder on a London bus. Blood on the razor was identical to Annette's rare blood group; hairs on the blade matched the girl's fur collar, and the bus conductor of the vehicle in which the razor was found remembered Freedman as a passenger. The jury quickly found him guilty and he was hanged at Pentonville on 4 May 1932 by executioner Robert Baxter.

1933 The Malevolent Dwarf: Stanley Eric Hobday

More than 45 witnesses were willing to testify against Hobday at his trial. Not one person came forward in his defence. Standing barely 4 foot tall in his socks, with a generally sour disposition, one witness described him as 'an overgrown dwarf'. Stanley had a long list of offences, although he was just 21 years old, and to these he added murder on 27 August 1933.

It was late on that hot Sunday night in Moor Street, West Bromwich, when a householder, Mrs Gladys Fox, who was having trouble sleeping in the heat, heard the sound of breaking glass. She nudged awake her 27-year-old husband Charlie, a metal cutter, who was none too pleased at having his sleep so rudely interrupted. Lighting a candle and dressed only in his vest and shirt Mr Fox crept down the stairs and into his living room while his nervous wife watched from the landing. The door at the foot of the stairs was ajar and Gladys shouted out, 'Oh look – somebody has been in!' One can imagine her horror when a gust of wind blew out the light of the candle. As she trembled in the darkness Mr Fox stumbled back up the stairs and without saying a word slumped onto the bedroom floor. Like a scene in some old 'B' movie, Mrs Fox crawled on her knees towards her husband and suddenly felt warm sticky blood. In the light of an early and soft summer's dawn she saw a knife sticking out of his back. Her screams attracted a printer on his way home from a night shift and he alerted the police. Charles Fox had been stabbed seven times.

That same early morning a butcher called Newton, who lived just a few streets away from Mr and Mrs Fox, found that he too had been the victim of a break-in. To his astonishment he found a bowl of soapy water where his razor had been used by the intruder to shave himself; a work basket had been taken from a cupboard, apparently to do sewing repairs; and the thief had even made breakfast and helped himself to the milk in the kitchen before absconding with a few pounds in cash.

Detective Inspector Fred Cherrill, Scotland Yard's great fingerprint expert, was soon on the case and found a perfect set of prints on a milk bottle. This led the BBC, for the first time in its history, to carry the description of a criminal 'wanted by the police in connection with a murder'. Hobday was not only remarkable for his small stature, but seems to have been none-too-bright, though he thought of himself as quite smart. His ineptitude at the scene of his crimes was only matched by his stupidity, or bad luck, while on the run from the law.

After the two burglaries, he had stolen a Jowett Jupiter saloon car and headed north. Being a very small man he had trouble reaching the pedals and his bad driving led to him turning the car in a complete somersault, much to the amazement of an Irish labourer who witnessed the whole scene at High Leigh in Cheshire (about 67 miles from West Bromwich). Unable to start the damaged vehicle, Hobday now set off on foot leaving his old suitcase in the car. He walked north avoiding main roads but in a country lane near Carlisle he blundered into a herd of cows. The actions of the little man were noted by cowman 'Watty' Bowman and he subsequently remembered the BBC announcement. Two hours later he told his employer, who phoned the police and the constabulary found the pint-sized Hobday and arrested him. When charged he said, 'I haven't done any murder' but he soon began incriminating himself during an interview.

His trial started at the Stafford Assizes on 14 November before Mr Justice Talbot. The prosecution case was damning: apart from more than 45 people willing to testify against Hobday, there was the fingerprint evidence; stubble on a razor used by the accused in prison was found to be identical to that on the razor left at Mr Newton's house; a footprint in the garden of one of the burglaries was found to be a size 4, a very small size for a man, but the man in the dock was a size 4; he was also able to describe all the items found in his suitcase, which was full of camping equipment, except for one missing item – a sheath knife. Hobday's skilled defence counsel, Sir Reginald Coventry, K.C., fought valiantly for his client without calling a single witness (as there were none). He tried to ridicule Cherrill's fingerprint evidence but the detective refused to give way. Coventry finished his closing speech by asking the jury if it was 'conceivable' a cold-hearted killer could burgle two premises on the same night and 'calmly' sit down and do sewing or shave himself before also stealing a vehicle?

The jurors clearly thought it *was* very possible and found Hobday guilty. He was executed by Thomas Pierrepoint at Winson Green Prison, Birmingham, on 28 December (some accounts say on the 29th). Charles Fox, the victim, had supplemented his income by working as a doorstep collector for the National Clothing Company. His weekly round was on a Saturday and his takings on the day before his murder had amounted to 14 shillings (about £40 today). That small sum was all Hobday had found at the house; it cost poor Mr Fox his life, but duly led his killer to the gallows.

1934 Corned Beef and Dead Dogs: Ethel Lillie Major

Mrs Major was executed at Hull Prison on 19 December 1934 for the murder of her husband, Arthur, who had died on 24 May. The cause of death had been strychnine poisoning. In his book on poisons the writer John Rowlands called strychnine 'the cruellest of all' in the way that it paralyses the nervous system and produces such excruciating pain that, typically, a victim's back arches spasmodically in a 'C' shape.

Ethel and Arthur had married in 1918 when she was 28 years old. Her father was a Leicestershire gamekeeper, living on the estate of an aristocratic family at Tumby near Horncastle. She had gone to the local village school, a typical working-class Victorian girl, and planned to be a dressmaker, but her mother's failing health required that Ethel stay at home and run the household. She also got herself pregnant at 24 years of age and an illegitimate daughter named Auriel was born. Ethel's parents were not told who the father was and they did what many other working-class families did in similar circumstances – they got on with their lives and brought up Auriel as if she was Ethel's sister.

Arthur Major had fought bravely in the First World War and had no fewer than 28 pieces of shrapnel in his body. After marrying Ethel he found employment as a gardener but occasionally was out of work and on these occasions the couple, with a son, Lawrence, born in 1919, moved in with Ethel's parents. In 1929 Ethel's mother died and the Majors settled in a council bungalow at Kirkby-on-Bain, while Ethel's father and Auriel went to live in nearby Roughton. That first decade of marriage was reasonably smooth, though some folks said Arthur Major was turning more to drink, while Ethel complained he was not affectionate enough towards their boy.

Not long after the move to Kirkby, a village gossip told Arthur the truth about Auriel. The row which followed pushed the Majors' marriage onto the slippery slope that ended in his murder. Mrs Major was now in her 40s, a mousey-looking skinny woman with thin lips and horn-rimmed spectacles. There were soon frequent quarrels. Lawrence later said that his father came home drunk almost every night. It must be added that several neighbours, including the local vicar, at the trial declared they had never seen Arthur worse for drink except one woman who had witnessed him fall off his bike into a ditch dead drunk. It was reported how on one occasion, after a row, Ethel followed Arthur and threw a brick at him. It missed. She threw another. It missed also.

Matters started to come to a head early in May 1934, three weeks before Arthur's death, after Ethel had found two love letters in one of her husband's jackets. She thought they had been sent by a neighbour, Mrs Rose Kettleborough. Ethel went on the war path and showed the letters to a visiting sanitary inspector and also the family doctor, to whom she declared, 'A man like that's not fit to live. I'll do him in.' Spitefully, she wrote to the chief constable accusing Arthur of often being drunk in charge of his lorry. She made the same compliant at the local police station. A solicitor was asked by Ethel to write to Mrs Kettleborough – who denied having anything to do with Mr Major – and request she stop writing letters to her husband. Arthur, who refused to discuss the matter, retaliated by putting a notice in a local newspaper saying he was not responsible for his wife's debts.

One can imagine that the situation in the Major home must have been difficult because, oddly enough, Arthur, Ethel and Lawrence still shared the bungalow. Arthur usually prepared his own food and on 22 May at 5pm he arrived home whilst Ethel was upstairs and made his own supper from a can of opened corned beef. A short time afterwards Lawrence saw his father trembling violently in the backyard. When he fell down both mother and son helped Mr Major up to bed, Ethel remarking that the corned beef must have disagreed with him. Before very long Arthur was in extreme pain, foaming at the mouth, and jerking his legs convulsively. Ethel made no attempt to call a doctor until her father, who happened to call by, saw the state of his son-in-law and insisted Dr Smith be roused. By 10pm, when the doctor visited Mr Major, he was a little better and privately Mrs Major said her husband had been having fits for a year or two. This was news to Dr Smith but he assumed that fits and foaming at the mouth meant Arthur Major was suffering from epilepsy. He prepared a sedative draught, which was given to the patient.

Next morning Arthur continued to improve but was off his food. Ethel brought him a cup of warm water, which he drank. Throughout that day Major lay partly in a coma and had periodic convulsions. At 2pm Mrs Major fed him a little gruel and at 9pm the patient had a cup of tea. Next morning Arthur seemed a little better and that evening Ethel gave him some more water. Around 10pm Lawrence noticed his father was getting worse again. The boy hurried downstairs to fetch his mother. A trembling Arthur Major clung to his wife and poignantly remarked, 'You have been good to me,' before heaving violently and dropping back dead. It was 10.40pm.

Ethel did not bother to tell Dr Smith about Arthur's demise until surgery hours the next day. He wrote out a death certificate saying the 44-year-old man had died of 'status epilepticus'. Two days later, as Ethel and the relatives were preparing to go to the funeral, a police inspector called to say the event needed to be cancelled. Ethel remarked that it looked 'as if they were suspicioning me'. The police had acted after an anonymous letter, signed 'Fair Play' (the author was never discovered), had been received by the coroner. The writer implied that Ethel had murdered her husband and fed the remnants of a meal on 23 May, during her husband's sickness, to a dog belonging to a neighbour, Mr Maltby. The dog had died afterwards. The remains of both Arthur and the dog were now exhumed and strychnine was found in both of them.

Many authors who refer to the case trot out a classic red herring; when Ethel was interviewed by Detective Chief Inspector Hugh Young of Scotland Yard she said, 'I did not know my husband had died of strychnine poisoning.' D.C.I. Young replied, 'I never mentioned strychnine. How did you know that?' Ethel answered, 'Oh, I'm sorry. I must have made a mistake.' This exchange of words is usually presented as evidence of her guilt. But at her trial defence counsel Norman Birkett showed that her solicitor had discussed strychnine with his client as early as 29 May – and the police interview was on 3 July. This information puts a different emphasis on Ethel's words.

Birkett was considered the greatest defence counsel of his generation. The poisoning of husbands by their wives had become a rather popular form of murder by 1934 and he had already saved two women in arsenic poisoning cases from an appointment with the hangman. Yet Birkett knew that the cards were stacked heavily against Mrs Major and she would likely make a poor showing in the witness box, so he advised his client not to give evidence at her trial before Mr Justice Channell, which started at the Lincoln Assizes on 29 October. Most damning was that a key, freshly polished, had been found in Ethel's purse which opened a box containing strychnine belonging to her gamekeeper father. He had lost the key some years earlier. The jury took only an hour to find Ethel guilty and, sad to relate, she had to be helped out of the dock and went to her execution in a terrified half-faint. Yet she made no confession.

This murder case has an epitaph more pleasant than most; in 2011 Hull Prison staged an exhibition of its history and Ethel's grandson was invited to open the display. Lawrence Major had only been 15 years old when his mother was executed and there had been a deep love between the two. Out of shame, he did not tell his own son that his grandmother had been hanged as a murderess until manhood. Construction was due to commence on the wing of the gaol where Ethel had been executed and apparently her grandson was overjoyed to see his grandmother's grave and for his sake, and that of his father, to pay her a small but heartfelt measure of respect.

1935 The Villa Madeira Murder: George Percy Stoner

The British, unlike the French or Italians, don't do *crime passionnel* very well. Strong passions, histrionic outbursts of love, jealousy and revenge seem alien somehow to the native character. The three greatest British *crimes passionnels* of the 20th century involved *femme fatales* – Edith Thompson, Alma Rattenbury and Ruth Ellis.

A young married woman of 28 years who took a younger male lover and wrote silly letters to him saying such things as, 'Yes, darlint, be jealous so much that you will do something desperate' put herself and Frederick Bywaters in the dock at the Old Bailey. Bywaters stabbed 32-year-old Percy Thompson to death one dark night in October 1922. Edith was completely innocent of the murder itself but was charged alongside him. Her trial and dreadful execution were major milestones on the path towards the abolition of capital punishment.

Ruth Ellis shot and killed her abusive lover. She was the last woman to hang in Britain and we will meet her later in this book.

Alma Rattenbury's case has some parallels with Edith Thompson's since both women took younger lovers, both committed adultery in an age when this act had strong moral significance and both were highly emotional women who lived to some extent in fantasy worlds of their own making. Alma was 28 years old and Francis Rattenbury was 56 when the pair met at the Empress Hotel, Victoria, British Columbia, in 1923. He was one of Canada's most eminent architects (though born in Leeds), responsible for designing the Empress Hotel and also the British Columbia Parliament buildings and the Vancouver courthouse. She was a twice-married Canadian citizen from Kamloops, British Columbia, a musical child prodigy on the piano and violin, described as 'beautiful, with a lovely oval face, deep hauntingly sad eyes and full lips which easily settled into a pout, at once fashionable and sensuous'. Alma's first husband and greatest love, an aristocratic British officer, died on the Western Front in 1916, just two years after their marriage. Inwardly scarred for life, she joined a nursing unit and later received the Croix de Guerre for her war work. In 1918 she met and had an affair with another aristocrat, a penniless Pakenham relative of Lord Longford. This marriage ended in divorce and Alma took custody of their baby son, Christopher, to whom she was devoted.

Francis Rattenbury was soon smitten by this artistic, flighty, attractive bird of paradise. He was married and well established in Vancouver society with a wife – and two children almost the same age as Alma. He started to take Alma to social events, much to the displeasure of some influential citizens. She had, by now, become his mistress and even moved into his palatial home, where the sick Mrs Rattenbury had rooms. Alma was in love with this older figure who was a V.I.P. and took her on Mediterranean cruises and generous shopping trips. Eventually a divorce was agreed and Alma and Francis married in April 1925. Canadian polite society, however, was slowly turning against Rattenbury and his new young wife. He found himself cold-shouldered by former clients and business associates, and work dropped away. After the birth of a son named John, the couple decided to relocate to England where Alma would try to re-establish her musical career and Francis, who had several investments, could enjoy a fairly comfortable retirement. So it was that in 1930 they rented the 'Villa Madeira' at 5 Manor Road, Bournemouth, a modest bijou villa with four upstairs bedrooms.

The couple were not sleeping together. Francis, now becoming increasingly deaf, was an alcoholic who downed a bottle of whisky a night. He slept in a bedroom next to the sitting room on the ground floor. Alma, who drank quite a number of whisky cocktails, found life in Bournemouth to be stultifying. She adored her two sons and was a very affectionate mother but she needed other interests too. She advertised for a maid and gave the job to 22-year-old Irene Riggs, daughter of a Bournemouth gravedigger. At last Alma had a young friend and Irene soon found that she was far less a maid and more a companion. In the way of women, the pair became inseparable, calling one another 'darling', shopping together and running the Rattenbury household. Irene was fascinated by her new employer with the soft Canadian accent; Alma was excitable, silly at times, talked, drank and laughed a lot, had absolutely no idea of the value of money and overspent her husband's generous allowance. She was also still interested in sex and implied to Irene that Francis was impotent and did not care if she found her pleasures elsewhere. She was diagnosed with pulmonary tuberculosis, and Alma's doctor was later to assert that treatment had increased her sex urge. She made passes at two male staff, who left hurriedly. Alma habitually wore her silk pyjamas under a loose housecoat or kimono.

In September 1934 George Stoner came to work at the Villa Madeira, a 17-year-old youth, short and stocky, with slightly bowed legs, but good looks. He was a working-class lad from the poor part of Bournemouth who had spent much time growing up at his grandmother's home. She later described him as 'an extraordinary good boy', an opinion confirmed by many other local folk. His main job was to be the Rattenburys' chauffeur. Alma never called him by his first name and simply referred to him as 'Stoner'.

The Rattenburys were by now often arguing over money matters; two months before Stoner's arrival they had a rare violent argument when both were the worse for alcohol. Alma screamed at her husband: 'Instead of threatening to kill yourself why, in the name of charity, don't you bloody well get on with it? At least with you gone I could get myself a real man. Go on, kill yourself...' He had then punched her and Irene was required to comfort Alma as she sobbed, 'You bloody coward, you drink-sodden bastard.' Next day Rattenbury, in typical fashion, apologised to his wife and gave her £100 (about £4,000 in today's money) to spend on anything she wished.

So it was that George Stoner arrived to form the third corner of a very odd triangle (if indeed a triangle has enough angles for this particular setup) at the Villa Madeira. Several things happened quickly. About a month after the chauffeur's arrival he took Alma on a visit to Oxford where she seduced him. Alma later said the romance was mutual, and the young man was obviously smitten by the advances of his employer and soon deeply in love with her. Then she arranged for her new lover to become a live-in employee, taking the spare bedroom upstairs close to her own. Irene Riggs naturally resented the way Stoner had supplanted her in Alma's affections and warned both of them that they were courting disaster if Mr Rattenbury found out. Alma, in the way of all hopeless romantics, cared not a jot. She and Stoner argued over their respective age differences – he was now 18 and she was twice his age – but the affair was at boiling point and people in love are blind to good advice and just about everything else except themselves. Lying to Francis that she needed to go away for a glandular operation, Alma squeezed £250 out of her husband and took Stoner to London on 19 March 1935 where they stayed at the Royal Palace Hotel, Kensington. She bought her lover expensive clothes in Harrods worth about £40 (Stoner's salary was £1 a week 'all found') and he, in turn, bought her a single stone diamond ring for £15 10s with money she had given him as a gift. So intense was their passion that it seems safe to assume that the diamond ring formed an engagement between them.

The couple returned to Bournemouth on Friday 22 March in the evening. Francis was drunk and already in bed. The next day passed quietly enough. It was at 1.15am on Monday 25th that a call was received at the local police station from Mr Rattenbury's doctor, William O'Donnell, saying that Francis had been taken to the local nursing home with head injuries that could not have been self-inflicted. A police constable, with the splendid name of Alfred Bagwell, now set out to check this story, then cycled around to the Villa Madeira at 2am. Alma, clad in her trademark pyjamas, excited and drunk on whisky and soda, met Bagwell at the door and blurted out she had found her husband unconscious when she entered the sitting room, blood running down his face as he sat in his armchair. Within minutes of an inspector also turning up, Alma was behaving in a very strange way. She said, 'I did it with the mallet. Rats has lived too long'; then she said her lover had done it, then Francis's son (who lived in Canada) was the assailant; she offered and then retracted the offer of a bribe of £10 to P.C. Bagwell, and even tried hysterically to kiss the unfortunate man, who was forced to put up his arms and say 'Easy on', especially since the copper was desperate to use the loo and after extricating himself from Alma's clutches exited into the front garden to relieve himself (where he was almost seized upon by another policeman wondering who was hiding in the bushes).

Alma soon became tired and wanted to sleep. Under caution she said, 'I did it. He's lived too long.' She was allowed less than three hours to rest and that same morning made a statement saying, 'I was playing cards with my husband when he dared me to kill him as he wanted to die. I picked up the mallet. He then said, "You have not the guts enough to do it." I then hit him with the mallet. I hid the mallet outside the house. I would have shot him if I had a gun.'

In his statement Stoner said he had gone downstairs after he heard Mrs Rattenbury's screams. He saw her husband slumped in the chair. He went to Dr O'Donnell's house (but the doctor was on his way), returned, cleared the blood on the floor after Alma's instructions and then took the doctor and Francis to the hospital. Taken into custody and cautioned again, Alma told detectives, 'That's right. I did it deliberately and would do it again.' She had left the Villa Madeira after a tearful farewell, little Johnny waving Mummy goodbye after a fond kiss. Stoner's last words to her were interesting: 'You've got yourself into this mess by talking too much.'

On 28 March Stoner went up to London and it is believed that he saw Alma at Holloway Prison. He had already startled Irene Riggs by going on a drunken binge (he normally never drank) and shouting, 'Mrs Rattenbury is in gaol and I've put her there', an incident she reported to the police. Irene also asked Stoner if his fingerprints were on the mallet and he told her that he had been wearing gloves. Several commentators see this as the obvious proof of his guilt, along with his confession to the crime, but it was never resolved whether Stoner was referring to wearing gloves when he moved the mallet. Francis Rattenbury died that day, making Alma a party to murder; as Stoner got off the London–Bournemouth train, he was arrested and similarly charged.

Their joint trial began in the Old Bailey's No. 1 Court before Mr Justice Humphreys on 27 May 1935. Alma now said that a jealous Stoner had killed her husband in a cocaine-fuelled rage. One might well ask how a country boy like Stoner got introduced to cocaine if not from his excitable mistress, but then George described the substance as brown with dark spots when the wider world knows the drug as being as white as 'snow'. Mrs Rattenbury could afford top lawyers to defend her. Stoner was represented under the Poor Persons Defence Act by J. D. Casswell, then at the start of a long career, not yet a silk or K.C., though a valiant defender of the underdog. Stoner chose not to go into the witness box and instructed his counsel to stick with the cocaine frenzy defence. In his summing-up the judge, who had been one of the prosecutors in the Edith Thompson case, took a different line with the jury than that sad lady's tough judge, Mr Justice Shearman, who had lectured them about the sins of adulterers. Humphreys warned the jury that Alma's sexual morals 'should not make you feel any more ready to convict her of this crime'. The jury was out for 47 minutes and returned to find Alma not guilty of murder. She almost fainted in the dock. George Stoner was found guilty and Humphreys donned the dreaded black cap to pronounce sentence of death.

Three days later, in a field of flowers near the River Avon at Christchurch, Alma stabbed herself repeatedly and fell into the water by a bank of irises, a latter-day Ophelia. Thousands attended her pink funeral – pink flowers being her favourites – and so she was buried as theatrically in death as she had lived her life. Among the notes she left was one that read, 'If only I thought it would help Stoner I would stay on. But it has been pointed out to me too vividly that I cannot help him. That is my death sentence.'

Stoner wept when he got the news. His appeal was dismissed and he seemed certain to hang. The Lord Chief Justice, toad-faced Gordon Hewart, called it 'a sordid and squalid case' and the appeal 'a mere waste of time'. Stoner had by now made it clear that he had confessed to the crime only out of love and loyalty to Alma. Now that she had been found not guilty, he was able to say that the cocaine business was a pack of lies. Francis had been in the chair when he entered the room. He pushed the mallet behind a chair and later hid it in the garden. He was not aware at first how badly Alma had incriminated herself but he decided to do all he could to incriminate himself rather than see her die on the scaffold. Many thousands petitioned for Stoner's reprieve and there was a public groundswell that he was the victim of an older woman's lust. On 26 June, 23 days after Alma's suicide, the Home Secretary agreed to let George Stoner live.

It does seem quite possible that Alma murdered her husband, although the conventional view is the one presented in court. The story has been the subject of several books and plays; Terence Rattigan in his play *Crime Celebre* suggested that Stoner had manipulated Alma. It is an enduring *crime passionnel* and mystery because we will never know the real truth. Stoner was a model prisoner and released after seven years on 20 May 1942, still a relatively young man of 26 years. He joined the army, served bravely at D-Day, got married, had a daughter and died in Christchurch Hospital, less than half a mile from the Villa Madeira, at the ripe age of 83 years in 2000. Alma and Francis' son, John, became a famous architect like his father, a disciple of Frank Lloyd Wright in America.

1936 Body Parts and Bloodstained Halls: Buck Ruxton

In some respects the Ruxton case might seem simple, with evidence stacked against the defendant. Yet this murder story, an open and shut case in some respects was also, as Colin Wilson wrote, 'the most remarkable feat of forensic reconstruction of the 1930s.'

Eighty years ago in an age long before the 'selfie' existed a rustic bridge was the perfect beauty spot to breathe in the scenery, or lean over and admire the sparkling fast-flowing water as it leaps over rocks by a pretty burn. One girl, Miss Susan Haines Johnson, looked over the little bridge of the Gardenholme Linn, a tributary stream of the Annan on the Edinburgh–Carlisle road just north of Moffat on 29 September 1935 and saw a human arm sticking out of some wrapping in the gully below.

Susan called her brother who went down to the stream and found parts of a body wrapped in newspapers and a sheet. The police were summoned and Sergeant Sloan of the Dumfriesshire constabulary discovered four grisly bundles. Wrapped in a mix of newspapers, some sheeting, a child's woollen rompers and a blouse were two heads, two upper arms, a forearm with a set of hands, two thigh bones, two lower leg bones, the chest portion of one cadaver, some 30 chunks of human flesh and one pair of feet. Maggots were feasting on the flesh and many human features in the faces had been obliterated with what appeared to be surgical skill.

The newspaper wrappings came from the *Daily Herald, Sunday Chronicle* and *Sunday Graphic*. The latter paper gave the case its first breakthrough since it was a special edition sold only in the Morecambe and Lancaster area. By a lucky coincidence on 9 October the Chief Constable of Dumfriesshire spotted in a Glasgow newspaper a report of a missing Morecambe lass, Mary Rogerson. He communicated with the Lancashire Police and the girl's mother recognised the blouse as that of her daughter. Forensic scientists had meantime decided they were dealing with the remains of two bodies and for a time suspected they belonged to a man and a woman. Other body parts continued to be found over the initial four weeks including a left foot, right forearm and hand. Teeth and bone samples, together with the steadily growing number of pieces, led the team to conclude that the cadavers were those of one young woman, aged 18–25 years, and an older woman, 30–60 years. Mary Rogerson was 20 years old. Her employer, Isabella Ruxton, was 36 years old, and she too had been reported missing by her common-law husband, Dr Buck Ruxton.

Soon Dr Ruxton, whose real name was Bukhtyar Rustomji Rantanji Hakim (he had changed his name by deed poll to Buck Ruxton), was the chief and sole suspect. He had been born in Bombay in 1899 to French-Indian Parsee parents, and had become an intelligent, handsome and well-liked man who held degrees in medicine and surgery and had worked for the Indian Medical Corps in Bombay, Basra and Baghdad. After a time at the University College, London University, he had bought his practice in Lancaster, setting up his home and surgery in a solid Victorian mansion at 2 Dalton Square in 1930. In those pre-National Health Service days, a skilled doctor such as Ruxton undertook minor surgery and even some dentistry in addition to his duties as a general practitioner.

Mrs Ruxton and the doctor were never married, though they had two girls and a son aged between two and six years of age. Isabella Kerr, as she was born, hailed from Edinburgh but had met the handsome

'Captain Hakim', as Ruxton sometimes used to call himself, in London in 1928. They stuck together despite a tempestuous relationship. Their Lancaster household was completed by the maid Mary Rogerson, a plain but cheerful girl, as well as three daily helps, charladies Mary Oxley, Elizabeth Curwen and Mabel Smith.

Forensic work on the body parts was a big job, a veritable jigsaw puzzle, and involved some of the top men of the time (though not, for once, Sir Bernard Spilsbury), led by John Glaister, Regius Professor of Forensic Medicine at Glasgow University. The killer had tried to destroy or remove any body parts that might aid identification. Curiously, the missing parts seemed specific to known features of Mary Rogerson and Isabella Ruxton. Mary, for instance, had a noticeable glide in one eye yet both her eyes had been removed. She had a birth mark on her right arm and the flesh had been cut out at this spot on the younger person's body. Miss Rogerson had also had freckles and the facial skin had been removed on the corpse. This sequence was repeated on the body thought to be Mrs Ruxton; she had a prominent nose, but it had been cut away, as had the ears, eyes and lips (which could show signs of strangulation); the area where she had a large bunion on her left big toe had similarly been cut away, and so on.

Yet science threw up useful clues. An entomologist was able to study the maggots and date the infestation to shortly after 15 September, the date of the *Sunday Graphic*, and also the date, the police soon learned, when Dr Ruxton had started to act very strangely. In a forensic first, Glaister compared life-size photographs of the heads of the two suspected victims with the skulls he believed to be theirs and various transverse and vertical measurements tallied exactly. After soaking one set of hands in hot water, he got a perfect set of fingerprints belonging to Mary Rogerson off them.

Cause of death was fairly clear; the taller, older woman had a broken hyoid bone in the neck, indicating strangulation. There were five stab wounds in the chest along with several broken bones and bruises. These all indicated a fight, possibly the result of a jealous rage. The younger victim's arms indicated bruising before death and there were two blows to the head from a blunt instrument. Since the body trunk was missing (and never found) the experts could not reach further conclusions. Had she witnessed the first murder and been quickly despatched with blows to the head? We will probably never know.

Dr Ruxton's odd behaviour on 15 September had included getting a charlady to wash down his wooden stairs and 'very dirty yellow' bath that late Sunday afternoon. His children were staying with friends and the doctor had been locked inside his house all day on some task. The cleaner, Mrs Hampshire, had found the place strewn with bits of straw; a heavily bloodstained landing and stair carpets, the latter already pulled up by the doctor who was apparently in a rush to be 'ready for the decorators'; two bedrooms locked at the top of the house, while she also spied a bloodstained shirt and some half-burned bloody towels. Ruxton was also going about waving a bandaged finger which he said he had cut opening a tin of fruit. Then, on Tuesday the 17th the doctor had a minor road accident near Kendal driving a specially hired Austin Twelve, a car much larger than his own Hillman Imp. This matter required a visit to the police to clear up insurance details. He claimed to have been on a trip to Carlisle but it was an odd route to take. That same evening Ruxton lit a bonfire in his backyard that produced a blaze so big it lit up the bedroom of two schoolgirls in a nearby house and caught their attention. Mrs Curwen, continuing the cleaning up, found the bedroom doors were now all unlocked and there was a 'dirty smell' in two of them.

As he was agitated and tearful at times, the cleaners and other folk could not fail to notice the doctor's highly strung manner. He made matters worse for himself by complaining to the police, 'What the hell' they wanted, inquiring about his private affairs. The Lancaster constabulary had met the doctor on at least two other occasions when he and Isabelle had been seen violently arguing. One time he had told a policeman, 'My wife has been unfaithful to me and I will kill her if it continues.' At his trial he summed up their marriage thosly: 'We were the kind of people who could not live with each other and could not live without each other.' Their love-hate relationship was fuelled by his paranoid jealousy and resultant rages. In reality Mrs Ruxton does not seem to have been carrying on with another man though she liked the company of men and flirted occasionally, especially at local social events, while the doctor simply sulked. Now Ruxton began telling anyone who would listen that his 'Belle' might be having a fling with another man but she would come back. He suggested that she had taken Mary away because the maid needed an abortion, a tall tale which appalled the girl's distraught parents.

On the evening of 11 October the doctor visited the chief constable of Lancaster, Henry Vann, and volunteered a long statement called 'My Movements'. It can be seen in hindsight that having done all he could to clean up his house and cover his tracks Ruxton penned this cunning essay to explain what had been going on. At 7am the next morning, after asking a few questions, Vann, much to Ruxton's surprise, formally charged the doctor with the murder of Mary Rogerson. He replied: 'Most emphatically not... What motive and why? What are you talking?' With Ruxton arrested, the forensic experts moved into 2 Dalton Square; bloodstains yielded more secrets and human fatty tissue was found in the drains. On 5 November Ruxton was also charged with his wife's murder.

Buck Ruxton's trial before Mr Justice Shearman opened at the Manchester Winter Assizes on 2 March 1936. The chief Crown counsel was Mr J. C. Jackson K.C., while Ruxton's defence was led by Norman Birkett K.C. The defence team faced a monumental task; the Crown had assembled 107 witnesses in addition to the wealth of forensic evidence. Ruxton spent a day and a half in the witness box but seemed to get trapped in his own web of lies and evasions. Frequently he burst into tears. When Birkett asked him if he had killed his wife, the defendant sobbed that it was a 'deliberate fantastic story'. Asked if he was responsible for Mary Rogerson's death he cried again and replied, 'It is absolute bunkum with a capital B... Why should I kill my poor Mary?'

On the last day of the trial – ironically Friday the 13th – the jurors took only 63 minutes to find Ruxton guilty. Shortly before the trial began he had given a letter to the *News of the World* newspaper, which was to be opened only in the event of his death. Ruxton was executed at Strangeways Gaol on 12 May and on the following Sunday the newspaper printed in manuscript facsimile form the following words: 'I killed Mrs Ruxton in a fit of temper because I thought she had been with a man. I was mad at the time. Mary Rogerson was present at the time. I had to kill her. B Ruxton.' It is believed the doctor got £3,000 from the newspaper, which was used to pay his legal costs. He had earlier told Birkett 'Thanks old man' and bequeathed him a set of fish knives in his will. A kindly fellow, Norman Birkett did what he could to help the Ruxtons' three orphaned children.

The spot where the remains were found near Moffat is to this day called 'Ruxton's Dump'. The house in Dalton Square was uninhabited for years and believed to be haunted. Eventually the interior was totally gutted and the place turned into offices. Ruxton, who had a considerable ego, would have been delighted to learn that he made it into the *Dictionary of National Biography*. The bath he used to dismember his victims still exists but has been put to much better use – it is the horse trough at the Lancashire police headquarters.

1937 Evil Uncle Fred: Frederick Nodder

Mona Tinsley was a petite 10-year-old girl with rosy cheeks, four prominent front teeth and bobbed dark hair. Dressed in a double-breasted tweed coat with frayed sleeves, worn over her blue woollen jumper suit, black wellington boots and carrying a grey handbag, she was last seen alive leaving the Wesleyan School, Guildhall Street, Newark, on the late and bitterly cold afternoon of 5 January.

The little girl's home was just 20 minutes' walk away. By 9.30pm her distraught father called the police. A search that night proved fruitless, but next day an 11-year-old boy said he had seen Mona with a man near the bus station, a woman claimed to have seen the child 20 miles away near a bus stop in Retford and a third witness said she had seen an ex-lodger of the Tinsleys' loitering near the school. This man, who had left the Tinsleys because of non-payment of rent, was traced by the police to a house called 'Peacehaven' at Hayton, near Retford. The man's real name was Frederick Nodder though he had called himself 'Frederick Hudson' during his stay with the Tinsley family. He was a squalid, drunken brute, a 44-year-old motor engineer by profession, who got along best with the Tinsley children who called him 'Uncle Fred'.

More witnesses came forward connecting Nodder to the missing girl. He denied everything at first, then in a second statement said he had foolishly picked her up as she left school and agreed to take her to see an aunt who lived in Sheffield. She had stayed at 'Peacehaven' one night before being put on a bus to Sheffield, a journey of 90 minutes. Nodder refused to say much more and was duly tried for abduction at the Warwick Assizes before Mr Justice Swift who observed after Nodder was found guilty, 'What you did with that little girl, what became of her, only you know. It may be that time will reveal the dreadful secret that you carry in your breast.'

Two months and 27 days later, the judge's words rang true. Mona's body was found by some people out boating on a summer Sunday on the River Idle. There was a mark of a ligature on the little girl's neck denoting death by strangulation but the remains were too decomposed to say if she had been sexually assaulted. Oddly enough, Mona's parents had consulted a clairvoyant after her disappearance and the woman, Estelle Roberts, had seen a small girl's body floating in a river somewhere.

Nodder was back in court, this time at the Nottingham Assizes, in November. Despite pleading 'not guilty', a jury did not accept his tale of putting Mona on the bus. The prosecution suggested that Nodder had probably sexually assaulted her before death. 'Justice has slowly but surely overtaken you,' remarked Mr Justice Macnaughten before passing sentence. Nodder was hanged at Lincoln Prison on 30 December.

1938 Sex and Stupidity: George Brain

Despite his surname, George Brain was one murderer who displayed remarkably little intelligence in carrying out a senseless killing.

In the dawn mist of a fine summer's day on 14 July 1938 a motorist driving along Somerset Road, Wimbledon, saw a woman's body lying in the road. It seemed as if she was the victim of a hit-and-run accident, the body having fallen almost opposite the side entrance of the famous All England Lawn Tennis Club. Police noticed a tyre mark on her right leg stocking near the ankle that appeared to have come from a Morris Eight or Austin Seven car. The victim was soon identified as a 30-year-old prostitute, Mrs Rose Muriel Atkins, nicknamed by her clients, 'Irish Rose'. Knife marks on the woman's body convinced detectives that she had been killed elsewhere. She was lying face upward on the road, dressed in black, a pair of black lace gloves on her hands, her head resting on the verge in a pool of blood. The victim's face was terribly lacerated with a number of head wounds. Her handbag was missing.

Soon the police were on the hunt for George Brain, a 27-year-old married man who was a driver for a firm of boot repairers. His employers accused Brain of embezzlement of £37, but the police were especially interested to learn that the missing man drove a green Morris van. A nationwide search was launched with Brain's picture in the newspapers and, on 27 July, he was caught in Sheerness. In a statement he said that he had picked up Rose Atkins for sex but she had threatened to tell his employers that he used his van after hours. In a fit of temper he had slapped the prostitute, 'then everything went blank' and Brain hit her with the starting handle. This was a stupid thing to say because detectives had already found a cobbler's knife hidden in the garage where Brain had tried to hide the Morris van, a vehicle which bore many traces of Rose Atkins' blood. In a small room attached to the garage they also found Mrs Atkins' handbag.

At Brain's trial before Mr Justice Wrottesley at the Old Bailey, the judge told the jury: 'It is no excuse to say "I did not remember doing it", or "I am not clear that I did do it."' The jury took just 15 minutes to reach their guilty verdict. Brain had many friends in the Wimbledon area and was known in several bars and cafes as a likeable guy; 16,500 people signed a petition asking that he be reprieved, but he was hanged on 1 November 1938 at Wandsworth Prison.

1939 The Murder of Mabel Bundy: Boon & Smith

At 6.20am on 5 July a dead woman's body was found near the staff entrance of the Moorlands Hotel at Hindhead, Surrey. She was a maid at the hotel, 42-year-old Mrs Mabel Bundy. Her head had been crushed, though cause of death was a broken nose and injury to the chin, causing a massive brain trauma. Detectives quickly ascertained that Mrs Bundy had been seen on the previous evening at the Royal Huts Hotel in the company of soldiers from Thursley Camp. There were 700 soldiers at Thursley – 500 regulars and 200 army reservists on a refresher course.

The 2nd Battalion North Staffordshire Regiment were put on parade and three witnesses accompanied Detective Superintendent Cox of the Surrey Police as they looked at each soldier. From this parade, the witnesses picked out a Private Stanley Ernest Boon who, in turn, named Privates Joseph William Goodwin and Arthur John Smith as drinking companions with him at the Royal Huts on the previous night.

All three men were committed for trial at the Old Bailey in September. By this time Britain had declared war on Nazi Germany and the Second World War had begun. Twenty-six-year-old Smith admitted that he and Mrs Bundy had consensual sex. They had been interrupted by a drunken and aggressive Boon, along with his pal, Goodwin, who had been spying on the couple. The woman had tried to get away but 28-year-old Boon had been insistent and raped her. All three men said Mabel had been very friendly at first, but Boon said (according to Goodwin), 'We shall have to knock her out to get what we want.' Goodwin claimed he had tried to pull Boon off Mabel after he punched her in the face. After deliberation the jury acquitted Goodwin but found Boon and Smith guilty of murder. The pair blamed each other for Mabel's death. They were executed separately at Wandsworth Prison, Boon's hanging taking place on 25 October and Smith's on the next day.

1940 The Breakfast Murder: Ernest Edmund Hamerton

Lancashire lass Elsie Ellington moved down to London from Blackpool and got a job as assistant manageress of a Camberwell Green café. Her boyfriend, 25-year-old Ernest Hamerton, a Blackpool hotel kitchen worker, trailed after her looking for employment. He found a room at the same lodgings, 93 Inville Road, Walworth, south-east London, but the couple started quarrelling. On 15 January 1940 Elsie told her landlady, 'I am finished with him.' Early next morning another row broke out. Then, while 28-year-old Elsie was preparing breakfast, Hamerton went upstairs, fetched a knife and returned to stab the girl in the face, arms and back. Her dying words were 'You bad bugger...' before she collapsed. The girl was found covered in a pool of blood in the scullery with the knife still stuck in her body.

Hamerton tried to flee back to Lancashire but was caught by vigilant police at Manchester train station. Brought back to London for his trial at the Old Bailey, Hamerton was quickly found guilty. After Mr Justice Wrottesley had donned the black cap, and passed sentence of death, the young man asked if he could say a few words and was permitted to do so by the judge. Hamerton asked for no leniency and said, 'Why I killed the girl I cannot tell you. Just some selfish lust I suppose. There must have been some kink from the start. I struck her once with the knife and straight away felt sorry for her. I could not stand seeing her in such pain and that accounts for the repeated stab wounds. I did not try to disfigure her face; that must have happened accidentally.' The prosecuting counsel then intervened to ask, 'You do not blame the girl at all?' 'I do not,' replied Hamerton, 'I did it wilfully, just through some fit of jealousy. That is all.'

Despite taking full blame on his shoulders, Hamerton tried to launch an appeal but this was rejected, due in part to his striking confession in the dock. He was hanged by executioner Thomas Phipps on 27 March 1940 at Wandsworth Prison.

1941–1950

The war seemed to bring with it a new darkness, not just the darkened streets, with all the dangers they contained, nor the risk of death from the skies, but a rage that manifested itself in a new kind of murderer – the psychopathic sex killer. Sex crimes were not new but from 1941 onwards with men like Morgan, Cummins and Heath it seemed as if a new chapter had started in the dark history of murder. After the war Britain was awash with firearms of all kinds. Violent crime surged upwards from 1944. The murder rate had stayed fixed during the war but violent offences such as grievous wounding rose by 65 per cent in 1945. Violent offences doubled again in the next 18 months and would see a tenfold rise during the next 30 years. Movies such as Brighton Rock, Cosh Boy *and* The Blue Lamp *emphasised (some said glorified) youth crime.*

To stop this upsurge the authorities came down hard on criminals carrying firearms. One 1946 amnesty in London resulted in 2 million rounds of ammunition being handed in. A new executioner joined the family firm at the start of the war in the person of Albert Pierrepoint who carried out his first execution in 1940. He was following in the footsteps of his father, Harry, and his uncle Tom. Albert would hang many of the major German war criminals and, in his 25 years in office, despatch more than 400 men and women on his gallows. Shortly after the war the Criminal Justice Bill was revived and, to general surprise, it was passed into law by a slender majority of 245 to 222 votes. The capital punishment abolition clauses were defeated in the House of Lords and since there seemed only modest support in the country for abolition, the matter was allowed to slide. During the decade as a whole 3,596 persons were charged with murder, attempted murder and manslaughter.

1941 Hanged by a Dirty Bandage: Samuel Morgan

Mary Hagan was a good girl, a rather plain but happy 15-year-old with dark hair who wore the kind of unattractive horn-rimmed spectacles that so many women had to endure in those days. At 6.40pm on 2 November 1940 she set off from her home in Waterloo Road, Liverpool, to get her father a copy of the *Liverpool Echo* and some cigarette papers at a nearby newsagent's shop. The blackout was in progress, though Liverpool had not so far been bombed, but negotiating the darkened streets was an uncomfortable experience. When Mary did not return Mr Hagan grew worried; a search was instituted and late that night her body was found in a disused cement blockhouse. She had been raped and strangled.

Forensic scientists set to work but the conditions were far from ideal; the dark blockhouse had a filthy floor strewn with discarded bits of paper, cigarette butts and many footprints. It was also partly under water and the fire brigade had to be called to pump it dry. Near the girl's body they saw the fresh print of a man's boot. A cast was made and soil samples taken. Other detritus close by included a handkerchief with the name 'Rimmer', a chocolate wrapper, a tiny dirty piece of material and some matchsticks. An indeterminate bloody thumbprint was found on the left side of the victim's neck, which must have come from someone with a bleeding thumb.

Although an extensive inquiry for anyone called Rimmer in Liverpool led detectives nowhere, the laboratory specialists had a breakthrough with the small piece of material. It turned out to be a bandage in three layers, the inner part of which was impregnated with an ointment called 'acrislavine' that was not generally available to the public and used primarily in field and service dressings.

On 15 November during a roundup of deserters and soldiers AWOL in London a Private Samuel Morgan, Irish Guards, based at Seaforth Barracks, Liverpool, was detained in connection with the robbery of a girl cyclist, Anne McVittie, by a Liverpool canal one month before the Hagan murder. Police noticed he had a circular cut on his right thumb. Morgan was returned to Liverpool and detectives soon found a number of interesting facts. According to his sister, who had first bandaged the wound with his field dressing, the 28-year-old soldier had cut his thumb badly on barbed wire on 31 October, two days before Mary's death. Minute traces of Mary's blood group were found on his uniform, and his boot matched the boot print. Most fascinating of all was that a piece of the original dressing had been found at Morgan's home. It bore a double row of stitching holes by the selvedge, the natural edge of the material. The manufacturers were able to confirm that this double row was unusual; under examination the warp and weft of the original bandage and the one found at the murder scene matched perfectly.

Other facts fitted into place such as the chocolate bar wrapper which had traces of the ointment on it. Mary had eaten the chocolate so it was clear whoever had given her the confectionery had been with her that evening. A witness came forward, a waitress, to say that Morgan had asked if he could clean up at her house, claiming to have been in a fight. At his trial it did not take a jury long to find the soldier guilty and he was hanged at Walton Gaol on 4 April 1941.

1942 The Blackout Ripper: Gordon Frederick Cummins

Each decade seems to bring forth a particularly gory or bloody crime. One might think of Robinson in the 1920s (one of a small group of ghastly 'trunk murderers' dismembering their victims); perhaps the best recalled in the 1930s was Dr Ruxton, spreading body parts in Scottish dells; the Second World War gave London a shiver from hell in the deeds of a genuine ripper and serial killer, the first of his kind since an unknown madman had terrorised Whitechapel in 1888. The new ripper also targeted good-time girls but preferred the teeming fleshpots of Piccadilly, Soho and the West End. Luckily his reign of terror lasted just a few days.

Early on the morning of 9 February 1942 a postman delivering letters in Montague Place, London W1, saw a discarded bicycle lamp lying just inside the entrance of an air raid shelter. Thinking he had found a small prize in those blackout days he stooped to pick it up and saw the body of a woman lying inside the shelter. It was later confirmed she had been manually strangled, and that a red and green knitted scarf had been tied tightly around her neck after death.

Detectives were soon on the scene led by D.C.I. Sydney Birch, assisted by Scotland Yard's foremost fingerprint expert, Superintendent Fred Cherrill. The woman, who had not been sexually assaulted, turned out to be 42-year-old Miss Evelyn Hamilton, a respectable spinster from Newcastle-upon-Tyne who had simply been in London for one night on her way to a new job. She had popped out from her hotel for a late supper and, so detectives ascertained, been attacked around midnight. Her handbag was missing.

The killer had left no clues save one – the bruises on Miss Hamilton's neck had been made by a left-handed person.

Barely had the detectives returned to Scotland Yard when the call came in that another murder victim had been found in the West End. This time the scene was truly hideous; Mrs Evelyn Oatley, who called herself 'Nita Ward', a pretty 35-year-old former Windmill Theatre showgirl (and part-time prostitute), had been found dead in her Wardour Street flat, spread-eagled naked across the bed. Her throat had been cut and a classic metal tin opener had been used to rip open the lower part of her abdomen. Fred Cherrill found a set of fingerprints on the handle of the bloody tin opener that did not belong to the murdered woman. He also retrieved an unidentified thumb print on a small mirror lying next to Evelyn's open handbag – both prints made by a left hand.

Three days later a concerned neighbour reported to police that Mrs Margaret Lowe, who lived alone in a small two-room flat in Gosfield Street near Tottenham Court Road, had not been seen for several days; a parcel lay uncollected outside her apartment and she was not responding to knocks at the door. When officers broke into the flat they found Mrs Lowe beneath the hump of her big, black eiderdown. Her clothes lay strewn across the floor. Under the eiderdown she was naked, strangled with an old darned stocking. What made the murder so appalling was that the killer had mutilated her body using a bread knife, two other knives, a long poker and a candle. One detective later recalled the body, 'stiff and arched and gashed like a crudely butchered carcass'. Fred Cherrill was able to get some excellent finger impressions off the glass candlestick. These came from a right hand; Cherrill deduced that a left-handed person, grabbing the candle with his left hand, would have steadied the candlestick using his right hand. A glass with some dregs of beer and a nearly empty bottle of stout also bore marks of a left hand.

While still at the murder scene detectives got a call that a fourth victim had been found in a tawdry flat in Sussex Gardens. When they arrived the body was still warm. The woman, 32-year-old Doris Jouannet, was the flighty wife of a 70-year-old hotelier. She had a reputation as a good-time girl with a string of lovers. She had been strangled with a silk stocking, while a bloodstained razor had been used to slash at her lower body. One of her nipples had almost been cut off in the murderer's frenzy. Examining the victim Sir Bernard Spilsbury commented to police, 'You've got a madman on parade here.'

Panic hit the streets of the West End. London's large wartime population of prostitutes who were making good money from the soldiers out for a good time, especially the American G.I.s who had money to burn, became extremely jittery. The press blazed headlines such as 'West End Search for Mad Killer'.

A break in the case came within hours of the Lowe and Jouannet murders; Mrs Greta Heywood, an attractive young woman, was eating at the Trocadero, Piccadilly, when a smiling, green-eyed R.A.F. officer cadet started talking to her. He continued chatting as they walked down the Haymarket and he offered Mrs Heywood money to sleep with him. She refused and he then pushed her into a doorway saying, 'You must at least let me kiss you goodnight', dropping his gas mask as he put his hands around her neck. His choking caused the woman to lose consciousness. The man was rifling through her handbag when he was disturbed by a delivery boy. He ran off leaving behind his gas mask case. Inside was a serial number which identified the owner as 28-year-old Gordon Cummins, a married man billeted with other cadets in St John's Wood.

Barely two hours later that same night Cummins picked up a prostitute in Paddington, went to her apartment, gave the woman £5 for sex and when there was a power cut tried to strangle her in the darkness. She screamed and kicked so much that Cummins ran off, leaving her another £5. The prostitute's description of the assailant matched that of Mrs Heywood's attacker. Detective Chief Inspector Ted Greeno, one of Scotland Yard's most intrepid bloodhounds, now had a name and a description. He visited Cummins and charged him initially with the assault on Mrs Heywood. A cool customer, Cummins did not deny hitting Mrs Heywood but insisted she had demanded money from him. Greeno noticed that Cummins signed his statement with his left hand. His fingerprints were taken and Cherrill saw immediately that the man's left little finger matched a print taken from the tin opener and his left thumb print corresponded with the mirror in the handbag, while his right fingerprints were the same as those on the candlestick. At Cummins' billet the police found a metal cigarette case belonging to Mrs Lowe, a fountain pen with Mrs Jouannet's initials and Evelyn Hamilton's rations book. Brick dust in Cummins' respirator case matched dust from the air raid shelter where the first body has been found.

A cunning killer, Cummins showed police a leave pass that proved he could not have committed the last three murders. Unfortunately for him, tests under ultraviolet light proved that the leave pass was a forgery. Cummins had been married, happily by all accounts, since 1936. He seems to have been a fantasist who was called 'the Duke' by some of his friends. He was in the habit of calling himself 'the Hon. Gordon

Cummins' and claimed he was the illegitimate son of a nobleman. What led this friendly man to begin a killing spree has never been established. Clearly he had a deep-rooted hatred of women and his psychosis was so bad, with multiple attacks on the same day, that he was spiralling totally out of control. Yet he had a wry smile, tried to evade the questions of detectives and even appealed his conviction on the grounds that 'the verdict was against the weight of the evidence'. A police sergeant who escorted the killer on remand from Brixton Prison recalled years later that 'he chatted to me on everyday subjects as though he had not a care in the world... he was not an obviously unpleasant person... He was deceptively gentle in manner and quite good-looking...'

After only 35 minutes' deliberation an Old Bailey jury in April found Gordon Cummins guilty of Evelyn Oatley's murder. The Lord Chief Justice rejected his appeal. He was executed on 25 June 1942, apparently the only murderer hanged during an air raid.

1943 The Wigwam Murder: August Sangret

A muscular, handsome 29-year-old Cree Indian from the Battleford area of Saskatchewan, Canada, August Sangret was a private in the Regina Rifles serving in Surrey and waiting, as were so many young men in other units, for the invasion of Fortress Europa.

Despite little formal education he seems to have been quite intelligent, a slow, methodical speaker of the cool and silent type many women find attractive. Sangret was well aware that his build, piercing eyes and thick, wavy dark hair made him irresistible to some women and he had several British girlfriends. One of these was a promiscuous teenager called Joan Pearl Wolfe.

It was on the morning of 7 October 1942 that the Royal Marines were exercising on Hankley Common – hilly moorland topped with heather, fir trees and silver birch – when Private William Moore approached a sandy dune, the ground all about rutted by tank tracks from a recent manoeuvre, and saw a hand jutting up from a mound of earth. The thumb and two fingers had been gnawed away as if by rats. Then he saw a foot protruding and realised a body lay in the ground.

Police and forensic scientists were called. One of the first to examine the body was Professor Keith Simpson, one of a trio of pathologists (the others were Francis Camps and Donald Teare) known as 'The Three Musketeers', whose fame was just starting to grow as Sir Bernard Spilsbury's declined. The stench of putrefaction was strong, flies buzzed in the sunshine and the body was crawling with maggots. This told Simpson that it must have been exposed to air long enough for the blowflies to settle and propagate. The clothing on the body was a soiled green and white summer frock, a slip, a vest, a brassiere and French panties. The victim's skull has been smashed in at the back, and her legs were grazed. Simpson told detectives that the victim had been killed by 'a heavy blunt instrument, perhaps an iron bar, or a wooden pole, or stake. I think she was dragged here, head first, probably by her right arm. I suppose her shoes fell off on the way.'

While Simpson and his secretary, Molly Lefebvre, had the grisly task of soaking the remains in a bath of carbolic at Guy's Hospital to kill the maggots, Superintendent Richard Webb of the Surrey police already had a good idea who the victim was – facts confirmed by Simpson's subsequent autopsy. She had been seen in his office five or six weeks earlier. Her name was Joan Wolfe, a 19-year-old tearaway who had been living in the woods in a little shack, improvised from branches and leaves by her boyfriend, August Sangret, who was stationed at nearby Witley Camp. Later the newspapers called this love nest 'a wigwam'. The couple had been dating since 17 July, Sangret told police, the affair starting in a pub at Godalming. They had sex that first night. 'She did not want to for a while but I persuaded her,' confessed the Canadian. Joan was an ex-convent girl who had first run away from home at the age of 16. Her father was dead but she maintained a good relationship with her thrice-married mother, who could not understand why her daughter wanted to be a drifter. A cheerful girl, Joan seemed to have many male friends and was hoping to marry a G.I. before she met Sangret, but he was suddenly transferred back to the U.S.A.

Soon she was madly in love with her handsome Canadian. She wrote him frequent letters. He could not read English but comrades read them aloud to him. Most nights he would slip out of the barracks to be with Joan in the woods. In one letter Joan wrote with all the gushing naivety of a teenager: 'I wish with all my heart that I could see you, it is so very lonely here without anyone to speak to and there is so much I want to tell you... I regret what we did now it is too late, for I still say it was wicked. I hope God forgives me... We were taught to have a baby before you was married was a sin... Oh dear, August, why did we do it, you will not want to marry me anyway, because we hardly know one another, and I do not know anything about babies... so au revoir (daddy).' It seems that Sangret had made his girlfriend pregnant (though her corpse was too decomposed for Professor Simpson to form a forensic opinion on the matter).

In one of the longest statements on record, taking five days to transcribe its 17,000 words, Sangret told police in detail that he had last seen Joan alive on 14 September. He could not fully explain her disappearance and admitted that they had quarrelled at times. Comrades and local people confirmed that he had thoroughly looked for her after she vanished. Completing his statement, Sangret told D.C.I. Ted Greeno from Scotland Yard, 'I guess you have found her? Everything points to me. I guess I shall get the blame.' 'Yes,' said the detective, 'she is dead.' 'She might have killed herself,' said Sangret. Joan, jealous, immature and seemingly pregnant, might have been even more upset if she had known that her lover intended to spend 14 days' leave with a widow from Glasgow.

Gradually the police case took shape; items belonging to Joan including her shoes were found on the heath as well as a heavy birch branch with human hairs adhering to it that matched those on the girl's scalp. Sangret's battledress trousers and a blanket gave a positive result for bloodstains. Keith Simpson thought the murder had taken place in a nearby dell or small ravine not far from the hillock where the body was discovered. Sangret refused to enter this dell with detectives. It was also noted how Cree Indians usually buried their dead in high places. Had Sangret returned to the murder scene and moved Joan's body in some kind of ritual?

A reconstruction of Joan Wolfe's skull led Simpson to the conclusion that she had been stabbed in the head, hand and arm before being bludgeoned to death. No ordinary knife made the wounds. The blade had a pointed tip resembling a parrot's beak. Finding the knife was vital to the Crown's case. Seven weeks after investigations began, the knife was accidentally found, stuffed in the waste pipe of the shower behind the guardroom at Sangret's camp. Just such a knife had been found near the 'wigwam' shack by a soldier who duly returned it to Sangret. He accepted it yet later denied it was the kind of knife that he and Joan had used. D.C.I. Greeno was of the opinion that Sangret had hidden the knife on the morning of his police interview when he excused himself to go to the toilet.

Sangret's trial began at the Surrey Winter Assizes on 24 February 1943 before Sir Malcolm Macnaghten. The trial lasted more than a week and the jury spent two hours in deliberations before returning a guilty verdict, 'but with a strong recommendation to mercy'. The Home Secretary chose to ignore the jury's recommendation and Sangret was duly hanged by executioner Albert Pierrepoint at Wandsworth Prison on 24 April 1943.

Circumstantial evidence took August Sangret to the gallows. The crime writer M. J. Trow, has argued in a book that the weight of evidence in the case should have been insufficient to hang Sangret, though he offers no other conclusive theories or a likely killer. Greeno, Simpson and Webb all thought differently (the former detective declaring that Sangret confessed before he died, though this report is unsubstantiated). Sangret was cool and methodical, not a likely killer. Joan Wolfe was very young and emotional. It seems reasonable to assume that the couple argued; perhaps Joan threatened to go to August's commanding officer about the baby unless he married her? Something snapped in the Cree's mind. He stabbed her seven times in the hand and arm, three times in the head. Joan staggered 100 yards before he finished her off with a birch branch. He then dragged her back into the dell, buried her under some leaves, and told friends he had been out blackberrying. A few days later, perhaps out of a sense of guilt or shame, he moved the body to the hillock and tried to give her a better burial.

It was almost a perfect murder if a tank had not upset the body – or that parrot beak knife had not been discovered.

1944 Strangler and Rapist: Ernest James Harman Kemp

'The Cabbage Patch Murder' investigation, as the newspapers referred to the case, began at 8.35am on Monday morning, 14 February 1944 when a special constable going to his allotment in Eltham, London, SE9, spotted a woman's body lying beneath her coat, shirt and pullover amid the cabbages. Below her piled clothing she was naked, having been raped and strangled with her own scarf.

Detectives and forensic experts soon concluded that Iris Miriam Deeley, a 21-year-old WAAF, had been dead for six or seven hours. She had been assaulted a couple of hundred yards away and the killer had dragged her body across the allotments. Iris's feet had made furrows in the soft earth – so had the killer's large size 11 shoes. Leading Aircraftwoman Deeley had left her parent's home in Wanstead, E11, after weekend leave. Her fiancé, a pilot officer, kissed her farewell at Bow Street underground station and Iris travelled via Charing Cross to Lewisham, arriving later than she had intended, close to midnight. From the train station she had a 4-mile walk to her camp at Kidbrooke since there was no late-night public transport.

The case was given to one of Scotland Yard's top murder squad detectives, D.C.I. Ted Greeno, famous for his jutting jaw, battleship manner and, like all policemen of his generation, the trademark drooping cigarette. He soon had scores of officers questioning people on evening trains 'at every station from Charing Cross to the ends of Kent'. Britain was swarming with soldiers of all the Allied nations and hundreds were interviewed. To further frustrate the investigation there were several hoax calls and false alarms. Then, finally, a good citizen named Mrs Margaret Macgregor came forward (much to the annoyance of her husband who thought she was wasting police time), to say that she had walked for part of the way from Lewisham station on the night of the murder with her brother-in-law and a pretty young WAAF who was holding a large book under her arm (Iris was reading *War and Peace*). She also clearly remembered a loud-mouthed soldier who was walking with them. She described him as 'a rough-tough individual with a light-blonde moustache, and an amazing paraphernalia of regimental flashes and glider's pilot's wing, four medals, sergeant's stripes and a gymnast's badge'. Mrs Macgregor recalled the soldier saying, 'I've walked this way a few times.' Greeno sent out a detailed description of the suspect along with information that Miss Deeley's wallet, silver cigarette case and a book of clothing coupons in her fiancé's name had all been stolen.

About 5am on 21 February a railway police sergeant of 30 years' experience called Charles Memory noticed a couple cuddling on the platform of St Pancras station. From his army days Sergeant Memory saw that the young man was sporting North-West Frontier and Palestine medals, which were old soldiers' decorations, as well as the strange combination of American G.I. army trousers with an American officer's valise. He arrested the young man and found on him a wallet, a Waterman pen and a book of clothing coupons with the front-page name removed. His explanations for having these items seemed dubious.

The man turned out to be Gunner Ernest Kemp, Royal Artillery, a cocky 20-year-old absentee soldier who seemed to have an answer for everything. He was on the run from the military police having escaped previous arrest by climbing through a toilet window. He had been born illegitimate and taken his mother's name. At their first meeting he told Greeno that he had indeed been the soldier walking with Iris Deeley, but that he had left her near a railway bridge outside her camp and then taken a 46 tram to Woolwich. Greeno noticed that Kemp, 'a big powerful chap', wore size 11 boots.

Once Greeno detained him in connection with the murder Kemp quickly confessed. 'I put my hand over her mouth and pulled her to the ground,' said Kemp in his statement. 'She tried to struggle so I twisted her scarf round her neck and pulled it too tight. She went out... I felt her heart and found she was gone. I got the wind up and dragged her into the cabbages and left her there.'

Kemp was tried at the Old Bailey in April before Mr Justice Cassels. No defence evidence was presented and the case against the accused seemed bleak. The jury, rather strangely for such a violent crime found him guilty but with a recommendation for mercy. There was also an appeal on the grounds that the judge had misdirected the jury, but the Lord Chief Justice rejected the appeal and the jury's recommendation. Early on the morning of 6 June 1944, while hundreds of thousands of other young men were launching the massive Allied assault on the beaches of Normandy, Ernest Kemp was hanged at Wandsworth Prison.

1945 Chicago Joe & Blondie: Karl Gustav Hulten & Elizabeth Maud Jones

The most notorious murder trial of that year, though pathetic in many ways, gripped the news-reading public. Celebrities thronged the courtroom and the BBC even sent a correspondent to sit next to the scandal sheet *News of the World*. 'It was a West London story of milk bars and super cinemas,' wrote Donald Thomas, 'street robbery and stolen guns, with a dash of Chicago and clubland striptease, the whole overlaid by the tawdriness of blackout and austerity.'

Private Karl Hulten was a 22-year-old American deserter of the 501st Airborne Division who was masquerading as 'Lieutenant Ricky Allen'. Elizabeth Jones, who liked to be called 'Georgina Grayson', was a failed blonde striptease artiste, just 18 years old. Her defence counsel described her as 'a fragile little person... a colourless, pathetic little creature, not at all my idea of what a striptease dancer should look like'. She had run away from her Welsh home at age 13, married an army corporal 10 years her senior at age 16, then left him on their wedding night after he hit her. Her one great love had been a Canadian bomber pilot but he had recently been killed in action. Not much of a stripper, nor a prostitute, Mrs Jones was surviving in a small Hammersmith flat on a weekly £1 15s 6d marriage allowance from the army. Then she met 'Ricky Allen'.

Karl Hulten had been born in Sweden but brought up in Massachusetts and was a grocery clerk, driver and mechanic before his war call-up. He had deserted the U.S. Army, taking with him a 2½-ton military truck. In court he surprised people by not looking like a gangster, just 'a young man who liked to have a good time, perhaps inclined to self-indulgence, but with no signs of brutishness or cunning in his face'. One of the witnesses, Elizabeth Jones's landlady, Mrs Evans, referred to him as 'a very decent chap'. Hulten bragged to Elizabeth that he had been a Chicago gunman and was now leading a London mob. He showed her his stolen automatic pistol. The girl warmed to the idea of being a tough gangster's moll. Their partnership lasted just six days and was marked by rash and brutish acts culminating in murder. The couple were not even sexually intimate. Later the press dubbed them as 'losers' but as one writer later noted, 'it was their consciousness of failure, even as criminals, that made them dangerous'.

The ill-fated pair first met at a café off Hammersmith Broadway on Monday 3 October 1944 and agreed to a late-night date. Hulten turned up in his stolen truck and headed west out of London. Elizabeth Jones got excited when he confessed the vehicle was stolen and he showed her his pistol. 'She said she would like to do something exciting,' he later said, 'like becoming a gun moll like they do back in the States. At first I thought she was kidding...' To impress his new friend, Hulten stopped a girl cyclist near Reading, shoved her away and stole a purse. The couple returned to London with their paltry haul of a few shillings and some clothing coupons.

On the Wednesday night they met again, but Elizabeth had a bad tummy ache so they had a night in. Hulten slept with her for the first time, though the pair went only so far as 'the next thing to sexual intercourse'. On the next evening, after a meal and a visit to the Gaumont Palace cinema in Hammersmith, 'Georgina' goaded 'Ricky' into a robbing a cab at gunpoint in Cricklewood, north London, but the presence of a passenger alarmed him and he fled the scene. Driving back through the blacked-out streets of the West End, the pair stopped to help a girl who needed to catch a train from Paddington to Bristol. Hulten offered to take her as far as Reading and the girl got into the lorry. In Runnymede Park, near Windsor, he stopped and insisted he had a flat tyre. Everyone got out and while the girl's back was turned Hulten hit her over the head with an iron bar. Her pockets were then rifled for a paltry five shillings before the duo dumped her body beside the edge of a stream. Luckily she survived.

Late on the Friday night Hulten and Jones hailed a taxi opposite Cadby Hall in the Hammersmith Road with the intention of robbing the driver. Around 2am and just past the Chiswick roundabout, heading west, Hulten told the driver, 34-year-old George Heath, to pull over to the kerb. Just as the cabbie leaned over to his left side, across the back of the front seat, to open the nearside door for his female passenger, Hulten fired his pistol. The taxi driver was shot through the middle of the back. 'Move over or I'll give you another dose of the same,' Hulten was claimed to have said, as he pushed Mr Heath out of the driver's seat. Hulten drove towards Staines and it took the cabbie 15 minutes to drown in his own blood while Elizabeth Jones callously went through his pockets, throwing out various belongings along the way, though retaining the man's wristwatch, cash, cigarette case, fountain pen and silver pencil. The pair dropped his body in a ditch on the outskirts of Knowle Green near

Staines, drove back to Hammersmith, wiped the taxi clean of fingerprints and had breakfast in a café before going to bed about 5am.

The first thoughts of the police after George Heath's body was found about 9am on 7 October was that it might be a gangland-related killing as the cabbie had a dodgy reputation. His killers meanwhile slept late that day, then sold the wristwatch, fountain pen and pencil for £5 18s 0d, took a taxi to the White City Stadium and bet on the greyhound races. After a meal, they saw Deanna Durbin in *Christmas Holiday*. Elizabeth rested her head on the American's shoulder. He had bought her a spray of flowers, pinned to her coat. 'This was their nearest approach to happiness.'

On Sunday 8 October the couple decided to have more exploits in the stolen Ford V8, using it as a hire car. Parking just off Piccadilly, Elizabeth said she wanted a fur coat. Hulten tried to grab one off the shoulders of a woman leaving the Berkeley Hotel. A constable came around the corner and Hulten rushed back to the vehicle and drove off.

The police already knew the number of George Heath's taxi and had circulated it across London. On Monday night they were waiting when Hulten approached the Ford. In his left hip pocket they found a Remington pistol, already cocked, and spare shells in his trousers. Soon he was whistling to the authorities about his friend, 'Georgina Grayson'.

Under the Visiting Forces Act the U.S. Army was entitled to prosecute Hulten but not Jones. At first it seemed that his court martial might wait until after her trial. This could have resulted in Mrs Jones being hanged before she could be called as a main witness in the American case. The matter, so legend has it, was referred to the president and it was agreed for the first time in British and American legal history that a United States serviceman could be tried for murder in a British criminal court. The pair appeared in the dock of No. 1 Court, Old Bailey, on 16 January 1945 before the elderly Mr Justice Charles. While in custody Elizabeth Jones had written to 'Ricky': 'What the police have against me is going through the man's pockets. Had you not ordered me to do so, I could never have done it... You know the condition I was in for hours afterwards. I was dazed, and still you threatened me, even when you knew I was too scared to go to the police. And there is another thing, you must tell the police, as you promised, *the truth about the body*. I did *not* help you to carry him to the ditch. You know that. Ricky, for God's sake tell the truth. You and God are the only two who know of my innocence. Half of the case is fresh to me... I did not know you were married and had a child. I did not know you had deserted the army...'

Was Elizabeth Jones manipulative and wilful, or naive and pathetic? Her counsel, J. D. Casswell K.C., was astonished that she seemed to think her worst offence was rifling a dead man's pockets and had no idea she would be charged with murder. In her home town, where many people were suffering war's deprivations, women's groups called for the girl to be executed.

Hulten's initial defence was that he intended to fire 'through the car, but I did not expect George Heath to rise to open the door just as I did it'. The victim had thus died accidentally. In court the American now changed this story to the gun going off without warning as his arm was jerked. He also fully involved his girlfriend in all his actions.

After a six-day trial the couple were both found guilty and condemned to death. Elizabeth Jones had to be dragged screaming and crying from the dock. Hulten took the news more stoically. He was executed at Pentonville Prison on 8 March 1945 just five days after his 23rd birthday. The war in Europe ended two months later. Elizabeth Maud Jones was reprieved just two days before her hanging was due. Even then she foolishly thought this meant she would be freed and wrote to her mum to lay out her best frock. She stayed in gaol until January 1954, by which time she was 27 years old, and is believed to have died in the 1980s.

1946 Psychopath: Neville George Cleverly Heath

Modern writers of crime fiction such as Brett Easton Ellis and Patricia Highsmith have popularised the idea of the smiling, intelligent and thoroughly amoral sociopath, a man who can stoop to murder without qualms or conscience. The 20th century's most notorious British example of this breed of real-life killer was the cheery, well-liked, handsome brute called Neville Heath. What shocked people in 1946 and is still frightening is the sexual aspect of Heath's murders, savagery masked behind the seemingly friendly exterior of this war hero and family man. That he was a habitual criminal and a crook without conscience was not the issue – even some of Heath's RAF friends thought him a likeable rogue – but the sadism of his killings appalled all who knew him and, one suspects, even appalled Heath himself.

He was born on 6 June 1917 during a German airship raid over his Ilford home. His parents, Bessie and William, were a loving lower-middle-class couple and to his dying day Neville never had a bad word to say about either of them. When he was two years old, the family moved to Merton and eventually settled in a solid villa close to Wimbledon town centre. A baby sister was lost to meningitis when Neville was six years old, but a much younger brother who always adored him (and to whom he tried to act the hero) came along in 1928. Bessie Heath seems to have been an over-indulgent mother who spoiled Neville to some extent. At an early age he learned quickly that a lie or smugly contrite answer could get him out of trouble. He proved not much good at academic subjects, but excelled at sports, served in his grammar school's cadet corps and, as one of his biographers notes, 'his yearning for upward social mobility, his self-aggrandizement and snobbery was ignited' by his grammar school's ambitions to turn him into a pseudo-public school boy. Heath studied the language and manners of the pre-war upper classes and began to 'ruthlessly exploit this'.

His tall, masculine good looks meant he was also popular with the local girls. One of them later recalled him as 'an unmitigated liar, show-off, a swank-pot... yet although all the girls knew his faults, he somehow managed to blend them into an unusual and charming personality, and we all liked him'. Around the time he was 15, Heath sexually assaulted a girl (he called it 'horseplay') at a party, but the matter was hushed up.

Reality hit Neville Heath hard in 1934 when, after failing his matriculation exam, which could have led on to university or officer entry into the services, he was forced to start work as a lowly warehouseman in the City of London. Six months later he enlisted as a rifleman in the 28th London Regiment, Territorial Army, immediately loving the camaraderie of service life, and filling out his uniform to perfection. His dream was to be an R.A.F. pilot. All went well at first; he attended the R.A.F. training school in 1935, was assessed as 'above average', got his pilot's 'wings' and in August 1936 was posted to 19 Squadron at R.A.F. Duxford. In November he became a pilot officer and his commanding officer wrote, 'This man has the makings of a first-class pilot...' Back home in Wimbledon, Neville got engaged to a local girl. His future looked bright. Money, or the lack of it, now proved the anvil that was to wreck Heath's life. He yearned to impress his richer officer friends and aped a lifestyle beyond his means. Soon he was lying about his background, stealing money from other airmen and passing dud cheques. Rather than face the music when found out, he simply disappeared. Caught, he tried to escape, was recaptured, court-martialled and dismissed from the R.A.F. – all within a year.

A cheque fraud spree was Heath's next scam and he stayed in various hotels calling himself the Earl of Dudley. When the inevitable meeting came with officers of the law it had a touch of farce about it. Drinking, pipe in hand, Heath was approached by a detective. 'Are you Lord Dudley?' 'Yes, I am, old man.' 'Well I am Detective Inspector Hickman of the C.I.D.' 'Then in that case I am *not* Lord Dudley.' Luck played along with Neville

Heath for several years; in court he contritely claimed to have learned his lesson and was put on probation. Soon he was back at his petty thefts and fraud and wound up in the dock of the Old Bailey on 12 July 1938 to be sentenced to three years inside a borstal (though he served less than two). Heath had more luck; he found himself sent to Hollesley Bay, a new kind of borstal institution where an enlightened governor believed in rehabilitation rather than punishment. Neville behaved impeccably like an overgrown schoolboy and later wrote, 'I was really happy there.' On release, with a war on, he was desperate to get back into the R.A.F. Luck stepped in again; early in May 1940 he joined an officer cadet training unit of the Royal Army Service Corps (passing out 9th of 34 cadets) and was soon posted to the Middle East, from where he lied and wrote to family and friends that he was once again flying.

Financial irregularities were soon cropping up again. In Cairo and Port Said a bored Heath, who wanted nothing more than to fight Italians and Germans, wasted his money, much of it acquired illegally, in beer halls and brothels. It seems that in some of the seedier whorehouses he may have discovered that he had a kink – he enjoyed inflicting pain on women. Arrested by the red caps, 2nd Lieutenant Heath managed to jump ship in Durban. Posing as a 'Captain Selway M.C.' he acquired £85 from a Barclays Bank, made his way to Pretoria and volunteered for the South African Air Force. Soon 'Lieutenant James Robert Cadogan Armstrong', ex-Harrow and Trinity College, Cambridge, was entering the happiest period of his life. He courted and then wed in February 1942 Elizabeth Hardcastle Rivers, an attractive Johannesburg girl from a wealthy family. That September his wife gave birth to a baby boy. Heath was now a respected flying instructor at the Central S.A.A.F. Flying School and life was good.

This idyllic existence came to an end when the South African C.I.D. finally caught up with him. He begged the S.A.A.F. to give him a second chance. They agreed to put him on six months' probation, provided his debts were repaid. Neville's wealthy father-in-law reluctantly obliged. In April 1944 Heath, now back in England, won his cherished dream of returning to the R.A.F. but he was seconded as a pilot to Bomber Command and not a fighter squadron. During a raid over Holland his plane was hit. He gallantly saved the life of his stricken navigator and bailed out last. All the crew survived and Heath led them to the safety of an R.A.F. station in south Holland. He was now eligible to join the Caterpillar Club – airmen who had parachuted out of a disabled aircraft and got home safely. Despite his many failings in life Neville Heath was now a bona fide hero.

The mental toil on bomber crews was enormous. With 65 per cent fatalities in Bomber Command, each man knew any hour in the air could be his last. Heath was by now drinking heavily. This was nothing new, but under the influence of alcohol he began to display unprovoked and frightening rages. Fellow officers complained of his abnormal behaviour added to which he started to have blackouts or relive in nightmares the terrors of a burning plane. After a spell in hospital, he returned to South Africa. His wife, who later blamed the murders on whisky and his Jekyll-and-Hyde persona, had decided the marriage was over. Elizabeth thought him 'a big teddy bear', but felt life for her and their son would be better off without him. This may have been a pivotal event; Heath later said, 'I think my divorce broke me completely. I have never felt the same since it happened and ever since have acted in a peculiar way on occasions.' Soon back perpetuating cheque frauds and dallying with various women, he was eventually dismissed from the S.A.A.F. and kicked out of the country.

No sooner had he arrived back in London than an incident occurred at the Strand Palace Hotel. Screams were heard in room 506 in the early hours of 23 February 1946. Staff entering the room found a naked woman tied face down on a bed while a naked man claiming to be 'Captain James Armstrong, S.A.A.F. and D.F.C.', also naked, stood over her. The girl stated that she had been knocked out, undressed and tied up against her will. She also asked for the whole incident to be hushed up, which the hotel was happy to do. Captain Armstrong left the next morning.

Around town that hot June, Heath was seen in several of his old drinking places wearing the uniform of a major in the S.A.A.F. and telling friends that he intended to become a commercial pilot. The famous theatre actress Moira Lister, who had known him and Elizabeth in South Africa, even went on a date with the handsome officer and later recalled how he behaved 'impeccably', a 'charming man'. This was the week another major disaster struck Heath – the Air Ministry told him that due to his dismissal from the R.A.F., they would never grant him a pilot's licence. All hopes of a new career and life were thus crushed.

Heath had started dating an attractive 19-year-old called Yvonne Symonds and even encouraged her to marry him. This did not stop him from eyeing and having an appeal to other women. On the night of 20 June 1946, after a heavy drinking bout, he took one of these, a good-looking bohemian arts lover and occasional film extra called Mrs Margery Gardner, to the Pembridge Court Hotel, Notting Hill Gate.

By the next morning Heath had gone but 32-year-old Mrs Gardner lay in bed. That afternoon staff entered the room and drew back the curtains to find one of the two beds covered in bloodstains. Margery lay under the bedclothes of the other bed to which she had apparently been moved. Naked, her ankles were tied tightly together and her wrists had at some stage been bound. A small amount of blood seeped from her vagina. On examination Professor Keith Simpson, the eminent pathologist, deduced that she had been gagged (although the ligature was missing). Mrs Gardner's chin and face were bruised as if hit by a fist, while a hand seemed to have held her jaw to keep the head still. Seventeen whip marks lay across her shoulder blades, buttocks, back, chest, abdomen and head. So strong were the blows that a diamond pattern of marks could be discerned. Simpson concluded that Margery had been beaten severely while still alive, then suffocated by having her head pushed into a pillow or the bedding. The woman's nipples had almost been bitten off. A 7-inch tear in her vaginal wall showed that a sharp implement had been thrust viciously into her body and rotated.

Heath had booked the room in the name of 'Lt-Col. And Mrs N.G.C. Heath' (perhaps an indicator that the murder was not premeditated), and detectives were soon hunting for him nationwide. The Sunday papers were full of the murder. Neville told his fiancée on the telephone that it was all some ghastly mistake, a mix-up over names and rooms. He would see the police and sort the whole matter out. She never heard from him again. He headed first to Worthing and then moved on to Bournemouth, taking a room at the Tollard Royal Hotel in the name of 'Group Captain Rupert Brooke'.

The weather that June was gloriously hot and sunny. During the course of the next few days, despite the hue and cry, the smart R.A.F. officer met and charmed a beautiful 21-year-old, Miss Doreen Marshall, recently discharged from the Wrens and enjoying a short holiday after a bout of measles. On Friday 5 July the manager of the Norfolk Hotel where Doreen was staying notified police that she had been missing for two days. Soon officers were interviewing the helpful, charming Group Captain Brooke. He even volunteered to go to the police station at 5.30pm where he ran into Doreen's worried father and tried to console him. D.C. Souter was struck by how the R.A.F. officer resembled the wanted man, Neville Heath, and it was decided to detain him. Heath asked if someone could fetch his jacket from the Tollard Royal. An obliging policeman did so but went through the pockets and found a cloakroom ticket for Bournemouth West station. Heath's suitcase was collected and found to contain a bloodstained scarf with several hairs from Margery Gardner's head, some articles marked 'Heath' and, worst of all, a leather riding crop with a criss-cross diamond weave and wire filaments exposed at one end. The whip had been washed but still bore traces of blood.

In the early hours of 7 July Heath was formally charged with Mrs Gardner's murder by D.I. Reg Spooner of Scotland Yard. Earlier that day a woman exercising her dog had found a body beneath some bushes in a heavily wooded valley called Branksome Chine, a popular walking spot about a mile west of the Tollard Royal Hotel. It was Doreen Marshall, who had apparently put up a terrific fight for her life. Some of the girl's fingers were cut where she had held back a knife. The killer had tied her wrists, hit her face and chest, then cut her throat. Roughly she had been stripped naked, her abdomen and private parts slashed with a knife, while a rough instrument, possibly a tree branch, had been thrust into her vagina and anus. The right nipple had been bitten off. The body had then been dragged 70 yards to the rhododendron bushes.

That Heath was guilty never seemed to be much in doubt. The question was whether he was sane or not. When his barrister, J. G. Casswell K.C., first met his client he mistook him for a handsome prison warder. 'Why shouldn't I plead guilty?' was Heath's first question. 'You've a mother, father and brother alive,' replied the barrister. 'Do you want it said that a man in his right mind committed two such brutal crimes?' Heath paused for a moment, then smiled and said, 'Put me down as not guilty, old boy.' The remark was so off-the-cuff that Casswell decided his client must be mad. In hindsight it seems clear that Neville Heath felt he had enjoyed his cup of life to the full and now drunk the dregs. The long path of lies, evasions, thefts, frauds, fun, frolic and happy days in the services had run their course. He had lost his beloved wife and child, been kicked out of two air forces and could never fly a plane again, which was the only worthwhile thing he had ever truly enjoyed or wanted to do. What triggered his urge to inflict pain and kill will never be known for sure and Heath did not go into details. Alcohol clearly fuelled his inner rages and he was seen to have consumed a lot of whisky on the nights of both murders. Resentment that his life was screwed up, an inner rage that his wife had left him – these may have led to his need to punish women. Going to the police when he did was likened by his barrister to entering the lion's den and makes one wonder if he wished to end the lie he had been living. He never expressed remorse and Casswell did not allow his client to speak at the trial in his own defence for fear that he might say extraordinary things. It seems though that Heath was finally shamed by his own bestiality.

On Friday 27 September 1946 at the Old Bailey sentence of death was passed on Neville Heath by Mr Justice Morris for the murder of

Mrs Margery Gardner. Awaiting execution in Pentonville he told his family not to visit, but his last letter was to his parents: 'I shall probably stay up reading tonight because I'd like to see the dawn again. So much in my memory is associated with the dawn – early morning patrols and coming home from night clubs. Well, it wasn't a bad life while it lasted, and I've lots to think about. Please don't mourn my going – I should hate it – and don't wear any black. I really mean that. Just wear your gayest colours and refer to me quite normally – that is the easiest way to forget. So now I'll leave you. Cheerio, my dear, and very many thanks for everything. All my love is with you both always.'

Minutes before his execution on 26 October the prison governor asked Heath if he had a last request. Perhaps a tot of whisky? With his old bravado, reminiscent of Errol Flynn off to fight the Huns in *The Dawn Patrol*, Heath replied: 'While you're about it, sir, you might make that a double.'

1947 Gun Guys: Charles Henry Jenkins, Christopher James Geraghty & Timothy John Peter Rolt

Britain, unlike the United States, has no major history of gun crime or of murder using a firearm. The period roughly 1945–55 saw, for the first time, the emergence of armed gunmen in what appeared to be growing numbers, young thugs who wanted to ape the manners and morals of their gangster movie heroes. With a long war at its end, it was hardly surprising that Britain was awash with guns of all kinds. In 1946 a Metropolitan Police amnesty in the capital alone saw 76,000 illegal firearms handed in with more than 2 million rounds of ammunition. In 1952 the cop killer Christopher Craig, a schoolboy of 16, boasted of owning 40 illegal firearms. He was later destined to be detained at Her Majesty's pleasure, while his henchman, illiterate and unarmed Derek Bentley, was executed, a case that fuelled the call for abolition of the death penalty. What tragically happened to Derek Bentley had its origins in 1947 after the public outcry following the death of Alec de Antiquis, a 34-year-old father of six children, who had once rescued a kid from a burning house. Using his motorcycle Mr de Antiquis tried to bar the path of three gunmen in Charlotte Street, London W1 after they fled a botched jewel robbery on the afternoon of 29 April. Two of the gang ran around the motorcycle but the third man, 'without hesitation or warning, raised his revolver and shot the motorcyclist in the head at point-blank range. In that second, the bungled jewel raid became capital murder.'

The case was given to D.C.I. Robert Fabian, the most famous of post-war Scotland Yard detectives (holder of the King's Police Medal for single-handedly defusing an I.R.A. bomb in Piccadilly in 1939 and later to be immortalised as *Fabian of the Yard* in an early TV cop show), a man who was noted for his painstaking and thorough methods. The Commissioner of the Metropolitan Police, Sir Harold Scott, demanded that this kind of gun crime in London streets had to be stamped out. In an extraordinary move, he assigned every detective in the capital not on essential duties to work on the case – at one point more than 4,000 officers were looking for the killers.

Twenty-three witness statements had been taken but they were confused and not much help. Then, three days after the murder, a cabbie named Arthur Grubb told police that he had seen two suspicious men, 'with handkerchiefs knotted under their chins', entering an office block at 191 Tottenham Court Road about 2.30pm on the afternoon of the murder. Soon Fabian had more statements from workers in the building. Behind a counter in a room full of rubbish, he found a raincoat, cap and scarf. Despite the makers' names having been removed D.C.I. Fabian had the very ordinary raincoat unstitched. This revealed a manufacturer's stock ticket and more good policing led detectives to the Deptford branch of Montague Burton, the tailors. Here the names of all those who had bought raincoats in the past year were examined against clothing coupons (Britain was in the grip of post-war austerity). Scanning names against criminal records in those pre-computer days turned up a Thomas Kemp, a petty criminal known to Fabian, whose brothers-in-law were well-known thieves: the eldest, Tommy Jenkins, was serving eight years for manslaughter after driving his getaway car over the body of Captain Ralph Binney R.N. who gallantly tried to stop a robbery on a jeweller's shop in 1944; younger brother Harry, aged 22, who liked to be called the 'King of Borstal ', had a reputation for violence and had come out of gaol just one week before the Antiquis murder.

Robert Fabian led a team to arrest Jenkins in Bermondsey on 11 May along with his best pals, Christopher Geraghty and Tim Rolt. Around this time a schoolboy trawling about the low water mark at Wapping found a .33 revolver loaded with five rounds and an empty case that later proved to be from the bullet which killed Alec de Antiquis. The Thames also soon gave up a rusty old .455 Bulldog revolver, loaded with six rounds, one of which had been fired inside the jeweller's shop in Charlotte Street.

To the annoyance of police, Jenkins was not recognised by 27 witnesses at an identity parade. Perhaps thinking he was in the clear he tried to lay the robbery at the door of Bill Walsh, another criminal with a long record. It later turned out that Walsh had double-crossed Jenkins over the loot from a robbery at a Queensway jeweller's on 25 April – hence his revenge. Walsh owned up to his part in that robbery and named other crooks including Geraghty, but he had a cast-iron alibi for 29 April. Jenkins, Geraghty and Rolt were all rearrested and taken in for more questioning. This time a very nervous Rolt, who was only 17, blurted out, 'I'll tell you what happened. Chris never meant to kill that man.' Soon he was 'singing' in detail. Geraghty also admitted his part in the robbery but refused to implicate Jenkins who seemed unconcerned and hummed Frank Sinatra songs in his cell.

The trial of the three men opened at the Old Bailey on 21 July before Mr Justice Hallett. Forensic and firearms evidence was provided by the old team of Sir Bernard Spilsbury (who committed suicide just two months later after a career spanning half a century) and Robert Churchill, the famous gunsmith. The judge had to remind the jury that under English law it did not matter who pulled the trigger – the law considered all the defendants equally culpable of murder. After one hour's deliberation, the jury found all three men guilty. Because of his age Rolt was detained during His Majesty's pleasure (and later released under licence in 1955) but Jenkins, who fired the fatal shot, and Geraghty, who had not, were both executed at Pentonville on 19 September.

1948 Behold the Beast: Peter Griffiths

The ultimate nightmare for a hospital nurse must be the loss of a child. This is what happened to Gwendoline Humphreys early on the morning of 15 May 1948. At twenty minutes past midnight her six tiny charges lay sleeping in their cots in Ward CH3 of the Queen's Park Hospital, Blackburn. One hour later the nurse found a porch door open and three-year-old June Devaney missing from her cot. Twenty-five minutes later the police were called. Officers fanned out to search the 70 acres of hospital grounds. It was at 3.17am that a constable spotted a terrible sight close to the boundary wall. It was the body of June. Her head had been smashed in and forensic examination would also determine that she had been sexually assaulted.

At 4am D.C.I. John Capstick of Scotland Yard was roused from his bed and told to take charge of the murder investigation. He was on a train heading north by 6.20am and that afternoon viewed the body. 'I saw it through a mist of tears,' he wrote later, 'years of detective work had hardened me to many terrible things, but this tiny pathetic body, in its nightdress soaked in blood and mud, no man could see unmoved, and it haunts me to this day.' The children's ward was fingerprinted and a bottle that had been moved from its usual position near June's cot gave a good set. A trail of footprints also led to an open office window. For starters the police interviewed and fingerprinted everyone who had access to the children's ward in the previous two years – all 642 of them. No luck. The fingerprints on the bottle also did not match anything in police files.

Utilising a huge public outcry, endorsed by Capstick, the Mayor of Blackburn and Chief Constable of Lancashire, it was decided to fingerprint every male over the age of 16 living in the town. This kind of thing had never been done before. Twenty detectives trawled 35,000 homes over the next two months but no killer was revealed. Capstick then decided to marry the fingerprint file with the post-war ration cards, one of which was owned by every citizen. This clever bit of detective work showed a shortfall of about 200 names. These people were also rounded up and on 12 August it was confirmed that the prints on the cot bottle belonged to a 22-year-old ex-soldier called Peter Griffiths – set 46253. Arrested by D.C.I. Capstick, the dark-haired, boyish-looking Griffiths made a statement admitting to the murder – 'She wouldn't stop crying. I just lost my temper then and you know what happened then. I banged her head against the wall....' He concluded by saying: 'I'm sorry for both parents' sake and I hope I get what I deserve.'

So much evidence was marshalled against Griffiths at his trial before Mr Justice Oliver at the Lancaster Assizes that it was really a question of whether a jury would accept his defence of insanity. It took his peers just 23 minutes to find him guilty of murder as charged. He was hanged at Liverpool Prison on 19 November 1948. Lancashire Police concluded that he may have committed several other child assaults including the murder of an 11-year-old boy stabbed and beaten to death two months before June Devaney's death. A poem found in Griffiths' bedroom shows a corner of his warped mind:

> For lo and behold, when the beast
> Looks down upon the face of beauty
> It staids [*sic*] its hands from killing
> And from that day on
> It were as one dead.

1949 The Acid Bath Murderer: John George Haigh

'He is a smart, polite, intelligent boy and has had a good education. He has an excellent character and his home environment is good.

I have every confidence in recommending him, feeling that he will give satisfaction to all he comes into contact with.' So ran an appraisal of a 17-year-old boy from Wakefield Grammar School, winner of the Divinity Prize, a charmer who was a skilled pianist and organist (Chopin, Mozart, Beethoven and Tchaikovsky preferred, thought not the 'irritating' 1812 Overture), a server at the High Altar of Wakefield Cathedral, a choirboy with 'the voice of an angel', someone later recalled. By the time he was 39, the lad had grown to a stocky 5 feet 8 inches, not unhandsome, with a slimly dashing moustache, magnetically twinkling blue-green eyes and an irrepressible smile forever playing around his lips. The occasional observer thought him a little too smooth, a tad too cheerful for their tastes; something about the fellow just wasn't quite right. But most people meeting him for the first time were bowled over by his wit, cheery good manners and obvious intelligence. The chap never touched beer or spirits and was always immaculately dressed in a smart suit, often of brown worsted set off with a vermillion tie or a carnation in his buttonhole. He lived in a classy hotel and drove a succession of flashy cars. Older and younger women found him very attractive. His business interests seemed secure, his manners impeccable, his friendliness quite genuine. A gifted inventor using remarkable self-taught engineering skills acquired from his father, he created a range of things including a self-expanding coat hanger, toy soldiers who could move and march, a child's car that could run at up to 12 miles an hour and designs for acrylic fingernails. This music-loving, inventive, immensely likable chap was John Haigh – who murdered at least six people and was described by the press in 1949 as a blood-drinking 'vampire', a serial killer who dissolved his victims in sulphuric acid with the motto, 'No body, no crime'.

Haigh's story, so far as the police were concerned, began on the afternoon of Sunday 20 February 1949 when a nervous and frail old lady called at Chelsea Police Station to report the disappearance of her friend, Mrs Olive Durand-Deacon, aged 69 years, who had been missing about 24 hours. It turned out that Mrs Durand-Deacon and the little old lady, Mrs Constance Lane, were resident guests at the Onslow Court Hotel, a smart address, where the two wealthy widows had lived for some years. Olive had failed to keep an appointment on the Saturday afternoon with a third resident, smart-looking Mr John Haigh, who had driven Mrs Lane to make her missing person's report.

Next day Sergeant Alexandra Lambourne climbed the steps of the imposing hotel to ask some questions. The smiling Mr Haigh was polite and helpful but for once his great charm failed him. For reasons she could not comprehend the policewoman instantly distrusted him. What was a man in his 30s doing living in an hotel full of so many old ladies? The hotel manageress said he was behind in his bill (though he had lived at Onslow Court for four years). Why had he also not been more concerned when Mrs Durand-Deacon failed to keep her appointment for a visit to his Crawley factory? Back at Chelsea Police Station the sergeant reported her suspicions to Divisional Inspector Shelley Symes and wrote a report noting 'apart from the fact that I do not like the man Haigh with his mannerisms I have a sense that he is "wrong" and that there may be a "case" behind the whole business.' D.I. Symes agreed to run a check on John George Haigh. The intuition of Sergeant Lambourne was well repaid – back came the news that Mr Haigh was not all that he seemed on the surface, but a fraudster and thief who had been sentenced to seven years behind bars in 1934.

D.I. Symes took the matter of Haigh and the missing old lady to D.I. Albert Webb, head of Chelsea C.I.D. He, in turn, asked Horsham Police to check out the factory of which Haigh claimed to be a director at Crawley. The three-man detective force in sleepy Horsham were trying to solve a crime wave all of their own, which seemed to be the work of a bent copper (he was duly caught red-handed breaking into a car showroom in the middle of the night), but Detective Sergeant Pat Heslin set off to find out what he could at Hustlea Products, 15 West Street, Crawley. There he learned from the owner, Edward Jones, that Haigh was not a director of his light engineering and tool-making business, although the two men were engaged in a joint venture to create a gadget to help people with poor eyesight to thread needles. Haigh was permitted to carry out some engineering work of his own at the factory, said Jones, and he also acted as an unpaid London rep for the firm.

One week after Mrs Durand-Deacon's disappearance the police investigation had stalled and D.S. Heslin decided to return to Hustlea Products. By chance he found out that Jones had other premises, a small building in Giles Yard at Leopold Road, which was used by Haigh as a workshop for the purpose of acid conversions. Straightaway Heslin got the spare keys from Mr Jones and set off. He found a grubby, unkempt yard full of broken and empty crates, rubble, heaps of sand, lots of ladders and a collection of ugly old oil drums. The small, two-storey Hustlea Products storeroom revealed no missing woman yet its contents were remarkable: three heavy carboys of acid; a stirrup pump; a rubber apron, mackintosh, rubber boots and gauntlet gloves; an Army-issue gas mask; an attaché case marked 'J.G.H.' full of clothing coupon books, ration books, passports, driving licences, diaries and other documents in the names of a Mrs Rosalie Henderson and Dr Archibald Henderson, and a family named McSwan; and a recently fired .38 Enfield revolver with eight rounds of ammunition. Fraudster Haigh clearly had some explaining to do.

Events now snowballed, thanks in part to wide coverage of the missing woman's disappearance in the national newspapers. A jeweller in Horsham came forward to say that a man resembling Haigh had sold him jewellery now known to have belonged to Olive Durand-Deacon. 'Right Albert,' said Superintendent Tom Barratt to D.I. Webb, 'bring the bastard in.'

Haigh remained calm under arrest. After a few minutes he asked Webb, 'Tell me, frankly, what are the chances of anyone being released from Broadmoor?' D.I. Webb refused to answer the question. Haigh went on: 'Mrs Durand-Deacon no longer exists. She has disappeared completely and no trace of her can be found again.' 'What happened to her?' asked Webb. 'I have destroyed her with acid,' said Haigh quite calmly and with some smugness, 'You will find the sludge which remains at Leopold Road. Every trace has gone. How can you prove murder if there is no body?'

From Haigh's subsequent statement and further police enquiries detectives began to unravel a grisly tale of greed and murder-for-profit. It began in Stamford, Lincolnshire, on 24 July 1909 when John George was born to Emily and John Haigh. The couple were devout members of the strict Plymouth Brethren sect, the father working as an electrical engineer. An only child, John's harsh religious upbringing, in a home where even newspapers were banned as sinful, clearly affected him in later life. Yet he seems to have had a lot of respect for his stern but loving father and adoring mother. To their credit the Haighs never rejected their son despite the shame he brought to the family.

After the bright start in life referred to in the opening paragraph, the adult Haigh decided early on to kick over the traces of his sheltered existence. He came to believe that all things were ordained and his life marked out for him by a higher authority. He discovered that people could be taken in by his smile and good manners. Prison spells taught him to become an excellent forger, a faculty that combined with his sharp mind to make him quite brilliant at faking letters and legal documents. For periods lasting several years he was capable of gainful employment, never giving his bosses any cause for concern, but sooner or later he would commit some act of fraud or be up to a dodgy trick.

The McSwans – elderly Donald, chatty wife Amy and bright son William, the same age as Haigh – were one such group of employers who grew fond of the intelligent engineer and promoted him to be manager of their Tooting arcade of pinball machines (a craze of the 1930s). After a time Haigh left their employ to once again try and live off his own skills as an inventor and businessman. Once again he ended up in prison. During one of these spells as a guest of His Majesty, Haigh heard about a Frenchman called Sarret who had murdered some people using sulphuric acid. This set him to thinking. He also read legal textbooks in prison and concluded: 'If there's no body, there's no *corpus delicti*. And if there's no *corpus delicti*, there's no murder!' He was so loud in making this announcement to fellow lags in Dartmoor that some prisoners started to call him 'Old *Corpus Delicti*'.

In the summer of 1944, about one year after his last term in prison, Haigh ran into William McSwan in a Kensington pub. Soon he was friendly again with the whole family – and a dark plot was forming in his mind. Using a basement workshop at 79 Gloucester Road, Haigh inveigled first William, then Donald, and finally Amy McSwan to visit his dingy premises on various pretexts before coshing each of them to death with a lead pipe. Their bodies were placed in drums and covered in sulphuric acid. This was a dangerous operation but Haigh improved his style of killing with each murder. The acid soon reduced the bodies to a thick sludge which Haigh poured down a main drain conveniently located in the basement floor. Using a skilfully forged yet quite legal Power of Attorney document, the sharp-thinking killer acquired various properties owned by the McSwans, their pinball machines and personal goods. Sales of these items netted him more than £6,000 (around £250,000 today), and he moved into Room 404 of the prestigious Onslow Court Hotel. On Friday 13 February 1948 Haigh repeated his earlier *modus operandi* at the Crawley address, though he now shot his victims, attractive Rosalie and ex-Army Archie Henderson, firing the doctor's old revolver at point-blank range. The couple were sludge within a couple of days and poured on to the waste dump at the back of the yard. Once again Haigh was able to acquire about £8,000 in assets. Unfortunately, rich living and a new obsession – gambling – saw this sum drop to zero by the start of 1949.

It was then that Mrs Durand-Deacon, one of the coterie of friendly old ladies at his hotel, frightfully rich with £36,000 in investments, talked to Haigh about an idea she had for starting a business selling fake fingernails. No doubt an engaging smile passed over Haigh's lips. It was truly a case of the spider and the fly. Dear old Olive made the fateful trip to Crawley in Haigh's speedy maroon Alvis roadster and ended up becoming Victim No. 6.

Haigh's boast that all trace of his victim had been obliterated proved quite wrong (although a few more weeks would have seen him to have been correct). The famous forensic expert Dr Keith Simpson had 475 lb of grease and earth carefully lifted from the yard in Leopold Road and transported to Scotland Yard. He had luckily spotted a gallstone on his visit to the murder site. Forensic work led to the discovery of two more gallstones, part of a foot, 18 bone fragments, a lipstick container, pieces of a handbag and a full set of dentures which were identified as belonging to Mrs Durand-Deacon.

Even before Haigh's trial the press were writing such sensational stuff that the *Daily Mirror* was charged with contempt. It had made references to Haigh as a murderer and also reported that he drank the blood of his victims along with his own urine. The Lord Chief Justice, Rayner Goddard, sitting alongside two celebrated defence and prosecuting counsel, now both judges, Norman Birkett and Travers Humphreys, were determined to make the point that even a man such as Haigh was entitled to a fair trial without prejudicial press coverage beforehand. Goddard, vilified (to this day) for his handling of the Craig-Bentley trial, lambasted the proprietors of the *Daily Mirror* who stood in court like errant schoolboys. To the shock of Fleet Street and delight of many, including John Haigh, the newspaper was fined the huge sum of £10,000 while the editor was sentenced to three months in prison.

Standing before 81-year-old Mr Justice Humphreys, a man whose record of trials stretched back to Oscar Wilde, Crippen and that other killer-for-profit, George Joseph Smith, the 'Brides in the Bath' murderer, Haigh's trial started at Lewes Assizes on 19 July 1949. It lasted just two days. The defence, led by Sir David Maxwell Fyffe, K.C. M.P. (his fee paid by the *News of the World*), as in the Heath case, was based on trying to prove that Haigh was criminally insane. No defence witnesses were called, save one psychiatrist who made a poor showing in court. Haigh, like Neville Heath, was not asked to give evidence, presumably because his lawyers thought he might incriminate himself still further (though, on reflection, he might also have convinced one or two jurors that he really was mad). The jury were asked by the judge to consider if Haigh was 'guilty or not guilty of murdering Mrs Durand-Deacon or do you find him guilty but insane?' After only 17 minutes they returned with a traditional guilty verdict.

While awaiting execution Haigh gave several interviews and wrote letters to many friends. He even permitted Madame Tussauds, the famous waxworks, to take his measurements for their Chamber of Horrors and donated one of his best suits with special instructions that the trousers be well pressed.

For some years he had been platonically dating an attractive girl almost 20 years younger than himself. She was devastated to find out that the man she loved was so evil. While he was in prison she angrily and understandably berated him saying that he might have killed her too some day. Coldly Haigh told her not to be so silly; his killings (he disliked the term 'murders') were simply business. He had tried to cause his victims as little pain as possible and by the time they were covered in acid they had become simply 'carcasses'. Yet he still maintained to the end that his blood drinking had been real. Bloodstains were found on a penknife in his possession yet he never explained how he managed to drink blood, which is a well-known emetic. Haigh's girlfriend, Barbara Stephens, was convinced that the vampire tale was rubbish. She blamed his vivid imagination. The trouble with Haigh, as Mr Justice Humphreys said at the trial, was that you never knew where the truth ended and the lies began. He had told the police of three other murders but the facts didn't add up. It all seems to have been part of his plan to save himself from the gallows by appearing as a homicidal nutcase and ending up in a cosy cell in Broadmoor. Haigh shows many signs of the classic psychopath but perhaps he was not 'mad' as interpreted by the Macnaghten Rules of British jurisprudence. The truth is that Haigh's murders, like his frauds, were carefully planned with profit in mind. He was no fool. Had he done no more killings after the McSwans he might have got away with the perfect murders.

His final letter was to his parents hoping 'your God of all loving kindness be very kind to you and heal your sore'. He went bravely to the gallows at Wandsworth on 10 August 1949 – 13 days after his 40th birthday. The elderly Mr Justice Humphreys retired not long afterwards and spent his final two years living at the Onslow Court Hotel, apparently unconcerned by the fact that he had sentenced to death the notorious former occupant of Room 404.

1950 The Edgware Mystery: Daniel Raven

Murder without apparent motive is a perplexing affair. It is all the more tragic when the man on trial for his life has so much to live for.

Early in the evening of 10 October 1949 a smartly dressed young man of 23 summers called Daniel Raven – 'Danny' to his friends – went to see his attractive 22-year-old wife, Marie, in a maternity home in Muswell Hill, north London. Four days earlier Mrs Raven had given birth to the couple's first child, a baby boy. This event should have been a cause for celebration, especially within a close-knit Jewish family. Also visiting Marie and the baby that evening were her parents, Leopold and Esther Goodman, a couple 'passionately proud' of their daughter and their new grandson. What was said around the hospital bed will never be known. Did the somewhat bluntly spoken Mrs Goodman voice an opinion, expression, attitude or prejudice that annoyed her son-in-law? Seemingly Daniel had a good job at an advertising agency. His pay was £20 a week, a fair wage in 1949, but Danny had debts and there was a bill of sale unpaid on the furniture in his house.

About 10.30pm that same night the police rang Mr Raven and asked him to visit his in-laws' home straight away. They had some bad news for him. The Ravens lived in Edgwarebury Lane just 500 yards around the corner from the Goodmans' house in Ashcombe Gardens, Edgware, Middlesex. Thirty-five minutes earlier, at around 9.55pm, Esther Goodman's brother-in-law, Mr Frederick Fraiman, had called at the Ashcombe Gardens address with his 17-year-old daughter June wishing to hear all the latest news about Marie and the baby. When knocking at the front, side and back doors elicited no response Mr Fraiman climbed in through an open rear window. In the blood-spattered dining-room he found the bodies of his relatives. Leopold was still alive, though unable to talk, and he died about 15 minutes later.

The murder weapon lay in the scullery sink – the heavy base of an aluminium television aerial that normally stood in the hallway. It had been used to batter Mrs Goodman's head seven times, while her husband had been coshed 14 times. Blood spatters ran all over the dining room wallpaper and the carpet was soaked. Mr Justice Cassels at the trial did not mince his words: 'Violence – extreme violence – had taken place. Somebody in that room, almost with the ferocity of a maniac, had struck the life out of those two persons... It must have been fiendish in the extreme.'

Raven arrived at the Goodmans' residence in a highly agitated state. Wearing a crisp shirt and light grey suit he sat on the stairs with his head in his hands and said: 'Why did they tell me to go? Why didn't they let me stay?' He admitted that he had visited his in-laws after their return from the maternity home, but stayed only a few minutes, driving home about 9.30pm. He had turned on his immersion heater and had a bath. The Goodmans, so Danny claimed, were nervous about being burgled. Leopold was a stateless Russian Jew who, so he hinted, was mixed up in shady international currency deals. He was known to keep large amounts of money, sometimes more than £3,000, in a safe in his bedroom. Detectives saw that the bedroom had indeed been ransacked though the intruder had ignored £6 in notes lying on a mantelpiece.

Detective Inspector John Diller told Danny to pull himself together. The young man continued to rave and volunteered the information that while he was on generally good terms with his father-in-law, 'Mrs Goodman and me didn't get on at all well.' D.I. Diller's suspicions of Raven deepened when a constable who had been interviewing other relatives drew attention to the agitated young man's smart appearance and the fact that a few hours earlier he had been wearing a different suit. Since Raven's home was nearby D.I. Diller asked Daniel for his house keys. He handed them over willingly, then thought better of it. 'No, why should you have them? Give them back.' Diller refused. Danny Raven was taken to Edgware Police Station for further questioning. About 11.45pm Diller entered Raven's kitchen and noticed that something was burning. Inside the boiler was a brown tweed suit half-consumed by the flames. The detective switched off the boiler and forensic experts were soon on the scene and able to study the charred suit spattered with the Goodmans' rare AB blood group. In the sink detectives found a bloodstained dishcloth and the garage yielded a pair of newly washed shoes with a clot of blood in an instep. The car's driving seat and controls also had AB bloodstains.

Daniel Raven's trial began at the Old Bailey on 22 November 1949 before a man who had been one of the great defence counsels of his generation, Jimmy Cassels, now Mr Justice Cassels. The defendant now claimed that after leaving the Goodmans alive and well he had called on a cousin nearby, who was out. He then returned to Ashcombe Gardens as he hoped to see the Fraimans. When his knocking was ignored Danny had entered through the rear open window and been horrified to see his dead in-laws. Blood got on his clothes and shoes, so he claimed, when he knelt down by Esther Goodman's body. He had then rushed home, consumed by fear, and tried to burn his suit and wash his shoes.

Raven seemed nervous in the dock. Mr Justice Cassels allowed him to say the oath in the Jewish fashion, head covered, and insisted that the defendant be given a glass of water, which he sipped regularly. In a low voice Raven admitted that the four statements he made to the police on the night of the murder were incorrect. He told how on entering the dining-room he saw Esther's face: 'I could see her eyes were open. I could see that face all... I felt sick.' He told his defence counsel, John Maude, K.C., that he went home in a 'complete state of fear'.

Cassels' summing-up took 150 minutes. He asked the jury to note the intruder theory: 'It may have been an intruder. It may have been.

Give it your careful consideration.' Then he went on to say: 'It was a strange intruder, wasn't it, who went to carry out such a design without any arms or weapons.' Warming to his subject Cassels said: 'The realm of speculation knows no limits. If one side speculates, the other side can speculate. Everybody can speculate, and even you can speculate if you like, if you think speculation is more important than looking at the evidence... why didn't the prisoner call for help? Why didn't he use the telephone? Why did he burn his clothes? Why did he tell lies to the police?' John Maude had talked of the Goodmans' death as possibly being a revenge killing for some shady deal gone awry. The judge pointed out that there might have been other motives – 'jealousy, temper, desire for gain or even a desire to enjoy a benefit that is the result of a death'.

After only 48 minutes' deliberation on 24 November, the jury found Raven guilty of the murders. He never confessed and was executed at Pentonville on 6 January 1950.

It has been suggested by some writers that Raven had sneaked into the Ashcombe Gardens house before his in-laws returned from the maternity home. He wanted the money in Leopold's safe and thought the key was kept under the mattress in the main upstairs bedroom. He was mistaken. While he was searching the room Mr and Mrs Goodman returned home. Trying to sneak out of the house he was accosted by Esther in the hallway. Daniel then panicked, grabbed the TV aerial and struck her down. Agitated and in a temper he then continued a frenzied attack and did the same thing to Leopold Goodman. In the scullery he threw the murder weapon in the sink, washed his hands and hurried on home.

Sixteen thousand people signed a petition demanding that Raven should not be hanged. No sane man, it was said, could have committed such an attack. This petition, as well as an appeal to the Home Secretary, were both rejected. The Lord Chief Justice declared that Cassels' summing-up had been unfavourable to Raven because the evidence was unfavourable to Raven. No defence of insanity was offered at the trial. It has since been discovered that Daniel did have a history of mental instability and hysteria, a man with a short fuse. Had this information been used at the trial it might have saved his life. Marie Raven was not in court to see her young husband condemned to death. Losing both her parents as well as the man she loved must have been a dreadful shock. Her son would never enjoy any memories of his father. Through the sale of the Ashcombe Gardens house, at least Marie Raven was made moderately well-off by the dreadful events.

1951–1960

It was a decade in which the British started to get used to having a welfare state. Deprivation was worse from 1945 until the early '50s than it had been in the war years. The loud-suited 'spiv' became a symbol of austerity Britain, though most folk needed his help to locate those special luxury items. Later, things started to improve as television and other new electronic products became household necessities. Citizens were told they had 'never had it so good'.

The number of persons charged with murder, attempted murder and manslaughter actually dropped to 3,091 men and women. A new Royal Commission on capital punishment 1949–53 concluded that hanging would remain the British way and there would be no gassing or use of the electric chair. Yet disquiet was mounting. Cases such as Derek Bentley and Christopher Craig, Christie and Evans (1953) and Ruth Ellis (1955) caused much furore. 'Cassandra', a columnist in The Daily Mirror, told people they should feel sick after the Ellis execution. A new Homicide Act in 1957 distinguished between capital and non-capital murder. Only six categories could result in a hanging verdict: murder in the furtherance of theft; shooting or causing an explosion; murder whilst under arrest or during an escape; killing a police officer; the death of a prison officer by a prisoner; and a second murder committed on a separate occasion in the British Isles. Albert Pierrepoint resigned in 1956, seven months after he hanged Ruth Ellis. The two men who succeeded him carried out 34 more executions before abolition. The last 18-year-old youth hanged was Francis Forsyth on 10 November 1960 and the last teenager, on 22 December 1960, was Anthony Miller.

1951 The Boastful Murderer: Herbert Leonard Mills

One of the maxims of director Alfred Hitchcock was that one never gets to know who a perfect murderer is, since to advertise the fact makes the deed less than perfect. There is the rub, a perfect Catch-22.

A young man who thought he had found the answer to this problem was 19-year-old Herbert Mills. A fantasist who fancied himself as a poet, he set out on 3 August 1951 to deliberately commit a perfect killing. His chosen victim was mousey Mrs Mabel Tattershaw, a lonely 48-year-old whom he met in the Roxy Cinema, Nottingham. She had little income but Mabel's one luxury was going to the cinema. Flirting and impressing the prematurely aged, skinny, working-class mother of two, Mills arranged to see her next day for a walk in the woods near Sherwood Vale. They stopped at an overgrown orchard known locally as 'the jungle', a popular spot for young lovers. Mabel got tired and sat down. The grass was sodden after recent rain. Herbert wrapped Mabel's coat around her when she complained of the cold, then gallantly offered his own coat. Next he put on his gloves, stating later that he thought the 'experiment' went off without a hitch. 'I think I did rather well' he wrote. 'The strangling was quite easily accomplished.'

So pleased was Mills that he went home to read about his crime in the newspapers. Day followed day and still the police made no mention of the body which lay undiscovered. Mills could stand it no longer. He wanted some recognition. So on 9 August he called the *News of the World* news desk saying, 'I've just found a woman's body. It looks like murder...' The paper got in touch with the Nottingham Police and gave the details of the caller. Soon detectives were following the teenager to Mabel's bludgeoned and strangled corpse. Mills talked of seeing a man with a limp in the woods, though his description was hazy, and in his pocket was a broken bead necklace that had belonged to the dead woman. After giving police blood and fingernail samples he was free to expound on his theories of the murder to *News of the World* crime reporter, Norman Rae. The young man wanted cash for his story and began a series of statements, each more exaggerated than the previous one, with corresponding increases in his payment demands. He told Rae: 'I like Shelley, Burns, Tennyson and Keats... I like crime stories too, and murders, if there's any preference. That's the irony of me running into a murder shortly after writing a sonnet.'

This bizarre behaviour culminated in a meeting at a Nottingham hotel between Rae and Mills on 24 August where the teenager made a statement of his own volition, having been warned in advance by the reporter, 'If it contains information material to the murder, I will take your statement and yourself to City police headquarters.' Mills wrote quietly for an hour, starting with the words, 'I had always considered the possibility of a perfect murder.' He went on to say how having selected Mrs Tattershaw and got her to the woods, 'I had not interfered with her, nor did I... I put on a pair of gloves... knelt with my knees on her shoulders. The coats were placed on her so that she would not clutch, nor gather any thread with her fingernails...' He was delighted that there was 'no motive, no clue. Why, if I had not reported finding the body I should not have been connected with the crime in any manner whatsoever.' He gloated, 'I am quite proud of my achievement.'

Herbert Mills was tried at the Nottingham Assizes in November before Mr Justice Byrne. His defence was that he accidentally found the body and invented his story to make some cash. A pathologist, Professor J. M. Webster, thought that Mills had struck his victim both before and after the strangulation. Hairs from Mills' head were found on Mabel's dress and fibres under her nails came from the blue suit he had worn on the day of the crime. The jury found him guilty as charged and Herbert Mills, not a perfect murderer, though an extremely boastful one, was hanged at Lincoln Prison on 11 December 1951. Rather curiously, although his neck was broken, it took 20 minutes before Mills' heart stopped beating.

1952 Child Killer: John Thomas Straffen

One of the longest life tariffs in British criminal history – more than 55 years –was served by John Straffen who died in gaol on 19 November 2007. The length of his sentence was relative to the dangers he posed to society, having killed two little girls, escaped from Broadmoor, and within four hours murdered a third child.

He was born in 1930 into a service family and spent a few infant years in India. At school in Britain he was a thief and also played truant. In 1940 he was sent to a school for mentally defective children. Seven years later he had matured into a gangling, slack-jawed youth with a shock of blonde hair. He assaulted a 13-year-old girl saying, 'What would you do if I killed you?' Afterwards he strangled five of her father's chickens. He was assessed as having a mental age of nine years and sent to an institution.

On 27 February 1951 he reached the age of 21 and was released on a certificate, provisional on his good conduct. Straffen detested this bond and blamed it on the police. His mother appealed to the Bath Medical Officer of Health in July but he refused to do anything for at least another six months.

That same day the newspapers were full of the murder of a girl who had been found raped and strangled near Windsor. In Straffen's warped mind a plan now formed – 'strangling a child obviously caused the police a lot of trouble so he would do the same'. On Saturday 15 July he was walking to the cinema when he saw five-year-old Brenda Goddard picking flowers in a field. He offered to show her where there were even more, lifted the youngster over a fence, took her to a copse of trees and strangled her. Deed done, he sat in the cinema and watched a thriller called *Shockproof*.

Straffen had been spotted by Brenda's foster mother and he was an immediate suspect. Since there were no apparent clues, he was released after questioning. Fate now took a nasty turn; Straffen's employer, a market gardener, fired him. Since the police had questioned this man about his movements Straffen blamed his dismissal on them. Eight days later he picked up nine-year-old Cicely Batstone in a cinema, took her to another cinema where they watched a Tarzan movie, then to a meadow. There he strangled her. A former workmate, a courting couple and the wife of a police constable had all seen the lanky guy playing with Cicely in the field. He was arrested the next day and laughingly said, 'She's dead, but you can't prove I did it!' This was a typically stupid comment since in his simple mind he thought a witness had to be an 'eyewitness'.

At his trial before Mr Justice Oliver, the mentally deficient man was deemed unfit to plead on the grounds of insanity and sent to Broadmoor criminal lunatic asylum. Six months later he escaped by climbing on some oil drums, to the roof of a shed, then stepping onto the institution's wall and jumping down. He was wearing civilian clothes beneath his overalls. The ease with which he escaped Broadmoor infuriated Mr Justice Cassels at Straffen's 1952 trial. The judge sarcastically told jurors, 'You might think that a notice could almost have been put up in the institution at such a place as this lean-to shed – a notice indicating this was the way out.'

Around 4.30pm Straffen had walked 7 miles from Broadmoor and reached a village called Farley Hill. One hour later he met five-year-old Linda Bowyer trying out her bicycle. He quickly strangled her and made no attempt to hide the body but headed to imposing Farley Hill House and asked for a glass of water. The good people actually gave him a tray with tea and biscuits. Straffen's 5 hours and 10 minutes of freedom were fast dwindling; given a lift to a bus stop, he ran into uniformed staff from Broadmoor. Running away, he was chased and ironically cornered by a gang of children before being forcibly detained. Under arrest he told D.C.I. Francis about his escape. 'Yes, we know all about that,' said the detective, 'but are you prepared to tell us what else you did and if you got into any mischief?' To this Straffen replied, 'I didn't kill her.' Choosing his words carefully, Francis responded by saying, 'What do you mean you didn't kill her? There's been no suggestion that anyone has been killed, injured or in any way attacked.' Straffen replied with the damning words, 'I know what you policemen are. I know I killed the two little children, but I didn't kill the little girl,' then added as if for good measure, 'I didn't kill the little girl with the bicycle.' Later he showed police his bitten-down fingernails and smirked, 'You're looking for flesh – they did that to me before – but you'll be unlucky this time.'

It was accepted that Straffen 'knowingly' killed within the meaning of English law. Despite tests that showed his brain had been damaged at age three, he was brought to trial at the Winchester Assizes in July. His judge, formerly the defence counsel of such famous criminals as Patrick Mahon and Norman Thorne, was Sir James Cassels, now Mr Justice Cassels. Evidence on the earlier child killings was permitted as evidence by Cassels. He noted that this was prejudicial to the defendant, yet added, 'When the word "justice" is used it's important to remember that the word has an application to both sides of the case.' A pathologist, Dr Robert Teare, told the jury that after examining Linda's neck he noticed that pressure had been 'applied at exactly the right points, as if by a person with some experience of killing', a neat job done in 15 to 30 seconds. All six doctors who gave evidence said that John Straffen knew what he was doing within the limits of his intelligence. Judge Cassels asked one of the psychiatrists, 'Did he know that if you squeezed a little girl's throat for long enough life would become extinct?' 'Yes,' replied the doctor who then explained how Straffen was seeking revenge on the police. 'If that's so,' replied the judge tartly, 'had he the intelligence not to select a policeman to strangle but a defenceless little girl?' 'Evidently,' admitted the psychiatrist.

The jury found Straffen guilty after only 29 minutes and Mr Justice Cassels donned the black cap and pronounced sentence of death. With the death penalty under review this was commuted by the Home Secretary to life imprisonment. Some might ask how a serial killer like Straffen could escape hanging while an innocent such as Derek Bentley went to the gallows. These arguments raged at this time and in poor Bentley's case have gone on ever since. John Straffen was considered too dangerous ever to be released. In gaol he was a loner and described by one inmate as a 'long, emaciated, miserable figure, like a dying butterfly or a caged animal'. He always denied killing Linda Bowyer. Perhaps hanging would have been more humane; he never saw the outside world again, dying in Frankland Prison, County Durham, at the age of 77 years.

1953 Ten Rillington Place: John Reginald Halliday Christie

It may be a dark tale of post-war austerity Britain, of strangling and prostitutes, abortions and lies, corpses packed like sardines in the walls, the whole sordid drama played out in a dank, gloomy West London slum house, yet for all that it is one of the greatest British real-life mystery stories. There is so much that went on in 10 Rillington Place that we will never know. Added to which is the incredible question – could two men, acquaintances but not friends, have lived together and killed in the same house, or did one of them die on the gallows an innocent man?

John Christie was described rather neatly by one of his biographers as 'a thin, bald, weak, neurotic, unlikeable person, a hypochondriac, a liar and one-time thief'. With an extremely high forehead made to appear even higher by his bald dome, beady eyes staring coldly out of round horn-rimmed spectacles, Christie was the kind of man who made people feel uncomfortable, a 'genteel Frankenstein monster'. Service in the Great War included being gassed twice and blinded for some months. He claimed that for three years he lost his voice and thereafter spoke in a low whisper, a mannerism that only added to his creepy quality.

He had been born in Halifax, West Yorkshire, in 1898, one of seven children. Known as a sissy, though fairly bright at school, John joined the Halifax police at 15 but very quickly lost his job because of petty pilfering. Pneumonia laid him low at 17, possibly an explanation why a girl that year cruelly called him 'Reggie-no-dick' and 'Can't-do-it-Christie'. In 1920 he married a Yorkshire lass called Ethel but they had no children. Various theft offences followed until in 1924 Christie got nine months' hard labour. He held down a clerical job for the next five years before ending back in prison for striking a woman with a cricket bat. The year 1933 saw him in gaol again for stealing a car. Somehow his wife, after what had been a 10-year separation, returned to her errant husband on his release from prison and joined him in London. Mrs Christie seems to have been an honest woman and the separation may have been caused by her objection to his immoral ways. He convinced her, apparently, that he would make a fresh start. In 1938 Ethel and John – 'Reg' to his friends – rented a three-room ground-floor flat in Rillington Place, Ladbroke Grove, West London. An elderly man called Mr Kitchener lived on the first floor and there was also an attic flat. The squalid building had one lavatory for all the tenants and was at the end of an ugly street.

In 1943, at the height of the Second World War, Mrs Christie made a visit to Sheffield. Reg Christie was serving as a War Reserve policeman and had a reputation as an officious type. He met a 21-year-old Austrian girl called Ruth Fuerst, invited her back to Rillington Place two or three times, strangled her during intercourse, hid the body in the outside wash house, and that night hastily buried it in the garden. We only have Christie's word for what happened. He told the police about the incident 10 years later, by which time his mind was confused, added to which he was an inveterate liar. No one can be certain how or why he killed Miss Fuerst, but kill her he did because her remains were later found.

In October 1944 he murdered another woman, 32-year-old Muriel Eady, a canteen worker at Ultra Radio in Acton, where Christie was working as a clerk. She too was buried in the back garden. Christie claimed to have devised a method of easing catarrh by using a mixture of gas and Friar's Balsam as an inhalant. Somehow he got the women to try this rather unpleasant mixture. Years later he was very vague about how Muriel died. What seems likely is that his gassing method using a jar and rubber tubing allowed Christie to indulge his sexual fantasies on the immobile and unconscious bodies of his victims, a form of sex which suited this secretive man who was aware of his own sexual inadequacies and ailments. Masturbation and intercourse with an inert and uncomplaining woman suited his nature. Possibly he did the same to Ruth Fuerst? He may only have killed the women when they resisted. The police later found tins containing hair and also pubic hair clippings, but not all the hair matched his known victims, so did Christie try out his gassing method on other women?

One odd fact is that Christie did not kill again – if one discounts Beryl and Geraldine Evans – for nine more years. Then he murdered four more women in four months. Possibly Mrs Christie was around more or less permanently? Perhaps prissy, nervous Reg realised he had done wrong and could not face killing again? Maybe he meant to change his ways; maybe...

On 30 November 1949 Timothy Evans, a 24-year-old Welshman, who had been living in the top-floor flat at 10 Rillington Place since Easter 1948, walked into a police station in Merthyr Tydfil and confessed to 'disposing' of his wife. Detectives duly found Mrs Beryl Evans, as well as the corpse of baby Geraldine, hidden in a corner of the wash house. In later confessions Evans, who was a notorious liar and braggart, a hard-drinking wastrel with a famously violent temper, blamed Christie for the murders. Evans's trial began at the Old Bailey on 11 January 1950 and ended two days later, the jury taking just 40 minutes to find him guilty of Geraldine's murder. He showed no signs of remorse for his dead family, but still maintained, 'Christie done it.' Mr Christie had been a witness at the trial and was seen to be crying in court when the death sentence was pronounced. There was no public outcry when Tim Evans was hanged. Feelings were summed up by his mother who had described him as 'no good to himself or anybody else ... his name stinks up here ... I am ashamed to say he is my son.'

The years rolled by; Reg was by now a martyr to fibrosis, enteritis, amnesia and insomnia; wife Ethel suffered from bad nerves and depression. In 1952, now aged 54 years, Mr Christie was advised to go into a mental hospital for anxiety treatment. On 14 December he murdered Ethel. He later claimed that she had taken an overdose of phenobarbitone (though no traces were found in her body), and he woke up to find her choking, so he eased her pain with strangulation. Why did Christie suddenly kill his wife after 19 years? We will never know. The event does not seem to have been premeditated.

Reg was in dire straits. He sold almost all of the furniture and for 10 bitterly cold weeks sat in his parlour with his mongrel bitch 'Judy' and the cat. His only source of income was £2 14s a week in unemployment benefit. During this period he murdered three prostitutes – Rita Nelson, Kathleen Maloney and Hectorina Maclennan. The women were gassed and strangled as they sat in Christie's string deckchair. One week after the last murder he illegally sublet his three rooms to a couple for £7 13s (three months' rent in advance), took his dog to the vet to be destroyed and with one battered suitcase left his home of buried corpses. The new tenants had just one night in the smelly rooms before the Jamaican landlord threw them out. Three days later Mr Beresford Brown, another Jamaican who lodged upstairs, was clearing out Christie's apartment when he knocked on a suspicious part of the kitchen wall and heard a hollow sound. He peered through a hole and saw a naked back. Dr Francis Camps, the country's most eminent pathologist, arrived at about 7pm. Inside the alcove, police found the trussed-up bodies of the three prostitutes. Rita Nelson, who was 25, had been six months pregnant. Spermatozoa was also found in all three vaginas. A full search unearthed Ethel Christie under the floorboards of the front room. She had been strangled but not sexually assaulted. Digging in the back garden uncovered the skeletons of Ruth Fuerst and Mabel Eady.

The newspapers had a field day with the 'House of Horrors'. Christie was found wandering the Putney embankment on 31 March, a sad figure. His trial began at No. 1 Court, Old Bailey, on 22 June 1953, before Mr Justice Finnemore. What put the cat among the pigeons was that Christie confessed to killing Beryl Evans, though not, it must be said, to murdering her baby. What muddies the waters is that it was very much in Christie's interests to include Beryl as one of his victims since he wanted to be seen as a mad homicidal killer. Only this way might he be found guilty but insane and get sent to Broadmoor Hospital. He admitted as much, saying 'the more the merrier'. In court he made a poor and seemingly confused defendant (though at times he was surprisingly sharp on dates and details so we cannot be sure), displaying a generally vague memory, speaking with long pauses and in a whisper that made it difficult at times to know what he said. Psychiatrists spoke for the defence and the prosecution. The trial ended on 25 June after the jury had deliberated for 85 minutes and found him guilty as charged. Christie was sentenced to death and hanged by Albert Pierrepoint at Pentonville (the same executioner had also hanged Timothy Evans) on 15 July.

There the matter might have ended except for some anti-hanging M.P.s who demanded an inquiry. It was decided that John Scott Henderson, Recorder of Portsmouth, should look into all the facts. This he did and duly reported that Evans had killed his wife and daughter. The anti-hanging lobby sensed a whitewash and articles in several influential journals demanded a second inquiry. This demand was reinforced by a hugely successful book, *Ten Rillington Place,* written by broadcaster Ludovic Kennedy. This work, also made into a creepy film with Richard Attenborough and John Hurt as the leads, presented Evans as a pitiable illiterate who had been under Christie's sway. A second inquiry was set up in 1965 under a High Court judge, Sir Daniel Brabin. This later reported that it was 'more probable than not' that Evans killed Beryl but not baby Geraldine. Since Tim Evans was hanged for his baby's murder he was given a free and posthumous pardon.

The doubts remain. The journalist Gordon Honeycombe, writing in 1982, found many aspects of the case deeply unsettling. He noted that there was no reason to suppose 'that Evans was dominated by the older man'. He noted how the Christies 'tended to keep themselves to themselves... There is also no reason to suppose that the police terrorised Evans into making a false confession – no complaint or allegation about this was ever made by Evans, by his lawyers, or by his relatives.'

In 1994 a book called *The Two Killers of Rillington Place* set out to destroy Kennedy's opus almost line for line. The author, John Eddowes, demonstrated with skill that the famous book, which did so much to gain Evans his pardon, is hugely flawed, full of distortions of truth and, in some cases, downright lies. Evans, it now appears, was much brighter than Kennedy's sad victim. More recently, in 2015, the historian Jonathan Oates, researching Christie's biography, viewing many documents not seen before, concluded that Evans killed his wife and child. Oates also showed how there are no hard facts to support the rumours that Christie was a back-street abortionist or a necrophile.

So did he kill Beryl and Geraldine Evans? Here are some things to ponder. In his first confession Evans said that he and Beryl had been fighting. He struck his wife 'across the face with my flat hand', before strangling her with a length of rope, 'in a fit of temper'. Dr Donald Teare, the eminent pathologist working on the case, noted how in his opinion the swelling on Beryl's face was caused 'by a single blow with the back of the hand'. Christie, on the day of the murder, was seen by his doctor. He could hardly walk with severe back pain. This hardly sounds like a man who climbs to the top of the house to try to abort a woman's baby (according to Kennedy), hits her really hard across the face (not his normal *modus operandi*), then assaults and strangles her and has the energy to somehow hide the body in a wash house. Workmen that day were also carrying out repairs on the property, sticking their noses in, asking for cups of tea. Mrs Christie was also at home until late afternoon. It seems an odd time for Christie to commit a murder. He then left to go to evening surgery and picked up Ethel at the library. They were apparently together for the rest of the night.

At Evans's trial Mrs Christie had said she heard noises that night while she and Reg were in bed, 'as if furniture was being moved about' upstairs. This is in line with Evans's first confession in which he claimed to have tied Beryl up with some string in a blanket and put her body under the wash house sink sometime after 10pm. Depressed after losing his job, it may be that Evans strangled Geraldine two days later because she would not stop crying. This reason was not stated at his trial but Evans gave this explanation to P.C. Trevallian, one of his guards.

There are many other small facts which, when viewed together, lead one to think that Evans was far from innocent. At the very least he was an accessory to murder, helping Christie dispose of the bodies. Besides Dr Teare, the two most eminent pathologists in Britain, Professors Camps and Simpson, both worked on aspects of the Christie case. Both thought Evans killed his wife and baby. All three were present when Beryl was re-exhumed and agreed that she had died of asphyxia and not Christie's carbon monoxide method (again, according to Kennedy). Dr Teare had a long-running debate in the national press with Ludovic Kennedy because he felt the campaigner had deliberately misconstrued some of his words in an autopsy report to imply something else or give the wrong emphasis to his findings.

The debate will never be settled to everyone's satisfaction, hardly surprising when so much is based on what was said by two pathological liars. In my own opinion, Christie may well have found out that Evans had murdered Beryl and agreed to help (the officious little man hardly wanted the police having any excuses to dig up the garden). Possibly he strangled baby Geraldine, making sure that one of Tim Evans's ties stayed around her neck. Possibly not.

Those who pooh-pooh the likelihood of two stranglers living in the same house discount improbability, yet improbable things happen all the time. In this book of just 119 murderers we have a Donald Neilson, a Dennis Nilsen and Ruth Ellis, formerly Ruth Neilson – history is littered with odd facts.

1954 Roast Beef and Cotton Thread: Thomas Ronald Lewis Harries

In a new murderous post-war age seemingly dominated by figures such as sadistic Heath, kinky Christie and Haigh with his acid bath, it was some relief to see a return to a classic crime in the story of Ronald Harries, a tale in which one clue and some of the methods employed by its lead detective were worthy of a Conan Doyle or Agatha Christie.

John and Phoebe Harries were a hard-working and elderly couple who farmed at Derlwyn, Llangynin, near Carmarthen, near the South Wales coast. On the evening of Friday 16 October 1953 they attended a harvest thanksgiving service at their local chapel and were never seen alive again. Three days later Ronald Harries, the couple's 24-year-old nephew, who lived at Pendine, some 10 miles away, was taking away their cows to his father's farm at Cadno and telling everyone that his aunt and uncle had gone on holiday. He said he had seen them off at Carmarthen Station on the Saturday morning. To most people he said they were in London for 10 days, adding on one occasion, 'They might be in America as far as I know.'

Neighbours and other relatives were suspicious. Ronald had a reputation as a liar. The disappearance of John and Phoebe Harries was reported to the local police on 22 October. They arrived at the farm, gained entry, and found it all looking quite homely. Then Detective Sergeant Watkins spotted an odd clue – peering inside the kitchen oven he found a weekend joint all covered in greaseproof paper and ready for cooking. It seemed remarkably odd that the Harries should rush away and leave their joint in the oven! Ronald Harries arrived a few minutes later and made a statement saying his aunt and uncle wanted their first holiday in 21 years; he had taken them in their car to Carmarthen, later returning to milk the cows. No one in Carmarthen had any recollections of a couple such as Mr and Mrs Harries catching a train that Saturday morning. Indeed, on the following days odd facts came to light while at the same time Ronald Harries kept changing aspects of his story. It turned out that on 16 October he had borrowed a hammer – still unreturned – from a friend saying, 'It's a beauty. I want it for a good heavy job.' A 15-year-old boy also told police that he had watched Ronald searching through drawers at the Derlwyn farmhouse during the morning of the 17th when he was supposed to be dropping off his relatives in Carmarthen. A strange cheque made out to Ronald Harries by his uncle also bounced at the bank; the amount appeared to have been altered from £9 to £909.

Local police searched Derlwyn Farm and 80 square miles of surrounding country without finding any signs of the missing farmer and his wife. Convinced that he was dealing with a case of murder, the Chief Constable of Carmarthenshire requested the help of Scotland Yard and Superintendent John Capstick took over the inquiry. Capstick was a bowler-hatted, pipe-smoking detective of the old school. He chatted genially with local farmers and was polite to Ronald Harries. He also noticed a buzzard with unblinking stare that sat day after day perched on some telephone wires staring intently into a field of kale at Cadno Farm. Working entirely on a hunch, Capstick decided one night to quietly arrive with his assistant, Sergeant Heddon, and run reels of black cotton thread around the hedges. Next they started their car engine very loudly. Sure enough a light appeared at Harries' bedroom window. Returning at dawn the two detectives found the thread broken in the kale field. Harries was clearly nervous of something. At the top of the field, a section of kale was wilting and there were tyre marks corresponding to Harries' Land Rover. Capstick had the whole area dug up and on 16 November 1953 the bodies of John and Phoebe Harries were found in a shallow grave, their skulls smashed in. After charging Ronald Harries with their murders Capstick and his team found blood samples on two of the suspect's jackets. Five days later the hammer was found hidden in one of the Cadno hedges. On first hearing the news that the bodies had been found Harries had said, 'I am sorry to hear that uncle and auntie are dead, as I was their favourite.'

Sent to trial at the Carmarthen Assizes in March 1954 before Mr Justice Havers, the shifty Harries gave a poor showing under an avalanche of questions. Indeed, the circumstantial evidence was overwhelming and the jury quickly concluded that he was guilty. He was hanged at Swansea Prison on 28 April 1954. The killer collapsed just before reaching the gallows and had to be partly carried to his execution by hangman Albert Pierrepoint and his assistant, Ronald Stewart.

1955 The Last Woman to Hang: Ruth Ellis

The murder of David Blakely by Ruth Ellis remains one of the great *crime passionnel* tales. It has been the subject of countless books, several plays and a well-acted motion picture. Because she was both glamorous and the last woman to die on the gallows, a fate she met with tremendous courage, Ruth's story is inextricably linked with the abolition of capital punishment in Britain. For many it is a classic tragedy.

Shorn of the emotion, the Ellis-Blakely killing is actually rather a sordid affair – a tale of smoky nightclubs, hostesses in thin stilettos, bleached blondes, red lipstick, lots of alcohol, fast cars, passionate sex, mutually cheating lovers, beatings and abortions.

Ruth was born at Rhyl, north Wales, on 9 October 1926 as Ruth Hornby but her father, Arthur, changed the family name to Neilson for business reasons. Arthur was a dance band cellist and a man of short temper. Her mother, Bertha, who delivered six children (Ruth being her fourth child), was a Belgian Catholic. Mrs Neilson found it difficult to cope with domestic and family matters. She preferred to accompany Arthur, who had a wandering eye for the ladies, on his travels. Little Ruth was mothered to a great extent by her older sister, Muriel, who took good care of her siblings.

Irascible and morose, Arthur went through a succession of jobs until, in 1941, he became a chauffeur in London. Ruth, a precocious 15-year-old, moved in with him, eager to sample the thrills of the big city. The skinny girl, 'as plain as hell' in glasses, had now begun to fill out a tight sweater and got a job with Muriel in a munitions factory. She spent her small pay packet on clothes, make-up and having a good time in the various dance halls where boys appreciated the 5-foot-2-inch bleached blonde with the curvy 34-inch bust. Ruth was determined to make the most of what wartime London had to offer, and in her case that meant lots of handsome young men in uniform, all of them having money to burn on a sexy girlfriend. Her mother called her 'dance mad' and she was out every night. Ruth was demonstrating a tough edge that remained all her life. Proud of the way she could handle men, she told Muriel after a row: 'You may be my older sister – but I'm ten bloody years older than you in experience.' When the family home suffered a direct bomb hit it was Ruth who dug her dad out of the rubble.

By Christmas 1943 Ruth was going through a variety of odd jobs including working as a photographer's assistant at the Locarno Ballroom in Streatham. Here she met, fell in love with and got pregnant by a French-Canadian soldier. He promised to marry her but it transpired that he had a wife and three children back in Canada. A baby was born on 15 September 1944 and called Andrea. Ruth was still only 17.

With the coming of peace Ruth decided to make the most of her figure and looks. She started doing nude modelling at photographers' clubs in Soho. The pay was good and she later explained: 'The men treated me very decently. Often, after work, one or other of them would take me to one of the clubs for a drink.' This was how in 1946 she met Morrie Conley, a fat, ugly but wealthy West End club owner who staffed his premises with young 'hostesses' who were 'encouraged to make men feel welcome and prostitute themselves'.

Soon Ruth needed a second abortion (others would follow). In 1950 she met George Ellis, a rich dental surgeon and alcoholic who seemed to spend most of his earnings in West End nightclubs. The couple had a whirlwind summer, living it up in Newquay before getting married on 8 November at Tonbridge register office. Despite her lifestyle Ruth craved the respectability that went with marriage to a professional man. Unfortunately for her, George's drinking got worse and he was violently abusive. Her dad had often walloped her but this was different. Ellis hit her when she was pregnant. During their numerous rows she called him 'a drunken old has-been' and he referred to her as 'a bloody bitch from Brixton'. After a difficult birth of their daughter, called Georgina, Ellis refused to pay for a pram and advised adoption. Ruth returned to working for Morrie Conley and the only easy way she knew of making money – milking men, or 'shits' as she called them, of cash. With the children living with her parents Ruth became a hostess at Carroll's Club and had sex with Conley (and others), who gave her a flat to share with some of his prostitutes in Gilbert Court, Oxford Street.

Early in 1953 she suffered an ectopic pregnancy. She had returned to working at Carroll's by September when one night a gang of motor-racing hellraisers turned up to party. The group included 33-year-old Desmond Cussen, a former pilot in Bomber Command. A bachelor somewhat older than the rest of the gang, Cussen lived in Goodwood Court, W1. With him was 24-year-old David Blakely, a rich Yorkshireman, son of a wealthy G.P. He had been brought up by his mother who divorced her doctor husband while David was at public school and married a wealthy man with a passion for racing cars called Cook. For his 21st birthday Mr Cook gave David a sports car. Soon the young man was living a playboy lifestyle on a £7,000 windfall left to him by his father, who had died in 1952. Blakely attended various motor-racing events, became a good mechanic, drove a fast car and liked to party even faster. He was charming, selfish and sulky, but extremely handsome, with long eyelashes and the lean frame of a 21st-century supermodel.

At first Ruth did not like David and thought him 'a pompous little ass'. She met him again in October when she was the manageress of The Little Club in Knightsbridge. This time the pair clicked. Within a fortnight they were sleeping together. She called David 'Loverboy' and he was soon telling his friends that Ruth was 'one of the finest fucks in town'. In February 1954 came another abortion, this one paid for by Ruth, who was still married to George Ellis and not sure how much she wanted Blakely despite his offer to wed her.

A racing friend later described Ruth, David and their tempestuous affair. She was in his opinion 'a typical club girl... very attractive... she didn't take money for sex and she always bought her round... She had a bloody sight more principles than Blakely...' David was a 'good-looking, well-educated, supercilious shit. But you couldn't help but like him.' Once their affair had ignited, 'Theirs was the absolute in love-hate relationships... They wanted each other, and the feeling was so diabolically strong that it excluded everybody else. If she was talking to somebody else or flirting with someone, it immediately sparked off an explosion. And of course she felt the same over his behaviour.' Then there was Desmond Cussen, 'a snaky bastard... well-dressed and suave,' who was 'madly in love with Ruth and hated Blakely's guts.'

Intense lovemaking led in turn to intense rows. Ellis and Blakely were in a giddy spiral of pleasure and pain known to all who have ever been involved in a truly passionate relationship where jealousy is a major component. There were black eyes, cuts and bruises especially after a fight in Cussen's flat (he was not there), on 6 February 1955. The jealous rows led inexorably to both David and Ruth sleeping with others. When she got pregnant again he was angry, suspicious that the child was not his. During one fight he punched her in the stomach screaming, 'You're mad – you're stark raving mad. One of these days I'll kill you!' 'You've done that already,' hissed back Ruth. She subsequently had a miscarriage.

Matters came to a head over the Easter weekend. David had gone to stay with friends called the Findlaters in north London. Ruth was convinced that he was bedding their 19-year-old nanny. She staked out their home, making constant and abusive phone calls from a nearby telephone kiosk. The police were called by the Findlaters to deal with this domestic rumpus. Tearful and jealous, by Sunday Ruth had not really slept much in three days. She was emotionally and physically distressed, having been on her feet for much of the time, drinking heavily and taking drugs. It is also worth remembering that less than two weeks earlier she had suffered a miscarriage.

On the Sunday evening, with Desmond Cussen's help as her driver, Ruth located David drinking with some of his friends in the Magdala Tavern, South Hill Park, NW3, on a corner of Hampstead Heath. When David left the pub at 9.30pm Ruth approached him and called out his name. He either did not hear her or chose to ignore her. She then took from her handbag a .38 Smith & Wesson revolver, yelled 'David' one more time and fired twice. The shots missed Blakely, who ran around his car and headed towards the hill. Ellis fired four more times, each bullet hitting its target. Her last shot was fired less than 3 inches from Blakely as he lay helpless in the road. One of the first two shots had hit a passer-by, Mrs Gladys Yule, though luckily only in her thumb, while the other shot went wild. Some witnesses said Ruth tried to turn the gun on herself but it was empty. When a plainclothes policeman who had been off duty and drinking in the Magdala approached her, Ruth said: 'Will you call the police?' He replied, 'I am the police' and took the revolver out of her hand.

Not long after being taken into custody Ruth told police officers, 'I'm guilty. I'm rather confused. When I put the gun into my bag I intended to go and find David and shoot him.' Detectives who interviewed her that night, lawyers who talked with her, even prison officials who befriended her in the weeks that followed – all were astonished by Ruth Ellis's calmness, charming manners and simple matter-of-factness. She spoke of 'a life for a life' and told Blakely's mother in a letter 'how deeply sorry I am to have caused you this unpleasantness... I shall die loving your son. And you should feel content that his death has been repaid.' In a confession published in the *Daily Mirror* she wrote of only vaguely being aware of firing the shots, intending to kill herself, yet watching David's blood flow 'in a completely detached sort of way...'

In Holloway Mrs Ellis was interviewed by two psychiatrists: one for the prosecution concluded that she was not suffering any mental illness when she fired her weapon; the other, for the defence, thought Ruth demonstrated a history of being 'emotionally immature'.

Her trial began at the Old Bailey before Mr Justice Havers on 20 June 1955. It lasted barely two days. Ruth appeared in court with her hair done, the classic platinum blonde, looking smart in a black suit and high-heeled shoes. Her defence counsel, Melford Stevenson, Q.C., was hoping that he could save his client by a defence of manslaughter because she had been 'driven to a frenzy' by jealousy and provoked into killing her lover. Stevenson did not help his client when he attempted to ask her if she could have controlled her impulse to kill Blakely. 'No,' answered Ruth. 'And you went up, and you in fact shot him? Is that right?' 'Yes,' said Ellis. Prosecuting counsel Christmas Humphreys (son of the judge in the Haigh case) asked: 'Mrs Ellis, when you fired that revolver at close range into the body of David Blakely what did you intend to do?' Ruth gave a damningly honest reply: 'It is obvious that when I shot him I intended to kill him.'

Ruth's one defence witness, psychiatrist Dr Whittaker, did his own unwitting part in sending her to the gallows when he told Humphreys that she had been 'sane' when committing the murder.

With the jury dismissed, Stevenson tried to convince Havers that Ellis was guilty of manslaughter. The judge disagreed and as the law stood in 1955, it is generally accepted that he was right. *Crime passionnel* does not exist as a defence in English law. The crime historian Edgar Lustgarten once explained how the law is 'an admirable instrument for ascertaining *facts*; it is much less efficient in dealing with psychology'. Next morning on the second day of the trial both Stevenson and Humphreys waived their closing speeches. This was almost a mutual act of solidarity against the judge's ruling. The jury retired at 11.52am and were back 23 minutes later with a guilty verdict. Mr Justice Havers donned the black cap and pronounced sentence of death. One reporter claimed that Ellis mouthed 'Thanks' under her breath. At the back of the court her father was weeping.

Brassy and tough, Ruth told friends who visited her in prison that she wanted to die. 'You may find this very hard to believe, but this is what I want.' She told one well-wisher that her execution was no more alarming 'than having a tooth pulled out'. Her solicitor described Ellis as 'tough as old boots,' though on at least one occasion before her execution she broke down in hysterics. Ruth seemed, on the whole, to be able with admirable sang-froid to see the grimly funny side of things. 'I gave David lots of rope,' she joked, 'come to think of it, he's giving me quite a bit now.' Early on the morning of 13 July 1955 she took the last rites of the Roman Catholic faith and later on enjoyed a glass of brandy. At 9am she walked bravely to the gallows where executioner Albert Pierrepoint later said she was the most courageous woman he ever hanged.

The Ruth Ellis story hardly ended with her death. Her many defenders have claimed that she was a badly wronged woman who had suffered years of abuse at the hands of her father, husband and lover. An emotional and physical wreck on the day of the killing, she deserved better from the English judicial system. Then there is the question of the revolver – how did Ruth come by it and what part did Desmond Cussen play on that fateful Sunday night? He always denied providing Ruth with the handgun, claiming she was an inveterate liar, yet she told her solicitor hours before her execution that Cussen had given her the weapon. One author has even suggested that Cussen actually pulled the trigger! It seems likely that she kept his name quiet because of some deal that he would provide for her children. He was attentive before her trial but avoided Ruth after the verdict.

It was not until two years after Ellis's execution that a change in the law allowed the new defence of 'diminished responsibility'. This might have saved her from the gallows. The final decision on whether Ruth Ellis would live or die rested with the Home Secretary, Sir Gwilym Lloyd George. Years later he explained his reasons for hanging Ellis: 'This was a public thoroughfare where Ruth Ellis stalked and shot her quarry. And remember that she did not only kill David Blakely; she also injured a passer-by. As long as I was Home Secretary I was determined to ensure that people could use the streets without fear of a bullet.' In the face of this kind of thinking, the 50,000 citizens who signed a petition asking for a reprieve were wasting their time.

Ruth Ellis basically went to the gallows because she wished to die. She would have been bemused and astonished by the fascination her life and death continue to hold for so many people. Whether it was right for her to die – morally and judicially – will continue to be argued for a long time to come. She, at least, held fast to her opinions and got the kind of justice that she craved. Tragedy, very sadly, seemed to afflict all her family in the years that followed. In the 1970s women who had been executed at Holloway were re-interred elsewhere. Ruth Ellis's remains now lie in the lovely little churchyard of St Mary's at Amersham, Buckinghamshire.

1956 Lucky Killer: Freda Rumbold

One year after the Ellis case another woman stood before a judge accused of a firearm murder. She also served time in Holloway's condemned cell but, luckily for her, won a reprieve and was sentenced to life imprisonment. This was 43-year-old Bristol housewife Mrs Freda Rumbold, who had shot her husband twice.

The Rumbolds' marriage had been bad for years. Mr Rumbold was frequently abusive. Freda decided one day that enough was enough. She went and bought a gun and on 22 August put two bullets into her husband while he was sleeping. For several days during that hot summer she did nothing with the body before finally contacting the police. To them Freda said that her husband had threatened to kill her and their daughter, the couple had wrestled and the gun had gone off. This was a stupid line of defence since the gun only carried one shot and to fire it twice required the act of reloading. Once this was pointed out to Freda she blamed the killing on the moon and her husband's constant demands for sex. She might so easily have been hanged, like Ruth Ellis, but her trial fell in an 18-month period, 1955–1957, during which there was a moratorium on the death penalty. Lucky woman.

1957 The Insulin Killer: Kenneth Barlow

During the night of 3 May 1957 police in Bradford received a call to go to a house in Thornbury Crescent where Mrs Elizabeth Barlow, two months pregnant, had apparently drowned in her bath. Her husband, a 38-year-old male nurse, said his wife had been unwell, sick in bed. Elizabeth decided to take a bath about 9.20pm. He had fallen asleep. Checking up on her two hours later, he found his wife submerged and unconscious. He had pulled the plug, drained most of the water and tried to give her artificial respiration before a doctor arrived.

It was noticed that Mrs Barlow's eyes seemed somewhat dilated though her body showed no signs of maltreatment. Four hypodermic punctures in the woman's buttocks looked more serious. Substances were taken from the body and when injected into mice produced an insulin reaction. It was later ascertained that 84 units of insulin must have been in Mrs Barlow when she died. She had no reason to use the drug and was not a diabetic. Police had found hypodermic syringes at the house but in view of Mr Barlow's occupation this was hardly unusual. What made them suspicious was that there was no water on the bathroom floor. Would not a dying woman have made some kind of struggle? Kenneth Barlow's pyjamas were also dry, which hardly tallied with his tale of holding his wife and giving her artificial respiration. At first the man denied using a syringe, then retracted this statement, saying he had given Elizabeth six injections of ergometrine to produce an abortion.

Duly charged, Kenneth Barlow was put on trial in December before Mr Justice Diplock. In poisoning cases a senior law officer always represents the Crown and Barlow faced the Solicitor-General, Sir Harry Hylton-Foster. One witness recalled the accused discussing with him two years earlier how an injection of insulin might make a perfect murder since the drug quickly dissolves in the bloodstream and is untraceable. A female nurse at East Riding General Hospital and a patient at Driffield Sanatorium had also listened to similar theories. Barlow had access to insulin in his work with diabetic patients at St Luke's Hospital, Huddersfield. He told the court that he was very much in love with his new wife and had no reason to kill her. Much of the time was taken up with the forensic evidence. The defence, led by Bernard Gillis, Q.C., came up with a novel theory that Mrs Barlow had slipped in the water and in a state of fear her body had produced a massive amount of insulin. Prosecution experts argued that for a human body to produce the amount of insulin found in the dead woman, it would have to secrete 'the unheard of quantity of 15,000 units.'

Sentenced to life imprisonment on 13 December 1957, Barlow served 26 years in gaol, being released in 1984, the second-longest life term up to that date after John Straffen. He still protested his innocence. One fact not revealed in court was that his first wife had died just 18 months before Elizabeth Barlow's demise, 'the doctors then being unable to determine the cause of death, although believing it to be from natural causes'.

1958 The Man Who Talked Too Much: Peter Thomas Anthony Manuel

Glasgow High Court had never witnessed anything quite like it – nor had the learned judge, Lord Cameron, or the jury, nor the assembled barristers in their gowns and wigs. It was the tenth day of what many in Scotland were calling the trial of the century. Just after 10.45am on 22 May 1958 the defence counsel, Harald Leslie, Q.C., told the astonished court that his client, Peter Manuel, on trial accused of multiple counts of murder, wished to present his own defence. Looking immaculate in a smart blazer and tie, his thick, wavy hair greased back '50s style, the man on trial for his life for eight murders sucked on a pencil and looked studious.

In the six decades since that trial Manuel's legend has grown. Intelligent, smart-looking, a smooth talker full of bravado and cunning, this stocky 31-year-old man who could croon a good tune and tickle the ivories, a man who always paid his round in the pub (almost always with stolen money), has come down over the years to represent the classic psychopath. Violence, especially violence directed towards women, seemed to excite him. His crimes follow no special pattern, however, and nor do his confessions. Loving the limelight, as he did, it was hardly surprising that he wished to show off in court even if his errors might take him to the gallows. Ultimately the man who seemed to think of himself as a George Raft movie-star-style gangster was shown to be nothing more than a vicious sexual predator and killer.

He had been born on 15 March 1927 in New York. His Scottish father, Samuel, had emigrated hoping for a better future for his family. Work on a car assembly line did not make him any richer and in 1932 the Manuels returned to Lanarkshire. Peter was getting into trouble almost as soon as he could walk. From the time he was 11 until he was 18 his behaviour, mainly breaking into and entering properties, earned him long spells in remand homes, approved schools and borstal. With each passing year he grew more violent; aged 15 he broke into a sleeping girl's bedroom, woke her up and hit her with a hammer. It seemed as if he wanted to terrify his victim as well as inflict pain. In 1946 he made three separate attacks on women, including a rape. He elected to defend himself on the rape charge, a bold move for a 19-year-old. His skills in court attracted some praise but only served to inflate his growing ego. The jury still found him guilty. Manuel was already on bail for 15 burglaries. The rape charge was added and he got nine years in Peterhead Prison, Aberdeenshire.

Astonishingly, perhaps, he was a model prisoner, winning full remission and stepping out of gaol a free man in 1953. One year later he met 'a lovely wee bus conductress' called Anna. Nine months later they became engaged and a wedding was set for 30 July. Manuel was charming to his fiancée and family. She was a good Catholic girl and it is unlikely that they had intercourse during this courtship. In fact he behaved like a perfect gentleman – until an anonymous letter told Anna O'Hara some truths about her husband-to-be, as well as some preposterous lies (some writers think Manuel was the author of this letter, though it hardly matters since he could not take communion, was not a practising Catholic and so the relationship was doomed). Hurt and bitter, Manuel's response to the end of his engagement was to drag a terrified woman into a field and beat her on the same day he was supposed to have been married. Arrested, he again conducted his own defence at Airdrie Sherriff Court. The jury returned that peculiarly Scottish verdict of 'Not Proven' which to Manuel's great delight meant that he walked out of the court. His ego grew even bigger.

His murders began on 2 January 1956; Anne Knielands, a 17-year-old girl, was found two days later with her head smashed in and clothing askew; one stocking and her knickers were missing. Manuel was interviewed by police and had scratches on his face, yet he somehow talked himself out of trouble. He lied and said that he had been in a fight over Hogmanay. His father provided an alibi. A pair of his trousers and a jacket were also missing but Manuel claimed he had given them to a friend.

That September three burglaries took place in which the housebreaker trashed the homes in a careless and unnecessary way. The third also involved the murder of a Mrs Watt, her sister, Mrs Margaret Brown, and her 16-year-old daughter, Vivienne. All three women had been shot in the head. Their clothes had been interfered with but there were no signs of rape. William Watt, Mrs Watt's husband, although away at the time on a fishing trip, was arrested and charged with the murders.

Three months later on 28 December (Manuel had been in gaol from 2 October to 30 November on burglary charges), Isabelle Cooke, an attractive 17-year-old schoolgirl, failed to meet her boyfriend on a date. Manuel later confessed to strangling her and stripping her naked, an act that excited him, before burying the body in a field.

On 10 January three more dreadful murders took place: a 45-year-old businessman, Peter Smart, his wife, and their 11-year-old son, Michael, were all shot in the head by an intruder at their Uddingston home. Police had strong suspicions that the killer was Manuel. Real proof was missing. They decided to turn the screws on his father, Samuel, by claiming he was the receiver of stolen property from some recent burglaries. This tactic has been denounced ever since but it did work; Manuel agreed to make a confession on 16 January. He told police that he had killed Anne Knielands, the Watt and Smart families and showed them where he had buried Isabelle Cooke's body near some brickworks.

His trial began on 12 May. Having given a long confession, Manuel now claimed that it had been forced out of him under duress. He accused Mr Watt, who was in poor health, of killing his family. In court he displayed great ability in cross-examination of the police and others. Lord Cameron later said in his summing-up that Manuel had demonstrated 'a skill that is quite remarkable'. But the jury were not fooled by the way his stories kept changing, nor his constant accusations that the police had set him up. After 15 days, the jury took exactly 141 minutes to find Manuel guilty of seven murders, though not guilty of the Anne Knielands killing.

With the black cap held above his head Lord Cameron pronounced the Scottish version of the death sentence: 'Peter Thomas Anthony Manuel, in respect of the verdict of guilty of capital murder and of murder done on different occasions, the sentence of the court is that you will be taken from this place to the prison of Barlinnie at Glasgow to be detained until the 19th day of June and on that day within the said prison at Glasgow and between the hours of eight and 10 to suffer death by hanging. This pronounced for doom.' Executioner Harry Allen hanged Manuel not on 19 June but at 8am on 11 July. In prison he confessed to three other murders although doubts attach to all of them; with Manuel there is a strong possibility that he just wanted to keep his name in the limelight.

An attempt to cheat the hangman by swallowing disinfectant, after his appeal failed, was stopped by a quick-acting prison official.

For many years afterwards Glasgow children knew him as the bogeyman – 'If you don't get to bed, Peter Manuel will come and get you!' The Dundee-born actor Brian Cox, who was 11 years old at the time of Manuel's trial, has claimed that his performance as cannibal psychopath Hannibal Lecter in Michael Mann's acclaimed film *Manhunter* was influenced by what he had had read and seen of this Scottish killer.

1959 The No Memory Man: Guenther Fritz Erwin Podola

Can someone who has no recall of the crime be found guilty of murder? This was the novel question posed by one of the most sensational trials of that year.

On 3 July the apartment of wealthy English-born American model Mrs Verne Schiffman was burgled in Poland Gardens, South Kensington. The thief got away with jewellery worth £1,785, a mink stole valued at £535 and three passports, including Mrs Schiffman's.

Four days later she got a blackmail letter in the post demanding $500. The matter was reported to the police and when a man rang at 3.30pm on Monday 13 July, Mrs Schiffman had instructions to try and keep the caller talking. Post Office engineers traced the call to a box in South Kensington underground station. Two detectives, Sergeants John Purdy and John Sandford, raced to the scene. Purdy saw a man in a telephone box and pushed his way in saying, 'Okay lad, we are police officers.' Purdy and Sandford took hold of the caller and led him to the street where they had left their car. Without warning the suspect suddenly twisted free and ran off down Sidney Place. The detectives followed and saw their quarry run into a new block of flats at 105 Onslow Square. They entered and found him cowering behind a pillar in the lobby. Purdy said, 'We are police officers and we are taking you to Chelsea Police Station.' The man's blue sunglasses were removed and he was told to 'sit on the window sill and behave yourself'. Sandford has crossed the hall to look for a porter when he turned and saw the suspect gingerly getting off the window ledge and putting his right hand inside his jacket. 'Watch out,' he shouted to Purdy, 'He may have a gun.' No sooner had he spoken the words than the man drew out a 9mm FB Radom V15 pistol and shot Sergeant Purdy at point-blank range through the chest. He died instantly. A 40-year-old father of three children, the well-liked sergeant was later called 'a gentlemanly sort of fellow' by his chief.

The killer fled into the sunny street while Sandford stayed with his colleague's body. The police now launched a massive manhunt for 'a young man about thirty, height about 5ft 10 ins, slim build, brown hair, speaking with an American accent, last seen wearing dark glasses, with a light sports coat, light grey trousers and suede shoes'.

The shooting was a sensation in the press. Fingerprints were taken off the window sill and circulated via Interpol. Within 24 hours, Scotland Yard detectives knew they were looking for Guenther Podola, a German who had recently been deported from Canada and arrived in Britain on 21 May from Dusseldorf. He was a known burglar and thief who sometimes affected an American accent and called himself – in true Mickey Spillane style – 'Mike Colato'. After the murder, Podola had returned to his room at the second-class Claremont House Hotel, 95 Queen's Gate, Kensington, refusing thereafter to leave his room. The manager, Thomas Harding, thought his guest in Room 15, 'Mr Paul Camay' from Montreal, was rather strange.

Police were combing the area and knocked on the door of Room 15 at 3.45pm on 16 July. That morning Podola's picture had appeared in all the newspapers. Once the door was unlocked seven officers burst into the room led by 16-stone D.S. Albert Chambers. The door hit Podola in the face as he fell backwards over a chair and onto the floor. Chambers blundered on top of him. Other policemen seized the suspect's arms and legs as he writhed on the floor. This struggle lasted four or five minutes. Podola was searched and found to be carrying no gun (it was later found in the attic with extra rounds of ammunition). He was handcuffed to the bed and seen to be bleeding from a wound above his left eye. Officers later recalled 'a peculiar trembling, which was most noticeable in his hands'. The German started twitching and shaking so much that even Chambers thought his condition was 'very pitiful'.

Some newspapers wrote that Podola had been beaten up by the police, but he never made a complaint, nor did his legal team. He seemed to be in a stupor and had to be admitted to hospital. Tests revealed no fractures, but for some days he seemed barely aware of his surroundings and acted like a man suffering from shock. He was finally charged with D.S. Purdy's murder on 20 July and replied, 'What do you mean, I shot somebody?' In conversations he claimed to remember barely anything about his life before 17 July.

On 10 September Podola's trial began at the Old Bailey before Mr Justice Edmond-Davies. The main part was taken up with the question of whether the defendant was feigning amnesia. Six defence doctors called by Podola's counsel, Mr Frederick Lawton, Q.C., thought the memory loss was genuine. Two prosecution doctors concluded he was a highly intelligent malingerer.

On 23 July the jury were told to consider if the amnesia was genuine or not. They returned after 210 minutes to say that amnesia had not been established. A new jury was now sworn in – with the same judge and lawyers – for the real murder trial, which took two days. The evidence was hardly in doubt.

Killing policemen has always merited severe punishment. Podola was found guilty and condemned to death. The appeal judge noted: 'Even if the loss of memory had been a genuine loss of memory, that did not render the appellant insane.' Podola was hanged at Wandsworth – the moratorium on the death penalty now over – on 5 November 1959.

1960 Peeping Tom: Patrick Joseph Byrne

Ask most people to describe a psychopath and nine out of ten will conjure up the kind of knife-wielding maniac in horror films such as *Halloween* and *Friday the 13th*. Thankfully these kind of night stalkers are rare, but they do exist. Just such a man was the deranged killer who perpetrated what the press in 1960 called the 'Youth Hostel Horror'.

It was one day before Christmas Eve 1959 at Eden Croft, a rambling old Georgian-style mansion serving as a YWCA hostel in Wheeleys Road, Edgbaston, Birmingham. Fifty girls normally stayed there but several had already left to spend the holiday season with families and friends. Around 6pm Margaret Brown, a pretty 21-year-old Scots lass, was ironing in the washroom in the main block was she heard the door behind her open. She turned to see who it was and the lights went out. Margaret just had time to make out the shape of a man before she was struck a blow on the back of her head, a vicious attack softened a little by her bun of long hair. The girl screamed loudly. Her assailant ran off. Police were called. Not far away they found a heavy stone wrapped in a brassiere taken from the laundry line.

Searching the various buildings of the hostel the police came to Room 4 and found it locked from the inside. Calls to open the door met with no response. An officer nipped round to the outside window and peered in through the curtains. He saw a pair of legs on the floor. Hurriedly, police now broke into the room and the sight which greeted them was awful enough to put one officer on sick leave with shock for the next two months.

The victim was Sidney Stephanie Baird, an attractive 29-year-old from Bishop's Cleeve, Gloucestershire. There were no obvious clues as to her killer, apart from Margaret Brown's sketchy description. Christmas Day that year fell on a Friday making it a four-day holiday. Many local people were away over Christmas, while at the same time Birmingham had lots of visitors, one of whom might or might not be the murderer. There had been sightings of a bloodstained young man seen that night on a No. 8 bus. Despite appeals, no one came forward with further information on this person and he was never found.

Pathologists led by the eminent Francis Camps (of Christie murder fame) deduced that Stephanie had been manually strangled. Her skull was fractured and there were numerous lacerations on her body. She had not been raped. Detectives now got to work: 4,000 butchers were interviewed, as well as 700 medical students; every man with a history of violence living within 50 miles of Birmingham was seen and accounted for; every mental patient in the British Isles was checked; in all 2,000 house calls were made and 50,000 statements taken.

Eventually the police knocked on the door of a lodging house in Islington Avenue, Birmingham, where the manageress said one of her boarders, 28-year-old labourer Patrick Byrne, had left suddenly just before Christmas and not returned. Three thousand men in Birmingham had done much the same thing, but detectives continued on their trail and traced Byrne to his mother's house in Warrington, Lancashire. He was out when police called. They left a note asking him to report to the local police station and he duly turned up that afternoon. With a cheery smile and thick wavy hair he hardly seemed a murderer and helpfully filled in a questionnaire. Just as Byrne was leaving D.S. George Welborn asked: 'Is there anything else you would like to say about your stay in Birmingham?' After a brief silence, Byrne turned around and blurted, 'Yes... there is... yes. I want to tell you about the YWCA. I had something to do with that.' Police are used to people making false confessions, especially to sensational crimes, but the story Byrne told was so full, horrifying and detailed that it seemed clear he was Stephanie Baird's killer.

A Dubliner, Patrick Byrne, known to his friends as 'Acky', came from a large, happy family. He was especially devoted to his mother. A quiet lad, he left school at 14, was a good worker and later was discharged from the Royal Army Ordnance Corps with an excellent service record. Friends noticed that he was shy around girls. One of them remarked, 'He was good with kids ... they liked him.' Jean Grant, a young Birmingham woman, recalled that at a local social club, 'I used to drag him out of his corner to join in the fun. He never put his arms around me or kissed me goodnight ... I used to tell him I would walk home alone, but he said somebody might jump out and attack me.' She summed him up as 'such a nice fellow'.

Byrne told police that he was 17 when a middle-aged woman seduced him. Confused in his mind, 'I began to hate all women, yet I badly wanted to have a steady girlfriend.' On the night of 23 December he had decided to have a peep through the YWCA curtains, something he had done before. He entered the building through a window, saw a light on in Room 4, then stood on a chair to spy on Stephanie through a small window above the door. She was wearing a slip and jumper. He got 'browned off' when she didn't take off more clothes and was about to leave when the girl opened the door. An angry Stephanie asked him what he was doing and threatened to call the warden. Byrne tried to kiss her. The girl screamed, and he pushed her backwards into the room, strangling her and falling on top of her. 'I heard a couple of small noises in her throat, but kept on kissing her.' Once dead, Byrne mutilated the corpse using a table knife, cutting off a breast and throwing it onto the bed. Finally, in an act of bestial horror, he cut off Stephanie's head and held it up to the mirror for a closer study. Before leaving the room he left a note. It read: 'This is what I thought would never happen.'

Highly sexually excited, Byrne decided, 'I ought to terrorise all women. I would like to get my own back for causing me nervous tension through sex... I felt I only wanted to kill beautiful women.' His lusts aroused after murdering Miss Baird, he had roamed the old building until he spotted Margaret Brown in the washroom.

The important matter at Byrne's trial before Mr Justice Stable at the Birmingham Assizes in March related to his state of mind. He was clearly sexually abnormal but was he insane or not? Byrne did not dispute the acts he had committed but his defence was one of diminished responsibility. Three doctors were of the opinion that he was legally sane when he killed Stephanie. Defence counsel Mr R.K. Brown, Q.C. asked Dr Percy Coats, senior medical officer at Brixton Prison, 'Are you saying there was nothing wrong with his mind except these depraved desires to which he surrendered?' 'Yes,' replied the doctor. Byrne claimed to have a dual personality, possibly the result of a head injury when he was eight years old. Byrne told the court that he had returned to his lodgings after the killing and stared at himself for a long time in a bathroom mirror, 'talking to myself and searching my face for signs of a madman, but I could see none'. The all-male jury took 45 minutes to find him guilty of murder and he was sentenced to life imprisonment. In July 1960 the Court of Criminal Appeal quashed the sentence and substituted one of manslaughter on the grounds of diminished responsibility. This in reality had little effect on Byrne's incarceration as he posed such a grave risk to society. He served 33 years in prison, finally getting released on licence in 1993, but his subsequent behaviour gave the authorities cause for concern. His licence was revoked and Patrick Byrne was returned to prison in 1999.

1961–1970

Supposedly it was the 'Swinging Sixties', though the 'swing' outside the big cities happened more gently. British musicians such as The Beatles and The Rolling Stones, fashion designers like Mary Quant and her miniskirt were dominating culture around the world. With them came a wider use of recreational drugs, the Pill, and greater sexual permissiveness. The Cold War also reached its peak in the Cuban Missile Crisis and the world tottered on the brink of nuclear Armageddon. At home, a cabinet minister hit the headlines when he slept with a call girl who was a 'friend' of a Soviet intelligence agent.

In 1965 long-time abolitionist Sidney Silverman introduced a Private Member's Bill in the House of Commons, which passed on a free vote by 200 to 98. It even passed in the House of Lords by 204 to 104 votes. The Murder (Abolition of Death Penalty) Act of 1965 suspended the death penalty everywhere except for Northern Ireland for five years and substituted a mandatory life sentence. After five years, the Act would be voted on by both houses of Parliament to make it permanent. This actually happened in December 1969. Four years later its provisions were also adopted in Northern Ireland. One of the first reprieved was Patrick McCarron, a Scotsman who had shot his wife. Ironically, he hanged himself in prison in 1970. In total 3,471 persons were put on trial for murder, attempted murder or manslaughter.

1961 The Identikit Killer: Edwin Albert Bush

On 3 March 1961 an assistant, Mrs Elsie Batten, was found stabbed to death in a curio shop at 23 Cecil Court, Charing Cross Road, WC2.

She had been killed with a ceremonial dagger, the 9-inch blade buried to a depth of 8 inches in her chest. Mrs Batten's husband, Mark, was President of the Royal Society of British Sculptors.

The shop's owner, Louis Meier, recalled a Eurasian youth on the previous day who had shown a lot of interest in a curved dress sword and several daggers. 'He told me he was Indian and it was a common thing to carry a dagger in India,' said Mr Meier. After interviewing the shopkeeper, Detective Sergeant Raymond Dagg, attached to Bow Street station, was able to compile a facial picture of the suspect using 'Identikit' – a set of facial features on transparencies developed by Hugh Macdonald of the Los Angeles Police Department during the war years. The system had never been used in Britain for a murder hunt.

Five days later P.C. Arthur Cole, on duty in Old Compton Street, Soho, barely 10 minutes' walk from Cecil Court, saw a man answering the suspect's description and arrested 21-year-old Edwin Bush. He admitted the Identikit picture looked a 'bit' like him but denied having anything to do with the murder. His mother said he had also left home for work as normal about 7.30am on the day of the killing. Mr Meier failed to pick Bush out of an identity parade but another Cecil Court shop owner, Mr Paul Roberts, recognised him immediately. After being charged Bush made a statement saying, 'I am sorry I done it. I don't know what came over me. Speaking personally, the world is better off without me.'

It turned out that the young man had a troubled childhood. During his teens he had been in and out of borstal several times for burglary and theft. On the day of the crime he had returned to the shop after seeing Mr Meier and looked again at the dress sword. He was infuriated when Mrs Batten insultingly said, 'You niggers are all the same. You come in here and never buy anything.' He stabbed the woman, clubbed her with a vase, then stole the dress sword which he tried to sell elsewhere.

His trial began at the Old Bailey on 10 May before Mr Justice Stevenson. It lasted just two days and a jury quickly found him guilty of murder. He was hanged at Pentonville Prison on 6 July, the first murderer caught using the Identikit system. One aspect of the case sometimes overlooked is that under the terms of the Homicide Act 1957 if he had not stolen property he would not have been hanged. It was taking the dress sword – not the murder itself – that took him to the gallows.

1962 The Jigsaw Murder: James Smith

There is something appealing about old-style sweet shops. It has a lot to do with the way all the stock is arranged; large glass bottles of multi-coloured candies on the shelves, silk-ribboned boxes of chocolates in a glass-fronted display, chocolate bars next to the counter and a big set of scales to weigh out these toothsome delights. Most of these small shops have long gone. Hopefully a few remain in odd corners of the British Isles.

Just such a shop was run by 58-year-old Mrs Isabella Cross on the corner of Hulme Hall Lane and Iron Street in the Miles Platting district of Manchester. That was until Friday 4 May 1962 when she was clubbed to death by a killer who got away with just a paltry £6 that had been in her till. The murder had been committed using five large glass screw-top bottles of orange and cherryade. Fragments of glass littered the floor behind the counter where the dead woman lay. She had a 9-inch fracture to the skull. Police soon found a perfect set of fingerprints on a door frame. The killer had also dropped some coins from his pocket. The prints were on file. They belonged to 28-year-old James Smith, a greasy-haired, £15-per-week rubber moulder and father of two children. The dabs, however, only put Smith in the shop. They did not make him the murderer. When arrested he told D.I. Tom Butcher, 'I'll bet you a fiver I don't hang.'

The glass fragments from the shop had been taken to the North West Forensic Science Laboratory at Preston. When Smith's house was searched microscopic particles of glass (found using a modified vacuum cleaner) were in some of his clothing and also down the sides of a settee. These minute shards of glass were carefully sifted at the Preston laboratory and the bottles were rebuilt using glue. It was a painstakingly slow task.

Smith's trial began on 15 October and lasted three days. He simply denied ever having been in the shop. The forensic evidence was overwhelming. The jury took just 20 minutes to find him guilty. He was another killer who could have lived under the terms of the Homicide Act 1957, but murder in the furtherance of robbery or theft was still a hanging offence. Smith's date with the executioner was on the morning of 28 November 1962 at Strangeways Prison, Manchester. The bottles that helped hang him are on display in the Manchester City Police Black Museum.

1963 Not to Be Teased: Ted Donald Garlick

One might wonder how many murders might have been prevented in those years before mobile phones became indispensable. On the evening of 11 October 1962 a 16-year-old girl called Carol White phoned her boyfriend from a telephone box in West Drayton. When she did not return home her father went to the red kiosk and found her purse.

Next day 25-year-old Ted Garlick was out exercising his dog with other members of the family near their rented home in Hayes, Middlesex, when the dog ran into a field. Ted gave chase, or so he told the police later, and he stumbled over the body of Carol White. She had been stabbed several times. At first the police thought nothing was unduly suspicious until they discovered that Mrs Garlick had died in mysterious circumstances; apparently she and her husband had made a suicide pact but after her gassing, he had survived. He was charged with murder at that time but later acquitted. His mother-in-law had commented: 'God forgive you. He'll kill again.'

It then turned out that Carol must have been killed around 9.00 to 9.30pm and Garlick had been seen walking home around 10.00pm. Further police questions trapped him in a web of lies and he finally confessed. He even showed detectives the murder weapon. He claimed to have seen Carol standing by the phone box and they had got into a conversation about sex. Somehow she made a comment about his sexual inexperience that made him see red. 'I don't know how many times I stabbed her,' he said.

The man who may have killed twice was tried at the Old Bailey in February 1963, found guilty and sentenced to life imprisonment.

1964 The Last Two to Hang: Peter Anthony Allen & Gwynne Owen Evans

To the long litany of tragic lasts in human history – the last person to jump off the sinking *Titanic*, or the last soldier to be killed in the First or Second World War – must be added the last condemned man hanged in Britain. As if to emphasise this tawdry event, it was two men, not one, involved in a pathetically senseless killing. Thus, as the law dictated, with each man accusing the other of having been the real murderer, they had a date with the hangman on 13 August 1964. So ended several centuries of British judicial executions.

It was 3.55am on 7 April that D.I. John Gibson of the Cumberland & Westmoreland Constabulary was roused from his bed to investigate 'a serious incident', the body of a 53-year-old bachelor, John West, found on the stairs of his home at 28 King's Avenue, Workington, apparently bludgeoned to death and lying in a large pool of blood. Found on the floor was a foot-long strip of metal piping, covered in rubber and wrapped in pyjama trousers. Forensic examination would also reveal a knife wound to the heart on Mr West's corpse. It was established that he died about two hours before the police had been called by anxious neighbours who had heard a disturbance. West, a van driver for the Lakeland Laundry, was a quiet, respectable man and not known to have any enemies.

Searching the house, which did not appear to be ransacked, detectives found a suspicious raincoat folded over a chair in a bedroom. Inside was a wallet containing the name of a teenager, Miss Norma O'Brien, a set of keys, and a Royal Life Saving Society medal to a 'G. O. Evans, July 1961'. A call to the R.L.S.S. showed no medallion had been awarded to any 'G. O. Evans'. Miss O'Brien was traced and contacted. She was shown the medallion and said it belonged to a man she had met called 'Ginger Owen Evans'. More important perhaps, she recognised immediately the same man's overcoat. It would take the police a few days to realise that this man was Gwynne Evans, a known criminal with convictions for theft and fraud.

Meanwhile in nearby Ormskirk a woman had gone to the police on 8 April to say she was uneasy about a man who had come to her door earlier in an agitated state. He had left his car, a Ford Anglia, outside in an abandoned builder's yard. The police discovered the vehicle had been stolen in Preston. They took fingerprints.

In one of those amazing occurrences that happen in real life, that same afternoon two young men – one of them not wearing a shirt or jacket – together with a young woman carrying two infants, one a baby of 10 months, travelled by bus from Ormskirk to Preston. With them on the bus was a baby lamb. That night from a vicarage in Preston, they called the local R.S.P.C.A. where the woman, a 'Mrs Allen', said: 'We found the lamb on the road and couldn't see any sheep about so we've brought it with us.' They were vague where they had picked up the animal and the R.S.P.C.A. inspector thought them all a little bit odd. Little did he know that Mrs Allen and the infants had been in the stolen car and had sat in the vehicle while Mr West was killed, that her holdall contained her husband's bloodstained shirt and jacket and that, after finding a stray lamb and taking pity on it, they had proceeded all day 'without the great British public raising an eyebrow'.

Inexorably the police net closed on Peter Allen and his lodger and friend, Gwynne Evans, two unemployed men both with minor criminal records. Something of a 'simple dope', Allen's life had been more deprived than depraved. He had no record of violence and when finally interrogated admitted that he wanted to tell 'the whole flipping world' the truth. He and Evans had 'pinched' a car in Preston, put his wife and infants in the back, 'but the wife didn't know what was going on', their aim being to steal from a bloke 'Sandy Evans' said 'had money lying about'. Allen said he had struck Mr West with his fists at first, then twice used the metal cosh. The men had hurriedly found some cash and cheque books in a bedroom and grabbed the lot.

'I'm glad you found me,' said Allen, 'Who am I to take a human life? All I wanted was £100 for a deposit on a house.' The police noted that the suspect made no reference to a knife or stab wound.

By contrast, Evans in his first interview talked of a knife, but said he was an expert at karate, so would not need a weapon to kill. He claimed 'Peter did all the hitting'. In a detailed statement Evans claimed that Allen 'always carried a knife or a cosh... the killing was all Peter's fault I never once hit him.'

In her statement Mrs Allen blamed both men for the deed. She had no idea of what they were planning that night. She explained that Sandy Evans had been in control. The police had found out that Evans was a congenital liar and fantasist – in fact he was not Welsh at all, though he adopted a phony accent in the dock at his trial, but had been born in 1940 at Maryport, Cumberland, and christened John Robson Walby. Evans told police that he was really a German and born in Innsbruck, Austria. Detectives found that as a child Walby/Evans had mental health issues and a psychiatric report noted him as 'showing a vivid imagination'. His skills at karate were minimal at best.

The trial of the two men began at the Manchester Assizes, No. 3 Court, on 23 June before Mr Justice Ashworth. The forensic evidence was overwhelming and linked both men to the scene of the crime. In his summing-up, the judge explained to the jury: 'Right at the heart of the case lies the problem who did murder West? Was it Allen or Evans or both? Let me give you this direction. If two men agree to kill or do grievous bodily harm to a man, and he dies, then both men are guilty of murder, even if only one deals the fatal blow. But, of course, the prosecution must prove that there was, in the minds of both men, the intent to kill or do grievous bodily harm.'

At the time the law allowed one of three possible verdicts: not guilty, guilty of murder and guilty of capital murder. It took the jury 195 minutes to find both defendants guilty of capital murder. Mr Justice Ashworth thus had no alternative but to condemn the two men 'to suffer death in the manner authorised by law...' In Walton Gaol, Liverpool, Peter Allen went totally berserk when his appeal was rejected, smashing up and his cell and breaking a bulletproof glass window. Evans got a last letter from Mrs Allen in which she wrote: 'Believe me, Sandy, all the lies you have told will do you no good.' Within two years she had married an old friend of her husband's, but died comparatively young, aged 37 years, in 1980.

Her none-too-bright first husband and his lying mate who had been dumb enough to leave his coat and wallet at the crime scene are now not quite forgotten. They remain footnotes in any discussion of the death penalty in England as well a source of fun for pub quizzes. Their case was full of little ironies, from the lamb they saved within hours of killing a man, to the awfully tragic fact that Peter Allen was executed for a senseless crime caused because he wanted a paltry £100 as a down payment on a house for his wife and kids.

1965 The Bubble Car Murders: Michael Copeland

A cyclist on 12 June 1960 was using an isolated moor path, part of Clod Hall Lane, near Baslow Hill, outside Chesterfield, and came across the shoeless and bludgeoned body of an elderly man. Earlier in the day, local police had found a small 'bubble car' (one of the motoring symbols of the late 1950s and early '60s) smashed into a lamp post in the town. The inside of the car was covered in bloodstains and a pair of men's shoes were on the floor. The police, naturally enough, at first thought they were dealing with the survivor of a traffic accident. The bubble car was traced to the dead man – 60-year-old bachelor and known predatory homosexual William Elliott, a resident of Baslow.

Forensic experts thought Mr Elliott's death was due to his head being stamped on by someone wearing heavy boots. A witness came forward to say she had seen a man answering Mr Elliott's description being chased up a dark alley on the day of the murder. There had been a scuffle. His assailant was a younger, skinny, dark-haired man. Police questioned several likely suspects including Michael Copeland, a 20-year-old conscript on home leave in Chesterfield. He had a minor criminal record, was reckoned to be violent and had bragged to a girl that he had murdered a man. Detectives could find no direct link between the soldier and the murder and he was allowed to return to his unit.

Four months later Guenther Helmbrecht, a 16-year-old German boy, was stabbed to death while strolling in a forest with his girlfriend near Verden, Germany. A few hours later Copeland staggered into his nearby barracks with a knife wound in his leg, later claiming he had fought off an attack from Guenther's deranged killer. The West German police and British Military Police were not so sure, but at an identity parade Mr Helmbrecht's girlfriend failed to pick Copeland out of a line-up and he was freed.

Completing his National Service, the young suspect returned home. On 29 March 1961, in what the newspapers quickly labelled 'The

Carbon Copy Murder', George Stobbs, a 48-year-old married industrial chemist, was murdered on the moor in almost exactly the same spot as the 1960 killing. His car, a Morris Oxford, was also found abandoned and there were injuries to the victim's head, at first listed as caused by a boot, but later confirmed as done by a hammer. Copeland was again under suspicion and put under careful surveillance. In October he went to the *News of the World* and they printed an article entitled 'Murder Seems To Follow Me Around But I Am Innocent' in which Copeland talked of 'police lies', of having a 'wonderful' girlfriend, a steady job and just wanting a normal life – 'surely, that's not too much to ask.'

Over the weeks and months D.I. Ernest Bradshaw of the Chesterfield Police had long talks with Copeland and became almost an uncle figure. In November 1963 Copeland finally confessed his three murders to D.I. Bradshaw. He said he regretted killing the German youth, but had been angered by the way that the boy was having sex with his girlfriend in the same way that he had seen his own mother have intercourse. Elliott and Stobbs had to die, he claimed, because they were homosexuals, 'something I really hated'. Elliott had tried to give him a blowjob in the bubble car, and Stobbs had also importuned him. Police discovered that Copeland was bisexual and his killings seemed to be triggered by a love-hate attitude to his homosexual tendencies and a rage triggered by sex acts. Six days before murdering Mr Elliott, he had raped a 64-year-old man and in the spring of 1961 committed a gross indecency on another elderly man. About this time a homosexual had been viciously attacked in a Chesterfield public toilet. He described his assailant as having a military background.

Tried at the Birmingham Assizes, Copeland now said that his confession had been a pack of lies – he had never made a formal statement – told deliberately to allow him to prove his innocence in public and get the surveillance lifted. A jury felt otherwise and Michael Copeland was condemned to death. With capital punishment under review in England, his sentence was duly committed to life imprisonment. It is believed that he spent some years in Durham Prison and also Broadmoor.

1966 The Moors Murders: Ian Duncan Brady & Myra Hindley

He thought himself a Nietzschean super-god. She was his queen. He told her that power was his aphrodisiac, power over the life and death of others, power to behave without any human constraints like a character in one of the novels of his beloved Marquis de Sade. Together they seemed unable to comprehend the simplest of facts – that with power comes responsibility.

Hindley died after 36 years in captivity. Brady died on 15 May 2017, Britain's longest-serving prisoner. He had said that he did not want to be released. The couple's murders of at least four youngsters, strangled, mutilated, buried in lonely spots on bleak moorland – along with the axe murder of a youth – are horrible crimes. Even more shocking is the sadistic delight of Brady and Hindley in these deeds: taking photographs, eating picnics on the graves of their victims and at least in one instance recording the screams and terror of a 10-year-old girl as they sexually assaulted and mutilated her body. Being in the Castle Courtroom at Chester Assizes on 19 April 1966 and hearing those obscene tapes was perhaps the most shocking moment in any British murder trial before or since.

Brady was born Ian Duncan Stewart in Glasgow on 2 January 1938. His mother was an unemployed tearoom waitress who married a Patrick Brady in 1950. By that time, Ian had spent most of his life in the foster home of a kindly local family named Sloan. The boy showed intelligence from an early age and did well at primary school. He later claimed his childhood was a happy one with lots of friends. Some writers insist that he was cruel to animals, but Brady always denied these accusations saying, 'I prefer animals to people.' At school his nickname was 'Dracula' because he loved horror movies. His only act of rebellion was to tell a Sunday school teacher that there was no God. He passed his exams and went to 'posh' Shawlands Academy where staff later recalled him as 'withdrawn, quite a clever boy'. At 12 his pet dog died and a visibly upset Ian renounced God and called himself an atheist. His early teens saw the start of his obsession with the Nazis and he began collecting Nazi memorabilia.

One year later he was accused of his first offences – housebreaking and theft – and got two years' probation. A further housebreaking charge saw him in the dock in 1952. He left school the next year and drifted haphazardly from menial job to job, frustrated and dissatisfied with life. In November 1954, after another court appearance for theft and housebreaking, a lenient judge allowed Brady to walk free. He immediately boarded a train to Manchester, got reunited with a mother he had not seen in six years and took on the persona of 'Ian Brady'. Twelve months later he was in court again on a charge of stealing the lead labels off banana boxes. Probably Brady anticipated a fine. He got, instead, two years in borstal.

On his release, using some skills in bookkeeping acquired while in borstal, Brady tried to get office jobs and finally settled in 1959 as a

£9-a-week stock clerk at Millwoods Merchandising, a small firm supplying chemicals to the cotton industry. It was here that he met 18-year-old Myra Hindley, who joined the typing pool in 1961. She was a 'slinky candyfloss blonde' who had left school happily days after her 15th birthday. In many ways Myra was a typical teenager of her class and generation. Her passions were pop music (especially Elvis Presley and The Beatles), along with jiving at the local palais, socialising with her girlfriends and toying with a succession of Mancunian lads.

Soon Myra was besotted with the stock clerk with the thick wavy hair and brooding lower lip. He seemed to know so much about books, films, music and a hundred other subjects. She also found him sexy. They began dating and gradually Brady led his lover into his world – a place where radio shows such as *The Goon Show*, TV satire in *That Was The Week That Was*, and movies such as *West Side Story* and *Dr No*, contrasted with readings aloud from the works of de Sade or books on sexual murders. Sitting in Myra's lounge (her Gran asleep upstairs), the pair would open a bottle of Liebfraumilch (the trendy wine of the early 1960s), listen to classical music, discuss philosophy and torture, then act out some of Ian's fantasies. These included urinating in Myra's mouth, anal sex, and occasionally allowing her to adopt a more dominant role by inserting a lighted candle in his backside. In public she was ordered by Brady to dress more provocatively in short skirts and leather jackets in homage to Irma Grese, the notorious Nazi concentration camp guard whom Ian adored. In the office at Millwards, colleagues thought them increasingly surly and unsociable. Frequently the couple would drive up onto high Saddleworth Moor outside the city and picnic. Here Ian began to talk of 'switching on the dark' – of closing their minds to normal emotions and conventions by murdering a child. In these talks he spoke little of paedophile urges but wanted Myra to join him in experiencing the sadistic delights of a child's suffering. The pair went to see the 1959 film *Compulsion*, about the 1924 U.S. killers Leopold and Loeb, who had tried to commit a perfect murder. Thus, as Brady later wrote, he and Hindley began to think of themselves as 'demon folk', above and superior to 'normal, mundane' people. Hindley, once a Roman Catholic who now embraced her lover's atheism, later wrote: 'We became our own Gods.'

They set a date for their perfect murder – 12 July 1963. That evening Myra in her car picked up 16-year-old Pauline Reade on her way to a dance. Brady followed on his motorbike. Outside the city, up on Hollin Brown Knoll, Saddleworth Moor, the killers sexually assaulted the girl, and Brady cut her throat, burying her in a peat grave. The pair then went to Myra's house and had passionate sex.

By autumn, Brady at least was thirsting to kill again. This time he wanted his victim to be a real child. On 23 November the pair managed to abduct 12-year-old John Kilbride from the marketplace at Ashton-under-Lyme with the offer of a lift home. Driving up to Hollin Brown Knoll, they asked the boy to help them look for a glove. Here, in this bleak place, Brady raped the child, then strangled him, throwing his corpse into a makeshift grave.

Eight months later Myra in her white Mini Traveller abducted another 12-year-old boy, Keith Bennett. Brady murdered and buried him in the same fashion as John Kilbride.

Lesley Ann Downey was an angelic-faced 10-year-old who enjoyed a happy Christmas Day with her three brothers and parents in their council flat in Ancoats, Manchester. On Boxing Day she went to a local fair. Brady and Hindley asked the little girl to help them carry some boxes to their car. She agreed. Lesley was seized and taken to Myra's home at 12 Wardle Brook Avenue, Hattersley, 10 miles east of the city centre. There her two tormentors stripped her naked and abused her. They recorded the child's terror and took solo pornographic pictures. A shocked courtroom would later have to listen to two tapes and hear such things as Lesley screaming: 'Please, God, help me please, oh,' and the girl whimpering as Hindley said roughly: 'Put it in your mouth, and keep it in... Shut up or I'll forget myself and hit you one – keep it in!' Who actually killed Lesley has never been cleared up. Brady insisted that on this occasion it was Myra who did the strangling. She later admitted 'there was blood everywhere'. The pair cleaned up, then curled up on the lounge sofa to make love. Above them on that Boxing Day, and while her own family were frantic with worry, Lesley's body lay trussed up in a bedsheet. She too was buried on the moors.

The police were now in full hue and cry but without any strong leads. Brady and Hindley, as yet unsatiated by their killings, now longed to have a disciple, a 'Peter' or 'rock' to join in their fun. They thought they had found him in David Smith, Myra's 17-year-old brother-in-law. What they got – at least in their eyes – was a Judas Iscariot. Smith had seemed fascinated by the Nazis, by Ian's lectures on power and the Marquis de Sade, but he was no cold-hearted murderer. At 11pm on 6 October 1965, Smith visited his relatives. He was talking to Myra in the kitchen when screams were heard and she asked David to help Ian in the lounge. Smith rushed in to see 'a young lad about 17-years-old... Ian was standing over him... a hatchet in his hand... the lad half-fell or half-wriggled off the couch, onto the floor, onto his stomach... Ian... kept hacking away at the young lad. I don't know how many times he hit the lad with the hatchet, but it was a lot... I felt my stomach turn... There was blood all over the place...' Hindley watched from the door. When it was all over Brady said, 'It's the messiest yet. It normally only takes one blow.'

That night in his own bed Smith lay shivering with the awful realisation that Brady and Hindley wanted to test him and see if he could be trusted. He was appalled by the crime and also the nonchalant way in which the killers had cleaned up the mess, laughed and joked about the murder over a pot of tea, and talked of other bodies buried up on the moors. Fearful for his life, at 6am on 7 October, David Smith called the police. Detectives found the bludgeoned body of 17-year-old Edward Evans. Brady and Hindley's spree-killing days were over.

The trial began at the Chester Assizes on 19 April 1966 before Mr Justice Fenton Atkinson. The case was world news and the prosecution was led by the Attorney-General, Sir Frederick Elwyn-Jones, Q.C. Accused of the Downey and Kilbride murders, Brady admitted 'games' with the children but said that he had left them unharmed. In the case of Evans he said there had been an argument. He basically claimed that Myra had done his bidding and the pair clearly banked that she would get a minimal sentence. It took a jury 150 minutes on 6 May to find Brady guilty of all three murders. Hindley was found guilty of the Downey and Evans murders and of assisting Brady in the murder of John Kilbride. For each murder they received a life sentence.

It was not until 1986 that Hindley confessed to the killings of Reade and Bennett. With Myra's assistance, Pauline's body was recovered from her moorland grave (Downey and Kilbride had been found before the trial). Brady had been asked many times to help with the search for Keith Bennett's remains. He was even allowed a trip to the moor, a visit denounced in the press. At times he had seemed to relish the power he still had and the police remain convinced that he knew exactly where he buried the body. They also think there may have been other victims. From his prison cell, Brady penned an extraordinary study of serial killers and defended his position: 'There is little intellectual or spiritual inducement for the captured serial killer to co-operate in any way. To all intents and purposes, his real life is over and done with, as he knows he shall never be free again, so why should he volunteer information...' Considering the pain and suffering his murders caused, especially to the Bennett family, who still have no release from their misery, Brady's self-centred remarks are typical of the sexual psychopathic killer, a man who thinks he is above normal morality and without any empathy for humankind. To the end he seemed content to die in gaol – Britain's most hated man.

1967 The Red Mini Murder: Raymond Sidney Cook, Eric Jones & Valerie Dorothy Newell

The most interesting murder case of 1967 was also a classic tale of detection. It demonstrated how even a humble police constable, if alert and intelligent, can do much to bring a murderer to justice.

About 10pm on 2 March a P.C. Sherlock – an apt name – stationed at Nettlebed near Henley-on-Thames was patrolling in a radio police car. He was ordered to the scene of a reported traffic accident on the road through Rummerhedge Wood, about 3 miles away. He found two cars lighting up a crashed red Morris Mini with its front bumper up against a beech tree. The two occupants of the Mini – a dazed male passenger and an unconscious female driver – had already been rushed to hospital. One of the men standing by the cars said that when he arrived a man had been standing over the woman. He offered to fetch some towels from his car but had driven away.

P.C. Sherlock noted that there was very little external damage to the crashed mini apart from the front bumper. The windscreen was intact. Inside the car, the driver's side was covered in blood. When he telephoned the hospital in Reading, he was told the woman was now dead and the man was comatose from alcohol. Off went Sherlock to the hospital where he heard that the woman had been admitted with severe head injuries and, though alive, had died a short time later. He concluded that the man was not really drunk but suffering from shock. He was Raymond Cook, a 32-year-old draughtsman, and the dead woman was his wife, 41-year-old teacher and mother of two boys June Cook. Sherlock offered to drive Mr Cook to his home in Spencers Wood, a suburb of Reading. During the journey he thought it odd that Cook was able to give very precise instructions to his address, but lapsed into vague mumblings whenever he brought up the subject of the accident. Next day Sherlock told his superiors that he did not think damage to the car could account for Mrs Cook's shocking head injuries. Why was her husband not injured at all, and who was the man who had driven away from the scene of the crash?

With these suspicions in mind, P.C. Sherlock went to see the red Mini in the garage where it had been taken. In the sunshine he noticed that the outside was spattered in blood. He spotted a hair soaked in blood sticking to the offside rear wheel. He also met with Cook's in-laws who lived in the house next door to him and their daughter. They gave Sherlock the impression that the marriage was on the skids and that Raymond was a philanderer. Cook volunteered a statement saying he had taken his wife for a meal in Pangbourne. On the way home he had felt sick and stopped the car. She took over the driving. Soon after, a car with dazzling headlamps had approached them and he remembered nothing more.

Luck now stepped in to help the police: a witness came forward to say he had seen a dark-coloured Ford Cortina leaving the scene of the accident; when Sherlock and Sergeant McMiken, the scene-of-crime officer, returned to the site to take photographs they planted the camera tripod quite by chance next to a large bloodstain on the gravel 75 yards from the damaged tree; a pathologist confirmed no woman could have walked to the car from that spot with such severe head injuries. When a detective called on Cook and asked to see the clothes he had worn on the night of the crash, he said that they had been cleaned and he had burnt his driving gloves. Further investigation revealed that in the previous autumn Cook had deserted his wife and gone to live with a younger woman, Valerie Newell, known as 'Kim', a nurse at a nearby mental hospital. A longer search of the crash site revealed skull bone fragments. After a post-mortem it was concluded that June Cook had died from blows to the head delivered by a blunt instrument. The case was now handed over to Detective Superintendent Ian Forbes of Scotland Yard's Murder Squad.

Publicity helped the case enormously; a house painter, Angus Macdonald, recalled a blue Ford Cortina being driven into Reading from the Oxford direction on the night of the murder. He even remembered noting the number – 7711 FM. Detectives learned that the Cook–Newell affair had not ended and Raymond had seen his girlfriend on the Saturday after his wife's death. Kim Newell was known locally as a sexy blonde with a string of lovers.

Eventually the Ford Cortina was traced to a plant hire firm in Wrexham. The driver, Eric Jones, claimed to have been in London on 2 March but was nowhere near Reading.

D.S. Forbes found that under the terms of June Cook's will, her husband would gain about £10,000 from her death. There was also a motor insurance policy for an extra £1,000 if she died in a traffic accident. On 17 March Cook was formally charged with his wife's murder. Putting pressure on Jones and Newell led the man to admit that she was his old flame and that he had visited her on the night of the killing in Reading but he still denied knowing anything about the crime. Newell soon told a different tale: Jones had been her lover when she was 16 and made her pregnant; she confessed that all three had planned the murder and Jones had killed Mrs Cook using a car jack. On 16 April Newell was arrested and later that same day Jones confessed to his part in the crime.

Cook, Jones and Newell were soon in the dock at the Oxford Assizes. Jones changed his plea to guilty to murder and gave evidence for the prosecution. He told the court that there had been more than one rehearsal for the killing. Newell was later charged as an accessory before the fact. All three were given life sentences. Murderers are not allowed to benefit from the wills of their victims and so June Cook's £10,651 went to her sons.

The press during the trial had a field day with 23-year-old Newell who was described as 'having the morals of an alley cat'. It was said that she made Jones abort her baby. To get him to kill Mrs Cook, she had blackmailed him using the abortion as the inducement with a threat to make it public. Throughout the trial, including nine hours in the witness box, she wore tight-fitting costumes that enhanced her busty physique and seemed to love the attention of the press photographers. In prison she gave birth to a baby boy fathered by Raymond Cook. (He was brought up by her mother in Wales.) Freed after 12 years, she returned to Wales and worked in a school. She died aged 47 years in 1990. Shortly before her death Kim Newell showed some remorse and said of June Cook, 'She didn't deserve to die.' Asked about her ex-lovers, Cook and Jones, she replied disdainfully, 'I never loved them. I only loved my dog.'

1968 Bad Seed: Mary Flora Bell

Thankfully, murders committed by children are exceptionally rare, multiple killings even more so. In 1968 the nation was shocked by an 11-year-old girl who was charged with killing two infants. To make matters worse she appeared to revel in the murders, admitted they had given her pleasure, and showed every sign of a severe psychopathic disorder. Her subsequent trial, incarceration, release and later life have all contributed to making Mary Bell Britain's most famous child killer.

On 25 May the body of four-year-old Martin Brown was found by some boys in a derelict house in Newcastle. It looked at first as if the toddler had eaten pills out of a bottle found at the site and an inquest recorded an open verdict. Two girls, Mary Bell and Norma Bell (not relatives), aged 10 (Mary's 11th birthday was two days away) and 11 respectively, had tried to follow the boys into the building. Told to go away, they called on Martin's aunt and gave her the news. Next day a nursery was burgled and trashed. A note was left which read: 'WE did murder Martain brown. Fuck of you bastard.' Three days later Mary Bell knocked on the Browns' front door and asked to see Martin. 'No, pet,' said Mrs Brown, 'Martin's dead.' 'Oh, I know he's dead,' said Mary, 'I wanted to see him in his coffin.' Mrs Brown slammed the door in the smirking faces and collapsed on the floor. Two days later Mary and Norma were caught inside the nursery but they denied the earlier break-in.

Brian Howe, a toddler of three years and four months, went missing on 31 July. Mary took part in a search and told the little boy's sister that he might be playing among some concrete blocks on wasteland. That evening, among the blocks, Brian's body was found covered with long grass and purple weeds. He had been manually strangled. A small pair of scissors with a broken blade lay near his body and the boy had puncture marks on his legs. A pathologist concluded that very little pressure had been exerted to strangle the infant and the hands used most probably were those of a child. The police sent a questionnaire to children in the area and the answers given by Mary and Norma led to them being interviewed. Mary talked of seeing an eight-year-old boy with scissors walking with Brian (the police had not released any information on the scissors), but it turned out that the lad had a perfect alibi. On 4 August Norma confessed that she had gone with Mary and viewed Brian's corpse. 'I squeezed his neck and pushed up his lungs,' said Mary, 'that's how you kill them.' It later was revealed that she liked to gently massage the necks of smaller children before applying more and more pressure. Norma led the police to a razor blade hidden under a rock at the site. Further forensic examination showed faint razor scratches on Brian's body, which made the letter 'M'.

Detectives found that on 10 May both girls had been playing with a toddler who was severely injured by a fall. In police files were complaints from three mothers that Mary had tried to squeeze the throats of their daughters. She had even been slapped by Norma's father after he caught her trying to squeeze the throat of a sister. Mary made a highly detailed statement blaming everything on Norma. Both girls were charged with Brian Howe's murder. Mary simply replied: 'That's all right by me.'

Mary Bell's background was a sordid one. Her mother was a young prostitute who specialised in female domination. It appears that Mary witnessed her mother inflicting pain on clients. Her father was a small-time crook who was frequently drunk. The little girl had often been dumped with relatives. Police found Betty Bell's house to be filthy and sparsely furnished. From day one, little love had been lavished on Mary and she grew up with little, if any, empathy for others.

The trial of the two girls began on 3 December 1968 at the Newcastle Assizes before kindly Mr Justice Cusack who allowed the defence team to sit with their client. The press noted Mary's 'intellectually very alive' and pretty face: 'All in court were to be amazed by her astonishing ability to assimilate what she heard witnesses say and turn it to her own advantage.' Both girls accused one another of Brian's killing and denied having anything to do with Martin's murder. The police, however, had found a very accurate drawing of Martin's death in one of Mary's school books. Four psychiatrists all attested that Mary was psychopathic, 'an unsocialised, manipulative personality'. They noted how Mary had chatted about the killings quite unemotionally. One of the doctors said: 'I've seen a lot of psychopathic children, but I've never met one like Mary: as intelligent, as manipulative, as dangerous.'

Slow-thinking and inarticulate Norma was quickly seen as Mary's foil and duly acquitted of all charges. Mary was found guilty of manslaughter on the grounds of diminished responsibility. During the trial she had made some interesting remarks to her warders. She told one that she wanted to become a nurse, 'because then I can stick needles in people. I like hurting people'; while on another occasion she said of sentencing: 'If I was a judge and I had an eleven-year-old who's done this, I'd give her eighteen months... Murder isn't that bad. We all die sometime anyway.'

The Home Office had no idea of how to deal with an 11-year-old psychopathic killer. Mary was sent to a 'secure unit' inside a boys' approved school (though she was later moved to an all-girls institution). In September 1977 she briefly escaped with two boys and later claimed to have had sex with one of them. She was released from Askham Lodge after 11 years in 1980 and given a new name. Mary was 23 years old. Four years later she gave birth to a baby girl. It was 16 years before the press broke Mary's anonymity and her daughter learned the truth. In 2003 Mary won a High Court battle to have her anonymity and that of her daughter extended for life. Any court order protecting the anonymity of a convict is now called a 'Mary Bell order'. In 2009 it was reported that Mary became a grandmother. On hearing this news the mother of Martin Brown commented: 'I will never see a grandchild from my son. I hope every time she looks at this baby she realises what my family are missing out on...'

The journalist Gitta Sereny wrote two important books on this case, with much help from Mary. Can a psychopath be 'cured' as Mary claims to have been, or is this a masking of truth, a distortion of her mental make-up? Whatever the answer, she will always remain an intriguing criminal, and worthy of study.

1969 East End Legends: Reginald & Ronald Kray

In 2015 the Kray Twins were honoured with a second major motion picture about their lives as East End gangsters. The film had scant regard for historical fact and was right only in respect of its title – *Legend*. It showed handsome actor Tom Hardy in the dual roles of kindly Reggie Kray and nutter Ronnie Kray. The boys loved their old mum, ran the story, were charitable to fellow cockneys, only beat up other gangsters such as the Richardsons and rang rings around the stupid police led by Detective Superintendent 'Nipper' Read, their nemesis. Such is the immortality of London's best loved bad boys, an image far removed from truth or the gritty reality of events in the mid-1960s.

The two murders most infamously associated with the Krays – the shooting of George Cornell in the Blind Beggar pub by Ronnie and the stabbing of Jack 'the Hat' McVitie by Reggie – were tawdry crimes carried out in full view of witnesses. Such was the fear the Krays exerted over their fellow cockneys and even their own gang members that it looked for a long time as if they could get away with murder. Read and his team were far from stupid; to close down London's most fearsome gang, with tentacles spreading into West End clubland and as far as the U.S. Mafia, required much time and diligence. Eventually the two brothers were arrested in dawn raids on 9 May 1968. Twenty-eight criminals were offered immunity from prosecution if they talked. Witnesses now started to come forward once they knew the Kray Twins were safely behind bars.

Their trial before Mr Justice Melford Stevenson, a tough judge, began at the Old Bailey in January 1969 and lasted 39 days. Reggie Kray declined to give evidence, since both brothers accused the police of stitching them up, but Ronnie stupidly shot his mouth off in the dock, calling prosecuting counsel Kenneth Jones, Q.C. 'a fat slob' and yelling at the judge, 'You're biased too!' While they were being sentenced to life imprisonment, Mr Justice Stevenson made a recommendation that the twins should each serve not less than 30 years. It was a hard sentence deliberately designed to frighten London's underworld and it worked a treat. Never again would one 'outfit' come to dominate the city's crime. Ronnie Kray died in Broadmoor Criminal Lunatic Asylum in 1995.

Reggie Kray, aged 67 years, was released in 2000 suffering the final stages of terminal cancer.

Such was their ill fame that books, TV documentaries and movies have been churned out. The historian Donald Thomas has suggested this is all perfectly natural as the Kray Twins fit 'neatly into a vogue for working-class history... as icons of the 1960s'. Sadly the allure of these two villains has quickly given them a gloss out of all proportion to their dreadful doings.

1970 Pigs Will Eat Anything: Arthur & Nizamodeen Hosein

For anyone who likes a good mystery one of the best in the latter half of the 20th century is the kidnapping and murder of Mrs Muriel McKay. Two brothers were given life sentences for her killing and yet no trace of a *corpus delicti* was ever found. The full story of why and how she was kidnapped, who masterminded the plot as well as where, when and how she died seems unsolvable.

Fifty-five-year-old Muriel was the wife of Alick McKay, deputy chairman of News Ltd, tycoon Rupert Murdoch's publishing group that included the world's biggest-selling Sunday newspaper, the *News of the World*. The McKays, like Murdoch, were Australians and had lived in England for 12 years, making their home at 20 Arthur Road, Wimbledon, in a smart, red-brick mock-Georgian mansion close to the Common.

Mrs McKay's fate was probably settled on 30 October 1969 when Murdoch was interviewed on television by presenter David Frost. The press baron had recently married a young and attractive wife and the programme made reference to her as well as Mr Murdoch's acquisition in the previous January of the *News of the World* for several million pounds. The show left no one in doubt that Murdoch was super-rich. Clearly, if his wife was kidnapped, he could afford to pay a king's ransom. Unbeknown to the plotters, Mr and Mrs Murdoch set off for Australia just before Christmas on six weeks' vacation. Alick McKay was left in charge as temporary chairman. He was also given use of the chairman's car, a chauffeur-driven dark blue Rolls-Royce.

On 19 December, as the Murdochs jetted off to Sydney, a 'dark-skinned man' turned up at County Hall saying his car had been in a slight accident with a Rolls-Royce ULO 18F and asked for the home address of the owner. The enquirer gave his name as Shariff Mustapha and an address in Norbury Crescent (police were to find the name unknown, but the address corresponded to friends of Nizamodeen Hosein, while the writing on the form matched an application he had at one time made to join the RAF).

Monday 29 December was the first day the shops were open after the long Christmas weekend. Mrs McKay rushed around Wimbledon, saw her dentist in the West End and drove her daily help home at teatime. She must have been back home by 5.40pm, settling down to a cup of tea and the evening papers. Around 5.50pm it is believed someone rang her doorbell. Ten minutes later a passing neighbour saw a dark-coloured car in the driveway. Alick McKay returned at 7.45pm and was surprised to find his front door unlocked (the family had suffered a burglary three months previously, losing most of Muriel's jewellery, and now locked and bolted the front door). In the hall the scene was described by a detective 'as if it had been set up for an amateur production of an Agatha Christie thriller...' The telephone cable was wrenched from the wall and the contents of Muriel's handbag scattered across the stairs. Her pet dachshund dozed undisturbed by a roaring log fire. Detectives noted some odd objects lying about – a ball of twine, a strip of 2½-inch adhesive tape and a wooden-handled farmer's billhook. Mrs McKay was missing along with £600 worth of her jewellery (about £18,000 today).

That same night at 1pm Alick McKay got a call from a public kiosk in Epping. The caller, who sounded American or Caribbean, said: 'This is Mafia Group M3. We are from America... We have your wife... We tried to get Rupert Murdoch's wife. We could not get her, so we took yours instead. Have £1,000,000 by Wednesday night or we will kill her!' Alick McKay was in a terrible dilemma. The threat gave him just 24 hours to appease the kidnappers and the ransom demand was colossal by 1970 standards (about £30 million today). Soon he and the McKay children would fall out with the police over their handling of the case; he accused them of being slow and they disliked the way the press were given too much information. Over the next 38 days the McKays were to receive another 22 menacing phone calls although the increasingly frustrated kidnappers altered their demands to £1 million in two instalments. Four letters were received from Muriel in her handwriting (postmarked Wood Green, London, N22). The first began: 'Dear Alick, I am deteriorating in health and spirit... I am blindfolded and cold. The earlier you get the money, the quicker I may come home.'

A Hertfordshire drop-off using two suitcases full of fake money and detectives dressed as a chauffeur and one of the McKay sons had to be aborted. Watching officers did notice a cruising Volvo with a nearside rear light not working. On the snowy night of 6 February a second drop near Bishop's Stortford also failed to produce a satisfactory result. Detectives noted a blue Volvo, XGO994G, cruising past the suitcases. Next morning a party of police led by Detective Superintendent Wilfred Smith descended on Rook's Farm, Stocking Pelham, Hertfordshire, a thatched and white-painted old farmhouse with 14 acres of grounds. Parked outside they noted the same Volvo seen on the previous night. Its nearside lights did not work.

The owner of the farm was Arthur Hosein, a 'vain and natty little man' who was known to be ambitious, boastful and volatile. He had emigrated from Trinidad in 1955 for a better life in Britain. At first things had gone badly but he had gradually built up a successful tailoring business, specialising in trousers, and claimed to earn £1,500 a week. Arthur had no criminal record, though he had absconded from the army. A main room in the beamed and chintzy farmhouse had been turned into a workshop. Arthur was married with two children. Also living at the farm was his younger brother, Nizamodeen, who worked simply as a labourer, apparently for pocket money. He was an introverted and highly emotional young man who had come to Britain only in 1969. The Hosein Brothers seemed an odd pair and had quarrelled so badly over Nizamodeen's 29-year-old girlfriend on Boxing Day that there had been a punch-up. A distraught Nizamodeen called the police but later declined to press charges.

Circumstantial evidence began to pile up around the Hoseins: the billhook found at Wimbledon was positively identified by a local farmer as one that he had loaned the brothers; stationery at Rook's Farm matched the ransom letters; Arthur's prints were found on a cigarette packet left in a ransom telephone kiosk along with a thumb print on one of Mrs McKay's letters. During interviews a distraught Nizamodeen at one point threatened to spill all the beans before clamming up. Arthur arrogantly denied everything.

The Hosein Brothers' trial began in No. 1 Court, Old Bailey, on 14 September 1970 before Mr Justice Sebag Shaw with the Attorney-General, Sir Peter Rawlinson, Q.C., leading for the Crown. One matter that had to be resolved was that Mrs McKay's body had not turned up, nor any trace of her. 'There is a *prima facie* case that she is dead,' admitted Arthur's defence counsel, Barry Hudson, Q.C., 'but, I submit, not one scintilla of evidence that she was at Rook's Farm, or met her death at Rook's Farm...' The judge pointed out that the evidence substantiated a *prima facie* case against the Hoseins for kidnapping and a note had said, 'If you don't pay, we execute her.' Thus it was for a jury to decide if they did, or did not, execute their threat. The trial ended on 6 October when, after four hours' deliberation, a jury found both Hosein Brothers guilty on all charges of kidnapping, extortion and murder. Arthur made a long speech from the dock berating the judge as a Jew with 'immense partiality' and declaring the verdict a huge injustice. Nizamodeen said nothing. The jury had recommended leniency in the younger man's case. Both were sentenced to life imprisonment. Nizamodeen served more than 20 years and returned to the family home in Trinidad (the farm had been sold and Arthur's wife had divorced him). Nizamodeen has consistently refused to discuss the murder. Arthur Hosein was repeatedly denied parole. This might have accelerated his mental problems. He died in Ashworth Secure Hospital in 2009.

Unresolved aspects of the case make it an engaging mystery. No trace of Muriel McKay was found in the farmhouse or its outbuildings – not one single hair or clothing fibre, not one trace of blood, not one item belonging to her including her valuable jewellery. Firemen drained ponds, police dogs searched hedgerows and officers scoured the fields. So what happened to Mrs McKay? Legend has it that she was killed within the first two days of her kidnapping as Mrs Hosein and her children were due home from a visit to Germany just after the New Year. Cut up, Muriel may have been fed to Rook Farm's seven Wessex Saddleback pigs. The boar and four sows were slaughtered in January, two sows and their litters on 26 February. Possibly police might have found traces of cortisone, a drug used by Mrs McKay, in their carcasses, but it was too late. There is a chance Muriel died of shock and her kidnappers had no option but to dispose of the body.

A rumour has persisted that other people were involved in the kidnapping plot and the Hoseins took the rap knowing that they would be killed if they told the whole story. One name bandied about was Robert Maxwell, Rupert Murdoch's bitter rival. This idea seemed fanciful in 1970 but, after Maxwell's mysterious death in 1991, his world was revealed to be an extremely shady one, peopled by many unsavoury characters. It is also interesting that a third, elder, Hosein brother, Adam, appeared briefly as a defence witness at the trial. He was an insurance broker in Surrey. Many years later Adam Hosein was implicated in the murder of a wealthy businessman in Florida.

1901 – Herbert John Bennett.

1903 – Samuel Herbert Dougal.

1905 – Albert Stratton. One of the first pair of murderers to be caught by the new science of finger-printing, this killer and his brother were a pair of street toughs who murdered a husband and wife couple for a paltry nine pounds.

1907 – Rhoda Willis. Baby-farming had already gone out of fashion when this woman suffocated a three-month-old baby. She admitted her guilt on the day before her execution.

1910 – Hawley Harvey Crippen.

1912 – Frederick Henry Seddon.

1915 – George Joseph Smith.   1918 – Louis Marie Joseph Voisin.

Above: 1922 – Herbert Rowse Armstrong.

Right: 1924 – Patrick Herbert Mahon. A real ladies' man, this killer made the bad mistake of dismembering his victim, something English juries dislike. He told the Court, "It is surprising what a room fire will burn...."

1925 – John Norman Holmes Thorne.

1927 – John Robinson. There was more than one trunk murder between the wars but the most famous case involved this ex-soldier who panicked when his assignation with a prostitute ended in a lethal fight.

1930 – Sidney Harry Fox.

1931 – Alfred Arthur Rouse.

1934 – Ethel Lillie Major. Strychnine - one of the nastiest of poisons - was this killer's weapon of choice. She was organising her husband's funeral when the police called.

1936 – Buck Ruxton.

1942 – Gordon Frederick Cummins.

1943 – August Sangret. He was a Canadian Cree Indian who spoke almost no English yet he left one of the longest statements on record. It did not save him from the gallows when the murder weapon was found and tied him to the victim.

1945 – Elizabeth Maud Jones.

1946 – Neville George Cleverly Heath.

1948 – Peter Griffiths. Psychotic and dangerous, this killer smashed a child's head in like a rag doll. The sight ever after haunted the lead detective.

1949 – John George Haigh.

1950 – Daniel Raven.

1952 – John Thomas Straffen. He had only a mental age of nine yet served one of Britain's longest ever custodial sentences after strangling three little girls to death.

1953 – John Reginald Halliday Christie.

1954 – Thomas Ronald Lewis Harries.

1955 – Ruth Ellis. The last woman to hang in Britain. Controversy has raged around her ever since but she seemed to want to die after shooting her lover.

1958 – Peter Thomas Anthony Manuel.

1959 – Guenther Fritz Erwin Podola.

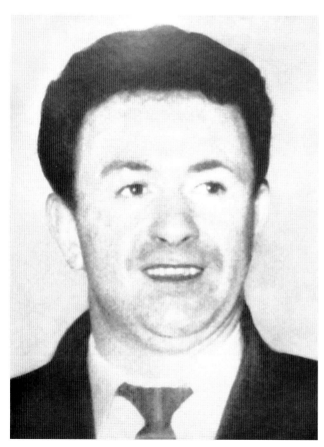

1960 – Patrick Joseph Byrne. A frightening killer, this seemingly pleasant man cut off the head of his victim and stared at it in the mirror. The police constable who found the body had to take sick leave.

1964 – Peter Anthony Allen.

1964 – Gwynne Owen Evans.

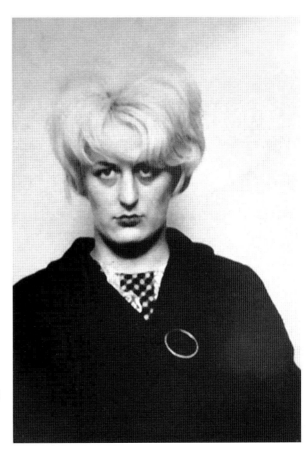

1966 – Myra Hindley. She
died in prison possibly
the most hated woman in
twentieth-century British
criminal history though it
could be argued that she had
tried to make some amends
for their crimes – unlike her
psychopathic lover.

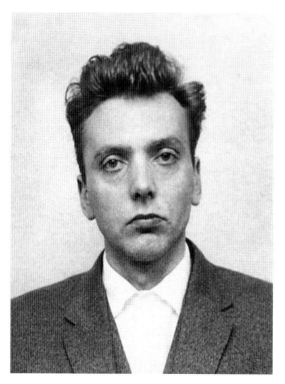

1966 – Ian Duncan Brady.

1970 – Arthur Hosein.

1970 – Nizamodeen Hosein. With his criminal mastermind brother he disposed of a victim so perfectly that the body has never been found. It did not stop him from being found guilty of murder.

1972 – Graham Young.

1973 – Mustapha Basseine.

1975 – Patrick David Mackay. A terrifying psychopath, he hacked his last victim, a priest, to death, then placed his body in a bath and played with the water before going to the cinema.

1976 – Donald Neilson.

1978 – Archibald Thompson Hall.

1981 – Peter William Sutcliffe. 'The Yorkshire Ripper' earned his nickname after using his favourite weapon - a ripping chisel. He murdered at least thirteen women and attacked several others causing a reign of terror across the North of England for years.

1983 – Dennis Andrew Nilsen.

1986 – Jeremy Nevill Bamber.

1992 – Albert Dryden.
It had to happen
sooner or later – a
murder on television –
though the actual crime
was tawdry and quite
senseless.

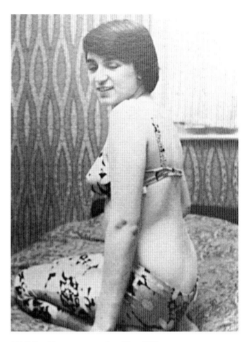

1995 – Frederick Walter Stephen West. 1995 – Rosemary Pauline West.

1995 – The house of horrors where Fred and Rose perpetrated their crimes – 25 Cromwell Street, Gloucester.

1971–1980

Putting aside the moral objections to capital punishment, it must be said that the abolition of the death penalty saw the number of men and women on trial for murder, attempted murder and manslaughter rocket in this decade to 5,003 – a huge jump of more than 1,500 persons. This would seem to indicate the fear that your life might be forfeit if you killed had been a deterrent; though there are other societal forces to be taken into consideration. In 1971 executions for those who committed an explosion in a naval dockyard, ship's magazine or warehouse were commuted to life imprisonment.

1971 The Murder of Ivy Virgin: Raymond Baxter

Mrs Virgin was a happily married woman from Boston, Lincolnshire, who had a wide circle of friends and, despite her 57 years, enjoyed an active social life. It was not uncommon for her to do the usual household chores such as making packed lunches for her husband and son, go off to the shops, be home in time to prepare an evening meal for the family and then be out again seeing friends. Around 11.30pm on the night of 19 November 1970 her husband heard what sounded like scratchings at the front door. On the doorstep he found Ivy covered in blood, the viscous liquid still spurting from her body. While Mr Virgin tried to stem the blood his son raced off to a telephone box to call an ambulance.

Mrs Virgin died at 1am despite all the efforts of hospital staff to save her. Four hours later a Home Office pathologist examined her body and concluded she had died from multiple stab wounds to her neck, left breast, shoulder and arm, committed, he thought, in a series of frenzied clubbing motions. An x-ray spotted something else – the tip of a knife embedded in her shoulder.

The following summer a shoplifter was arrested in Boston and found to be carrying a knife with a missing tip. His was 15-year-old Raymond Baxter. The Forensic Laboratory at Nottingham examined the weapon and found the knife and tip matched exactly. Baxter, it turned out, was a peeping Tom who liked to watch courting couples through house windows. He had been planning to spy on the Virgins when Ivy returned home, and saw him in her garden.

Being a juvenile, Baxter was found guilty of Ivy's murder, but was ordered to be detained 'at Her Majesty's pleasure' for an unspecified period. He was released during his 20s. Not long after he violently raped a woman and was quickly caught. This time he went to prison with a long sentence.

1972 Obsessive Poisoner: Graham Young

During the second half of the 20th century poisoning cases seemed to dwindle in murder trials. The days of lethal Victorian doctors such as Pritchard and Lamson dispensing antimony and aconitine, or serial killers like Mary Ann Cotton wiping out all and sundry with arsenic, were long gone. The main reason was that advances in forensic detection made it almost impossible to kill someone with a large dose of an organic or inorganic compound without microscopic analysis giving the game away. The 'art' remains to do it slowly in modest doses that parody any number of ordinary bodily complaints. Graham Young saw his poisonings as experiments using his family, friends and workmates as human guinea pigs as he administered to them small doses of antimony sodium tartrate, antimony potassium tartrate and thallium – the antimony to punish and the thallium to kill. He murdered at least three people, probably more, taking their lives coldly and without pity. He also poisoned at least 30 others who thankfully recovered.

Young began his killings while still a child. He was born in Neasden on 7 September 1947. His mother died from tuberculosis just 15 weeks after Graham's birth and for his first three years the infant was cared for by his father's sister. In 1950, after Fred Young remarried, Graham and his elder sister, Winifred, returned to the family home. In her book on the case Winifred Young says Graham 'loved our stepmother', but other writers have noted how even as an infant he showed signs of being emotionally disturbed. On one occasion Mrs Molly Young smashed her stepson's collection of model aeroplanes in retaliation for some misdemeanour. The boy grew increasingly withdrawn and secretive, though bright at school.

Around the age of 11 his father – who no doubt later rued the day – bought Graham a chemistry set. The boy was fascinated by the little phials and started to show a morbid interest in poisons. Within two years, as Winifred recalls, 'he grew odder and odder,' collecting bottles with strange contents, sniffing ether, carrying acid in his school blazer, lecturing the family on Black Magic and the Nazis, drawing macabre doodles (one was of a gravestone labelled 'In Hateful Memory of Molly Young, Rest in Peace'). Besides Hitler his greatest hero was Dr William Palmer, the so-called 'Prince of Poisoners', who used antimony to kill his victims. When his sister pointed out that this wicked Victorian was eventually caught and hanged, Graham replied that the death penalty no longer existed and had had been replaced by life imprisonment – and 'that's nothing'.

In April 1961, aged 13, Graham bought 25 grams of antimony from a local chemists. Molly discovered it in his bedroom and a row ensued. Undaunted, the boy simply started using another pharmacy and hid his collection in an old allotment shed. He acquired quite a mix that included atropine, digitalis, aconite, antimony and thallium. Completely self-taught, Graham immersed himself at the local library, reading every book on toxicology and famous poisoners that he could lay his hands on. Next it was time to experiment and observe.

On one occasion he administered 50mg of atropine (sometimes called belladonna, an ancient poison derived from the deadly nightshade plant), to his sister in her breakfast cup of tea. She only sipped it and thought it tasted vile, but on the way to work she felt extremely dizzy with blurred vision and enlarged pupils. Her bosses sent Winifred to the Middlesex Hospital who soon diagnosed her as suffering from belladonna poisoning. She went home mystified but her know-all brother insisted the poison had come from one of her shampoos.

Young's real weapons of choice were antimony and thallium. Antimony emetic (antimony potassium tartrate) with its faint yellow crystals has two advantages for a poisoner: first, it is soluble in water with a mild metallic taste easily masked by something like coffee; secondly, it used to be stocked by most pharmacies and was much used to treat sick animals (it is very good in small doses at promoting sweating and lowering a body's temperature). Its chief problem for the poisoner is antimony's unpredictable toxicity (Mozart may have been a victim). Since it causes almost immediate retching doctors have confused antimony poisoning with gastroenteritis or some viral infection. 'The successful antimony poisoner needs to persist with frequent doses ... each time the symptoms recur, they are passed off as a relapse,' writes John Elmsley. 'Soon the victim begins to weaken physically and waste away.'

Thallium is an element discovered by the British chemist William Crookes in 1861. It is not especially rare and is obtained today mainly as a by-product of zinc and lead smelting. While Graham Young was to receive much publicity as the first British murderer to use thallium it had been employed by a German murderess in the 1930s as well as cases in Australia and the Netherlands. It is a cumulative and tasteless poison that attacks the nervous system. A fatal adult dose is just 800mg (less than one-quarter of a teaspoonful). For the first day a victim might feel he or she has a cold coming on. On the second day there are stomach pains and pins and needles in the feet. Then, as the days progress, pain around the body and joints intensifies, sleep is made impossible, there is profuse sweating, facial paralysis and a smelly odour from the hands and feet. The heart, liver and kidneys degenerate and the victim may die of respiratory disorders such as pneumonia or heart failure. Little wonder that thallium can be confused with a number of normal complaints. The would-be poisoner has two problems: hair soon starts to fall out (this is the normal giveaway sign), and tallium is stored in the bones, even after cremation, though it is virtually undetectable unless bone and body tissues are studied.

Throughout 1961 Graham Young gave small doses of antimony to his family and a school friend, Chris Williams. All of them blamed their recurrent stomach problems and vomiting on a bug. Molly was even admitted to hospital with a suspected ulcer. Eventually, after watching his stepmother suffer for 14 months, Graham gave her a fatal 1300mg of thallium in an evening meal on Good Friday, 1962. The post-mortem did not reveal the element and Molly was duly cremated. It was not until 1971 that Young confessed to her murder.

Next Graham poisoned his father with repeated doses of antimony. Fred Young had to be spend much time in hospital and grew progressively weaker. Tests eventually showed the presence of antimony and Graham's aunt accused him of poisoning his father. At school Graham's science teacher had his suspicions too – even fellow classmates called him 'The Mad Doctor' – and on 22 May 1962 he was interviewed by a psychiatrist. Graham couldn't resist showing off his knowledge of toxicology, much to the doctor's alarm, who informed the police. Young was arrested next day at school. A bottle of antimony sodium tartrate was found inside his shirt. Young confessed to trying to poison his father and others and showed detectives his stock of poisons. Before his appearance at the Old Bailey on 5 July 1962 he told a psychiatrist: 'I am missing my antimony. *I am missing the power it gives me*' (my italics). He was sent to Broadmoor, the third schoolboy sent there since the grim institution opened in 1864.

During his nine years in the high-security mental hospital it is interesting to note that Young made no friends and was quite content to stay a loner. He displayed no homosexual tendencies nor missed a girlfriend. During his Broadmoor years a fellow patient, John Berridge, was killed by cyanide. The verdict was suicide though it was a mystery how he got hold of the poison. Young later confessed to Berridge's murder, saying he had distilled the cyanide from laurel bushes growing in the grounds. Foolishly allowed to act as a teaboy, Young tried to poison some of the 'goons', as he arrogantly called the other patients, by putting lavatory cleaner in the tea urn and a number of people were sick. He even repeated this tea poisoning when he had access to sugar soap whilst cleaning paintwork. Some inmates beat him up as punishment.

Nurses noted that Young was 'always very intense and appeared mentally much older than his age'. He had a dry sense of humour, made macabre jokes, and once told a staff member that 'he only poisoned people whom I really liked ... I don't want to get to like you because I know you have a family.' Inmates steered clear of a youth they labelled as 'mad as a hatter'. During Young's trial Dr Donald Blair had said: 'I fear he will do it again,' but Graham had a champion in Dr Edgar Udwin, a Broadmoor psychiatrist who wrote after nine years that Young had 'made an extremely full recovery and is now entirely fit for discharge'.

Shortly after his release Young got a job as an assistant storeman at John Hadland's Photographic Instrumentation factory at Bovingdon, Hertfordshire. The authorities had not told his employer that he had been in Broadmoor for murder. On 10 May he clocked on. Within one week or so fellow workers started to go down with stomach complaints and these soon grew to be so prevalent that it was called 'the Bovingdon Bug'. It later transpired that within days of leaving Broadmoor on 8 February Young had poisoned a young man who befriended him called Trevor Sparkes. His weapon was probably antimony. On 18 April, using London University notepaper, seemingly a Bedford College research student, he bought 25 grams of antimony potassium tartrate. During his six months at Hadlands the arrogant, know-it-all expert on all matters medical (though a useless storeman) poisoned a number of his workmates, killing two of them, Bob Egle and Fred Biggs. The Hadlands workforce gradually grew increasingly suspicious and took their concerns to the managing director. He went to see the police and Young was arrested. Among his belongings was found a 'diary' with initials for his closest colleagues. Graham had written 'F (Fred Biggs) is now seriously ill... In a way it seems a shame to condemn such a likeable man to such a horrible end. But I made my decision and therefore he is doomed to premature decease... It is better that he should die. It will remove one more casualty from the crowded field of battle.' When Fred lingered, Young wrote: 'It is extremely annoying. F is surviving far too long for my peace of mind.'

Graham Young's second murder trial began at St Albans Crown Court on 19 July before Mr Justice Eveleigh. In the dock a confident Young enjoyed scoring points off the prosecution and said his diary entries were notes for a novel. The jury, under British law, were not told of his earlier trial and crimes but nevertheless found him guilty of murder. His defence counsel then said that Young did not wish to return to Broadmoor and preferred to be sent to a prison. He was duly sent to Parkhurst on the Isle of Wight. Over the next two decades he was moved occasionally and at one point struck up a friendship with Ian Brady, the Moors Murderer. The vision of these two psychopaths amicably discussing their Nazi heroes is a horrible one. On 22 August 1990 Young was found dead in his cell. Cause of death was never really ascertained and put down to heart failure. This seems highly improbable (he was only 42 years old); with his vast toxicological knowledge it seems likely that Young fathomed out a way to kill himself.

His sister, Winifred, always thought there was nothing personal in her brother's murders and wrote: 'I don't believe he was a sadist. I think he was too *cold* a person, in the emotional sense, to let mere feelings sway him. His, I believe, were the crimes of an arrogant intellectual; his approach that of the objective scientist' who clearly knew what he was doing. After his second arrest Young had told detectives that he understood his acts were revolting, yet he did not see himself as a monster because his poisonings had been carefully planned to let a few victims die and most live. He clearly revelled in this power to play God, a fixation shared by many psychopathic killers. Graham's problem was that he could not leave poisons alone – they obsessed him. He realised this and saw a black humour in it all. He told his sister in 1970 before his Broadmoor release: 'Just think, Win, another few months and your friendly neighbourhood Frankenstein will be at liberty once again!!!'

There is a sad coda to the Young case; in 1995 a motion picture was released called *The Young Poisoner's Handbook*, a semi-comic biographical piece. Ten years later, in November 2005, a Japanese schoolgirl was arrested for poisoning her mother with thallium. She had apparently enjoyed the film, was obsessed with Graham, and even kept an online blog in which she listed the dosage and reactions in much the same way as Young's infamous diary.

1973 Interpol to the Rescue: Mustapha Bassaine

While it still persists in Russia and other parts of the world, one crime that has diminished in Western Europe in the 21st century, thanks to legislation, is that of 'queer bashing' – the victimisation of homosexuals. A particularly grisly example of this was the Bassaine case in which a cunning murderer thought he could evade British justice but Interpol and the long arm of the law proved him wrong.

On the morning of Monday, 21 December 1970, the servants of Lord Bernstein, chairman of Granada TV, returned to his house in Wilton Crescent, Belgravia, to find rooms ransacked. The Bernsteins were vacationing in Barbados and the only occupant of the house over the weekend of 18–20 December had been the family butler, 61-year-old Julian Sesee, a tall, smart-looking Belgian known to be quiet and respectable, a familiar sight in Wilton Crescent as the perfect manservant in his striped trousers and black jacket. Mr Sesee was also missing and the door to his bathroom was locked. Police were called and on breaking into the room they found the butler lying in a bloody mess in the bath. There were wounds to his head as well as slashes to his abdomen and throat, yet the killer had wrapped his body in towels. Thrown into the lavatory bowl were the weapons – a bloodstained meat cleaver and a kitchen knife. Quickly returning from the Caribbean and taking stock of her home, Lady Bernstein found £80 was missing from a drawer in her bedroom.

It looked at first as if the butler might had been murdered because he had disturbed intruders. Searching through Sesee's belongings, the police found several letters from young men. These made it clear that he had several homosexual relationships. Fifty pounds had been stolen in cash from the butler's flat as well as items of personal property. The police wondered if he had been the victim of a homosexual blackmail plot gone horribly wrong.

An inquest was formally opened and adjourned no less than eight times because 'enquiries are still proceeding'. Thanks to a member of the public, 23-year-old nightclub hostess Jean Fitzgerald, the police were fairly certain who the murderer was just 10 days after the killing. The man they wanted to talk to was Mustapha Bassaine, the 27-year-old son of a Moroccan government official. Bassaine, an intelligent but highly strung young man, had flown home to Morocco on 22 December. He was well aware that his country had no extradition treaty with Great Britain.

Miss Fitzgerald had gone to the police after worrying about her boyfriend's possible involvement in the murder. They had lived together in Tufnell Park, London N7 for some time. Despite menial employment, Bassaine usually seemed to have money. 'He said something about going with "queers", drinking with them and getting money from them,' said Fitzgerald. 'He showed me a picture of Mr Sesee and told me that the butler often gave him money.' Bassaine had left Jean on 19 December saying he was going to see a friend. He did not return, but on the next night telephoned and asked her to meet him in Wilton Crescent. She refused to go, explaining to detectives, 'I was frightened of Bassaine because sometimes he was vicious and I was afraid he would beat me up as he had done before...' When Bassaine did return to the flat in Anson Road, Tufnell Park, he seemed drunk and tearful. Jean noticed that he was wearing some of Mr Sesee's clothes that were too big for him, and that there was blood on his shoes and scratch marks on his hands. He showed his girlfriend a bag containing an odd assortment – a watch, a camera, a ring – and claimed the butler had given him these things as Christmas presents. Next morning Bassaine threw the clothes and some papers into a dustbin and told Jean he was flying home that day to see his sick mother in Morocco. She noticed he was flush with cash when he bought a one-way air ticket. At the airport he asked her to let him know if there was more in the newspapers about the murder.

Forensic scientists were able to identify Bassaine's fingerprints in Julian Sesee's flat. They also recovered some of the bloodstained clothing worn by the killer. Nearly 10 months after the butler's death an inquest returned a verdict that Bassaine had murdered Mr Sesee. In charge of the case was an indefatigable detective, Chief Superintendent John Hensley of Scotland Yard. Using Interpol (the international crime-fighting organisation which Britain joined in 1928), Hensley asked police forces across Europe to watch for the young Moroccan. Eighteen months later this vigilance was rewarded when news arrived that Bassaine intended to visit Holland and Germany. Within minutes of stepping off a plane at tiny Rotterdam Airport on 28 June 1972, Bassaine was taken into custody and a month later, after extradition proceedings, flown to London in the company of C.S. Hensley.

The trial of Mustapha Bassaine was held at the Old Bailey in February 1973, more than two years after the murder of Julian Sesee. The Moroccan despicably tried to blame the butler's death on Jean Fitzgerald who, he claimed, was jealous of Sesee and wanted 'the old bastard' dead. He denied the killing and thefts. He had seen the butler on the weekend of his death but left him fit and well, he said. Forensic evidence spoke otherwise and a jury found him guilty on all charges. The judge, Mr Justice Forbes, sentenced Bassaine to life imprisonment saying: 'This was a brutal murder and you have been convicted on the clearest possible evidence. Your attempt to shift some of the blame on to Miss Fitzgerald has received the treatment it deserves.'

1974 The Real 'Hannibal the Cannibal': Robert Maudsley

The story of Robert Maudsley can be viewed, depending on your attitude towards murder and British justice, as either a striking example of the need to restore the death penalty or a condemnation of an inhumane penal system. His horrific crimes and special glass-walled cell have led, not without reason, to Maudsley being dubbed 'Hannibal the Cannibal'. One thing is certain, as Maudsley has written: 'I am left to stagnate, vegetate and regress... My life in solitary is one long period of unbroken depression.'

Robert was born in June 1953, the fourth and youngest child of a Liverpool coal lorry driver and his wife. Home life was so bad that before his second birthday the infant was taken into care due to parental neglect. After nine years in a Roman Catholic orphanage the Maudsley children were returned to parents who barely knew them (and in Robert's case not at all). 'All I remember is the beatings,' Maudsley has written of his family life, especially a father who 'used to hit me with sticks or rods and once he bust a .22 rifle over my back'. Eventually removed by social services, Robert then stayed in a succession of foster homes. He drifted to London as a teenager, slept rough, got a drug habit and was in and out of various psychiatric hospitals after several repeated suicide attempts. He told doctors that voices in his head told him to kill his parents.

Working as a rent boy in 1973 the 19-year-old Robert was solicited by homosexual labourer John Farrell. According to Maudsley he was horrified when Farrell showed him photos of children that he had abused. In a rage Maudsley strangled the man. Doctors declared him insane and after a brief trial hearing he was sent to Broadmoor Criminal Lunatic Asylum. In 1977 he and another patient named Cheeseman took hostage a third inmate, David Francis, a convicted paedophile, and barricaded themselves in their cell. For nine hours they tortured Francis before garrotting him as Maudsley rammed a broken spoon into the man's ear until it penetrated his brain. Gleefully they held the corpse aloft so that staff could see the body through the door's spyhole. When the siege was over it was said that the victim's skull was 'cracked open like a boiled egg' with a spoon hanging out of it and part of the brain missing. Newspapers have consistently said that Maudsley ate part of Francis's brain but he denies it.

Deemed too dangerous even for Broadmoor and now – ironically – fit to stand trial, Maudsley was duly convicted of manslaughter on the grounds of diminished responsibility and sent to Wakefield Prison. Within weeks of his arrival Maudsley, who is reckoned to have a genius IQ, planned to kill seven inmates in a single day, or so fellow convicts said. He made them nervous 'with madness in his eyes'. During a morning period when cell doors were unlocked Maudsley lured into his room wife murderer Salney Darwood, cut his throat and hid his body under a bed. Later that morning 56-year-old convict Bill Roberts entered the cell. Maudsley smashed his head several times against a wall before hacking the man's throat open with a makeshift knife. Two murders done, he then calmly reported to prison staff that there would be two less names for roll call.

Convicted of this double murder, Maudsley was not returned to a secure mental hospital, where he might benefit from treatment, but was sent back to Wakefield, a severe Victorian building sometimes called 'the Monster Mansion' because of the numbers of violent offenders and serial killers incarcerated there. At his final trial in 1979, Maudsley told the court that he often raged about his parents: 'If I had killed my parents in 1970, none of these people need have died.' Maudsley apparently loves classical music, poetry and art. He has asked for, and been denied, a pet budgerigar. Supporters say he is gentle, kind and highly intelligent. Psychiatrists think he can be managed but is incurable. His cell is a two-unit glass cage 'that bears an uncanny resemblance to the one featured in *The Silence of the Lambs*', although it was constructed for Maudsley seven years before the movie was released. Its only furnishings are a table and chair made of compressed cardboard, a concrete slab bed, and a lavatory and sink bolted to the floor. He can be observed 23 hours a day (one hour being allowed for solitary exercise) in his thick Perspex-walled cell behind a solid steel door.

Maudsley has demanded better conditions but is currently still held at Wakefield Prison. He has defended his actions saying, 'I killed rapists, paedophiles and sex offenders, no other types of person...' He has been denied a television, stamps to write to his family or lawyers or, most importantly, better psychiatric help. There seems little hope for him, despite a campaign mounted in 2000, which is all but forgotten today. Maudsley will die in gaol officially classified as 'Britain's most dangerous prisoner'.

1975 Maniac: Patrick David Mackay

If Robert Maudsley is highly dangerous, some might say that Patrick Mackay is an even bigger menace to society. Vicious and cruel from an early age, Mackay went on a killing spree in the early 1970s that saw him committing some hideous murders. His punishment was a whole-life tariff and headline notoriety as one of Britain's most frightening psychopaths.

Mackay was born on 25 September 1952. His parents had met in South America and Marian Mackay was Guyanese. Patrick's father, Harold, was a seemingly mild-mannered accounting clerk until he touched alcohol, then he turned into a violent lout. He kicked his wife in the stomach while she was carrying Patrick, would often beat her up after a Friday night in the pub and soon was using his fists on the little boy. Harold Mackay died when Patrick was just 10, but the son, a chronic bed-wetter until well into his teens, often had nightmares about his father and thought him still alive. Patrick was not shown his father in his coffin nor did he attend the funeral, so it seems he had difficulty accounting for the loss. There were frequent tantrums.

At school Patrick was a big boy for his age, a bully and a thief. After his father's death he began to exhibit sadistic tendencies – roasting his pet tortoise alive, staking birds out on the road so he could watch them being squashed by tyres, torturing a cat and a rabbit. In 1964, aged 11, he set fire to a local church and beat up another child. He found himself in court on 21 charges and got three years' probation. This period of his life was spent in borstals and various psychiatric wards. At 15 a psychiatrist certified him as a schizoid psychopath. By now he was over 6 feet tall yet still took a doll to bed with him at nights. He sometimes asked other people to kiss it.

After his release, his mother tried to be supportive but Patrick was impossible to control. There were constant rows between him, his sisters and his mother. Police were frequent visitors to the home where the boy smashed up furniture and made several suicide attempts including stabbing himself with a bayonet. Mrs Mackay tried to take her family back to Guyana but the trip was a disaster and they all returned after just three weeks. In October 1968 Patrick violently assaulted a young boy and was sent to Moss Side High Security Hospital, Liverpool.

In 1972, aged 19, Mackay was released again. He went to stay for a time with two aunts, but began to drink and do drugs, on one occasion trying to strangle an aunt. He was told to move on. A Carmelite priest, Father Anthony Crean, tried to befriend Patrick. This kindness was rewarded by

Mackay breaking into the priest's cottage and stealing some money. The police pressed charges though Crean was willing to forgive and forget.

Detectives were later to be impressed with Patrick's intelligence and plausibility. He was an excellent liar. At times he could seem almost normal, but alcohol, especially whisky, made him 'excitable', as he called it, or on edge; the smallest thing could then send him into a rage with homicidal repercussions. Odd in other ways too, Mackay created his own Nazi-style uniform, calling himself 'Franklin Bollvolt the First', a world dictator. He made models of Frankenstein and burned out the monster's eyes. A photograph of Himmler was by his bedside.

The police later thought him responsible for as many as 11 murders. This tally may be exaggerated but it seems likely that he pushed an au pair under a train near New Cross in July 1973, battered a woman to death in Kentish Town that same month and threw a tramp who annoyed him one night off Hungerford Bridge and into the Thames. He later confessed to killing a tobacconist, 62-year-old Frank Goodman, on 15 June 1974, hitting him 14 times over the head with a piece of lead piping as he was closing his shop. Mackay showed police where he threw away his bloodstained boots. Blood samples were analysed and corresponded to both Mackay and the dead man.

From the autumn of 1974 and into 1975 Mackay began a wave of muggings. He especially targeted old ladies living in the Chelsea area. On Valentine's Day 1975, after another suicide attempt, he met 84-year-old Isabella Griffiths and carried her shopping bags to Cheyne Walk. A few days later he turned up at Mrs Griffiths' door and asked if he could do any shopping for her. We don't know what was said but she refused to let him in her apartment. In a rage Mackay snapped the door chain and strangled the woman. Later he took a knife and pushed it deep into her chest, then sat with the body, rearranging it 'to make her comfortable'. Her corpse was not discovered for 12 days.

On 10 March, Mackay charmed his way into the apartment of 89-year-old Adele Price in Lowndes Square. He said he was faint. She offered a cup of tea. He said a glass of water would be fine, thank you – then strangled her. He used just his left hand to show how powerful he was, later telling police, 'I felt hellish and very peculiar inside.' Once again he sat for a time with the corpse and had a doze, escaping only in the nick of time.

Eleven days later Mackay went on a visit to his mother in Gravesend. He decided to call in on Father Crean who lived nearby in the village of Shorne. According to Mackay in his statement he wanted to talk to the priest about repaying the stolen money. He let himself into Crean's unlocked cottage and surprised the priest on his return. Clearly frightened of the tall and dangerous intruder, Crean and Mackay were soon fighting in the hallway. Terrified, Crean ran upstairs and tried to barricade himself in the bathroom. Mackay, in a scene reminiscent of Jack Nicolson in *The Shining*, grabbed an axe used for chopping kindling and maniacally broke into the room, slashing at 63-year-old Crean with a knife, then going berserk with the axe, raining blows onto his victim's head. The senior detective, Chief Inspector Ken Tappenden, later described how the top of Crean's skull was mashed, revealing his brains. Blood had spattered all over the walls and floor. Mackay took the dying priest and pushed him into the bath, put in the plug and turned on the taps. For an hour (he returned later for a further 15 minutes), he sat by the corpse trailing his hands in the bloodstained water. 'I was just watching him sinking and floating about in the bath,' he said. Later Mackay enjoyed a chicken dinner with his mum and went to the cinema.

The Mother Superior found Crean's clothed corpse floating in the bath and called the police. D.C.I. Tappenden remembered the strange young man from the earlier incident with Crean and detectives caught him two days later. He quickly confessed. The problem was what to do with him. Mackay was eventually charged with the murders of Mrs Price, Mrs Griffiths and Father Crean. He admitted two robberies and asked for 24 more muggings to be taken into consideration. At the Old Bailey on 21 November 1975 Mackay pleaded guilty on the grounds of diminished responsibility. Psychiatrists attested that he had a 'severe psychopathic disorder', while the Superintendent of Broadmoor doubted if Mackay was 'adequately motivated to the extent that he would accept or be susceptible to treatment'. He was sentenced to life imprisonment. In Mackay's case this has meant a whole life tariff and he is still in a high-security gaol. His solicitor has gone on television to say that while his client never expressed remorse he could not understand why at times he had such a rage to kill. D.C.I. (later Chief Superintendent) Tappenden calls him a loner, though not insane, but once he is in a rage someone has to die. 'He is a monster,' says Tappenden. 'If free, he would kill again.'

1976 The Black Panther: Donald Neilson

Can you imagine the awfulness of being woken up in the middle of the night by a stranger in your room, an apparition clothed in black, wearing a black hood with razor-slit eyeholes, while the twin barrels of a sawn-off shotgun are shoved in your face? This was the ordeal of 18-year-old Richard Skepper about 4.15am on 15 February 1974. The intruder wanted safe keys, which Richard thought were downstairs in the corner shop cum sub-post office run by his parents, Donald and Joanna Skepper, in Harrogate. A search, first by the burglar and then with Richard in tow, failed to produce the keys. Richard said he thought they might be in his parents' bedroom. 'You go get. Me watch at door. No noise,' hissed the man in the hood. Knowing that his mother was a light sleeper, Richard protested, 'They'll wake up if I go into their room.' 'You go,' insisted the masked figure.

Sure enough, Mrs Skepper opened her eyes and switched on a light. 'Put that light out,' screamed the intruder. He flicked a switch on the wall but only made matters worse by turning on an overhead bulb. Richard told his father that the man wanted his safe keys. Seeing clearly that the burglar was alone the 54-year-old Methodist lay preacher shouted, 'Oh, does he? Let's get him!' As he swung his legs out of bed the burglar blasted him with both barrels. A 2½-inch wound opened up in Mr Skepper's chest. Grabbing his bag the gunman ran off, while Richard and Joanna tried to comfort Donald, who died in his wife's arms. It was her birthday.

The masked killer would finally be caught by a stroke of luck but not before committing four more murders and a string of more than 400 burglaries. He well deserved his nickname of 'the Black Panther' – a cold, remorseless criminal who dressed in black and worked only at night. His real name was Donald Neilson.

Thirty-seven at the time of the Skepper murder, Neilson had been born Donald Nappey, son of hard-working Yorkshire textile workers. A frail child who never grew to be more than 5 feet 6 inches tall, young Donald was constantly tormented at school by classmates who called him 'Nappey Rash'. A mother's boy, he was broken-hearted when this kindly figure died in 1947. This traumatic event affected him psychologically and he broke into a local Co-op and was caught. He vowed never to be captured by the police again. As he grew older, the boy grew more introspective in his loneliness. Failure at school led to failure at work; he went through a succession of jobs as a joiner.

National Service for two years in the King's Yorkshire Light Infantry began after his 18th birthday and it transformed Nappey. Despite being nicknamed 'Short arse' because of his stocky build, Donald became a keep-fit fanatic and took to the disciplines of army life as a duck to water. Later he claimed he had flunked his Bren-gun course so that he could do the whole thing twice, and it was true that playing with weapons became an obsession. Serving during the emergencies in Kenya and Cyprus, he later said, 'I enjoyed disciplining myself.' Before joining the army Donald, who was light on his feet and a good dancer, had met a nice girl called Irene Tate. The couple had a quiet wedding on 30 April 1955 – no guests, no parents and no reception. Back in Bradford after demobilisation, Donald was unable to settle in a job. He hated immigrants and 'lazy' bosses. In January 1960 a daughter, Kathryn, was born. Two years later Donald decided to work for himself. In 1965, not wishing his child to go through the humiliations he had suffered at school (and psychologically wanting to turn over a new leaf), he changed the family name to Neilson.

Dogged by cash flow problems, so often the bane of the self-employed, Neilson took in lodgers and tried various part-time jobs. Nothing worked. An unfair society, as Donald saw it, rewarded scroungers and this now turned him to crime. He decided to rob post offices. 'The money I took was Government money,' he later said, 'as far as I'm concerned I've never robbed anybody.' On 11 September 1967 he tried to rob a sub-post office in Nottingham, his first such robbery, but the postmaster put up a stiff fight. It would be three years before Neilson tried to rob another post office (securing £3,064), but by then he had refined his techniques based on careful preparation for each burglary and a study of all possible escape routes. During these years he targeted middle-class homes, took only cash, used no middlemen or helpers, studied police routines, used public transport and varied the direction and pattern of his crimes. At first he was called 'the Red Shadow' by the press (he wore red on some early raids), but soon got the sobriquet of 'the Black Panther'. This persona inflated Neilson's lifelong bruised ego. 'People saw me as the Black Panther and I didn't speak in normal voices,' he later told detectives. 'It wasn't me... it's an act – and I'm the principal actor. I've got to convince them that I'm in control.'

To prove he was in control Neilson grew increasingly ruthless. Seven months after the Skepper raid he killed again when Derek Astin, an ex-Royal Marine, tried to stop him from robbing his sub-post office at Higher Baxenden in Lancashire. Despite a shotgun blast in his shoulder Mr Astin managed to push Neilson down the stairs. In fury the Panther pulled out a .22 pistol and shot Astin from below, the bullet ripping upwards through his stomach. Derek died on the way to hospital.

Despite setbacks such as the Harrogate and Higher Baxenden raids, Neilson was by now averaging three successful post office burglaries a year and the authorities were offering £5,000 in reward money. Irene and Kathryn Neilson had no idea that Donald was the Black Panther. Despite a haul of more than £30,000 he was not flash with his loot. At home he was a disciplinarian, but family weekends were often spent playing war games, doing fitness runs, or military-style hide-and-seek in battle dress on the moors. It seems that Neilson's family accepted such diversions as part of his obvious military mania.

On 11 November 1974 Neilson committed his last raid, and third murder, at a sub-post office at Langley, west of Birmingham. It seems that Neilson's planning for once went awry. For reasons never fully made clear he shot and killed 56-year-old postmaster Stanley Grayland. Peggy Grayland found her husband dying, then saw a man framed in the doorway. He was unmasked. Perhaps nervous that Mrs Grayland might identify him, Neilson repeatedly smashed the middle-aged woman's head until she lay in a thick pool of blood. Miraculously she was found by a passing constable, rushed to hospital, and later gave detectives a description of her attacker.

This incident clearly unnerved Neilson; the reward money now rose to £25,000 and he was sick of the risks. He decided to try a new *modus operandi* – he would kidnap someone and net in ransom money a fat sum far in excess of his burglaries. He had, in fact, been planning the perfect kidnapping for some time. The Hosein case inspired him and Neilson later admitted, 'I studied the McKay kidnap closely. The police made such a balls of it, and I worked on the principle of learning from their mistakes.'

The intended victim was Ronald Whittle, the 28-year-old owner of a West Midlands coach firm that had been started by his wealthy and recently deceased father. Some time between 10pm and midnight on 13 January 1975 the Black Panther slipped into the home of Ronald's mother, Mrs Dorothy Whittle, at Highley, near Wolverhampton. Ronald and Dorothy were both away but resting in her bedroom was 17-year-old heiress Lesley Whittle, Ronald's younger sister. A much-liked and attractive girl, Lesley had no false airs and was a typical teenager, though she was due to inherit £82,000 (about £1 million today) on her 21st birthday. Lesley had spent the evening watching TV and altering the hem on a pair of jeans. Mrs Whittle returned from seeing friends at 12.45pm. She did not realise that her daughter was missing until the next morning and it was late in the day when a member of the family found four Dymo Tape messages in the lounge demanding £50,000 ransom to be delivered to the Swan Shopping Centre, Kidderminster. To the Whittle family's horror the message said: 'YOU ARE ON A TIME LIMIT IF POLICE OR TRICKS DEATH.'

Ron Whittle decided that it was best to contact the West Mercia Police, despite the threat to his sister. The note had advised him to go to a Kidderminster telephone box and find further clues. A game of cat and mouse now began that was to be disastrous. Neilson would not be caught for 11 months, the case would involve over 150 detectives, cost more than £1 million and elicit 30,000 witness statements. One of the worst aspects was the West Mercia Police's handling of the media, which was an unmitigated disaster. Neilson had thought the kidnapping would be kept secret. Due to slip-ups at police H.Q., the drama was soon national news. The Panther, despite later claiming to have learned techniques from the Hosein case, botched his own plans by providing a succession of unpunctuated Dymo Tape messages that were confusing and made sense only to him and not those trying to interpret them. A pair of false kidnappers tried to blackmail the Whittles and waste police time. One night, while hoping to get his ransom, Neilson was accosted in a car park near Dudley Zoo by a worker who demanded to know what he was doing there. In a panic the Panther shot 44-year-old Gerald Smith four times (a murder he was never charged with since Smith lingered with his injuries for 14 months and at the time a victim had to die within 12 months to bring the charge). Detectives realised, however, that the .22 shells they found matched those of the Black Panther killings. Poor Ron Whittle tried to make sense of the Dymo Tapes and in the early hours of 17 January found himself directed to Bathpool Park near Kidsgrove, Staffordshire. Told to flash his headlights, Ron waited 30 minutes but all seemed fruitless and he drove home. Neilson had been watching him, but was spooked by what he thought was a cruising helicopter (later denied by the police) and a patrol car.

It is likely that Lesley Whittle was still alive at this time. When she died will never be known. The police searched the park in daylight but found nothing. The kidnap messages ominously stopped. Then, on 23 January, the police found an abandoned green Morris 1300 at Dudley. It contained a 'plethora' of Black Panther clues and at last detectives realised that 'the most dangerous criminal at large in this country' had taken Lesley Whittle.

In March some schoolboys came forward and admitted to finding a Dymo Tape and a torch in January, near a concrete pillbox capping a deep shaft in Bathpool Park. On the afternoon of 7 March, some 55 feet below ground level, police found a narrow platform, 26 inches wide and 5 feet long. This had been the teenage girl's fiendish prison. A mattress and a few objects littered the platform. Lesley's naked body hung below in the darkness. A wire noose in the form of a locked collar was around her neck. It had snagged on a metal stanchion. A sleeping bag and slippers were found at the bottom of the shaft just inches below the dead girl's feet. A pathologist concluded that she had died of 'vagal inhibition' or shock to the vagal nerve and carotid artery in the neck, the result of falling off the platform – or of having been pushed.

Despite the massive hue and cry over the callous death of a lovely teenage girl, the police trail went cold. It was resolved on the night of

11 December when two police constables, Tony White and Stuart Mackenzie, were patrolling in their panda car through the sleepy village of Mansfield Woodhouse, Nottinghamshire. A small, wiry man hurrying along with a holdall seemed to avert his eyes from the crew of Panda Six and P.C. Mackenzie said, 'He looks worth a check.' When the officers stopped the stranger and asked to see the contents of his holdall the man – Neilson – whipped out a sawn-off shotgun and levelled it at P.C. White's head. 'Fucking hell,' said Mackenzie. Neilson ordered White into the back of the car and got into the front passenger seat of the vehicle next to driver Mackenzie. Near Sherwood Forest, where both policemen reckoned the gunman meant to kill them, Mackenzie took a huge gamble and pressed hard on his brakes. The shotgun instantly went off through the roof. Pellets hit White who muttered, 'The bastard's shot me!' Mackenzie and Neilson began fighting in the car as the officer shouted, 'I'll kill you, yer bastard!' Luckily for him customers at a nearby fish-and-chip shop saw what was happening and dragged Neilson out of the car, where the fight continued on the pavement until the gunman was at last subdued.

In custody, a somewhat battered Neilson did not at first admit to being the Panther but he did give detectives his real address. A search of the family home, according to one of the officers involved, yielded 'so many exhibits at the house that we didn't need him to confess'. At last the police knew they had captured the Black Panther.

Neilson's trial began at Oxford on 16 June 1976 before Mr Justice Mars-Jones. The case centred on the murder of Lesley Whittle. For many in court the most important question was whether Neilson had deliberately killed the girl. He pleaded guilty to blackmail and kidnapping but denied the murder charge. Defence counsel, Gilbert Gray, Q.C., tried to paint Neilson as a Walter Mitty character and a man who would not callously kill a young girl who was much the same age as his own daughter. He pointed out that the hangman's noose was padded with Elastoplast to avoid chafing the neck, Neilson had given Lesley a rubber mattress, a sleeping bag, magazines and small luxuries. Referring to the girl's body, Mr Gray said: 'This is not something the defence has made up. Her height from the neck was 4 feet and there was a 5-feet length of ligature giving an overall length of 9 feet. The drop from the landing to the floor of the tunnel was 6 feet 11 inches so that if it had not been for the unforeseen snagging which shortened the tether there would have been 2 feet to spare and she would have landed on her feet at the bottom of the shaft.' He described Lesley's death as 'unlooked for misadventure, unplanned and undesired. Neilson started something that went hideously wrong.'

Neilson told the court that Lesley had died accidentally on the night of the 17th when he stepped onto the platform and she moved to her right and accidentally rolled off. 'I froze, then panicked,' he said. This story – then and now – fails to convince many people. The autopsy showed that Lesley had not eaten for some days before her death. While it is possible that she died accidentally, or that Neilson murdered her, there is a strong possibility that he left the poor girl to her fate in that dank, dark place that became her tomb. Terrified, starving, half out of her mind, she may well have committed suicide.

The jury took five hours and five minutes to find Neilson guilty of Lesley Whittle's murder. During sentencing Justice Mars-Jones told the defendant: 'The enormity of your crimes puts you in a class apart from almost all convicted murderers in recent years.' Irene Neilson, who denied knowing about her husband's criminal career until 1975, was sentenced to one year in prison for cashing some of the stolen postal orders. Officers Mackenzie and White both received the Queen's Gallantry Medal. More than 34 years of incarceration followed for Neilson. Then, on 17 December 2011, he was taken from Norwich Prison to the Norfolk and Norwich Hospital suffering from incurable motor neurone disease. Gasping for breath and guarded, the 75-year-old killer, who had once been Britain's most notorious man, died there the next day.

1977 Mad Rampage: Thomas Neil McCulloch & Robert Francis Mone

The bloodbath perpetrated by McCulloch and Mone led to both men receiving some of the longest sentences in Scottish legal history. Very recently the question of parole for these convicted killers has also been a source of tension.

The two men were inmates of the Carstairs State Mental Hospital near Glasgow. Both were under strict supervision for earlier crimes and violent behaviour. Mone, born in 1948, was a handsome young man deemed schizophrenic by psychiatrists in 1967 after he had burst into a Dundee secondary school, sexually assaulted two schoolgirls, tried to shoot a student nurse with his shotgun and finally murdered a 26-year-old pregnant teacher, Mrs Nanette Hanson, shooting her in the back. One of the schoolgirls whom she tried to protect said in 2007, 'She was the bravest person I've ever met.' There would have been more deaths if Mone's gun had not had a faulty firing pin. McCulloch was 20 when a psychiatrist decided that he had a violent psychopathic disorder.

That was on 15 May 1970. The next day, after some heavy drinking, the Glaswegian burst into the city's Erskine Bridge Hotel brandishing a shotgun, a .45 revolver and a bandolier of ammunition slung across his shoulders. He ran through the building firing off rounds and injuring two people before police managed to disarm him.

With McCulloch providing the muscle and Mone the brains the duo planned to escape from Carstairs on 30 November 1976. Mone, who was of above-average intelligence (he held three Higher Certificates in Education and had been studying Law at the Open University), masterminded the breakout. During his eight years and 11 months in the mental wards Mone had been certified as 'a sadistic schizoid psychopathic personality', a man 'arrogant, supercilious and argumentative' with an 'always evident' potentiality for aggression. McCulloch had seemed to be improving under supervision and demonstrated quiet skills as a painter and decorator. In 1973 he struck up a friendship with Mone that may have had homosexual overtones. In the autumn of 1976 they began to seriously plan their escape.

Both men were members of a dramatic society within the mental hospital. About 5.40pm on 30 November McCulloch was escorted to class with Mone. The former man carried two boxes. Inside them were an array of weapons including an amateur axe, knives decorated with S.S. runes and garrottes made of violin string. The boxes also held disguises – false moustaches and beards, fake identity cards, male nurses' caps and a makeshift ladder. Armed with bottles of paint stripper stolen from the paint shop, McCulloch and Mone went into an office where Nursing Officer Neil MacLellan was talking to another patient, Ian Simpson, an older psychopath double murderer who was deemed unfit to plead and sent to Carstairs in 1962. Mone squirted the paint stripper in MacLellan's face and McCulloch did the same to Simpson. Then, without warning, McCulloch began hacking at Simpson with a knife. A melee erupted with blood squirting everywhere as the four men grappled first in the office and then in the hallway. At one point a furious McCulloch even hit Mone on the back of the head with the flat of his axe. Finally, Mone managed to jab and puncture Simpson with a garden fork while McCulloch leapt on a dying MacLellan in a frenzied tango of stabs and slashes. While Mone cut the telephone wires McCulloch returned to the victims and hacked away at them with the axe until both men were dead. He even cut off Simpson's ears.

Using their disguises the two lunatics used MacLellan's keys to get outside the building. They walked across a brightly lit area, pushed their rope ladder against a fence and somehow got over the barbed wire at the top, ran across a railway line and some fields and made it to Carstairs

Junction. The time was about 6.30pm. The bloody scene inside the mental hospital was not discovered for almost half an hour and it was another 30 minutes before the sirens were sounded.

Mone had cunningly planned the escape for around 6.30pm because he knew this was the busiest time of day on the road that ran through the Carstairs grounds. About 6.40pm, with Mone lying in the middle of the road, McCulloch flagged down a car driven by Mr Robert McCallum. McCulloch claimed there had been an accident. Mr McCallum got out of his car to help and was just due to become Murder Victim No. 3 when a police car pulled up. The two officers in the panda car, John Taylor and George Gillies, got out and McCulloch repeated his tale of an accident. When Taylor shone his torch in McCulloch's face the axeman leapt upon the police officer and Mone jumped up from the road. A terrified McCallum got back into his car and managed to drive off as the two violent offenders attacked the officers. McCulloch axed away at Taylor, who was a big man, while Mone stabbed Gillies. Somehow, despite his wounds, Gillies jumped an embankment and landed in a boggy ditch. Twenty-seven years old and a father-of-six, P.C. Taylor was less lucky; he staggered along the road and collapsed into the path of an oncoming bus. He died later that night on his way to hospital.

The two escapees now set off in the stolen police car. It was to be a chase like no other in Scottish criminal history and resembled something in a gangster film. Mone did not know how to drive and McCulloch had only rudimentary skills and went at a breakneck pace. The roads were icy and at one point on the A702 heading south, the car skidded badly and rammed an embankment. Two men in a van who offered help after this accident were hit and stabbed for their pains and thrown into the back of the van as Mone and McCulloch set off again. A short time later the van got bogged down in a muddy field when the fugitives tried to evade the police. So they set off on foot, waded through the freezing River Clyde and surprised a farmer and his family, demanding the keys to their Austin Maxi. They sped away, but the farmer's bright 12-year-old daughter had managed to slip into a back room and dialled 999. Van-loads of armed police spotted the Maxi on the A74 near Dumfries and gave chase to the Scottish border south of Gretna Green. Cumbrian police were waiting just over the border with a road block near Carlisle. Ninety miles from the scene of their murders, McCulloch and Mone's car was rammed off the road by a police vehicle at Roundabout 43. It was 9.14pm.

In February 1977 McCulloch and Mone faced Lord Dunpark in the High Court of Edinburgh. Mone pleaded guilty to the murder of

P.C. Taylor and McCulloch pleaded guilty to three charges of murder and three attempted murders. During sentencing the judge told the two men that he would recommend that they should not be released from prison 'unless, and until, the authorities are satisfied, if ever, that you have ceased to be a danger to the public'.

How long is a life sentence – especially in the case of demented men and serial killers? Mone's name in particular stayed in the headlines: in January 1979 Christopher 'Sonny' Mone, father of Robert, showed the family trait for aberrant psychopathic behaviour by murdering three women and boasting that he wanted to be more famous than his son; in 1981 Robert Mone staged a rooftop protest about prison conditions; two years later the elder Mone was stabbed to death in Craiginches Gaol, Aberdeen; in February 1995 Robert Mone got an extra six months on his sentence for attacking another prisoner with some boiling water; in May 2002 he won a victory using EEC human rights laws to demand his sentence be cut to 25 years; there was talk in 2007 of his eventual release and move to an open prison, but in 2011 it seems this release was stalled after concerns over his behaviour.

Once inside an institution again, Thomas McCulloch responded to treatment and after almost 43 years' incarceration was released in May 2013. He settled in the Dundee area with the girlfriend who had corresponded with him behind bars. A parole board has decreed that he is no longer a threat to society. In 2012 Neil MacLellan's son, John, commented: 'Life should be life. He was sentenced to die in gaol and I don't see why that should have changed. He gets another chance, but there's three people in the cemetery who won't because of what he did.'

1978 The Butler Did It: Archibald Thompson Hall & Michael Anthony Kitto

In her celebrated 1955 psychological thriller *The Talented Mr Ripley*, author Patricia Highsmith introduced us to her anti-hero, a likable, plausible, musical, thoroughly amoral young psychopath. Just such a sociopath was Archibald Hall, a larger-than-life character who clearly saw himself as a latter-day 'Raffles', the Edwardian gentleman jewel thief made famous in stories by E.W. Hornung. Hall robbed only the rich, planned and executed some audacious thefts, stayed in only the best hotels, tipped staff generously (with other people's money of course), and was an expert on fine wines, good food and rare antiques. As a man who totally avoided violence in his first 36 years of professional crime, there is a fine irony in the fact that his first murder was precipitated because he was being blackmailed to commit a robbery he did not want to do. His second murder, a foolish act, was done in a panic. From then on each murder led to another and in a few short months the callousness of these deeds would lead to him, and his accomplice Michael Kitto, being caught with a body in the trunk of their car.

Hall was born in Glasgow on 17 July 1934, son of a post office sorting clerk and his wife. Home in those formative years was a tenement block on the city's south side. Later they had rooms in a better middle-class district and by the time of Archibald's teens, his parents were renting an impressive six-bedroom house near the university. Both parents were loving; the boy had an adopted sister, Violet, whom he adored (and they remained close all his life), and a younger brother, Donald, born in 1941, whom he grew to loathe. An artistic child with a vivid imagination, Hall loathed his Christian name, 'Archibald', and from quite an early age asked people to call him 'Roy'. His favourite movie star was Joan Fontaine, so he began saying his name was 'Roy Fontaine' and he used this persona throughout his life.

Hall began his life of crime at an early age. He offered to collect door-to-door for the Red Cross and delivered to the charity a box brimming with copper coins from the poorer neighbourhoods. A second box, full of notes and silver coins collected from rich apartment buildings, he kept for himself. He had a first brush with the law aged 13 and, four years later, was sentenced to 60 days on two charges of theft and one of uttering a false document. A 1943 court appearance saw him being sent to a mental hospital for a short spell. He was certified again as a psychopath one year later, after being charged with three cases of housebreaking. His punishment was two years in the Perth Criminal Lunatic Asylum.

For the next three decades Hall's life took on a certain form; periods when he was at liberty consisted of him either working as a butler (invariably with excellent forged references) or posing as an antiques dealer or a rich aristocrat. To some extent he enjoyed his butlery duties, being an excellent cook and fastidious about cleanliness and his personal appearance. Prison allowed him time to educate himself in the library, learning about fine wines, antiques and other bits of knowledge that he could put to good use on the outside.

Like all the best thieves, audacity was Hall's watchword. On one occasion he disguised himself as an Arab sheikh and stayed at a plush London hotel so that he could steal from some of the country's top jewellers. In 1951, while working as a butler in Stirlingshire, he posed as his employer at a garden party at Holyrood Palace in Edinburgh, even turning up in the family Bentley. He fooled everyone. Everything Hall did, he did in style. Even some of his antique shop victims whom he robbed grew fond of the charming man with the cut-glass accent and gentlemanly ways. He always remembered to tip hotel and restaurant staff generously, once gave a cashmere coat to a beggar shivering in a shop doorway, and followed the underworld code of never 'ratting' on his colleagues. Women found him very attractive; he had several sexy girlfriends in the Swinging Sixties, married, had a common-law wife and fathered a little girl whom he adored (she was brought up by his relatives). He was also bisexual and completely unbothered by his sexuality.

In January 1964 he was sentenced to 10 years' detention for a series of jewel thefts and sent to a new prison, Blundeston Maximum Security Gaol in Suffolk. It did not take Hall long to exploit a weakness in the ventilation system and with two other convicts in tow he made a daring escape. On the run from the law, his adventures continued; in the West Country, after a jewel robbery, he found his hotel swarming with police and hid under a maid's bed in the attic for two hours until she saw him and screamed. Somehow he got away, managed to hail a taxi and tell the driver he had been in an accident and needed a hospital in Exeter. When police stopped the car at a road block Hall pulled a rug over his dirty trousers and calmly lit a cigar. The police waved them on their way. Giving the taxi driver a substantial tip, Hall talked to a nurse just long enough to see the cab depart, then slipped into a hotel for a shave and some sandwiches before slipping out again and onto a London-bound train. This was the kind of life he lived up to the hilt.

Early in 1977 Hall/Fontaine got a job as a butler to Lady Mary Hudson on her Kirtleton estate near Waterbeck, Dumfriesshire. Now in his 50s, the butler-cum-thief appeared to be settling down. His duties were not arduous, the pay more than sufficient for his needs, and he grew fond of his employer. She, in turn, found him to be very efficient. Things might have gone along very well (although it is hard to believe that Hall would not have robbed his employer eventually), but one day a young ex-con called David Wright turned up. This bad penny had known Hall in Long Lartin Gaol. Lady Hudson agreed to allow Wright to stay in her butler's apartment and gave him a few odd jobs to do around the estate. Wright, a petty thief, kept badgering Hall to help him steal some loot from the big house. The butler refused. Wright ignored him and took a silver tray and a ring. Suspicious of Wright, Hall did some detective work of his own, traced the ring to a girlfriend of his visitor, got it back and duly returned the item to her ladyship's jewel box. When Wright found this out he broke into the wine cellar while Lady Hudson was away and got drunk on fine champagne. Next he went to Hall's bedroom, where the butler was fast asleep, and fired his shotgun into the headboard, inches from the man's face, before collapsing into a sobbing heap on the floor. Hall was shocked. Blood poured from a face wound caused by the pellets as he realised that Wright had almost killed him.

The butler now knew that the stupid petty crook might upset all his plans if his erratic behaviour somehow escalated. The champagne was replaced by an even better vintage, the headboard was repaired and on the following day Hall invited Wright to go rabbit shooting with him. Conserving his ammunition, the butler let his guest blast away at some rabbits before shooting him three times in the head. He buried the body near a stream in the woods of the estate. Well aware of the enormity of his crime, Hall muttered to himself as he dug the grave, 'David, your troubles are over. Mine have just started.'

Less than one month later, Hall was fired by Lady Hudson on a tip-off that he had a criminal record. Three months later he found new employment as butler to an enormously wealthy couple, 82-year-old Captain Walter Scott-Elliott, an ex-Etonian former M.P. and his Anglo-Indian wife, Dorothy. The pair owned a Knightsbridge flat, a house in Scotland and villas in Italy and France. Their homes were stashed with antiques, many of them oriental treasures acquired cheaply by Scott-Elliott in India at the end of the British Raj.

Around midnight on 8 December 1977, one month after starting work for the Scott-Elliotts, the butler took a fellow ex-con, 39-year-old Michael Kitto, a quiet, smart-looking thief, on a tour of the Knightsbridge apartment. The pair had plans to case the joint. Mr Scott-Elliott was fast asleep in his room and his wife was supposed to be away at a nursing home. Hall was badly mistaken. Dorothy Scott-Elliott surprised the two men in her bedroom and indignantly demanded to know what they were doing there. For the first time in his career Hall now did something in a blind panic – he knocked the small, middle-aged lady to the ground and tried to stifle her screams with a pillow. Kitto took over and eventually their victim stopped breathing.

Michael Kitto had a 51-year-old lady friend called Mary Coggle. This petite woman from Northern Ireland, separated from her husband, a frequenter of Kings Cross pubs where she was often seen chatting up anyone who would buy her a Bacardi and lemonade, was brought into the plot as the two murderers decided to rob the Scott-Elliotts of as many of their valuables as they could. They began a car journey to Scotland with Dorothy in the boot and her husband sitting in the back seat and heavily sedated with sleeping pills. Next to him sat Mary Coggle, wearing a blonde wig and doing an impersonation of Mrs Scott-Elliott as she wrapped one of the lady's £4,000 mink coats around her. In this odd getup Mary waltzed into hotels along the way sounding and looking like a strange Irish duchess while Hall and Kitto acted obsequiously to Walter Scott-Elliott and called the senile old man 'sir'. All three criminals knew that the old man would have to go. His wife was hastily buried in a deep ditch by a snow-covered Perthshire road. A few days later in gloomy Glen Affric, Inverness-shire, after a lunchtime pub stop in Blair Atholl, they helped Captain Scott-Elliott out of the car to have a pee, then tried to strangle him. The old soldier put up quite a fight for his life until Kitto smashed his head in with a spade on Hall's orders. This time the killers did not even bother to bury their victim's body and merely covered it with branches and some foliage.

Victim No. 4 was Mary Coggle who refused to listen to Hall's advice that all the property they had stolen must be sold. She had fallen in love with some of Dorothy Scott-Elliott's furs. Hall found Mary an embarrassment; she acted vulgarly, to his way of thinking, in hotels and if she kept wearing the fur coats it was obvious that questions would be asked sooner or later. When Hall attempted to burn the coats Mary tried to stop him. He struck her over the head with a poker, then went on striking her as Kitto held the woman's arms behind her back. Her dying words were directed at Kitto: 'It's your turn next!'

Once again the killers sought out a lonely stretch of Scottish road and dropped Mrs Coggle over a bridge and into a stream near Lockerbie, Dumfriesshire. They then systematically began stripping the Scott-Elliotts' London home of its antiques, selling them to dealers in the Midlands and Edinburgh. That Christmas, flush with money, the two men joined Hall's relatives and showered everyone with expensive presents. The villains who had so recently been battering, smothering and shooting people to death took over the kitchen and personally served the Christmas turkey. Staff at the nearby luxury hotel where they stayed noted how Hall 'ordered two rounds of smoked salmon sandwiches and then insisted upon buying drinks for all the bar staff... He was very well-dressed and had a beautiful gold watch and a fine pair of silver cuff links. He spoke with an upper-crust accent and was very polite and proper...'

On 13 January 1978 Donald Hall, Archibald's younger brother, was released from prison after a three-year stretch for housebreaking. 'Roy' disliked his sibling, who had been arrested several times for petty theft and child molestation. Staying with his brother at the same cottage in the Lake District where Mary Coggle had died, Donald wanted to know how his brother and his friend had acquired their new-found wealth. The questions irked Archibald Hall/Fontaine. On his second day at the cottage Donald Hall offered to show the other two how it was possible to tie someone up so they could not escape. He offered to be the guinea pig and got down on the floor, inviting the others to tie his hands. It was an opportunity that Hall/Fontaine could not let pass by; he chloroformed his brother, then suffocated him with Kitto's assistance. Next morning, with Donald in the boot of the car, the two killers set off once more for Scotland. It was a snowy day and by 7pm, with treacherous driving conditions, they decided to stop the night at the Blenheim House Hotel, North Berwick; both men booking in under false names. The manager of the hotel, Norman Wright (ironically the same surname as Hall's first victim but no relation), now became the demon butler's nemesis. He noted the pair were travelling very light and conveyed his suspicions to the local constabulary. It was discovered that their Ford Granada had an incorrect tax disc. Two officers turned up at the hotel just as Hall and Kitto were ending a fine meal with some brandies and asked the men to accompany them to the local police station. Once there a very cool Hall asked if he could use the toilet. The portly 53-year-old then managed to squeeze through a small window and make good his escape. He knew it was only a matter of time before the police opened the boot of the car and found his dead brother. Hall hailed first a car and then a taxi, gave the occupants convincing tales of distress and spent three hours driving around East Lothian before he was captured at a road block. In true Hall style, stepping out of the taxi, he remembered to pay the cabbie his fare plus a handsome tip. It was to be a last gesture of freedom.

During questioning by detectives Hall and Kitto told their remarkable tale, though the latter man claimed he had been in fear of the butler, something Hall later dismissed as rubbish. Fontaine/Hall even told the police of the David Wright murder, a crime they knew nothing about, and took them to the lonely spot where he had hidden the corpse. Due to the geography of their crimes the pair were put on trial in Edinburgh's High Court in May 1978 and at the Old Bailey six months later. Hall admitted to the David Wright and Walter Scott-Elliott murders and was sentenced by the Scottish judge, Lord Wylie, to serve a minimum of 15 years, while the length of Kitto's sentence was left open. At the Old Bailey, Hall pleaded guilty to murdering Mary Coggle and his brother but not guilty to the death of Dorothy Scott-Elliott. In a rare legal move it was decided that the charges to which the men pleaded not guilty would be left on file as there were already sufficient guilty pleas to earn them both long sentences. The Recorder of London, John Miskin, Q.C., threw the book at Hall; this time it was Kitto who got a minimum of 15 years while Hall was told, 'You shall not be considered for parole during the rest of your natural life save in the case of serious infirmity.' In retrospect, since Kitto had taken an active part in four of the five murders, it must be said that he got off lightly. Despite muttering 'Jesus Christ' under his breath, Hall took his sentencing with tight lips and dogged determination. His life was lived in three acts: a long first part as a sophisticated jewel thief; a short, dark, second one of violence; and a third and lengthy final quarter-century lived in solitary confinement. He never was released and died of a stroke aged 78 years in Kingston Prison, Portsmouth, in 2002. Three years before his death he tried to tell his side of events in an autobiography. He called it, possibly with some irony, *The Perfect Gentleman*.

1979 Lies and Life Sentences: John Henry Childs

There is a grave danger when villains start 'grassing' to the police that they lie, distort events and generally try and blame other people for their actions. Detectives have no easy way of knowing what is real and what is false. This is especially true if the criminals involved are known hard men. John Childs has been described as Britain's 'most prolific hit man'. A judge has also called him 'a pathological liar'.

In June 1979 Childs was arrested in connection with a series of bank and security van robberies in Hertfordshire. He was 44 years old, a known petty criminal with untidy fair hair and a scruffy beard who wore spectacles and spoke with a cockney accent. The other gang members were also arrested and one of them, Philip Cohen, told police that Childs and the ringleader, Henry Mackenney, had committed two murders. When these matters were put to Childs he gave officers an extraordinary statement saying that Mackenney – an Essex businessman known as 'Big H' (due to his 6-feet-4-inch height), with another former prisoner, Terry Pinfold, had started a British version of 'Murder Inc.' and killed anyone for a profit. In some cases Childs confessed to killing with Mackenney's help, such as with Victim No. 4, Robert Brown, a former professional wrestler known as 'the Angel', a convict on the run from Chelmsford Prison when 'Big H' shot him twice in the head, then used an axe, while his accomplice stabbed him with a diver's knife. Victim No. 5, Frederick Sherwood, was killed for a contract payment of £4,000, claimed Childs, who hit the victim with a hammer while Mackenney shot him as the *coup de grace*. A fee of £1,800 was paid for the murder of haulage contractor, George Brett. According to Childs, the vicious Mackenney shot the Essex contractor, then put a Sten gun bullet through the head of 10-year-old Terry Brett who was clutching a teddy bear. The killers disposed of bodies by cutting them up, burning chunks in a council house fireplace or putting them through a mincing machine.

On 4 December 1979 at the Old Bailey a nervous Childs faced Mr Justice Lawson and after pleading guilty to six counts of murder was sentenced to six concurrent life terms. Childs then turned Queen's Evidence against Mackenney, Pinfold and two other men (the unnamed being acquitted), whose trial began in October 1980. Found guilty on 29 November, both Pinfold and Mackenney got life sentences with a recommendation that 'Big H' should serve a minimum of 25 years. The hulking criminal was so incensed that he had to be restrained in the dock after sentencing.

Cracks soon began to appear in the case. In 1986 Childs wrote an affidavit admitting that Penfold was 'only convicted because of my perjured evidence'. In 1998 he claimed in *The Daily Mirror* to have committed five more murders. Pinfold and Mackenney unsuccessfully appealed their convictions in 1981 and six years later were denied leave to appeal again. Finally, in 2001, Pinfold was released on bail and in 2003 both men had their convictions overturned by the Court of Appeal. Lord Woolf, sitting with Mr Justice Aikens and Mr Justice Davis, ruled that Childs' evidence had been unreliable. A forensic pathologist, David Somekh, concluded that Childs was a compulsive pathological liar and that police had known this at the time of the original trial but failed to inform the jury. Mackenney was now 72 years old and suffering from emphysema, while Pinfold at 70 had recently had six strokes.

To make matters worse it seems that one of the victims whose death had been described by Childs, a toy manufacturer called Terry Eve, had not been murdered at all and prehaps went on the run after a warrant for his arrest was issued in connection with the hijacking of £75,000 of stereo equipment. The investigating officer had been told by Commander Bert Wickstead, head of the Serious Crimes Squad, to add Eve's 'murder' to the list. Wickstead, known in criminal circles as 'the Old Grey Fox', was a tough copper from the pre-Second World War school of detectives and not squeamish about bending the rules to get a conviction. In Wickstead's opinion the end often justified the means.

It is hard to know what to make of the case. Bodies of the six victims have never been found and 'Big H' Mackenney was no pussycat. During the course of their enquiries detectives raided a house in Woodford, Essex (Mackenney lived in Romford), and found a Sten gun, 5 revolvers, a tear gas pistol, 2 rifles, 4 shotguns, 992 rounds of ammunition and 24 tear gas pellets. They also found a silencer hidden in a bucket of cement in a school playground.

The web of lies and confessions made by some villains becomes so tangled that the real truth vanishes in a haze. John Childs, in prison with a full-life tariff, is the living proof.

1980 The Murder of Clare Hutchison: Kenneth Kirton

In May 1980 a 23-year-old painter and decorator, Kenneth Kirton, raped an 18-year-old girl near Farnham in Surrey. He pushed her onto scrubland near Frensham Big Pond, made her strip naked while he held a knife, then he raped her. The girl might have become a murder victim, but she was able to get away and run naked to some nearby dog kennels where she worked.

On 5 June, while working on a house in Burnt Hill Road, Lower Bourne, Kirton grabbed a passing secondary school girl, Clare Hutchison, forced her into his hired van and drove to a secluded wooded spot near Old Frensham Road. Here he forced Clare out of the van, attempted to rape her and cut her throat with his painter's knife. The 14-year-old was later found naked, face down in the mud, with a few tufts of grass and stray earth thrown over her in a half-hearted and hurried attempt to hide the body.

Three days later Kirton tried to kidnap a 16-year-old girl at knifepoint in Haslemere. Luckily, a passer-by intervened and the girl got away. She ran home and on the kitchen table used a lipstick to write down the van's licence number. This allowed police to apprehend Kirton that same evening. He confessed in a statement to murdering Clare – a crime the police knew nothing about as the girl was simply listed as a missing person – and he showed them where he had left her body.

On 31 October 1980 at the Old Bailey the young man pleaded guilty to rape, murder and attempted rape and was sentenced to life imprisonment with a recommendation that he should serve at least 25 years. When searching Kirton's home detectives found a copy of *Reader's Digest* magazine in the lounge opened at an account of the 1943 Wigwam Murder that took place in the same part of Surrey. In the loft they found a copy of Professor Keith Simpson's autobiography, *Forty Years of Murder*. Kirton had carefully noted one photograph that showed a body positioned after death and then left Clare Hutchison in this manner. It is clear that he could not control his rape spree and would certainly have become a serial rapist and murderer if that bright and remarkably composed young woman had not had the presence of mind to remember the licence number.

1981–1990

British society was changing and gradually becoming less sexist as the decade rolled on. The murder, attempted murder and manslaughter rate continued to rise to 5,400 persons. Forensic science was starting to leap forward again and in 1987 a man called Colin Pitchfork was convicted of strangling two girls in 1983 and 1987 based on strands of genetic DNA. Soon the police would be able to use DNA profiling in the investigation of homicides.

1981 The Yorkshire Ripper: Peter William Sutcliffe

About 10.50pm on Friday, 2 January 1981, two policemen were patrolling the red light district of Sheffield in a car. Suspicious of a brown Rover 3500 saloon parked in a driveway, the officers, Sergeant Robert Ring and probationary constable Robert Hydes, pulled up to talk to the male and female occupants. The man gave his name as John Williams of Rotherham; the woman was a 24-year-old convicted prostitute with a suspended sentence. A check showed that the number plates on the Rover were false and the man was told he was under arrest. While the officers were dealing with the woman, the man edged away into the darkness towards a low wall by an oil tank. 'What were you doing there?' asked the sergeant. 'I've fallen off the fucking wall,' said the man, 'I wanted to piss.'

At Hamerton Road Police Station the man admitted that his real name was Peter Sutcliffe and that he had stolen the licence plates of the vehicle. Under questioning Sutcliffe, who seemed very anxious to get away from the police, made the officers suspicious; he lied clearly and badly about his knowledge of prostitutes. They decided to hold him for more questioning.

On his Saturday shift Sergeant Ring went back to the Lights Trades House driveway where he had arrested Sutcliffe. It was already dark. Finding a space between the wall and the storage tank he shone down his torch and saw a ball-peen hammer lying in the leaves. Realizing what this discovery meant he called on his radio for assistance. P.C. Hydes arrived with Inspector Paddy Hopkirk. The three men looked again in the narrow, leaf-strewn gulley. 'Is it the handyman's?' asked Ring rhetorically as they stared at the hammer. P.C. Hydes saw the gleam of something below the hammer. 'Well, the hammer might belong to the handyman,' he said, 'but who does the knife belong to?' 'Oh, Jesus Christ,' someone said. The three officers knew it was an historic moment. The Yorkshire Ripper was at last in custody.

It had taken 5 years and 3 months to catch him but one of the worst killers in British history was finally going to face justice. The search for him had seen the largest manhunt ever mounted by British police, with more than 250,000 interviews, 32,000 witness statements and 27,000 vehicles searched. The Ripper had bludgeoned, stabbed and mutilated at least 20 women aged between 16 and 47 years, with occupations ranging from student to prostitute. Thirteen of them had died. During this long period every woman in the North of England, on both sides of the Pennines, had lived in fear every night they had to walk anywhere after dark.

Several times Sutcliffe had come into the crosshairs of the police and yet always luck had been on his side. Even before his first murder he was already in the police filing system, a complex and colossal collection of filing cards in boxes and drawers that grew out of control during the 63 months of the investigation. It was not just the West Yorkshire Police as a whole who were overwhelmed; the chief investigator, George Oldfield, was under immense strain to catch the killer and took the whole business personally, which is a dangerous thing for a detective to do. Oldfield was supported in all his actions by Ronald Gregory, the egocentric Chief Constable of West Yorkshire.

Thirty-four-year-old Sutcliffe was from Bingley, the town 6 miles along the Aire Valley from Bradford. With thick, dark, curly hair, long sideburns and a beard he looked like a satanic Tom Jones. He had been married for six years to his 30-year-old wife, Sonia, a reserved, house-proud woman of Czech-Ukrainian parentage who had trained as an art teacher. One of Sutcliffe's brothers described Sonia as 'a pillock... she certainly thought she was *well* above everybody else. That's what I couldn't stand.'

The loathing was mutual. At home Peter Sutcliffe seemed well under his wife's thumb. She seemed to be constantly expecting him to do yet more home decorating, until the early hours of the morning, even after he had been driving his lorry all day.

A mummy's boy as a child, Sutcliffe was raised a Catholic in a solidly working-class neighbourhood. Considered the quiet one of the family, he left school at 15 and had a series of menial jobs including stints as a gravedigger. This allowed him to steal from the corpses. In 1975 he trained to get a heavy goods vehicle licence. Six months after starting work for a tyre firm he was sacked for stealing used tyres. In October 1976 he joined T. & W.H. Clark (Holdings) in Bradford as a long-distance lorry driver. He liked his job and according to friends was said to drive his lorry fast and recklessly. In 1977 he and Sonia moved into a three-bedroomed house in Heaton, a suburb of Bradford. Sonia kept the home spotlessly clean (detectives later described it as 'sterile').

Police astonishingly let Sutcliffe off his first assault on a prostitute in 1969 since the woman did not want to press charges. In July and August 1975 he attacked three more women, including 14-year-old Tracy Browne.

What prompted Sutcliffe to behave so violently will never be known for sure. He later claimed to have heard voices from God while he was a gravedigger. Clearly he is a complex individual. His odd behaviour manifested itself in many little ways; for instance, he could never sit still in someone's house and liked to wander from room to room, including bedrooms, opening drawers and cupboards, having a rummage. He also had a strong sense of the macabre and would sometimes drive to Morecambe on the Lancashire coast to visit a tawdry old seafront waxworks that had, besides its Chamber of Horrors, a grisly collection of medical monstrosities called the Macabre Torso Room. Here he would gaze for hours at the diseased penises, cancerous vaginas and deformed foetuses.

His major reason for killing seems to have been a hatred of all women he thought were prostitutes (he later admitted some of his victims had been 'mistakes'). It is interesting that about the time of his first attack in 1969 he had visited a prostitute who cheated him out of sex and a £5 note. 'I felt outraged and humiliated and embarrassed,' he later said, 'I felt hatred.' He vowed that no 'dirty whore' would ever make him a 'laughing stock' again. Hookers also gave him a dose or two of a sexually transmitted disease (it seems to have been gonorrhoea). Rather than accept responsibility for this misfortune, he blamed 'the mucky bitches'.

On 30 October 1978, a cold, damp and misty night, a 28-year-old drunken prostitute called Wilma McCann, mother of four children, extremely poor, was picked up by Sutcliffe in Meanwood Road, Leeds, shortly after 1am. He then parked his car near some playing fields. She offered him sex for a fiver. 'I was expecting to be a bit romantic,' he told police, 'I had to be aroused. But all of a sudden she said: "I'm going. It's going to take all fuckin' day. You're fuckin' useless."' In a rage he replied: 'Can we do it on the grass?' Wilma got out of the car. Sutcliffe followed but first he took hold of a hammer. From behind he hit her over the head. 'She made a lot of noise and kept on making noise, so I hit her again.' He sat in his car and watched the dying woman jerking on the ground. Then he took a knife and stabbed her 14 times in the abdomen and chest, and once in the throat, exposed her breasts and pulled her white slacks down below her knees. Satisfied that everyone would recognise her as a whore, he set off home.

By the middle of January 1976 there were 137 officers working on the McCann case, 530 statements had been taken and 53,000 police hours devoted to the crime. Sixty-one days after Wilma's death Detective Chief Superintendent Dennis Hoban, head of Leeds C.I.D., was called to another murder scene where 42-year-old Emily Jackson, a casual prostitute, was found with similar hammer blows to her head – and 52 separate stab wounds. This time the killer had plunged not a knife but a crosshead screwdriver into his victim. Soon the media was saying that a new Jack the Ripper was on the loose.

The murders in Leeds, Bradford, Manchester, Huddersfield, Halifax and Farsley continued at terrifying frequency – four in 1977, three in 1978, two in 1979 and two in 1980, the last being that of 20-year-old Jacqueline Hill of Leeds. A hoax tape sent in 1979 by a man dubbed 'Wearside Jack', due to his accent, taunted Assistant Chief Constable Oldfield, heading the West Yorkshire inquiry. It led to a vast amount of resources being spent looking for a Sunderland killer. It allowed the real villain to go on killing. So large was the scale of the inquiry that Sutcliffe was interviewed by the police several times, including twice in 1979. At one point, due to a £5 note passed by him to a victim, Sutcliffe was considered one of 300 likely Ripper suspects, yet that vast card system of information was too overwhelming for the police and forensic clues were not properly followed up. Even the PhotoFIT pictures of the killer, if viewed in unison, bore a striking resemblance to Sutcliffe, yet no one was able to join the dots in the case together.

One of the highlights of the case happened when Sutcliffe was told to strip in police custody after his arrest. Shocked detectives saw that he was wearing a lady's V-necked sweater as leggings, the knees padded so that he could kneel by his victims, the 'V' leaving his genitals exposed for quick intercourse, or more likely, masturbation.

Regina v. Sutcliffe began in the Old Bailey's No. 1 Court (moved from Yorkshire to ensure a fair trial) on 29 April 1981. Sutcliffe's defence was one of manslaughter on the grounds of diminished responsibility. After two weeks, despite the efforts of James Chadwin, Q.C., defence counsel, to prove his client was not guilty of murder, he was convicted on all counts by a majority verdict of ten to two. Mr Justice Bingham sentenced Sutcliffe to a minimum of 30 years, adding: 'I express the hope that when I have said life imprisonment, it will mean precisely that.'

After the trial there was huge criticism of West Yorkshire Police. Oldfield was forced into retirement, his No. 2 in the case demoted to traffic duties. A damning inquiry by the Inspector of Constabulary, Sir Lawrence Byford, was kept secret until 2006.

Sutcliffe began his sentence at Parkhurst but was moved to Broadmoor Hospital in 1984. He has been attacked on at least three occasions; in 1997 he had a pen shoved in his eyes causing severe loss of vision, and in 2007 was stabbed in the right cheek. He has also developed diabetes. In 2015 it was announced that Sutcliffe, now a Jehovah's Witness, has been declared sane by psychiatrists and can be moved back into a normal prison.

While awaiting trial his younger brother, Carl, asked him bluntly why he had murdered all the women. Sutcliffe smiled as he replied: 'I were just cleaning the streets, our kid, just cleaning the streets.'

1982 The Paraquat Poisoner: Susan Barber

The weed killer Paraquat is now banned in most developed countries, especially after a spate of almost 350 deaths in Japan in just four years, 1998–2002, most of them suicides. Murders using Paraquat are comparatively rare. The most famous is that of 35-year-old Michael Barber by his wife, Susan. The weed killer causes fibrosis of the lungs when ingested, also attacking the vital organs and burning the throat. Two teaspoonfuls is a lethal dose and there is no known antidote. Smaller amounts can cause a lingering death. Unfortunately for the would-be poisoner, Paraquat is relatively easy to detect in the body.

Mr Barber's death is also a lesson in the dangers of spousal abuse. He had returned home early from a fishing trip to find his wife in bed with a neighbour from three doors down the street, Richard Collins. Angrily the cuckolded husband punched Collins in the mouth before whacking his wife over her right ear. She later needed some medical attention while a clearly shaken Mr Collins got the message and fled all the way to his brother's house in Scotland for a fortnight. What Michael Barber did not know was that Susan had been seeing her factory worker lover for more than a decade; they had started having sex within weeks of her marriage in 1970, when she was 17 (and already a mother) and Richard Collins had been just 15 years old.

The Barbers lived modestly in a pre-war terraced house in Osborne Road, Westcliff-on-Sea, Essex. Thirty-seven-year-old Michael was an unskilled worker in a cigarette factory. He also had a minor criminal record for car theft, traffic offences and indecently assaulting a six-year-old girl. After the ruckus the Barbers tried to patch up their shaky marriage; Susan agreed not to see Richard anymore, though in fact the pair kept up a clandestine postal correspondence. On 4 June Michael said he had a bad headache. Next day his pain continued and was accompanied by stomach ache and nausea. Three days later he was admitted to hospital with breathing problems and had to be put into intensive care. On 17 June Mr Barber was transferred to the Hammersmith Hospital with a severe kidney condition. The subject of Paraquat poisoning was discussed there by specialists, and blood and urine samples were sent to the National Poisons Reference Centre and also to ICI, manufacturers of the weed killer. Due to a mix-up it was first thought that the results were negative. Michael died on 17 June. His death certificate listed cardiac arrest, renal failure and bilateral pneumonia as the symptoms. It was his post-mortem, carried out by Professor David Evans, that finally proved that Michael had died of Paraquat poisoning, though judgement was reserved until September when histology slides became available.

Susan, meantime, had quickly discarded her widow's weeds, or any sense of mourning her spouse. Richard Collins was filling her bed within a week of Michael's decease. Then in October she got a £15,000 death benefit from her late husband's employers along with a £9,900 refund in pension contributions for her three children. Susan now went on the razzle, pushing aside Richard for other lovers in an orgy of drink and partying. She even bought a Citizen Band (CB) radio and used the call sign 'Nympho'.

A net was slowly encircling her as the police gathered together all the evidence. Nine months after her husband's death Susan was arrested and on 1 November 1982 she found herself in the dock of Chelmsford Crown Court before Mr Justice Woolfe, charged with murder, conspiracy to murder and administering a poison with intent to injure. Alongside her was Richard Collins on the charge of conspiracy to murder. Both pleaded not guilty. Susan's defence was that she had put Paraquat in the form of a commercial weed killer, Gramoxone, in a steak and kidney pie and watched her husband eat it, but had merely intended to make him ill. Both were found guilty. She was sentenced to life imprisonment and Collins got two years due to his previous good behaviour. Susan had claimed that she wanted Michael 'to suffer as I have suffered', but Mr Justice Woolfe dismissed this plea as rubbish saying, 'I cannot think of a more evil way of disposing of a human being.'

Less than a year after starting her sentence Susan was briefly allowed out of Holloway Prison to marry one of her CB fans. It is believed that she was released after serving 10 years.

1983 The Man Who Killed Because He Was Lonely: Dennis Andrew Nilsen

Dyno-rod engineer Michael Cattran was having a bad day. It was not until 6.15pm on the dismal winter evening of Tuesday 8 February 1983 that he got to 23 Cranley Gardens, Muswell Hill, North London, where the tenants had been complaining for some days of bad smells in the house, which seemed to emanate from the drains. Most of the pleasant suburban street of semi-detached houses were family homes but No. 23 was rather different; for a start it was broken up into flats, although only three were occupied; the house and garden, also unlike its neighbours, were run-down and neglected, the shabby hallway and stairs did not even have a light bulb while the rear of the property was a jungle of weeds and trash.

Mr Cattran decided the problem lay below ground and would have to wait until daylight. Deciding to take a quick look, he prised open a manhole cover at the side of the house that led to the main drain. A foul smell wafted upwards. Climbing down the 12 steps into the sewer Michael shone his torch around and saw on the floor and sticking out of the pipe leading from the house what appeared to be 40 to 50 small pieces of flesh. To Jim Allcock, one of the occupants of No. 23, he said: 'I may not have been in the game for long, but I know that isn't shit!' Back inside the house Cattran telephoned his suspicions to his manager. The occupants had by now all gathered around him in the hallway. The plumber turned to 37-year-old Des Nilsen, a bachelor who lived in the attic flat with his one-eyed mongrel dog, 'Bleep', and bluntly said: 'You've got a dog, haven't you? Do you put dog meat down the toilet?' Mr Nilsen had written that same day to landlord's agents complaining of an over-flowing toilet and 'unpleasant odours' in the house. He vehemently protested that he had no idea what was the source of the mystery.

Des – Dennis was his real name – was being far from truthful. Around midnight he sneaked outside, prised open the manhole cover, climbed down and cleared up all the flesh in the sewer and threw the pieces over the back garden hedge. Jim Allcock and his girlfriend, Fiona Bridges, in a ground-floor flat heard him moving about outside. 'There's somebody having a go at the manhole,' said Fiona, 'I bet it's him upstairs.' Jim went to investigate and met Des coming into the house. 'I just went to have a pee,' he said. Later Nilsen got drunk on Bacardi and slept close to his beloved dog, 'the last warm and lovely influence in my life', before falling asleep.

Forty-five minutes after Nilsen left for work next day, Mr Cattran arrived with his boss. To their surprise the lumps of flesh had all gone. Down in the sewer Cattran put his hand inside a drain and pulled out a small piece of meat similar to a chicken wing along with four pieces of bone. The police were called. That afternoon the forensic lab at Charing Cross Hospital declared that the tissue was human, probably from a man's neck; the bones came from a hand. By 4.30pm Detective Chief Inspector Peter Jay was back at Cranley Gardens with D.I. Stephen McCusker and D.C. Jeremy Buller. Mr Nilsen walked in at 5.40pm.

The officers and Des all went up to his flat where the pleasantries lasted only a few minutes before Jay said: 'Don't mess about. Where's the rest of the body?' 'In two plastic bags in the wardrobe next door,' replied Nilsen, 'I'll show you.' He admitted that he had a lot to tell detectives but preferred to talk at the station. Jay administered a caution and arrested him. Later that evening David Bowen, Professor of Forensic Medicine at London University, would open the bags and find a ghastly collection of body parts including two torsos, a skull whose flesh had been boiled off and a second head retaining some flesh, along with a Sainsbury's bag containing a heart, two lungs, spleen, liver, gall bladder, kidneys and intestines, 'all mixed together in a disgusting, impersonal pottage'.

Worse, in a manner of speaking, was revealed by Nilsen on his way to Hornsey Police Station. Sitting in the back of the car with him, D.C.I. McCusker asked: 'Are we talking about one body or two?' Dennis Nilsen replied: 'Fifteen or sixteen since 1978.' The hairs shot up on McCusker's head, an electric moment. At Hornsey Nilsen explained that he had killed three people at Cranley Gardens and a further 13 at his previous address, 195 Melrose Avenue, Cricklewood. The most shocking thing for the police was that they had in custody a serial murderer but had no idea who his victims were.

Dennis Nilsen was born on 23 November 1945 in Fraserburgh, a lonely town on the most north-easterly tip of Aberdeenshire, Scotland. His father, Olav, was an officer serving with the Free Norwegian forces stationed in the town. His mother, Betty Whyte, was a good-looking young woman, daughter of a fisherman. Olav was a wanderer and in 1948 he wandered out of Betty's life when the couple were divorced. She raised Dennis and his brother and sister in one room of her parents' home. The boy's grandparents were loving but deeply religious. As a child Dennis was a quiet lad prone to wandering off along the lonely beaches, streams and heather-clad hills. His love of the outdoors was combined with a love of animals, sometimes rescuing young gulls who had fallen from their nests.

Betty Nilsen remarried and was to have four more children. 'Des', as he liked to be called, later wrote that his mum was 'very house-proud and I suppose she could not tolerate animal hairs around the house or on the carpet (I got the feeling sometimes that she didn't want me around on the carpet either)'. An Army Cadet at 14, Nilsen enlisted as soon as he was able and spent the next 11 years as a soldier. It was the happiest period of his life. In 1964 he joined the Army Catering Corps and served in various parts of the globe including Germany, Cyprus and Aden. He passed all his catering exams, was commended as being an 'exemplary' soldier and promoted to corporal. Had he signed on for another spell his life would have been so different. As it was, he returned to civvy street and in December 1972 joined the Metropolitan Police Training School at Hendon. Soon he was Police Constable Q287 and was based at Willesden Police Station for one year. It was during his police period that Des accepted a fact that he had tried to hide in the army – he was drawn to other men. He started to have relationships and, when they failed, an increasing number of casual one-night stands.

An excellent police officer, Nilsen suddenly resigned in December 1973, working temporarily as a security guard before getting a position as a clerical officer with the Department of Employment in May 1974. At the time of his arrest he was an executive officer at the Job Centre in Kentish Town. His social life was non-existent; apart from a mild interest in some socialist causes, Dennis simply watched television in the evenings, walked his dog, occasionally drank in homosexual pubs and hated himself for his own promiscuity – 'It's like compulsive gambling; you know that you will lose, but you go on regardless.'

By the winter of 1978 Nilsen was thoroughly depressed and 'defeated on all fronts'. He spent a lonely Christmas in his flat, hating the world, feeling that he had no friends apart from his mongrel, 'Bleep'. On 30 December he decided to go out for a drink. In a pub in Cricklewood he met an Irish lad aged about 17. That night, as he told police, 'things began to go terribly and horribly wrong.' Back at his apartment Nilsen strangled the teenager with a tie. He then washed the body in the bath, dressed him in clean underpants and tried unsuccessfully to have sex with the corpse. On New Year's Day he buried it under the floorboards. One week later he resurrected the stiffened corpse, bathed it again, placed it on the living room carpet and masturbated onto its stomach. Hanging the cadaver upside down, Nilsen masturbated again the next day before deciding to cut up the body. After eight months under the floorboards the smell was too much; he burned the Irish youth on a bonfire in the back garden.

Before he left Melrose Avenue in October 1981 Des Nilsen would kill 11 more young men, of whom only four could be identified by the time of his trial. Butchery skills learned in the army would help him to dispose of their bodies. They were generally destitute, homeless, homosexual, with mental and emotional problems of their own, young men easily forgotten and lost in a big city. Two more bonfires would see their bodies reduced to ash and bone fragments. He made by his own admission at least seven other attempts at murder, but either his victims fought him off, or he managed to snap out of his killing trance. He also had a number of casual one-night encounters without any compulsion to kill. Between his first recorded murder and the second, for instance, almost one year elapsed. Nilsen never had intercourse with his victims but masturbated over them. He also liked to bathe them, cover them in talc, and sit them – for days sometimes – on his bed or in a chair. Alcohol in every case was a stimulant for his murder attacks.

Later Des tried to describe his feelings: 'Even if I knew the body to be dead I felt that the personality was still within, aware and listening to me,' he wrote later, adding, 'sex was not a factor of continuity with the victims... The only similarity was a need not to be alone. It was to have someone to talk to and be with.' Frequently, if he is to be believed, Nilsen felt he was living in a bad dream, yet knew that unless he was stopped he would have gone on killing – 'I had no other thrill or happiness.' In more lucid moments he knew that 'killing is wrong ... my murders were for no useful ends as murders never are.' Society, he felt, 'has a right to call me a cold-blooded mad killer', yet he did not feel mad.

Nilsen's trial began at the Old Bailey on 24 October 1983 before Mr Justice Croom-Johnson. The defendant was accused of six murders and two attempted murders. The killings were not in dispute. What had to be decided by the jury was whether the murders were the act of a sane man or not. Psychiatrists for the defence explained that Nilsen had a severe schizoid paranoid tendency, a man deeply lonely and suspicious of others, whose own self-loathing and urge for self-destruction was directed elsewhere. The prosecuting counsel, Allan Green, summed up the whole case: 'The defence says: "He couldn't help it." The Crown says: "Oh yes, he could."'

On 3 November the jury retired to consider their verdict. They were unable to reach a unanimous decision but at 4.25pm next day returned to deliver, by a majority of ten to two (the same as in the Yorkshire Ripper case), a verdict that Nilsen was guilty of murder and one attempted murder. The judge sentenced him to a minimum of 25 years' imprisonment. In gaol, where he remains, Nilsen is said to spend his time painting, composing music, reading and writing to correspondents. Some writers have complained that he is manipulative, cunning, and has not told the whole truth, but it must be said that as an intelligent person Dennis Nilsen has tried to be more introspective about his crimes that most killers. He once said: 'Am I mad? I don't feel mad. Maybe I am mad.'

1984 Bloodstains Trap a Serial Killer: Arthur Hutchinson

It had been the day of her sister's wedding. Beautiful 18-year-old Nicola Laitner had been a bridesmaid for elder sister Suzanne, and the reception had been held in a marquee erected on the lawn of her parents' luxury home in the South Sheffield suburb of Dore. Secretly watching the guests as they chatted, laughed and drank champagne was a man hiding in the bushes. He became captivated by Nicola's good looks and convinced himself he had to have her.

That night, 23 October 1983, a tired but no doubt happy Nicola went to bed. She was woken some time later by loud sounds on the landing and then her mother's screams. Wondering if she was really awake or in some strange nightmare, a dazed Nicola saw her bedroom door opened and a torchlight was flashed in her face. She could not see much beyond the glare in her eyes, but a man with a north-eastern accent said, 'Scream and you are dead!' It was to be the start of a very real horror story. Calmly the man told Nicola that he had killed both her parents, then added, 'I don't want to kill you – I want to fuck you!'

Wearing only her flimsy nylon nightie the girl was hustled at knifepoint out of her room and down the stairs. On the way she had to step past her father lying headfirst down the stairs. The man took Nicola to the marquee, scene of such a wonderful event a few hours earlier, where he raped her. She would never forget the smell of his sweat, his 'horrible' narrow face, cropped curly grey hair and stubbly chin, nor the fact that he wore brown trousers and a bloodstained blue T-shirt. When the teenager started to whimper the man got annoyed. He pointed out that he was only having sex with her. 'You've got to enjoy it, or I'll kill you,' he said, then added, 'That's where your Mum went wrong – she made a fuss.' After her ordeal a terrified Nicola was pushed back inside the house and up to her room. The man had committed multiple murders just to possess her body and he was not quite finished. In the bedroom he raped her twice more. Finally sated he told her before leaving to 'tell the police it was a black man'. He had left his traumatised victim tied up, but after some hours she managed to break out of her bonds. Workmen that Sunday morning, hired to take down the marquee, were startled by a tear-streaked teenage girl who ran onto the lawn in a blood-streaked nightie.

Police quickly arrived and found the murder scene was worse than Nicola had described. The killer had first entered an upstairs bedroom by mistake (he later admitted that the sight of a bridesmaid's dress hanging on the door had confused him) and assumed the lone figure in bed was Nicola. The room was that of her 28-year-old brother, Richard, whom the killer stabbed through the heart as he lay sleeping. Basil Laitner had just returned to the house and he heard odd sounds in his son's room. The killer heard him coming and was ready to strike. He plunged his knife deep into Mr Laitner's neck, then continued stabbing as the 59-year-old solicitor fought for his life. The struggle continued on the landing. Finally the killer drove his knife so hard into Mr Laitner's back that the tip came out at his chest. Avril Laitner had been in her bedroom on the ground floor but came out to see what all the commotion was about. She shouted to the murderer to leave. Waving his knife he chased her into the bedroom. Probably it was rape that was on the man's mind, but when Avril resisted he stabbed her 26 times, before cutting her throat. It was then that he gone in search of Nicola.

The house was awash with bloodstains. In Nicola's bedroom a team of forensic experts, led by Alfred Faragher from the serology department at the Home Office Forensic Science Laboratory at Wetherby, were skilled in the study of blood. Mr Faragher found one stain that seemed to come from a person at knee level kneeling or squatting on the bed. Since Nicola had no cuts to her legs it seemed likely that this clue belonged to the murderer. 'Blood fingerprinting', as the press called it, was in its infancy in the 1980s, yet it offered a new advance in which protein analysis of serum could reveal a factor found only in a percentage of the population. Faragher was able to discover a combination of factors in the stain that would be present in the blood of just one in 50,000 of the population. Cross-checking cases held at Wetherby led to a match with a County Durham man, 42-year-old Alfred Hutchinson. This petty criminal and recently suspected rapist had escaped via a toilet window while being questioned at Selby Police Station a few days earlier.

The media, including national TV, soon began issuing descriptions of the wanted man. Hutchinson, within 12 days of the murders, had moved all over the North staying in boarding houses in Barnsley, York, Scarborough and Manchester. Ten police forces were looking for him. He was finally cornered in a turnip field near Hartlepool, his home town. After his arrest Hutchinson tried, but failed, to stab himself. Detectives found an audio tape on which he boasted of his criminal career and the way he could outwit the police: 'However crackers I might be, I've walked past them several times... I'm a master of disguise.'

Clearly loving all the media attention, Hutchinson told interviewers several lies and kept altering his story. At his Sheffield Crown Court trial, which began on 4 September 1984, he admitted to the sex but said it had been consensual after meeting Nicola in a pub with two of her girlfriends. He tried to put the blame for the killings onto a crime reporter for a Sunday newspaper. A palm print on a champagne bottle in the marquee clearly showed that he had been there. Other identifying marks, such as the bloodstain in Nicola's room and teeth marks in a piece of cheese in the kitchen refrigerator placed him in the house. Then he changed his story and said that he had returned to the house after the sex and discovered the grisly killings. Hutchinson's defence counsel argued that if his client had been the murderer he would not have left Nicola alive. The jury were not impressed; they had listened for 210 minutes as the teenage girl had recounted her terrifying ordeal and insisted she had most definitely not offered her body freely to Hutchinson. The murderer was found guilty, as charged, on 14 September. The judge, Mr Justice McNeil, sentenced him to three terms of life imprisonment, eight years for rape and five years for aggravated burglary, with a recommendation that Hutchinson should serve not less than 18 years in prison.

After his conviction the Home Secretary, Leon Brittan, placed Hutchinson on a new list of prisoners whose life sentences could mean life. In 2008, still in gaol, the killer lodged two appeals in the High Court, but both were rejected. In July 2013 the European Court of Human Rights ruled that 'a whole-life tariff' was a breach of human rights. This inspired Hutchinson to be the first British prisoner to demand that he be freed due to this ruling. To his dismay, however, on 3 February 2015 the same court rejected his appeal on the grounds that 'whole-life tariffs were appropriate in certain cases'. Four months later the prisoner made an appeal to the Grand Chamber of the European Court of Human Rights, his last line of appeal, and his case was heard on 21 October 2015. To date no ruling has been delivered and as this book goes to press Hutchinson is still in prison after 32 years.

1985 Devious, Dangerous and Determined: Graham Backhouse

Things had not been going well for 43-year-old farmer Graham Backhouse. Once he had been a successful hairdresser, but then he had bought Widden Hall Farm in the hamlet of Horton near Bristol. There he tried to build up a top-class herd of Friesian cattle. Two years of crop failures on the farm had landed Graham with a £70,000 debt to his local National Westminster Bank.

Up to March 1984 there had been a life insurance policy on Margaret Backhouse, Graham's wife, for £50,000. That month he encouraged her to take out a further policy for the same amount so that £100,000 would be forthcoming in the sad event of her death or serious injury.

Mr Backhouse was not well liked by local villagers, or so he maintained. Proof of his assertion seemed obvious on 30 March when his herdsman found a sheep's head impaled on a farm post with a note that read 'You next'. Backhouse complained to the police after this incident and declared it was just the latest in a string of anonymous phone calls and poison pen letters. Local crime officers knew he had a reputation as a Don Juan although he and Margaret had been married for 10 years. An attractive woman of 38 years, Mrs Backhouse somehow stuck by her man, though well aware of his sneaky romances and philandering ways.

On the morning of 9 April 1984 Graham asked Margaret to use his Volvo – her own car had starting problems – to pick up some livestock antibiotics. Mrs Backhouse got into the vehicle just as her husband and his herdsman entered the nearby cattle shed. She turned the ignition key and a blast – later reckoned by forensic experts to be similar to a sawn-off shotgun propellant loaded with 4,500 pellets – ripped upwards from the seat beneath her. Margaret Backhouse, who was to lose half a thigh, somehow succeeded in opening the car door and falling onto the ground. Someone had turned a radio on in the cowshed so it was several minutes before Graham or his farm worker knew of Margaret's predicament. She was rushed to hospital and stabilised. Detectives found that her survival was due to the Volvo's construction which had caused most of the blast to be compressed downwards.

Mr Backhouse told police that he could not think of anyone who hated him so much they would want to kill him. He did, however, admit to several local affairs and said there could be a vendetta against him. When another threatening letter arrived it was sent to the Birmingham Forensic Laboratory. A documents expert, Mike Hall, saw that the letter writer had cunningly disguised his handwriting by going backwards and forwards over each letter. An examination of the 'You next' note showed the imprint of a doodle, which had been on another sheet of the writing pad. This was soon to prove very useful in the investigation.

Detectives were given a list by Graham of possible business associates and villagers who might bear him a grudge. One who was listed was Colyn Bedale-Taylor, aged 63, a local carpenter who had quarrelled with Backhouse over a right of way. Graham also listed a local quarryman who had access to explosives. Concerned for the farmer's safety, the police put him under protection for nine days, but this was withdrawn at Backhouse's own request after an angry phone call to D.C.I. Peter Brock in charge of the case. The police warned Backhouse not to take the law into his own hands. The farm was connected by an alarm to the local police station.

That alarm rang on the night of 30 April. Police Constable Richard Yeardon rushed to the farm where he found Backhouse covered in blood with knife wounds to the left side of his face and a deep gash at his shoulder that stretched down to his stomach. Lying dead in the hallway was Mr Bedale-Taylor with two gunshot wounds in the chest. According to Graham his neighbour had turned up on the pretext of repairing some furniture, then said he was sent by God and blamed the farmer for the death of his son, Digby Bedale-Taylor, who had died in a car crash two years earlier. The two men had got into a fight, Bedale-Taylor slashing with a Stanley knife he had been carrying, before Graham Backhouse managed to reach and fire his shotgun.

Initially the police found Backhouse's story all very convincing. They even found a length of pipe from which the bomb had been made on Mr Bedale-Taylor's property. It was then that Dr Geoff Robinson, a forensic biologist, noticed that the Stanley knife had the initials 'B. T.' scratched crudely on the handle. This seemed a little odd since all the dead carpenter's tools seemed in place in his workshop and had smartly engraved handles. Robinson was not happy with the blood spots which were all the wrong shape; they were round and neat as if sprinkled from above whereas if the two men had been fighting there would have been 'trails' as the blood flew around. Mr Backhouse had no defensive wounds to his hands. There was no trail of blood down the hallway, which the scientist found extraordinary in view of the farmer's claim that he had run to escape his assailant.

A forensic pathologist, Dr William Kennard, was puzzled how the knife was clasped so tightly in the dead man's hand. He also could not understand how the large amount of blood on Bedale-Taylor's shirt front came from Backhouse unless the farmer had actually stood over the other man's body.

Doing further research Dr Robinson examined the first threatening letter Backhouse claimed to have received. Some wool fibres were found under the microscope. These fibres were trapped in the gum which the man had licked to seal the envelope. Detectives found these fibres matched the wool in one of Graham's jerseys.

Next it was the turn of the documents examiner, Mike Hall, who was sent a notebook found in a drawer at the farm. To his surprise he found the very doodle that had been on the next page to the 'You next' note.

All this evidence was meticulously explained to the jury when Backhouse appeared in the dock of Bristol Crown Court in February 1985. The prosecuting counsel, James Black, Q.C., described the farmer as 'a devious, dangerous and determined man who had carefully planned both crimes and carried them out in cold blood'. While being held before his trial Backhouse even wrote to his wife claiming that the police 'are fabricating evidence against me... So please help me. I must get out of this hell hole.' He made the bad mistake of smuggling a letter to the *Bristol Evening Post*, protesting his innocence. Forensic examination showed that the handwriting of this letter matched some of the threatening letters. The jury were out for five and a half hours before finding Graham Backhouse guilty by a majority verdict of ten votes to two. Mr Justice Stuart-Smith sentenced the prisoner to two terms of life imprisonment for the attempted murder of his wife and murder of Colyn Bedale-Taylor. Watching impassively as sentence was passed was Margaret Backhouse who had kept her composure as the plot to kill her unfolded in court.

In June 1994 Graham Backhouse suffered a fatal heart attack after playing in a prison cricket match. The wife he had tried to kill died in her sleep just nine months later. She was only 48. The Backhouses sadly left two teenage children as orphans.

1986 The White House Farm Murders: Jeremy Nevill Bamber

Police work entails a variety of dramatic situations. In the early hours of 7 August 1985 a three-man unit led by Sergeant Christopher Bews headed from Witham Police Station, Essex, in response to a call received via Chelmsford that a Jeremy Bamber needed assistance at his father's farm at Tolleshunt D'Arcy, a small village some 10 miles away.

Bamber drove into the farmyard minutes after the police arrived. He told the officers that there were five people in the house: his two parents, his stepsister Shelia, aged 27, and her two six-year-old twin sons. Shelia had a history of mental illness. 'I don't like her and she doesn't like me,' Bamber told the police, 'She's a nutter!' He said that his father, 61-year-old farmer Nevill Bamber, had phoned him earlier saying, 'Your sister's gone crazy and she's got the gun,' before the line went dead. Officers were alarmed that there were several shotguns known to be in the house as well as two .22 rifles.

At 5am an armed squad from the Essex Police Tactical Firearms Unit arrived but the actual assault did not take place until 7.25am. Bursting into the kitchen they found Nevill Bamber dead: 'His badly battered head was buried face down in the Aga fuel hod.' The room was full of smashed glass and overturned furniture. Clearly the victim, a big man of 6 feet 4 inches, had fought tenaciously for his life. Upstairs his wife June was found spread-eagled on her back, shot in the head. Blood stained her light blue nightdress. Lying on the floor of the same bedroom and also in her nightdress was Shelia (Mrs Shelia Caffrell). She had two bullet wounds beneath her chin apparently the result of self-inflicted injuries since a .22 rifle lay on top of her with the woman's right hand near the trigger. Her two sons were found in an adjoining bedroom, both shot dead at point-blank range. Given the dreadful news that all his family were dead, Jeremy Bamber closed his eyes 'and began to cry'.

Despite the carnage it looked at first like an open and shut case. Shelia had spent spells in several mental institutions and had a long history of depressive-related illness. Twenty-five shots had been fired, 15 from close range and seven of them directed at June Bamber. There were no obvious signs of a break-in and Shelia's fingerprints were on the gun, suggesting that she was the last to die. A quick inquest concluded that she had died by her own hand though it was impossible with any certainty to say for sure if she had killed the others in the house. National newspapers were less queasy; 'Family of Five Killed by Suicide Mother' ran the headlines.

Initially the police did not suspect 24-year-old Jeremy, a handsome, well-spoken young man who showed every sign of sadness. The media worldwide flashed his image in tearful grief at his parents' funeral as he stood crying by the graveside, smartly attired in a Hugo Boss suit, his hands tightly clenched in those of trainee school teacher girlfriend Julie Mugford, an attractive brunette.

Relatives, as in so many murder cases, were the first to have doubts. Jeremy's uncle, Robert Boutflour, slept uneasily as he recalled an odd conversation with his nephew following a mysterious break-in at a caravan park owned by the family (this robbery later laid at Jeremy's door). There had been talk of mounting a vigilante patrol to safeguard the place but Mr Boutflour thought this might engender more problems. 'Oh no, Uncle Bobby, I'd have no trouble in killing anybody,' Jeremy had blurted out, 'I could easily kill my parents.' 'Don't be stupid,' replied Mr Boutflour. Now he went to the police with his suspicions and told them, 'I am convinced that Jeremy has sold his soul to the Devil. A consuming greed, envy, and possibly the immediate need for cash to support an already expensive lifestyle (possibly involving a dependence on expensive drugs such as cocaine) has driven him to take this dreadful crime.'

Soon the police were starting to have doubts. These suspicions magnified when Julie Mugford contacted detectives and told them how her highly sexed (and bisexual) lover had talked constantly during their 20-month relationship of acquiring the family's £400,000 fortune. She claimed he had spoken of two plans: one involved feeding sleeping tablets to his family and then burning White House Farm down around them; the other plan was even scarier and required shooting all of them and pinning the blame on 'barmy' Shelia. At 10pm on 6 August, according to Julie, Jeremy had called her and said it was now or never. She told him he was being foolish and assumed he was drunk or on drugs and playing some attention-seeking game. After the murders she asked him if he had killed his family. Jeremy had chuckled and denied the shootings, but admitted that he had paid a man £2,000 to kill them. Miss Mugford told police that she had kept this story to herself for one month while her affair with Jeremy went off the boil. At his trial the defence would claim that she had invented her tale to spite her ex-lover, but Julie denied this, saying she had kept quiet out of fear.

Bamber was duly arrested and his trial began at Chelmsford Crown Court on 2 October 1986 before Mr Justice Drake, an ex-wartime hero and holder of the D.F.C. The trial lasted 19 days. Despite compelling circumstantial evidence from Boutflour, Mugford and others, the real Crown case rested on the forensic evidence. A local plumber, named by Bamber as the hitman, was able to prove conclusively that he most certainly was not the killer.

A pathologist, Dr Peter Venezis, explained how it would not have been possible for Shelia to have fired the first bullet into her neck using a silencer fitted to the rifle, then packed it away, climbed the stairs and killed her mother and children. Nevill Bamber had been attacked with a rifle butt; tiny Shelia was known as 'Bambi' by friends and seemed an unlikely assailant for such a powerfully built man. Despite broken glass and bloodstains on the floor, Shelia's feet were quite clean, a very odd coincidence.

A ballistics expert, Malcolm Fletcher, said that Shelia had been shot with a silencer fitted to the rifle. Experiments with women volunteers had been carried out, but they found it 'physically impossible to press the trigger'. There was no tell-tale blood on Shelia's nightdress, which ought to have been the case if she was the killer, nor was there any oil or soot such as is normally left as residue when a gun is fired. This was remarkable if Shelia had fired 25 shots. Another expert told the court that Shelia had just a millionth of one gram of lead on her hands whereas the volunteers had much higher amounts. Her fingernails were also undamaged.

On 28 October 1986, after jury deliberations of more than nine hours, Jeremy Bamber was found guilty by a majority verdict of ten to two. Mr Justice Drake sentenced him to life imprisonment for each death, with a recommendation 'that you serve a minimum – I repeat a minimum – of 25 years'.

Today Bamber is still in gaol serving out his tariff in harsh Wakefield Prison. He has continually protested his innocence and has an active website that promotes the discrepancies in the case, especially the way crime scene photographs suggest that Essex Police inadvertently damaged the scene. In 1993 his lawyers contacted Professor Herbert MacDonell, 'America's foremost expert in forensic ballistics', author of *Bloodstain Pattern Interpretations* among other works. MacDonell compiled a report but it failed to exonerate Bamber since the expert showed Shelia's right arm had been moved after she was shot. He also deduced that with a silencer fitted it was impossible for Shelia to have reached the trigger and killed herself. He wrote: 'She did not commit suicide but, like the other four victims, was shot to death by someone else.'

A calculating killer or an innocent man? Jeremy Bamber and the White House Farm murders continue to fascinate criminologists and armchair sleuths alike.

1988 The Hungerford Massacre: Michael Robert Ryan

A lone gunman stalks through a town shooting people at random, dispensing death coldly and methodically until he, too, is dead. Stories of such atrocities seem almost monthly events in America where the freedom to own guns is enshrined in the constitution. In England such events are thankfully rare but in the 20th century they did happen. The first took place on 19 August 1987 when Michael Ryan slaughtered 16 innocent people (11 men and 5 women) and wounded many others in the picture-perfect and otherwise tranquil country town of Hungerford, Berkshire.

Twenty-seven at the time he committed the murders, the killer had been born in nearby Savernake Hospital and grown up in the genteel town with its broad Georgian High Street, antique shops and red-brick clock tower. Hungerford was home to 5,000 residents. The lazy River Kennet, famous for its trout, flows through the town, there are vistas of the lush Berkshire Downs, while ancient Savernake Forest with 6,000 acres of leafy glades spreading across the Wiltshire–Berkshire border is not far away.

Ryan's parents, Alfred and Dorothy, were pillars of the local community; the father was Clerk of Works to the local Rural District Council, the mother, who doted too heavily on her only child, was a much-liked waitress at a nearby hotel. As a kid Michael was spoiled by his parents. To outsiders he seemed a quiet, withdrawn child who did not make friends easily. Later some folks would say that he had always seemed a strange lad but, in truth, he was in many ways a normal boy with a loving family. What made him stand apart from fellow playmates, even at an early age, was an almost fetishistic obsession with guns. He liked Action Man toys and was delighted when his mum bought him an air rifle. 'He would shoot at anything, would Ryan,' recalled another boy years later. Sports and academic subjects at school bored Michael. He preferred to collect weapons including antique swords, though guns were his real passion. Hours were spent in the garden shed greasing, oiling, polishing and stripping his assortment of firearms. Under British Law at the time he was allowed to own up to five guns – Ryan had two rifles and three handguns by summer 1987 – but he was constantly changing his little arsenal, much to the annoyance of the local police. In his bedroom Ryan stored his large collection of gun and ammo mags, and books on famous weapons and survival techniques.

Dorothy gave her boy whatever she could afford. He was spoiled with a new motorbike and later a succession of flashy cars that he treated badly. In 1986 he joined the Dunmore Shooting Centre in nearby Abingdon to help improve his marksmanship, later joining another gun club in Devizes, Wiltshire. A neighbour recalled Michael in his 20s as 'a bit of a military freak and always wore combat gear. He would tend to his guns the way most people would tend to their plants.' Even when he went to the pub Michael drank alone. 'I don't think he was a loner by chance,' recalled a local publican, 'mind you – just that he seemed inadequate.' Ryan left school at 16 with no diplomas. By 1987 he had been through a line of menial jobs and was on the dole after leaving his last employment on 9 July. Six days later he bought, for £310, a Chinese 'Norino' version of the Russian Kalashnikov AK47 semi-automatic assault rifle (under British Law at this time these fearsome weapons were perfectly legal), nicknamed 'the widowmaker'.

What triggered Ryan's killing spree will never be known. A combination of factors seem to have exploded in his brain. Only 5 feet 6 inches tall, with a rapidly receding hairline, beer gut and light beard, Michael knew he was no Adonis. He seems never to have had a girlfriend and may well have been a virgin. He knew people thought he was a mother's boy and some called him a 'wimp'. He had grown even more introspective after his father's death in 1984. Perhaps he thought it was time to show people he was somebody, that he was a real man, to make himself known, to have an adventure. One theory also postulated after his death was that Ryan was a fan of a fantasy war game that urged him to kill. Was he unable to distinguish between reality and fantasy? Before his death he told the police, 'I know it's happened. I'm not stupid.'

A fellow gun club member recalled Michael as 'very polite. Just a nice pleasant lad who liked to talk to people about guns.' On that sunny Wednesday morning of 19 August this 'nice pleasant lad' complained of a headache and took two paracetamol. He got into his Vauxhall Astra and headed for Savernake Forest. Here, waving his Beretta self-loading pistol, he accosted 35-year-old Sue Godfrey and her two young children who were preparing a picnic. Told to leave her two- and four-year-olds at gunpoint, the petite housewife, nicknamed 'Little Sue' by friends, was led deeper into the trees. Police later conjectured that rape must have been on Ryan's mind. Who knows? Possibly Sue made a dash for it. The gunman shot her dead (the children later found another family and told their horrible tale). He returned to his car and sped off. At an isolated service station on the A4 he pulled up, fired some shots through the window, then marched into the shop. 'Please don't, please don't,' begged Mrs Kakoub Dean, the manageress, who crawled under the counter. Ryan stared at her coldly and pressed his trigger 'four or five clicks' but there was no sound of firing. The killer was out of ammunition.

Ryan fled back to his home. He must have been aware that his murderous activities would soon be reported. It was too late to go back on anything. He doused his family home with petrol and set it ablaze. In his car were a survival kit along with battledress trousers and a balaclava helmet with eye holes. He took with him the Beretta pistol, an M1 carbine and the Kalashnikov.

What happened that afternoon in Hungerford might have been entirely different if Ryan had been able to drive away. This seems to have been in his mind but he could not get his car to start. He had always treated the vehicle badly. In a fury he sprayed it with five bullets, narrowly missing the petrol tank. So it was that he now caused a trail of death through his home town kitted out in an olive green armoured waistcoat and armed to the hilt as he jogged off down the road. His first victims were neighbours Roland and Shelia Mason; the last to die was 34-year-old Ian Phayle, clerk to the magistrates at Newbury, who was killed by a single bullet in the throat as he was driving his car to get away. It would be repetitive to list all Ryan's killings and woundings, as well as possibly upsetting survivors and loved ones who are still alive. One of the saddest and most terrible deaths was that of Dorothy Ryan who, like any loving mother, tried to stop her son. She yelled at him, 'Michael, why are you doing this?' There was no reply but he raised his Kalashnikov. 'Don't shoot me,' said Mrs Ryan. Her son put four bullets in her back. She was the eighth to die that day.

The shootings ended at a local school where Ryan found himself cornered by police marksmen. In a surreal conversation with negotiators the gunman admitted that 'Hungerford must be a bit of a mess' and 'it's like a bad dream'. He was concerned especially to know if his mother was alive or dead as her shooting 'was a mistake'. At one point Ryan said, 'It's funny. I killed all those people, but I haven't got the guts to blow my own brains out,' yet at 18.52 there came a muffled shot from a classroom. Michael Ryan, who had never expressed remorse for any of the deaths, had killed himself with a single round from his 9mm Beretta. His body was cremated on 3 September 1987. There were only seven mourners and two floral tributes. Feelings in Hungerford ran high. The national *Daily Star* newspaper next day reported the funeral with a three word headline – 'Fry in Hell'. Due to the outcry, Parliament passed in 1988 the Firearms Amendment Act which banned the ownership of semi-automatic centre-fire rifles as well as the use of shotguns with a capacity of more than three cartridges.

1988 The Railway Killers: John Patrick Duffy & David Mulcahy

Rape is a particularly ugly crime. The police investigating such cases are always aware of the possibility that they might be dealing with a serial rapist. These offenders often turn increasingly violent and can transform into murderers. Thankfully rare are predatory rapists working in pairs. When such men turn killers, it is a nightmare for the forces of law and order – and their communities.

It was in June 1982 that two men raped a woman near Hampstead Station. The following 12 months saw the pair rape 18 more women within a 5-mile radius of north London. One of the attackers was short, the other tall; both wore balaclavas. Then the attacks stopped. During the second half of 1984 they began again, though now they featured just the small man. Police were mystified and confused; what had happened to the other rapist – had the pair fallen out, the man changed his job or moved away?

In July 1985 three women were attacked separately during one night in the Hendon and Hampstead areas. It was after these crimes that detectives realised they were dealing with a serial rapist with a distinct modus operandi: he chatted up his victims before leading them at knifepoint to a secluded spot; their hands were tied with coarse string usually in a tourniquet and the man ended his rape by wiping the victim's genitals with paper tissues, or combing her pubic hair, as if trying to reduce the forensic evidence. Detective Superintendent Ken Worker was placed in charge of Operation Hart and told to catch this rapist. Soon officers saw a pattern in 27 attacks stretching from Camden Town northwards. Many of the rapes took place near railway lines and the culprit seemed to enjoy the power he wielded and was not averse to using violence.

Operation Hart soon had 4,784 suspects in a database. Hard police work reduced this figure to 1,593. In July 1985 suspect 1,594 was added; this was John Duffy, a 30-year-old Irish-born Kilburn man who attacked his estranged wife and then used his karate skills to rough up her Hungarian boyfriend. Duffy was brought in for an identity parade after a rape in September but the traumatised victim failed to recognise her attacker.

Just before New Year, a 19-year-old secretary, Alison Day, left her home in Hornchurch, Essex, to travel by train to Hackney to see her boyfriend – but she never arrived. Alison's disappearance sparked a huge murder hunt. Seventeen days after she vanished Alison's body was found in the River Lea – tied up, strangled and raped. Most forensic evidence had been destroyed by the long immersion in water but the girl's sheepskin coat bore fibre samples that might have come from her killer. Detective Superintendent Farquhar in charge of the investigation liaised with the Hart team and similarities with some of the other rapes made officers realise that the 'Railway Rapist' had turned to murder.

Four months later, on 17 April 1986, 15-year-old Maartje Tamboezer, daughter of a wealthy oil executive, was forced off her bicycle near the railway line in Horsley by a fishing line strung across the path. She was then dragged into some woods, cruelly beaten and raped before being strangled. A sock was stuffed into her mouth. The girl's hands were tied in a tourniquet in a manner identical to the knot used on Alison Day. Burning paper tissues had been forced into the girl's vagina to eliminate sperm samples. Witnesses came forward saying they had seen a small man wearing a blue parka and running to catch a train. Two million tickets were examined in the hope that he had left his fingerprints behind but without success. At least police scientists were able to discover that he was a 'Group A Secretor' – someone whose blood group can be determined from bodily fluids. Using an enzyme called PGM they were able to eliminate four out of every five suspects.

On 18 May – one month after Maartje's death – Ann Lock, a 29-year-old secretary with London Weekend Television, disappeared while on a walk. Ten weeks later her badly decomposed body was found in undergrowth near Brookmans Park Station, Hertfordshire, not far from her home. She had been raped, suffocated and, once again, an attempt had been made to burn out the sperm.

The day before Ann's disappearance John Duffy had been arrested for loitering at North Weald Station. He was found to be carrying a butterfly knife similar to one described in some of the attacks. He denied any involvement in the rapes and was duly released. Two months later he returned for further questioning and in the presence of his solicitor refused to give a blood sample. Detectives from Hart were starting to realise that Duffy, with his pockmarked features, small build and penetrating cold blue eyes, fitted the description of the man mentioned in many of the attacks.

In October 1986 a 14-year-old schoolgirl was attacked and raped near Watford Station. Duffy was still roaming around and had wasted police time claiming mental illness. Rapidly he was becoming Operation Hart's chief suspect. Around this time Professor David Canter, a behavioural psychologist, presented the police with a report he had compiled on the Railway Killers. The profile contained 17 characteristics and Duffy fitted 13 of them. On 11 November he was put under 24-hour surveillance and 12 days later he was arrested. Thirteen fibres from a jumper in his wardrobe matched those of clothes worn by Alison Day. Detectives found a collection of knives as well as 33 door keys stolen from some of the rape victims. Five of the victims unhesitatingly picked Duffy out of an identity parade.

On 26 February 1988 at the Old Bailey Mr Justice Farquharson sentenced Duffy to 30 years' imprisonment. The judge called him 'little more than a predatory animal' and gave him seven life sentences. D.S. Farquhar told reporters: 'He is without doubt one of the most evil characters in the history of British justice. Duffy is a walking advertisement for the return of the death penalty.'

Duffy's imprisonment was by no means the end of the case. Police still wanted to find his tall rapist accomplice. For a decade Duffy refused to divulge his name. Then, in March 1999, he pleaded guilty to further rapes between 1975 and 1986 including the attack on Ann Lock. Duffy was asked: 'Did you carry out all these offences on your own or with another on occasions?' He replied: 'With another on occasions,' before naming David Mulcahy as the man. He went on to implicate Mulcahy in all three murders.

The pair had met at Haverstock Secondary School and became inseparable friends. As kids they had shot at passers-by with air rifles and always enjoyed 'scaring people'. Once they were banned from school for bludgeoning hedgehogs. Duffy explained how they went 'hunting' for women to rape, at first treating the attacks as a game, before things turned serious. Early victims had referred to the tall man – Mulcahy – as 'the horrible one' and Duffy as 'the nice one'. According to Duffy it was Mulcahy who had strangled Alison Day, their first murder victim, because she made him angry by trying to run away. Mulcahy was turned on by the power to decide life or death, calling it 'almost God-like'. Miss Tamboezer was strangled first by Mulcahy and then by Duffy, the former killer being 'excited like a schoolboy' when he attempted to burn the body.

Mulcahy's trial at the Old Bailey lasted five months. He was presented as the chief perpetrator of the murders, a killer for whom sexual stimulation alone lacked the added thrill of murder. Both men were shown to be sadists. Duffy had frequently forced his wife to participate in bondage sex against her will and his hatred of women seemed to have been fuelled by his low sperm count and inability to father a child. The little man got his kicks from humiliating and raping women, but Mulcahy enjoyed far more the exercise of power over his victims, the opportunity to terrorise and the sheer sadism of inflicting pain. He would run his knife over nipples and threaten to gouge out eyes, then ask tenderly as he kissed a victim's neck, 'Are you a virgin?'

Duffy was convicted of 17 more rapes. Mulcahy was given a life sentence for each of the three murders and 24 years on each count of rape and conspiracy to rape. His wife, the mother of his four children, watched from the gallery and continued to assert her husband's innocence. Both men are unlikely ever to be released, though in 2015 Mulcahy, now 55 years old, was still protesting his innocence and planning a fresh appeal.

1989 Sicko: Anthony Arkwright

What triggers someone to go on a killing spree? Twenty-two-year-old Arkwright had always seemed a little dotty to his friends but no one could have guessed the insane savagery of his murder rampage.

Known to local South Yorkshire police as a petty criminal, the young man with a shock of upright blonde hair had served a 30-month term for burglary and was frequently argumentative with his neighbours. The son of a miner, he was born and grew up in Wath, a small mining community. His childhood had been spent in children's homes and authority care after his mother left him when he was just four years old, though he kept in touch with his dad. Tantrums and petty crime marked his childhood and teens. Clearly this unstable upbringing left deep scars on Arkwright's mind. A loner, he sometimes stayed at his father's flat in Denman Road or in hideouts he constructed by the railway line, where he liked to fantasise that he was an SAS-style survivalist.

On Friday, 26 August 1988, Arkwright was sacked from his job in a Mexborough, Doncaster, scrapyard due to his bad attendance record.

His anger drove him over the edge of sanity. At 4.30pm and after several drinks, he located his grandfather, 68-year-old Lithuanian-born Stasys Puidokas, on the old man's allotment in Ruskin Drive. Arkwright incorrectly believed that Mr Puidokas was his father, after having an incestuous relationship with his mother. Accusing the older man of incest he first stabbed him in the neck, severing an artery that quickly left Puidokas unconscious, then hit him with an axe and a 14lb lump hammer before locking the body in a shed.

That night Arkwright got drunk in several pubs and dropped hints to anyone who would listen about the murder. At 3am on the Saturday morning he entered the flat of his next-door neighbour, 45-year-old ex-teacher Raymond Ford. A depressive, Ford seemed to spend his days drinking cheap cider and doing crossword puzzles. Earlier that week Arkwright had burgled Mr Ford's flat and stolen a microwave oven and a clock. Totally naked save for a 'Prince of Darkness' mask, the young man stabbed Mr Ford no less than 250 times – some accounts say 500 times – over all parts of his body. Clearly having read of the Jack the Ripper killings, he neatly disembowelled his victim and, just as in the 1888 murder of Mary Jane Kelly, draped the entrails around the room and scattered some internal organs in the hallway and corridor.

Four hours later Arkwright was arrested on suspicion of the Ford burglary. The police had no idea at this stage that they were dealing with a psycho-killer. He was kept for 12 hours in custody before being released to appear at court on the following weekend. Within hours, on 28 August, Arkwright murdered a friend, 25-year-old Marcus Law, who he felt had scrounged too many cigarettes off him. Law was a big man but wheelchair-bound as a result of a recent motorcycle accident. He could not defend himself as Arkwright rained down more than 70 stab wounds, then stuffed cigarettes in his victim's ears and mouth, gouged out his eyes and placed unlit cigarettes in the sockets.

Next day Mr Law's mother called at his home in Denman Road and found the awful murder scene. Arkwright was quickly found and arrested on suspicion of murder. Detectives realised that there was something very odd about the young man when he sat at the interview table and pulled out a four of hearts playing card with the words, 'This is the master card. It means you have four bodies and a madman on the loose.' The police wanted to interview everyone in Denman Road and P.C. David Winter went to see Mr Ford. It was Winter's misfortune to be the first officer to see what one policeman called 'the most brutal act of slaughter I have ever seen'. Referring to Arkwright's handiwork he said: 'It is all the more chilling when you realise he must have spent at least half an hour inflicting these terrible wounds.' Another detective is quoted as saying that Arkwright was 'the most dangerous criminal I ever met in 25 years on the job'.

The young killer pleaded guilty to the three murders and was gaoled for life at Sheffield Crown Court by Mr Justice Boreham, with a recommendation that he should serve at least 25 years. In 1990 the Home Secretary imposed a whole-life tariff, meaning that Arkwright will never be released. At his trial he had pleaded not guilty to a fourth murder, that of his grandfather's housekeeper, elderly Elsa Konradaite, but it was felt that this case can stay on file. Arkwright never fully explained his actions so the deeper reasons for his murder spree will never be known. He has also gloated to police and prison officials, clearly revelling in his own notoriety. A sad postscript relates to Mr Law's father, a retired engineer, who was haunted by his son's murder. Fourteen years later he committed suicide in a fit of depression.

1990 The Killer from Manilla: Victor Castigador & Paul Clinton

An illegal immigrant from the Philippines, Castigador had entered Britain in 1985 when he was 31 years old. It was claimed at his trial that he had formerly been a hitman for President Ferdinand Marcos. In London he tried various jobs before getting employment at Leisure Investments Amusement Arcade in Wardour Street, Soho, a business staffed and managed mainly by Latinos. Castigador started to feel bitter towards his employer when he was passed over for management. His grudge developed into a plan to rob the arcade.

According to one employee, he had actually just been fired when he led a gang of four young accomplices into the building around midnight on 2 August 1989. The place had just closed for the day and the relief manager, Yuri Gomez, and cashier, 26-year-old Deborah Alvares, were counting the day's takings – about £9,000. At gunpoint Castigador's gang helped themselves to the cash, then forced Mr Gomez, Ms Alvares and their two Sri Lankan security men, aged 21 and 28 years, into the inner 'cash cage' of the strong room. Three of the robbers withdrew at this point leaving Castigador and a 17-year-old thug called Paul Clinton alone with the victims. Calmly the handsome Filipino with the cold dark eyes tied up his former workmates and with Clinton's help poured white spirit over them. Matches were lit and tossed at the hostages as the two robbers locked their victims in the strong room. It was their clear intention to murder those who had seen the raid and burn down the building.

The two guards died of burns and asphyxiation but somehow both Yuri Gomez and Deborah Alvares managed to survive. Both suffered 30 per cent burn injuries over their bodies and 'full thickness' burns to their faces, yet they were able to put out their own flames and take breaths of air through a keyhole. Their rescue came not until next morning, after suffering the pains of their ordeal all through the night, when staff arrived for work. Castigador was quickly identified and the other gang members also arrested.

After their Old Bailey trial, which ended on 28 February 1990, Castigador and Clinton were convicted of two murders, two attempted murders and one charge of robbery. The Filipino was given a recommended sentence that he serve not less than 25 years but the Home Secretary changed this to a whole-life tariff. The three lesser gang members all got gaol sentences and Clinton, who might also have ended up in prison for life, was given 20 years due to his youth.

During June 2016, as this book was being completed, Castigador was in court again charged with murdering a fellow inmate at Long Lartin Prison. The 61-year-old killed Sidonio Teixeira, aged 59 years, who had been gaoled for life in 2008 for murdering his three-year-old daughter and attempting to murder his nine-year-old son. Castigador apparently crept up on Teixeira on 26 June and smashed his head in with a rock hidden in a sock.

Victims in these cases are all too often forgotten yet they live the rest of their lives with terrifying memories. In 2009, when Clinton was due for release, Deborah Alvares had told a daily newspaper: 'I just want Clinton to stay in there... It was a horrendous ordeal... I used to walk a lot but now I can't walk that far because of my injuries. It becomes painful. I have down days like everyone, but I like listening to music – it makes me feel better.'

1991–2000

The murder, attempted murder and manslaughter figures were now running at more than double the figures of 40 years previously. The decade saw them rise to 6,470 persons on trial. It was an ugly decade with several notable sex murderers including Ireland (1993), Black (1994) and the Wests (1995). At the end of the decade came Dr Shipman (2000), a surprisingly old-style killer using that ancient tool – poison. His list of victims would dwarf anything yet seen in the British Isles and show how poison remains the most deadly weapon in the murderer's arsenal. For their part, detectives now had an impressive armoury of their own with improved fingerprinting, blood analysis and DNA techniques, yet many people seemed to think they could get away with murder. Cold cases such as Diedrick (1999) showed that they had less and less chance and that the law can catch up with them. Murder has never been such a risky business.

1991 The Body in the Bags Killer: Malcolm Green

Released to kill again, Green is a double-murderer from Ely, a suburb of Cardiff, who used the same *modus operandi* in each case – dismemberment of his victim.

On 5 November 1971, aged just 25 years, he was convicted of the brutal slaying of a 41-year-old Cardiff prostitute named Glenys Johnson. Green cut up her body and dumped the parts on waste ground off Wharf Street, Cardiff, close to the docks. He then phoned the police and taunted them saying, 'Have you found the body yet? There will be four more. This is the Ripper.' Despite his threats Green was soon caught and at his trial was sentenced to life imprisonment.

He was paroled 18 years later in 1989. Within five months, he killed again after befriending a young New Zealand tourist called Clive Tully. He bludgeoned his victim over the head with a hammer before sawing up the body. The grisly remains were discarded across South Wales. Police had to deal with a torso found in Rogerstone and a head and limbs at St Brides Wentlooge in the lonely marshlands between Cardiff and Newport. The head was so damaged that a graphic artist was successfully employed to produce a computer-enhanced photograph of the victim. This led to people coming forward and naming the missing Mr Tully. Green was a suspect due to the earlier murder. Detectives visited his home and saw bloodstains on the stairs and under his bed.

In 1991 he stood once again in Cardiff Crown Court and was sentenced to a minimum of 25 years for Mr Tully's killing. The Home Secretary subsequently extended this to a whole-life tariff, meaning Green will probably die in prison. Psychiatrists interviewing him came to the conclusion that Green's obsession with mutilation and death may be triggered by an awful experience he had as a child of 12 when he witnessed the accidental death of his brother, who was decapitated by a train.

1992 Murder on Television: Albert Dryden

It was bound to happen sooner or later – someone would be murdered in front of reporters and television cameras. The actual event was an avoidable and sad affair in which a decent man lost his life because of a squabble over plans to demolish an ugly little bungalow.

The murderer, Albert Dryden, was a 51-year-old self-employed small landowner, a bushy-bearded eccentric who had constructed a largely completed bungalow – he also termed it an 'atomic fallout shelter' – on a plot of land he owned in Eliza Lane, Butsfield, a small village just off the A68 between Castleside and Tow Low, Sunderland. From the mid-1980s when he purchased the land, Albert always seemed to be in dispute, either with neighbours, or the local Derwentside District Council. Planning officer Harry Collinson, also a local man, tried at first to be sympathetic to Albert's scheme to establish a smallholding on the site. He even helped him acquire some saplings, but the cantankerous landowner was soon constructing various ramshackle buildings such as greenhouses without much glass in them.

Dryden had set his heart on building his own bungalow and believed that if the top of the building was less than 6 feet above normal ground level then he did not need planning permission. To this end he excavated a large hole, dumped huge mounds of earth around his property and started construction down in the hollow. The local planning department was adamant that 'ground level' was the height measured from the foundations of the building. An appalled official visited the site and reported that 'the structure was built in a higgledy-piggledy fashion, part of it in brick and part of it in breezeblock, with some sections of the wall even made of wood. There was a random, haphazard distribution of windows and the roof was only partially tiled, interspersed with bits of rusting corrugated tin and Perspex sheets.' Dryden was saying it would be a fine bungalow when finished but the 'amateur, dangerous and ramshackle structure' was currently home to a family of goats.

Derwentside Council said the bungalow would have to be demolished. Mr Dryden refused to tear it down. Official letters whirled between the warring parties. Years passed. More disturbed as time went by, Albert seemed to view Harry Collinson and his planning team as enemies; anonymous phone calls were made to home numbers threatening lives. Dryden told people that he had booby-trapped his land with explosives. Since he was known to be a keen gun enthusiast, the local police were also concerned that matters should not get out of hand.

Demolition of the bungalow, at least in official circles, was finally set for 20 June 1991. The planning officers mobilised a bulldozer and met two days earlier with the Consett police. Mr Collinson asked that no one should touch or provoke tetchy Albert, whatever the provocation. Several local newspapers had decided to cover the event as well as a camera crew from BBC North East led by reporter (and usually the studio's news anchor-man) Tony Belmont, who was covering for a colleague with another commitment.

The reporters began that sunny morning by interviewing Dryden who was confident that an appeal he claimed to have lodged with the Department of the Environment would see him victorious. A self-righteous kind of man, he lectured his audience like a barrister and said it would take another five weeks to get a government decision.

Not entering Dryden's property due to a locked gate, Mr Collinson, a balding 46-year-old workaholic, arrived and pointed out that he had a valid enforcement notice to demolish the bungalow. Arguments ensued between Albert and Harry across the gate as Dryden was concerned about damage to his property and livestock. When told he would be liable for 'any damage subsequently caused as a result of you preventing us', Dryden stared at Collinson and slowly said: 'Well, you might not be around to see the outcome of this disaster. Now you've been warned.' When the bulldozer moved down the lane towards his land Dryden grabbed a western-style gun belt from under the wheel of an old caravan, walked up to Harry Collinson and pointed a pistol at him. Quite calmly the planning officer turned to the BBC cameraman and said: 'Can you get a shot of this gun?' The remark seemed to galvanise Dryden into action; perhaps he saw it as a provocation, because he squeezed off a round that hit Collinson squarely in the heart. The planning officer fell back into a drainage ditch. Pandemonium now broke out as local government officials, police, reporters and members of the public all ran for their lives. TV reporter Tony Belmont was shot through the arm and P.C. Steven Campbell was hit in the back before Dryden returned to Mr Collinson's body and fired two more rounds into the dying man's face and chest. Calmly, as if nothing had happened, he returned to his caravan and started brewing a pot of tea. He was captured later after a stand-off of a few hours by armed police officers wearing body armour.

Dryden's trial began at Newcastle Crown Court on 16 March 1992 before a female judge – Mrs Justice Ebsworth. The defendant was charged with one count of murder and three counts of attempted murder. Thirty-one witnesses were called by the prosecution and six for the defence, including Dryden himself. The defendant said that he had been suffering from acute head pains on the day of the tragedy. Admitting that he fired the fatal shots, Dryden blamed the officials for refusing to 'back off' and not waiting a few more weeks. He showed no signs of remorse over the murder. The jury of six men and six women listened to psychiatrists with varying opinions on whether the accused was suffering from 'diminished responsibility' at the time he pulled the trigger. It took the jury just two hours and four minutes on 31 March to find Albert Dryden guilty on all charges. In passing sentence Judge Ebsworth said 'the state of your mind on the day of the shooting was abnormal, but not sufficiently abnormal to diminish your responsibility for your actions... you are a dangerous man.'

No minimum sentence was placed on Dryden's term. He was freed in late 2017 on grounds of ill health. Six days after he began his sentence the bungalow was demolished, the hollow was filled in and the land restored to its former leafy natural state. Dryden died in 2018.

1993 The Man Who 'Hated Queers': Colin Ireland

An inner rage was what fuelled Colin Ireland's murders. While it is true that he stated that he 'hated queers', as he dismissively called homosexuals, the man was a rumbling volcano of violence who needed an excuse to unleash his homicidal tendencies. After his arrest he was at pains to tell detectives that he had not killed under the influence of alcohol or drugs, was not gay and did not participate in any sexual activity with his victims. He had targeted the homosexual community because they were easy prey and in his eyes vermin to be destroyed.

Ireland was born in 1954, son of a shop assistant at Dartford, Kent. His childhood was spent in various places with his mother and grandmother including a council house in Myrtle Road. At school he was frequently bullied, partly because he was a loner; 'a thin, lanky little runt, always getting the worst of it' was how he later remembered those years. When he was 12 Colin's mother, who seems to have been a kind-hearted woman, remarried and the family moved to the Isle of Sheppey. Some accounts say that the boy's new stepfather was a disciplinarian who beat him, others that he was a good parent. Whatever the truth, Colin's personality was starting to change. He became so difficult at school that he had to be sent to a special one for maladjusted children. The boy tried to burn down a similar institution. Soon he was turning to petty crime and was put in the charge of the local authority. A conviction for theft led him to a borstal institution and further charges of robbery, burglary, extortion and attempted deception meant spells in prison. According to Ireland, he had tried at one point to enlist in the French Foreign Legion but was rejected.

After two ruined marriages (he ran out on one wife after stealing her pub takings), Ireland had ended up by 1992 working at a night shelter for the homeless in Southend-on-Sea, Essex. Just before Christmas he had a row with a homosexual man at the shelter and, as a result, lost his job. This may have been the trigger that unleashed Ireland's desire to get his own back on society.

On 8 March 1993 he deliberately went for a drink at the Coleherne pub in Earls Court, West London, a popular hangout for homosexual men, especially, reportedly, those into kinky games. Ireland carried with him a knapsack containing his murder kit – nylon cord, a knife, gloves and a change of clothes. Men at the Coleherne carried colour-coded handkerchiefs to indicate the kind of sex they liked. Ireland, posing as a 'top' or 'dominant master', was looking for those into sadomasochism and especially passive masochists. Peter Walker, a 45-year-old theatre choreographer, walked past Ireland and accidentally spilled his drink. 'I pulled him up about this,' Ireland later said, 'he asked me to beat him; it may seem strange, but that's what he wanted. I said to him: "Don't worry. I'll take care of that."' Back at Walker's flat in Vicarage Road,

Battersea, Ireland tied up his victim on a bed, put a plastic bag over the man's head and started to suffocate him. Partial asphyxiation is a special bondage game but Walker at some point realised that it was all going too far. Ireland explained to police: 'It was a fate thing, and he said to me: "I'm going to die." And I said: "Yes, you are."' After the murder the killer stayed in the apartment watching television. He stole £200, placed two teddy bears in a 69 position on Walker's body and then, for some bizarre reason, singed the man's pubic hairs, 'just to see what it smelt like'.

Like many other murderers, Ireland was desperate to see his crime immortalised. He made an anonymous phone call to the *Sun* newspaper saying: 'I did it.' The body had actually been discovered six hours earlier after Mr Walker failed to turn up at a West End theatre rehearsal. Ireland also made two phone calls to the Samaritans, telling them about the murder and saying that Walker's two Labrador dogs needed feeding.

Several weeks later, on 28 May, Ireland returned to the Coleherne looking for someone new to kill. His choice was 37-year-old Christopher Dunn, a librarian and masochist. Once Dunn was tied to a bed in his Wealdstone flat Ireland stole money from the man's wallet and demanded to know his bank card PIN. When Dunn refused to tell him Ireland started burning his victim's testicles with a cigarette lighter. Once he had the number he then strangled the helpless man using some nylon cord. After the body's discovery the murder was thought at first to have been the result of an erotic sex game gone wrong. Only after more killings was it linked to Ireland.

Ireland was back at the Coleherne six days later and looking for a third victim. This time the man he chose was a Texan sales director called Perry Bradley III. The American did not want to be tied up but somehow Ireland convinced him that it would all be part of a fun S&M ritual. Once Bradley was helpless he rifled through the man's wallet. Bradley agreed that next morning he would take Ireland to a cashpoint machine. The killer lulled his victim into taking a nap before strangling him. He placed a doll on the dead body, stayed in the apartment all night and left in the rush of morning commuters.

Now on what he later called a 'roller coaster', Ireland picked up his fourth victim at the Coleherne just four nights later. This was 33-year-old Andrew Collier, warden of a block of sheltered accommodation in Dalston, East London. Ireland now made his first mistake by taking off his gloves and accidentally leaving a fingerprint on a window grille. Rummaging around the flat Ireland found out that Collier was HIV positive. This made him go 'fucking crazy'. He burned part of his victim's body, hanged the man's beloved cat before his helpless eyes, then strangled him. The cat's tail was placed in Collier's mouth and the animal's mouth around his penis, both tail and penis sheathed in condoms. Once again the murderer stayed in the apartment all night and melted into the morning rush hour.

Enraged that his spate of murders were not getting more attention in the press, the killer anonymously rang up both Kensington and Battersea police to complain, 'Doesn't the death of a homosexual man mean anything to you?' He told detectives that he wanted to be a serial killer and claimed to have studied 'the F.B.I. manual' for details and the minimum body count. 'I know how many you have to do,' he told the police. On 12 June, five nights after his fourth murder, Ireland left the Coleherne again with Emmanuel Spiteri, a 41-year-old Maltese chef who liked wearing black leather. He was soon suspicious of Ireland, especially after the spate of murders. Eventually Mr Spiteri got Ireland to confess that he was the man who was killing homosexuals. The murderer later admitted that the chef was 'a very brave man, but I couldn't afford to let him stick around and recognise me, so I killed him with a noose'. The Spiteri murder was Ireland's second mistake because the victim's home in Hither Green meant travelling via Charing Cross where the pair had been captured on security cameras. Once again Ireland phoned the police to brag about his five killings. Asked 'What was your aim in all that?' he chillingly replied: 'Just to see if it could be done.'

Co-ordinating police efforts was Detective Chief Superintendent Kenneth John. On 29 June he issued a description based on the video fit. The murderer was 'white, aged between 30 and 40, heavily built and 6 feet or more in height. Clean shaven with a full fattish face, short dark brown hair, and dirty, discoloured teeth. He was casually dressed in a dark jacket and jeans.' Actually the police were somewhat stumped; the gay community, fearful of repercussions since S&M acts were not entirely legal, was not being helpful while the senior forensic pathologist, searching for clues, admitted that it was a 'bloody difficult' case. Newspapers were now dubbing the killer 'The Gay Slayer' and asking why the police were saying so little.

By 20 July the case had stalled. That day Ireland walked into a solicitor's office in Southend and after a talk, agreed to make a statement to the police. He claimed that he was the man in the Spiteri video taken at Charing Cross (this footage had been released to the media on 2 July), but that the murder victim had been 'alive and well when I left him'. After several hours of being grilled by detectives Ireland at last made a full confession. He was initially charged with the Collier murder and subsequently all the others.

At the Old Bailey on 20 December Ireland's trial was a short one as he pleaded guilty to all five murders. Mr Justice Sachs handed down five life sentences saying: 'To take one human life is outrageous. To take five is carnage. You expressed your desire to be regarded as a serial killer – that must be matched by your detention for life. In my view it is absolutely clear that you should never be released.' He never was. Colin Ireland died in Wakefield Prison on 21 February 2012. A post-mortem ascribed his passing to 'pulmonary fibrosis' caused by a fractured hip that had not healed after a fall earlier that month. It is rumoured that while in prison he strangled to death a cell mate. He was never charged for killing this convicted child murderer since he was already serving life without parole, the harshest penalty under British Law.

1994 Suffer Little Children: Robert Black

Every country seems to have some sexually related social and moral dilemma that escalates into a national obsession. America, for instance, still finds abortion a headline issue, one that can lead to heated debate and even murder, while in Europe the subject is hardly news and barely raises an eyebrow. In Britain the emotive topic is paedophilia. This national fear of child molesters and killers is due in part to some high-profile cases and among these one of the best known and worst is that of Robert Black. He was convicted of the kidnapping, rape and murder of four young girls and at the time of his death in 2016 was being arraigned on a fifth killing done in 1978. He may well have committed many other child murders in Britain and on the European mainland between 1969 and 1987, making him one of the most notorious murderers in late 20th-century Britain.

One of the saddest aspects of Black's case is that he was clearly abused himself as a child and his obsession with young girls began when he was very young. No institution, no doctor, no psychiatrist was able to control Robert's impulses. His obsession with female genitalia led to his crimes and they in turn grew increasingly brutal.

He was born illegitimate in Grangemouth, Scotland, on 21 April 1947. Six months later he was placed in the foster home of Jack and Isabel Tulip, an experienced middle-aged foster couple who lived in Kinlochleven. For the next 11 years, Black had a home of sorts. Jack died when the child was five and Isabel passed away in 1958. She seems to have been a good woman but on occasions was not above belting or slippering Robbie, who was a young scamp. Even at an early age he was quite taciturn and on occasions displayed aggression. He also never showed much interest in personal hygiene, much to Isabel's annoyance, and at school was called 'Smelly Bobby Tulip'. He later claimed that at age five he and a girl compared their genitalia. This was a pivotal moment in Black's life and led to an obsession with female vaginas and anuses. He was angry that he had not been born a girl. From the age of eight, he started experimenting with inserting objects into his anus. When they raided his flat 35 years later, police found photographs Black had taken of himself inserting a chair leg, a telephone receiver and other objects.

After Isabel's death in 1958 young Robert was placed with another local foster family. That year he dragged a young girl into a public lavatory and assaulted her. This led to him being moved to a mixed-sex children's home in Falkirk. Here he regularly exposed himself to girls and led a gang who tried to rape one of the females. As a result he was sent to an all-male home in Musselburgh called the Red House. Robert was bright enough to study at the local grammar school but he made few friends. One classmate later recalled him as 'a bit of a loner with a tendency to bully'. His dream was to be a professional footballer, a wish he held dear until his 20s when failing eyesight spoiled all chances. At the Red House, Black was regularly abused by an elderly male staff member and for years he had to give this paedophile blowjobs.

In 1963, aged 16, he moved to Greenock and got a job as a butcher's delivery boy. If he found any young girls alone at home on his calls Black would sexually fondle them. He later confessed to 30–40 such assaults though none were ever reported. On 25 June 1963 he found himself in court after abducting a seven-year-old girl whom he had found in a playground; in a deserted air-raid shelter he throttled the child until she lost consciousness, then masturbated over her body. Astonishingly the court let Black go with a reprimand because a psychiatrist thought he would not re-offend. Not long after this, he began dating a young woman whom he had met at a youth club. The affair lasted several months and Robert was devastated when she broke off the relationship, due in part to his sexual demands. In 1966 Black's landlords in Grangemouth found out that he had repeatedly molested their nine-year-old granddaughter. They did not notify the authorities. He was not so lucky at his next digs when he molested the six-year-old daughter of the owners, who called the police. The 19-year-old youth was now sent to borstal.

Black's borstal time was probably very grim and it is almost certain that he was abused there. Despite telling psychiatrists later about the abuse at the Red House he always refused to say anything about the borstal. In 1968 he moved to London and did various casual jobs. One was at Hornsey Swimming Pool where, true to form, he was fired for fondling a young girl. At night, when the baths had been empty, Black used to swim lengths with a broom handle stuffed in his anus. In 1972 he started renting an attic flat in Stamford Hill. Here he remained a quiet, if rather smelly tenant, until his arrest 18 years later. During this time and unknown to his landlords Black amassed a large collection of child pornography. Gradually fantasising and masturbating over such images led him to want to try the real thing.

In 1976 Black got a permanent job as a long-distance van driver. His employers found him conscientious. Later, some colleagues would remark on how he varied his appearance – sometimes bearded, sometimes close-shaven, occasionally totally bald. Black also owned and wore a large collection of spectacles. The rear of his van was always covered with black opaque curtains.

The first murder he is known to have committed is also the last one for which he was convicted – that of nine-year-old Jennifer Cardy. She was abducted on the afternoon of 12 August 1981 in Ballinderry, County Antrim. Her body was found six days later and some 16 miles away by two duck hunters. She had been raped, strangled and drowned, probably within four hours of being abducted.

Fifty weeks later, on 30 July 1982, 11-year-old Susan Maxwell from Cornhill-on-Tweed was abducted as she walked home from the local tennis courts. Three hundred officers took part in a search for the missing child and fell teams scoured 80 miles of mountainous terrain on the Scottish–English border. Eventually, on 12 August, Susan's badly decomposed body was found in some undergrowth near Uttoxeter, some 264 miles away from her abduction. She had been gagged with sticking plaster, the girl's underwear removed and neatly placed under her head. Alive or dead, she must have been in Black's van for at least 24 hours.

On 8 July 1983 the killer struck again. Five-year-old Caroline Hogg was abducted while playing outside her home in Portobello, a suburb of Edinburgh. The Lothian and Borders Police launched the largest search up to that time in Scottish history with 2,000 volunteers and the Royal Scots Fusiliers assisting a massive police operation. Several witnesses came forward to say that they had seen a grubby, balding, 'furtive-looking' man wearing horn-rimmed glasses who was watching Caroline at play. He had followed her towards a local fun park and a 14-year-old witness saw the same man holding Caroline's hand. Ten days after her disappearance, the little girl's naked body was found in a ditch close to the M1 at Twycross some 310 miles from where she was last seen alive (and just 24 miles from where Susan Maxwell's body had been found). Caroline's body was too decomposed to precisely determine the cause of death.

Detectives were fairly certain that they were dealing with a killer who was a van or lorry driver. The fact that Susan and Caroline had been abducted on a Friday also suggested that their murders were linked to a delivery or production schedule of some sort. Four police forces were now involved. Luckily, they were able to co-ordinate their efforts very well. Having learned a thing or two from the botched Yorkshire Ripper enquiry, all information was fed into a computerised database at Bradford. Soon it held information on more 189,000 people, 220,000 vehicles and interviews with over 60,000 members of the public. Three extremely useful confidential hotlines were set up in 1984.

Around 8am on 26 March 1986 a 10-year-old girl, Sarah Harper, disappeared after having bought a loaf of bread and two packets of crisps near her Victorian terraced home in the working-class district of Morley, Leeds. Police were soon looking for a suspicious Ford Transit van. Twenty-three days later Sarah's partially dressed body was found floating in the River Trent near Nottingham. She had been gagged. Pathologists concluded that she had been brutally beaten and raped before being drowned.

Now six police forces were after the killer. The F.B.I. was invited to make a psychological profile, which proved very accurate. The police database, now called HOLMES, was used to check every person convicted in Britain of child murder, attempted murder, abduction, attempted abduction and assault of a minor since 1972. This gave a list of 40,000 names, but Robert Black was not among them, since his previous conviction had been in 1967.

The first breakthrough in the case came on 23 April 1988 when Black tried to grab a 15-year-old girl, Teresa Thornhill, in Radford, Nottinghamshire. She was small for her age but tough; Teresa fought back, kicking and screaming, even managing to hit Black in his testicles to which he replied, 'Oh, you... bitch!' Teresa's boyfriend, Andrew Beeston, heard the commotion and ran towards the van shouting, 'Let go of her, you fat bastard!' Black released the girl and drove off at speed. The teens were able to give police a good description of the balding and overweight 5-foot-7-inch killer.

Two years and two months later Black tried to abduct a six-year-old girl in Stow. David Herkes, a 53-year-old retired postmaster, saw what was going on and noted the vehicle's registration number. Mr Herkes then helped the girl's distraught mother to call the police. Within minutes six squad cars had reached the village. Suddenly a blue Transit van came down the road. 'That's him, that's the same van,' yelled Mr Herkes. Officers caused the van to swerve to a halt. Black was quickly handcuffed. In the back of the Transit was a sleeping bag containing the little girl. Her wrists and legs had been tied, sticking plaster was over her mouth and a hood was over her head.

Black's trial for abduction lasted just one day. In court he agreed that he was a danger to children and needed treatment. The judge, Lord Donald Ross, sentenced him to life imprisonment. Once their suspect was behind bars the police began to bring together sufficient evidence to charge Black with child murder. He refused to co-operate with them in any way. On 13 April 1994 at Newcastle Crown Court he finally stood before a judge, Mr Justice Macpherson, on 10 charges of kidnap, murder, attempted murder and preventing the lawful burial of a body. Black pleaded not guilty. His defence counsel, Ronald Thwaites, tried hard to find holes in the accuracy and memories of some of the witnesses and their statements. Three hundred items had been retrieved from Black's van and London apartment but Thwaites got the forensic experts to admit that the length of time since the murders made the forensic links in this evidence very weak.

The prosecution was forced to rely largely on circumstantial evidence but it was enough for the jury to find the defendant guilty on all charges. Judge Macpherson referred to Black as 'man at his most vile' and handed down a term of life imprisonment with a recommendation that he serve a minimum of 35 years on each murder charge.

It was not until September 2011 that Black was put on trial for the murder of Jennifer Cardy at Armagh Crown Court. Six weeks later a jury found him guilty. Mr Justice Weatherup imposed a minimum term of 25 years. The police think Black may have been responsible for at least 13 other abductions and murders in England, Ireland, France, Germany and the Netherlands. Black appealed his sentence and also refused to help investigators. A psychologist summed him up: 'He's the sort of person for whom it's all about power and control. Having information about what he's done gives him power. He has no desire to ease his conscience.'

Robert Black died of a heart attack in H.M. Prison Maghaberry on 12 January 2016. His body was cremated and the ashes spread at sea.

Shortly before his death he told one man who was granted an interview that he viewed his crimes as more of a sickness and that he was 'disgusted I've got this thing about girls'.

1995 The Cromwell Street Murders: Frederick Walter Stephen West & Rosemary Pauline West

The German term for a sex killing is *lustmord*. It is a word better suited to Fred and Rose West than anything the English language has to offer. The Wests are unique among British serial killers because they were a husband-and-wife team. They didn't kill to get rich, or because they heard voices from God, they didn't hate women, or want to revenge themselves on society. The Wests murdered simply out of enjoyment as part of a lust to enslave, sexually humiliate, rape, mutilate and torture young women to death.

Fred, 52 years old at the time of his arrest, was a curly-haired, stocky, smiling gnome of a man who was the instigator of all that happened. Rosemary, his wife, 12 years younger, had been an attractive slim brunette with big eyes and a saucy manner when she met Fred at 16. She put on weight as she put on the years, raising a brood of children, gradually becoming the equal and then, it seems, dominant partner in the relationship. The nasty business of disposing of their victims was left to Fred. It was, after all, a man's job, like wringing a chicken's neck or slaughtering a pig. Fred was happy just to rape their victims and dream up nasty perversions for them such as sex with animals, bondage, buggery and other delights while Rose got her thrills from S&M, especially whipping the trussed-up victims, faces usually masked in tape with a tube up their nostrils so they could breathe, terrified in the darkness of what tortures might follow next as she beat, masturbated, burned and cut them. Astonishingly, it all took place in a house where the Wests' growing band of children also ate, slept, watched television and did their homework.

Fred West was born on 29 September 1941 at Much Marcle, a Herefordshire village best known for its cider factory. Walter West, Fred's father, was a giant of a man. He worked as a cowman and raised his family alongside his buxom wife, Daisy, in a three-bedroomed tied cottage at Moorcourt Farm. Blue-eyed Freddie was the apple of his mother's eye, though she was not averse to belting him on occasions. School did not suit Fred. 'I was as thick as two short planks,' he later said, 'all I was interested in was farming.' He also claimed, 'We were a close-knit family, a very happy family.' Perhaps a little too close-knit because it has been suggested that Daisy ended her son's virginity one winter's night before his 13th birthday by taking him to her bed. Sex soon became not just Fred's hobby but his all-consuming obsession. Walter was also a highly sexed man who, according to Fred, confessed to having had sex with a sheep and taught that all women 'were begging for it'. As soon as he was old enough Fred bought himself a motorcycle and despite a spill or two was able to impress the girls of nearby Ledbury enough to have plenty of nocturnal adventures.

Just before his 18th birthday Fred ventured off to become a deckhand on boats out of Bristol. He returned home to Much Marcle in 1960. Within three months a 13-year-old girl was pregnant and it was being whispered that Fred West was the cause. He found himself on trial at Hereford Assizes but, luckily for him, the case was stopped. In April 1961 he was fined £4, however, on two charges of theft. One year and a few rapes later, Fred got a job driving a lorry for a local farm co-operative. In a Ledbury café that autumn he met a Scottish waitress, Catherine Costello, known as Rena by her friends. Eighteen years old, Rena had been working as a prostitute in Glasgow and was now pregnant by her pimp. West offered to abort the baby. His attempt failed but somehow the couple's sexual chemistry ignited. They returned to Glasgow where he married Rena. She went back to whoring, got pregnant by her Pakistani shopkeeper-pimp and gave birth to a little girl whom she called Charmaine. Fred demanded sex every day and beat Rena if she refused. She was a tough, streetwise lass and refused to kowtow to him. 'She knocked me cold on three occasions with one blow,' Fred said somewhat admiringly of his wife. He became an ice cream van man and if clients turned up for Rena, 'I was given £5 to fuck off, and I went.'

'It was a marriage of opposites,' Geoffrey Wansell has written, 'the country boy and the city girl, the poacher and the prostitute, bound together by a fascination with sex.' In 1964 Rena gave birth to Anna-Marie, a daughter fathered this time by West. Things rapidly went downhill after Fred ran over and killed a small child with his ice cream van in 1965. He lost his job, was hounded by a motorcycle gang and ended up splitting from Rena and taking the kids to Herefordshire where the girls were taken into care.

Rena turned up in due course and the tempestuous relationship of arguments and beatings continued. Fred by now was seeing a new love in his life, a Scottish lass called Anna McFall, his 'angel'. A jealous Rena got her children back from the authorities and moved into a caravan at

Brockworth near Gloucester. By the spring of 1967, Anna was pregnant. Fred could not afford to support another child. She was last seen alive at the caravan park in July. We do not know how she died but afterwards Fred dismembered her body, cut off and disposed of her fingers and toes (presumably to make identification more difficult), removed the foetus from the womb, then buried mother and child in a field near Much Marcle.

In the summer of 1968 Fred was arrested for theft from a house in Cheltenham, then lost his latest job also on a suspicion of stealing money. It was about this time that he met Rosemary Letts. Bill Letts, her abusive father, loathed Fred and forbade Rose from seeing him. She was sweet sixteen and not a virgin when she met Fred. Then she fell in love. Apart from her looks and fulsome figure, Rose was cunning and stubborn. The pair agreed to have a baby and run away together. When he found out Bill Letts was furious, threatening to 'knife' the lovers, but it was too late. Fred was now working for a tyre company and thinking of entering the building trade. He and Rose began life together sharing a flat with his two children. Rose took an instant dislike to mixed-race Charmaine and frequently slapped the seven-year-old. Fred did nothing to stop her. On 17 October Rose gave birth to a baby girl who was christened Heather Ann. Fred was absent that Christmas, a guest of Her Majesty on more theft convictions. Rose, though only 17, was developing a vicious temper probably inherited from her father. She frequently beat her stepchildren and on one occasion even smashed a cereal bowl across six-year-old Anna Marie's head.

That summer, freed from prison, clearly on the urgings of Rose, Fred West strangled Rena who had come back on the scene. He buried her also in a Herefordshire field. Charmaine, the child Rose hated, was also strangled. She was dismembered and buried in a small hole barely 2 feet square under the kitchen area of their home at 25 Midland Road. No one can be certain what exactly happened to Charmaine; she may have been raped by Fred before death, though he said that Rose had stabbed the child.

On 29 January 1972 Fred and Rose got married at Gloucester Register Office. That June a second daughter, Mae, was born. In September came the move to 25 Cromwell Street near the centre of Gloucester, a house of three storeys. Fred soon began work on an extension with building materials he had stolen. He also enlarged the cellar. In time it was a fairly sizeable property. To pay the bills the Wests took in a succession of short-stay lodgers. In due course Fred encouraged Rose to take up prostitution.

The couple used a van and also a top-floor bedroom garishly decked out with a lacy four-poster bed as her bordello.

The younger Wests grew up in an environment where sex dominated everything. 'His whole life revolved around sex,' daughter Mae said of her father, 'sex had to be every night or he'd think Mum didn't love him... He'd come down in the morning and say: "I had your mother last night."' As his daughters got older Fred would say, 'Your first baby should be your Dad's.' Insisting he watch them shower naked, refusing to allow them sanitary towels, exposing himself, constantly groping the girls, Fred saw his paedophilia as quite natural. 'Basically I lived in fear of being raped,' said daughter Mae (who was in fact raped by a visitor to the house when she was eight years old, her parents quite unbothered by this behaviour). With her father she thought rape was 'inevitable'. He had raped Anna Marie many times.

Both parents beat their children (though they were careful not to hit them in places where it might show at school), but they saved their real aggression for the casual female visitors who passed through the house. A nanny, Carol Raine, was abducted, beaten and raped by them. Seven teenage girls are known for certain to have been murdered at Cromwell Street. They started with a 19-year-old seamstress, Lynda Gough, in April 1973 and ended with 17-year-old Alison Chambers in September 1979. Five others aged between 15 and 21 years would also die in the cellar at 25 Cromwell Street, all victims of bondage, torture and mutilation before death. Most were found with feet and knee bones missing, the limp, bound and helpless playthings of the West's perverted lusts.

It was the murder of another of Fred West's offspring, first-born Heather, that finally saw the husband-and-wife killers brought to justice. The 16-year-old girl disappeared in June 1987 and was reported missing to the police. Heather had always resisted her father's sexual advances, the sibling most in revolt. The fear that she might expose their abuse and thereby throw light on the murders made Fred and Rose decide to eliminate her. Her brothers and sisters were told that Heather had run away to a job in Devon. Knowing their parents as they did, the older children were not surprised.

The mills of God grind slowly – on 6 August 1992 Fred was arrested on charges of rape and buggery against one of his daughters. Rose was charged with 'causing or encouraging the commission of unlawful sexual intercourse with a child'. A distressed Rose tried to commit suicide two days later. On 7 June 1993 they appeared in court on these charges, but two witnesses refused to give evidence against them and the judge entered formal verdicts of not guilty.

Despite their jubilation, nemesis in the shape of Detective Constable Hazel Savage was about to strike. D.C. Savage had been told to search for the whereabouts of Heather West. She thought it curious that the girl could not be traced anywhere – no claims for sickness or unemployment benefit, no attempt to change her name or acquire a passport, no visit anywhere to a doctor or dentist. Hazel had also heard the family joke – Heather was 'buried under the patio'. On Thursday 24 February 1994 the police arrived at Cromwell Street in force and with a search warrant. This time they were not after pornographic videos. Next morning Fred confessed to killing Heather. It was the first in a series of calculated gambles and lies by him aimed at diverting attention from Rose, 'who knew nothing at all', but over the succeeding days the full horror would be revealed. Soon forensic experts were finding bodies in the cellar and garden. Heather's remains were found under the patio, just as Fred had always joked. She had been decapitated, dismembered and disarticulated.

Before his trial Frederick West managed to hang himself in his cell at Winson Green Prison, Birmingham, on 1 January 1995. At a recent court appearance Rose had blanked him, an experience that devastated Fred. He left no suicide note, but it seems that he hoped that by his death the law might deal less harshly with Rose. He was mistaken. Her trial on 10 charges of murder began at Winchester Crown Court on 3 October before the severe-looking Mr Justice Mantell. All the evidence against her was circumstantial. On 21 November the jury unanimously found her guilty of three murders and the next day also of the remaining seven. Judge Mantell's sentencing was as damning as it was brief: 'Stand up. Rosemary Pauline West, on each of the ten counts of murder of which you have been unanimously convicted by the jury, the sentence is one of life imprisonment. If attention is paid to what I think, you will *never* be released. Take her down.'

In 1996 the Cromwell Street house was demolished as an ugly blot on Gloucester's fair city. Rose West was given a whole-life tariff in 1997. The fact that apart from killing Heather the Wests stopped murdering 15 years before their arrests has led many to conjecture that they killed other girls. Their children were, of course, growing up and there were more of them. It was not so easy to use the cellar for their kicks without arousing suspicion. Yet most serial killers find it impossible to stop after nine murders. Fred boasted in gaol that he had killed as many as 30 women. To date no further bodies have been found.

1996 The Dunblane Massacre: Thomas Watt Hamilton

Nine years after the appalling massacre at Hungerford, Berkshire, another small-town community was to be torn apart by a similar act of senseless savagery. This time the place was Dunblane, a small cathedral town of just fewer than 8,000 inhabitants, a royal burgh a few miles north of Stirling in Scotland. It is a quiet backwater with hardly any supermarkets, a middle-class retreat for commuters working in Stirling, Edinburgh and Perth. The old town boasts, in addition to its ancient cathedral, the oldest private library in Scotland.

By 1996 Thomas Hamilton was well known in the community and largely disliked. He was a balding and bespectacled 43-year-old with a chubby face and a deep resentment towards authority. The son of a bus driver who left his wife when their child was just 18 months old, Thomas had been brought up by his mother's adoptive parents. In later years he was estranged from all of them, especially his paternal relatives, though he was fond of his mother. Locals in Stirling later recalled him as a quiet, softly spoken man with an oily charm, usually well dressed in a shirt and tie, and sympathetic to local sick pensioners. In 1970 he had set up a DIY store in Stirling specialising in fitted kitchens. The chubby shopkeeper's first love, however, was the Boy Scout movement. In 1973 he became leader of the 4th Stirling Scout Group, but one year later he was forced to give back his warrant because of 'inappropriate behaviour after a Scout camp'. This humiliation was to drip like acid into Hamilton's psyche.

Nothing daunted, he set up the Dunblane Rovers in the 1980s. In 1984 Hamilton was told he could no longer use the local high school for its meetings due to complaints from some children and parents. The boys had nicknamed him 'Mr Creepy' and it was rumoured that he took inappropriate photographs of the lads bathing and getting undressed. Hamilton's DIY business collapsed soon after, and he blamed his problems on the way some locals were giving him a bad name. His paranoia started to grow and grow. In 1988, 1993 and 1994 he tried, and failed each time, to rejoin the Scout movement. These matters became the subject of police inquiries. Undaunted, Hamilton advertised and was able to somehow run summer camps for local boys as well as coaching a young football team weekly. A week before the killings he set out his grievances in letters to some local parents, the Secretary of State for Scotland and even H.M. the Queen. In these rambling epistles he claimed that Scout leaders were 'jealous' of his success with the boys' clubs and that he was the victim of a 'sinister witch-hunt'.

Then, on the morning of 13 March 1996, it seems that mounting pressure and paranoia caused Hamilton's sanity to snap. Wearing a dark jacket, corduroy trousers and a woolly hat with ear defenders, he set off in his van for Dunblane Primary School. He arrived at about 9.30am, parking his van next to a telegraph pole. He cut the telegraph wires with a pair of pliers before walking across the car park and entering the school. In each hand Hamilton held a pistol and altogether he was carrying four legal weapons – two Browning 9mm HP pistols and two Smith & Wesson M.19 .357 magnum revolvers, as well as 743 rounds of ammunition.

It is believed that he began his assault by firing a shot at the girls' toilets and another at the assembly room before entering the school gymnasium where a junior class was in progress. What followed was truly a massacre of the innocents. Hamilton shot and killed 16 children, all but one of whom was five years old – eleven little girls and five boys. The P.E. teacher, Eileen Harrid, was shot in the arms and chest but somehow managed to survive. Less lucky was 45-year-old Gwen Major, teacher of Primary Class 1, who was shot and killed instantly. An assistant teacher, Mary Blake, was hit in the head and legs but somehow managed to get to a store cupboard with several children in front of her.

The gunman next walked across the playground, letting off several rounds before entering a mobile classroom and then returning to the bloodstained, glass-shattered gym. Thirty-two people had been hit in three to four minutes, 17 of them fatally. Hamilton dropped one of the pistols and took out a Smith & Wesson magnum, put the barrel in his mouth pointing upwards and pulled the trigger, instantly killing himself as the top of his head exploded.

In the Parliamentary outcry that followed two Firearms (Amendment) Acts were rushed through in 1997. These laws effectively banned all .22 cartridge handguns in England, Scotland and Wales, leaving only muzzle-loading and 'historic' handguns legal, plus a few sporting handguns. School security also came under review with many premises adding extra fencing, gates and security doors.

Among the mourners at memorial services were H.M. the Queen Mother and Prince Charles. Within Dunblane Cathedral a poignant stone memorial has been raised to honour those who lost their lives. The issue is still an emotive one in the town after two decades; rightly so, since 16 young lives were snuffed out (and a brave teacher's), 16 young people who today would be getting married and starting families of their own. Immediately after the massacre the manager of the local ambulance service, John McEwan, said: 'One of the images I think will stay with me is, not so much the dying, although that is bad enough, but there were five-year-old children looking unbelievingly at bullet holes in their arms and legs. They just could not comprehend what had happened to them.'

Thomas Hamilton's body was quietly cremated and his ashes scattered 'a long way' from Dunblane.

1997 Horror beyond Imagination: James Patterson Smith

It is unusual for an author to ask his readers to consider skipping a section of his or her book but I feel that I must warn those of you with a delicate constitution that what follows is gruesome in the extreme – so bad that one website refers to it as the most horrible murder of all time. I thought long and hard about including this killer in my book, but finally I concluded that there are lessons to be learned from this awful case – even if those lessons question our very understanding of what it is to be human.

Kelly Bates was a petite 14-year-old schoolgirl when she met Smith. He was an unemployed divorcee living in Gorton, a suburb of Manchester. Her mum, Margaret, described Kelly as 'bright and bubbly... She didn't walk; she bounced.' Kelly met Jimmy Smith, whom she called 'Dave', when she was babysitting for a friend. It seems the teen was the kind of girl who finds older men attractive. Smith was a house-proud, well-groomed, teetotal non-smoker who bore a rather down-at-heel resemblance to the country and western star John Denver, with straggly blonde hair reaching to his shoulders. What few people knew was that Smith had been married, but this had ended in divorce in 1980 due to his bullying and beatings. For the next two years he dated a 20-year-old whom he used as a punch bag even when she was pregnant; Tina Watson said: 'At first it was now and again, just a little tap, but in the end it was every day. He would smack me in the face or hit me over the head with an ashtray. He would kick me in the legs or between the legs.' On one occasion Smith tried to drown Tina in the bath. Moving on to a 15-year-old girl, Wendy Mottershead, the misogynistic Smith tried to drown her in the kitchen sink besides administering regular beatings.

Two years after they started dating, when Kelly was 16 and ready to leave school, she moved in with Smith at his Furnival Road, Gorton, address. Up until this point her parents knew nothing, but now Kelly had to tell them and introduce 'Dave', whom she claimed was 32 years old (Smith was actually 47). Margaret and Thomas Bates took an instant dislike to the man. 'As soon as I saw Smith the hairs on the back of my neck went up,' said Mrs Bates, 'I tried everything I could to get Kelly away from him.' When Mrs Bates found out Smith's real age she confronted him. He replied: 'I didn't tell you because I thought you wouldn't want me being with Kelly.' Mrs Bates agreed that was indeed the case but Kelly insisted her boyfriend was 'alright'.

In November 1995 Kelly returned to live with her mum and dad after some arguments with Smith. They noticed she seemed withdrawn and depressed. In December she left her part-time job at a local graphics firm. In March 1996 birthday and wedding anniversary cards arrived for Mr and Mrs Bates, but they noticed the cards were signed by Smith. When Kelly's brother called at the Furnival Road house Smith refused to let him in saying that Kelly was out.

What exactly happened between mid-March and mid-April 1996 will never be known for sure, but on 16 April Smith went to the police. Kelly, so he claimed, had committed suicide in the bath after an argument. Officers led by Detective Sergeant Joseph Monaghan went to Smith's home expecting to find the body of a dead girl floating in a bath of water but, as Monaghan later told the jury, 'I have been in the police force for 15 years and never seen a case as horrific as this.' For a start the home was covered in blood stains. Kelly's sightless body had been bludgeoned, burned, scalped, and drowned with over 150 separate injuries. Dr William Lawler, the Home Office pathologist said: 'In my career I have examined almost 600 victims of homicide and never come across injuries so extensive.'

Dr Lawler deduced that for a month prior to her death Kelly had been tied up by her hair to a radiator or to a chair. Her knee caps had been smashed, so that she could not walk or run, let alone escape. She had been starved and the healthy girl who used to enjoy hockey weighed at her death just 7½ stone. It was the tortures that were remarkable: scalding to her buttocks and left leg where boiling water had been poured on the girl; burns on a thigh caused by a hot iron; a fractured arm; multiple stab wounds caused by a knife, fork and scissors; crushed hands; mutilations to her ears, nose, eyebrows, lips and genitals; stab wounds inside her mouth; severe bruises as a result of being hit by a spade and pruning shears; partial scalping; both eyes had been gouged out by hand – then stab wounds were made in the bloody sockets.

It was some months before Smith came to judgment but finally in November 1997 he stood before Mr Justice Sachs at Manchester Crown

Court. With incredible arrogance Smith, who pleaded not guilty, claimed that Kelly 'had a bad habit of hurting herself to make it look worse on me'. His girlfriend had dared him to hurt her, putting him 'through hell winding me up'. A consultant psychiatrist, Dr Gillian Mezey, told the court that Smith had a 'severe paranoid disorder with morbid jealousy' and lived in 'a distorted reality'. On 21 November, after one hour's deliberation, a jury found Smith guilty of murder. Mr Justice Sachs sentenced him to a minimum of 20 years saying: 'You are an abuser of women and I intend, so far as it is in my power, that you will abuse no more.' The judge thanked the jury who were so shaken by the photographs they had viewed of Kelly's injuries that every one of them asked for professional counselling.

The case is horrifying in many ways. Smith had coldly, methodically, slowly and sadistically tortured his victim just about to the ultimate length that any human being could go. Finally he had hit her over the head with a shower attachment and drowned her. Death must have been a merciful release for the sad, blind girl who had suffered unbelievable torments at Smith's hands. As Peter Openshaw, Q.C., prosecuting counsel, told the court: 'It was as if he deliberately disfigured her, causing her the utmost pain, distress and degradation.'

Smith will soon complete his original sentence but is unlikely to be released anytime soon, if ever. He is now 69 years old. He had told police: 'I know I'm going away. I know there is no point. I'm going to get found out anyway.' This sounds like an admission that he realised, after exhausting every sadistic act he could upon poor Kelly, that ultimately he would have to go to prison for the rest of his life.

1998 The Stolen Identity Murder: Albert Johnson Walker

In a decade remarkable for twisted sex killers, sadists and paedophiles such as Ireland, Smith and Black, it almost comes as a surprise to unmask an old-style murderer interested in committing the perfect crime. To try and take over another person's identity as part of a business scheme is audacious. Albert Walker almost got away with it too, had not fate in the shape of a fishing trawler unravelled in its net a dead body and put paid to his machinations.

It was late on a summer's afternoon in 1996 when the trawler *Malkerry* hauled in its net. The father-and-son team of John and Craig Topik had been out fishing for more than 10 hours and it had been an uneventful day. Then something seemed to have got snagged in their net and they decided to haul it in. Both fishermen thought it was most likely a porpoise. When the net was opened on the watery deck they saw to their astonishment the body of a fully clothed man.

Once the boat had moored at Brixham, Devon police took the corpse to a mortuary. Immersion in the water made the task of identification far from easy. The man's pockets contained nothing, he had no wallet and no identifying tags on his clothes. Two features remained that were to prove useful: the dead man had a tattoo on the back of his right hand and he was wearing an expensive Rolex Oyster Perpetual gold watch. Detectives knew that such expensive watches costing many thousands of pounds can be individually identified by serial numbers. Sure enough, the Rolex trail led police to a Harrogate jeweller who identified the watch as belonging to a 51-year-old TV repair man called Ronald Platt. Police also noticed that the watch had stopped at 11.35am on 22 July 1996. Since it had a 40-hour run from the time of the last winding, this suggested that the man had died on or between 20 to 22 July.

Initially the case was not treated as murder but forensic evidence, with the odd circumstances, soon pointed to foul play. Mr Platt had a deep gash at the back of his head. This would have been sufficient to render him unconscious though a pathologist concluded the cause of death was drowning.

So a murder investigation slowly got under way. Painstaking detective work led police eventually to Chelmsford, where Platt had rented an address. There the landlord was able to offer some extra help; a David Davis had agreed to act as a reference for Mr Platt and left his mobile telephone number on the back of the rental agreement. Police called Mr Davis who was shocked to learn of his friend's death. He confirmed that he had last seen Ronald Platt alive in June.

A short time later officers decided to ask Mr Davis a few more general questions to help tie up loose ends. Devon and Cornwall Constabulary asked the Essex Police at Chelmsford to help them clear up the business. Detective Sergeant Frank Redman set off fully briefed on the Platt case. When he got to the village of Woodham he found himself lost in an unsurfaced country lane with four farmhouses none of which seemed to have a name. Proceeding on foot, D.S. Redman knocked at a door. 'Could you tell me if this is Little London Farm?' he asked. The owner, elderly Frank Johnson, replied: 'No, it's not... it's over there,' pointing to another farm partly hidden behind a copse of trees. 'Is that where Mr Davis lives?' asked Redman. 'Wrong again,' smiled Mr Johnson, 'It's where Mr Platt lives with his lovely young wife, Noelle.' D.S. Redman thanked the farmer and tried to take stock of the astonishing news. Platt or Davis? Whoever the man was at Little London Farm he had a lot of explaining to do.

Detectives re-assembled and on 31 October, when a taxi left the farm at breakfast time, it was stopped at the bottom of the lane by a phalanx of police cars. D.S. Redman told the male passenger: 'Mr Davis, I am arresting you on suspicion of the murder of Ronald Platt in Devon on or around 21 July 1996.' While Davis was taken off to Chelmsford, officers entered the farm and found to their amazement various piles of cash containing pounds and Swiss francs along with a stack of gold bars. 'Noelle Davis' was found in a room filling a bag with even more money. The cash did not seem to relate to any robbery yet it made detectives uneasy. Davis had a North American accent and was identified as a Canadian citizen. As a courtesy, his fingerprints were sent to the Canadian embassy with the information that one of their citizens had been arrested in connection with a murder. Quickly the news came back that Platt/Davis was, in fact, Albert Walker, an international fraudster on Interpol's most wanted list. David Wallis Davis was just one of several aliases he was in the habit of using.

Walker had been born in the steel town of Hamilton, Ontario, in 1945. He married in 1968, raised three daughters and a son, and became a church elder and Sunday school teacher. When he started an investment business, friends and local pensioners soon swelled its coffers to nearly $12 million. The charismatic Walker was soon wearing designer clothes, driving a new Jaguar and telling everyone he had been educated at Oxford University (the truth was he had not even finished his secondary education). In the late '80s the business collapsed owing some 70 citizens in excess of $3 million. By this stage Walker's marriage was on the rocks. After one row in November 1990 he was arrested for trying to kick down the door of his estranged wife's house. It was at this point that he had to give his fingerprints.

Fearing the wrath of ruined investors and with a vengeful wife on the warpath, Walker decided to skip Canada. He took with him his 15-year-old daughter, Sheena, and they went first to Switzerland and then the U.K. Once in London and staying at the Ritz, the pair effectively went off the radar – Walker started calling himself David Davis, a Canadian national and international businessman. There was a real Mr Davis, an old friend, but Walker had acquired copies of his birth certificate and national insurance details without him knowing. Eventually Albert and Sheena, who now claimed to be his young wife, ended up in Harrogate, Yorkshire's famous spa town. There they struck up a conversation with Eileen Boyes, a middle-aged receptionist. She told them how her boyfriend, Ronald Platt, had lived in Canada as a boy and longed to return. The gullible, friendly, good-hearted Yorkshire couple were exactly what a master con-artist like Walker was looking for and he saw immediately that with cunning he could acquire a new identity. The handsome and moustachioed Walker told Eileen and Ronald that he was an international banker and thinking of starting an antiques business. He offered Eileen the job of receptionist and a starting salary of £15,000 a year. The four got along very well and the generous 'businessman' took his dupes to London for an *à la carte* weekend of luxury hotels and £400 meals.

A little antiques business was done but Walker talked more and more to the couple about emigrating. At Christmas 1992 he surprised them with a lavish gift – the promise of airline tickets to Canada to make a new start in life. Before emigrating Eileen and Ronald opened U.K. accounts to further their business with 'Mr Davis'. Somehow Albert got hold of copies of Ronald's birth certificate and driving licence. The big Canadian Dream did not last long; Ronald had difficulty getting a job and Eileen was homesick. She returned in July 1993. Mr Platt tried to stick it out for two more years but then he also returned in summer 1995.

The return of Ronald was a big problem for Albert Walker who had assumed Mr Platt's identity and was using his name. Ronald had no idea what was going on and the pair remained friends. 'Mr Davis' helped him get an apartment in Chelmsford. Something had to be done, and Ronald now hatched his murder plan. He told Sheena that Platt would be moving to France to run a joint business they had set up. At the same time he invited Ronald to take a holiday with him in Devon on a boat he owned called the *Lady Jane*. On the morning of 20 July the two men boarded the yacht, left the Dart Estuary, and sailed into the English Channel. Exact details can never be known but 6 miles out to sea, Walker hit Platt over the head with a new anchor he had bought for the purpose. He emptied his victim's pockets, stuck the anchor in his waist belt as an extra weight and threw him overboard. In his haste to dispose of the body Walker made one fatal error – he forgot to take off Platt's watch.

Walker's case was heard before Mr Justice Butterfield at Exeter Crown Court on 28 April 1998. Despite a plea of not guilty, the evidence was overwhelming: Walker had bought the anchor on his own credit card; a witness recalled the couple at the marina and the man with the American accent; some of Platt's hairs were found on the *Lady Jane* and the yacht's navigation system showed that at 9pm on 20 July it had been very close to where the body was found. Before passing sentence of life imprisonment, Judge Butterfield described the murder as 'carefully planned and cunningly executed with chilling efficiency'.

In February 2002 Albert Walker was transferred back to Canada to face additional charges of fraud, money laundering and theft. On 23 July 2007 he received a further five years on these charges. In 2013 he was transferred from Ontario to serve the rest of his sentence in British Columbia. Sheena Walker claimed she had been 'hypnotised' by her father and, it must be said, seems to have got off very lightly. She was deported to Canada with her two children. The paternity of the children has never been revealed but she had no known boyfriend in England.

1999 Homicidal Stalker: Anthony Diedrick

In 1986 a bright medical student called Joan Francisco started dating a West London man called Anthony Diedrick. Joan was a convent-educated high achiever. She was black, beautiful and proudly represented a new, multi-cultural, middle-class British society. At first she was crazy about her new lover, but he failed to impress her mother, Venus, or elder sister, Cecilia, especially after he threw a violent tantrum on a trip with them to Los Angeles. 'He is a walking time bomb and, honey, your time is running out,' wrote Cecilia to Joan with some perception. 'Is the end of your career worth it for Tony?'

During the early months of 1989 Joan finally split from her boyfriend after she heard that he had picked up a woman in a bar. She soon found a new boyfriend named Harold Ejegi. Diedrick began stalking the couple. On one occasion he broke through the glass patio doors in Venus Francisco's lounge screaming, 'I'm going to kill you!' He and Harold Ejegi wrestled on the floor while a terrified Joan called the police. By the time officers arrived, Anthony had run off. He later admitted criminal damage and was let off with a warning.

Years passed, over five of them, a long time. Joan, meantime, qualified and became a specialist in obstetrics and gynaecology. Still unmarried, she had a busy social life and was friendly with the boxer Lennox Lewis and footballer John Fashanu. Diedrick, despite her fears, had become a distant memory. Anthony's life had not gone so well; he did not get the kind of computer studies degree he really wanted and drifted through a succession of dead-end jobs. Gradually depression and schizoid fantasies took over and began to obsess him, especially the idea that Joan had been the love of his life and that he should try and win her back.

The stalking started again. He found and began spying on Joan's address in St John's Wood, a ground-floor flat, where she lived alone. One day he managed to sneak into her garden while she was out and plant a tiny Dictaphone machine through an open window. He began listening to all her calls. He even got her ex-directory number by telling British Telecom that he was her doctor and needed to get in touch. The obsessions got worse: Anthony began writing Joan love letters, then harassing her at work with numerous phone calls, followed by apologetic notes: 'I don't mean to frighten you... I just thought you might speak to me if you heard me.'

Joan was nervous but she ignored Anthony in the hope that he would go away. On Boxing Day morning she was in a good mood, ready to fly that afternoon to see one of her sisters in California. Having listened to her calls Anthony thought Joan might be intending to move to the U.S.A. When she opened the door of her apartment he was standing outside. 'Leave me alone, Anthony,' she screamed. Something snapped inside Diedrick's head – he caught Joan by the throat, pushed her inside the flat, grabbed a length of vacuum cleaner cable and strangled his ex-girlfriend. When Joan failed to answer her phone Venus got worried. The police found the dead woman at 1pm.

Diedrick was obviously their main suspect. He insisted that Joan had been out of his life for six years. Police asked questions, but finally had to release him for lack of evidence, although a search of his home had turned up one or two odd items such as listening devices. No fingerprints were found at the murder scene. Despite a major surveillance operation in the months that followed Anthony Diedrick said or did nothing that linked him to Joan's death. The Francisco family decided to pursue him through the civil courts. In March 1998 they brought an action, the first in British legal history, against someone who had never been charged with murder – and they won! Mr Justice Alliott said: 'I find assault and battery, in effect, murder, to have been proved.' Diedrick was ordered to pay Joan Francisco's relatives civil damages of £50,000 on the grounds that he had been responsible for her death.

Joan's sisters set up a foundation in her memory to help train black doctors. The family met with the Commissioner of the Metropolitan Police and the Crown Prosecution Service decided to re-open the case. It was three pin-prick sized specks of blood on the cerise T-shirt Joan had been wearing when she died that finally brought her killer to justice. She had worn the garment inside out, but when bagged by the police they turned it the right way around, and so forensic experts had thought the spots at the neck were Joan's blood. DNA now showed the blood belonged to Diedrick.

On 13 October 1999 Anthony Diedrick faced Mr Justice Hallett at the Old Bailey. Prosecuting counsel Nigel Sweeney told the court that there was a one in 170 million chance of the blood specks matching anyone else. Had the T-shirt been washed, the tiny specks would have been lost. Found guilty by a unanimous verdic, the prisoner was told that he would have to face a minimum of 15 years behind bars before being eligible for parole. Diedrick was taken to the cells shouting, 'I am innocent. I will fight.' Outside the court Mrs Francisco told reporters that she hoped Joan's soul and spirit might finally rest in peace.

2000 Doctor Death: Harold Frederick Shipman

'When a doctor goes wrong he is the first of criminals,' said Sherlock Holmes, 'he has nerve and he has knowledge.' The gaslit age of the great detective was notorious for its medical murderers such as Drs Lamson, Pritchard and Cream, skilled users of aconitine, antimony and strychnine respectively. At the start of the 20th century we have already documented Dr Crippen and murder by hyoscine, but it was almost 150 years since 'Palmer the Poisoner', a medical practitioner, had serially killed several patients and friends.

While Harold Shipman was still at school the crime writer Michael Hardwick had written prophetically: 'The doctor driven to murder has a unique choice of methods... He has unrivalled knowledge to assist him in the tricky task of disposing of the remains; he knows, and can state with authority, a false reason for death which is likely to deceive all but the most earnest inquirer; he can aggravate natural illness or retard recovery; he wears a concealing cloak of professional mystique, and enjoys ready-made advantages of social standing and implied personal respectability.'

In the spring of 1998 the manageress of a firm of undertakers in Hyde near Manchester, Deborah Massey, was concerned that something was not right at Dr Shipman's practice since he seemed forever to be giving her cremation forms for his elderly women patients. She raised the matter with Linda Reynolds, a rival doctor in Hyde, who in turn alerted the coroner for South Manchester. This high death rate among Shipman's patients was reported to the police who then conducted a relatively discreet investigation but could not find sufficient evidence to charge the doctor.

Between 17 April 1998, when the police dropped their investigation, and 24 June the doctor with the trim beard, spectacles and nice bedside manner was to kill three more times. His last victim was 81-year-old Mrs Kathleen Grundy, a wealthy widow and former lady mayoress of Hyde. Dr Shipman would probably have gone on murdering patients almost up to the present day if greed had not got the better of him (oddly enough it was the same reason that the Victorian doctors Lamson, Pritchard and Palmer were caught). Over the years, it later turned out, he had stolen items of jewellery from several patients. In Mrs Grundy's case he attempted to rush her death and forge her will. Apparently healthy, mentally and physically, Kathleen still did two half-days a week helping out in a charity shop. The doctor visited her, ostensibly to take a blood sample. He was the last person to see her alive and when phoned by the police said he had popped in 'only for a talk'. As her G.P., he then carried out a cursory examination of the dead woman and listed her cause of death on the certificate simply as 'old age'.

What Shipman did not know was that Kathleen's daughter, Angela, was a solicitor and was astounded to discover, 12 days later, that her mother had recently made a new will leaving her entire estate to Dr Shipman. It seemed an odd will too because it failed to mention Mrs Grundy's other properties. A badly typewritten letter had also arrived at Mrs Grundy's lawyers requesting that her body be cremated. Angela knew that her mother had always talked of being buried. Extremely suspicious of the will and letter, as were Mrs Grundy's solicitors, she took her concerns to Detective Inspector Stan Egerton at Hyde C.I.D.

A post-mortem had revealed no obvious cause for Mrs Grundy's death. It was therefore decided to exhume her body. That same day detectives raided Dr Shipman's surgery and home. A typewriter from his office was forensically shown to be the same machine that had typed both the will and covering letter. The police even found a print of Shipman's left-hand little finger on the will, but not Mrs Grundy's or those of the two 'witnesses'. An examination of the hard drive in the doctor's office computer also yielded a lot of incriminating information. Shipman acted, as he did throughout the months that followed and including his trial, in an arrogant manner. He accused the police of harassment and wasting his time. On 2 September a toxicology report confirmed that Mrs Grundy had died of a diamorphine overdose. Police now realised that their fraud inquiry had escalated into one of murder. Shipman suggested that Mrs Grundy had been a heroin addict, a ridiculous claim that hardly fitted a sweet old lady and former Conservative councillor. His computer showed false entries, his handwritten notes on Mrs Grundy were declared by a handwriting expert to have been added later, and dates when he was supposed to have been treating the elderly lady for her 'addiction' were proved to have been falsified.

Shipman had been born on 14 January 1946 to working-class parents at Bestwood, a council estate in Nottingham. He was the second of four children and brought up in a clean and thrifty home. His father was a lorry driver and both parents were practising Methodists. Harold was a quiet boy, good at grammar school, fond of rugby, who decided to study medicine at Leeds, graduating in 1970. After a few years working at Pontefract General Infirmary he became a general practitioner (G.P.) in 1974. One year later he was fined £600 for forging prescriptions of pethidine for his own use. This embarrassment did not end his career and in 1977 Shipman moved to Hyde as a G.P. He began his own single practice at 21 Market Street in 1993. By this time he was married and the father of three sons and a daughter.

By the time of Mrs Grundy's murder Dr Shipman had been a regular face in the community for 21 years, serving on various local committees, being interviewed on a Granada TV documentary about the mentally ill, organising charity collections and donating prizes to the rugby club. He seemed a perfect example to many of that dying breed – a doctor who has time for his patients. Old ladies were especially fond of him. Whether it was a late-night emergency call or some urgent weekend visit, Dr Shipman seemed the kind of G.P. who was always ready to come to your home and see if he could help. The size of his practice – more than 3,000 – reveals his popularity. One woman later said: 'When you were in his surgery he treated you like the only patient he had. When I was down, he was always there for me. He'd hold my hand and talk me through my problems.'

Once they had the doctor in custody police began examining some of Shipman's more suspicious deaths. Eventually they decided to prosecute him over 15 of these. His *modus operandi* seemed to be to target old ladies. The reasons he killed will never be known for sure. He seems at first to have carried out what he probably deemed to be 'mercy killings' of the terminally ill, then graduated to killing babies, young women, men and his speciality, elderly women. Later research carried out after his trial suggests that Shipman began killing patients as far back as 1971. Power play, the thrill of deciding who should live and who might die, seems to have motivated much of his killing; it was sufficient just to annoy Shipman for him to end someone's life, though he singled out those he thought idiots, time-wasters, irritable people and the wealthy; all were fair game for the man who liked playing God. An injection of diamorphine (basically heroin), two to four times stronger than morphine, was his weapon of choice.

On 5 October 1999 Shipman's trial began at Preston Crown Court before Mr Justice Forbes, an ex-Navy man. The doctor was charged with 15 counts of murder committed between 1995 and 1998. On 31 January 2000, after six days of deliberation, the jury found him guilty of all the killings as well as forging Mrs Grundy's will.

Back in 1957 a balding, tubby, bespectacled doctor, John Bodkin Adams, had been charged with killing 160 of his patients. Many criminologists think he was guilty, but at his trial Adams was acquitted. Six reports known as the Shipman Inquiry were chaired by Dame Janet Smith. They tried to evaluate how many people Shipman had really killed in his long career and to make recommendations to prevent further abuses of the medical system. It was finally agreed that he had murdered at least 250 patients and his biographers suggest a figure of 284 killings. Either way he is probably the biggest murderer in British criminal history (the Victorian baby killer Amelia Dyer might run him a close second).

On 13 January 2004 the doctor committed suicide in Wakefield Prison on the eve of his 58th birthday. He tied some bed sheets together and hanged himself. *The Sun* newspaper ran a headline next day, which his victims might have applauded – 'Ship, ship, hooray!' Shipman had clearly been depressed in Wakefield, possibly Britain's toughest gaol, but it also seems likely that he wanted to give his wife of 37 years, Primrose Shipman, a chance to apply for a full N.H.S. pension which, if he had reached his 60th birthday, she would have forfeited.

So it was that at the very end of the 20th century Britain's worst serial killer died by the noose, albeit by his own hand, 40 years after the last murderers hanged in England. An accident of fate perhaps, but a supremely ironic one.

Further Reading

Books

Adamson (I.). A MAN OF QUALITY A Biography of The Hon. Mr Justice Cassells. London 1964.

Anon. FAMOUS CRIMES THAT SHOCKED THE WORLD. London 1999.

Appleyard (N.). LIFE MEANS LIFE Jailed Forever. London 2009.

Beales (M.). DEAD NOT BURIED Herbert Rowse Armstrong. London 1995.

Bilton (M.). WICKED BEYOND BELIEF The Hunt For The Yorkshire Ripper. London 2003.

Blackie (D.). DEATH ON A SUMMER'S DAY The True Story of the Murder Britain Watched on Television. London 2006.

Blundell (R.) & Wilson (G.) ed. TRIAL OF BUCK RUXTON. London 1937.

Bingham (J.). THE HUNTING DOWN OF PETER MANUEL Glasgow Multiple Murderer. London 1973.

Bolitho (W.). MURDER FOR PROFT. London 1926.

Brady (I.). THE GATES OF JANUS Serial Killing and Its Analysis. Los Angeles 2011.

Briffett (D.). THE ACID BATH MURDERS. Horsham 1988.

Browne (D.) SIR TRAVERS HUMPHREYS A Biography. London 1960.

_____ & Tullett (T.). BERNARD SPILSBURY London 1941.

Burn (G.). SOMEBODY'S HUSBAND, SOMEBODY'S SON The Story of Peter Sutcliffe. London 1984.

Cannell (J.). NEW LIGHT ON THE ROUSE CASE. London 1927.

Capon (P.). THE GREAT YARMOUTH MYSTERY The Chronicle of a Famous Crime. London 1965.

Casswell (J.). A LANCE FOR LIBERTY London 1961.

Cherrill (F.). CHERRILL OF THE YARD. London 1954.

Clarkson (P.). STALKERS Disturbing True Life Stories Of Harassment, Jealousy And Obsession. London 2007.

Connell (N.). WALTER DEW The Man Who Caught Crippen. Thrupp 2005.

Cooper (W.). SHALL WE EVER KNOW? The Trial of the Hosein Brothers for the Murder of Mrs McKay. London 1971.

Creasey (J.) ed. THE MYSTERY BEDSIDE BOOK. London 1960.

Critchley (J.) ed. THE TRIAL OF NEVILLE GEORGE CLEVERLY HEATH. London 1951.

Cullen (T.). CRIPPEN The Mild Murderer. London 1977.

Dunboyne (Lord.) ed. THE TRIAL OF JOHN GEORGE HAIGH (The Acid Bath Murderer). London 1953.

Eddowes (J.). THE TWO KILLERS OF RILLINGTON PLACE. London 1994.

Elmsley (J.). THE ELEMENTS OF MURDER. Oxford 2005.

Falk (Q.). THE MUSICAL MILKMAN MURDER. London 2012.

Felstead (S.). SIR RICHARD MUIR Memoir of a Public Prosecutor. London 1927.

Fido (M.). MURDER GUIDE TO LONDON. London 1986.

Fielding (S.). HANGED AT PENTONVILLE. Stroud 2008.

Furneaux (R.). FAMOUS CRIMINAL CASES 2. London 1954.

_____ FAMOUS CRIMINAL CASES 6. London 1960.

_____ GUENTHER PODOLA. London 1960.

Gaute (J.) & Odell (R.). MURDER 'WHATDUNNIT' An Illustrated Account of the Methods of Murder. London 1982.

_____ THE NEW MURDERER'S WHO'S WHO. London 1989.

Godwin (G.) ed. THE TRIAL OF PETER GRIFFITHS (The Blackburn Baby Murderer). London 1950.

Goodman (J.) ed. THE SEASIDE MURDERS. London 1985.

_____ THE MOORS MURDERS The Trial of Myra Hindley & Ian Brady. London 1994.

Greeno (E.). WAR ON THE UNDERWORLD. London 1960.

Grout (J.) & Fisher (L.). MURDER WITHOUT MOTIVE 88 Days That Shocked a Nation. London 2009.

Guttridge (R.). DORSET MURDERS. Wimborne 1990.

Hardwick (M.). DOCTORS ON TRIAL. London 1964.

Hawkes (H.). THE CAPTURE OF THE BLACK PANTHER. London 1978.

Honeycombe (G.). THE MURDERS OF THE BLACK MUSEUM 1870–1970. London 1982.

_____ MORE MURDERS OF THE BLACK MUSEUM. London 1993.

Humphreys (T.). CRIMINAL DAYS Recollections and Reflections. London 1946.

Hyde (N.). NORMAN BIRKETT The Life of Lord Birkett of Ulverston. London 1964.

Jackson (R.). THE CHIEF The Biography of Gordon Hewart, Lord Chief Justice of England 1922–40. London 1959.

Jackson (S.). MR JUSTICE AVORY. London 1935.

_____ JOHN GEORGE HAIGH. London 1953.

Jakubait (M.) & Weller (M.). RUTH ELLIS My Sister's Secret Life. London 2005.

Jesse (F.) ed. TRIAL OF SAMUEL HERBERT DOUGAL. Edinburgh 1928.

_____ TRIAL OF SIDNEY HARRY FOX. Edinburgh 1934.

Jones (E.). THE LAST TWO TO HANG. London 1966.

Jones (R.) ed. THE MAMMOTH BOOK OF MURDER. London 1989.

Josephs (J.). HUNGERFORD One Man's Massacre. London 1994.

Jowitt (Lord.). SOME WERE SPIES. London 1955.

La Bern (A.). HAIGH The Mind of a Murderer. London 1964.

Lane (B.) ed. THE MURDER CLUB Guide To North-West England. London 1988.

_____ Guide to The Midlands. London 1988.

_____ Guide to South-East England. London 1988.

_____ Guide to London. London 1988.

_____ Guide to South-West England & Wales. London 1989.

_____ Guide to The Eastern & Home Counties. London 1989.

_____ THE 1995 MURDER YEARBOOK. London 1994.

_____ & Gregg (W.). THE ENCYCLOPAEDIA OF SERIAL KILLERS. London 1992.

Lee (C.). ONE OF YOUR OWN The Life and Death Of Myra Hindley. Edinburgh 2010.

_____ A FINE DAY FOR A HANGING. Edinburgh 2013.

Lucas (N.). THE SEX KILLERS. London 1974.

_____ & Davies (P.). THE MONSTER BUTLER. London 1979.

Lustgarten (E.). THE MURDER AND THE TRIAL. London 1960.

_____ THE JUDGES AND THE JUDGED. London 1961.

Macdougall (P.). MURDER IN KENT. London 1989.

Majoribanks (E.). THE LIFE OF SIR EDWARD MARSHALL HALL. London 1929.

Masters (B.). KILLING FOR COMPANY The Case of Dennis Nilsen. London 1985.

Morland (N.). BACKGROUND TO MURDER. London 1955.

Morton (D.). A CALENDAR OF KILLING. London 1997.

Napley (D.). MURDER AT THE VILLA MADEIRA The Rattenbury Case. London 1988.

Nash (J.). WORLD ENCYCLOPAEDIA OF 20TH CENTURY MURDER. New York 1992.

Nicol (A.). MANUEL Scotland's First Serial Killer. Edinburgh 2008.

Normanton (H.) ed. TRIAL OF ALFRED ARTHUR ROUSE. Edinburgh 1931.

Oates (J.). BUCKINGHAMSHIRE MURDERS. Thrupp 2012.

_____ JOHN CHRISTIE OF RILLINGTON PLACE. Barnsley 2012.

_____ JOHN GEORGE HAIGH A Portrait of a Serial Killer & His Victims. Barnsley 2015.

O'Connor (S.). HANDSOME BRUTE The True Story Of A Ladykiller. London 2013.

Odell (R.). EXHUMATION OF A MURDER The Life & Trial of Major Armstrong. London 1975.

_____ MURDERER'S ROW An International Murderers' Who's Who. Thrupp 2006.

Owens (A.) & Ellis (C.). KILLER CATCHERS. London 2004.

Robbins (J.). THE MAGNIFICENT SPILSBURY AND THE CASE OF THE BRIDES IN THE BATH. London 2010.

Rose (A.). LETHAL WITNESS Sir Bernard Spilsbury. Chalford 2007.

Rowland (J.). POISONER IN THE DOCK. London 1960.

Selwyn (F.). NOTHING BUT REVENGE The Case of Bentley & Craig. London 1991.

Shore (W.) ed. TRIAL OF FREDERIC GUY BROWNE AND WILLIAM HENRY KENNEDY. Edinburgh 1930.

Simpson (K.). FORTY YEARS OF MURDER An Autobiography. London 1978.

Skelton (D.). BLOOD ON THE THISTLE A Casebook Of 20th Century Scottish Murder. Edinburgh 1992.

Smith (D.). SUPPER WITH THE CRIPPENS. London 2005.

Sounes (H.). FRED & ROSE The Full Story Of Fred & Rose West And The Gloucester House Of Horrors. London 1995.

Thomas (D.). THE ENEMY WITHIN Hucksters, Racketeers, Deserters, and Civilians During The Second World War. New York 2004.

_____ VILLAIN'S PARADISE Britain's Underworld from the Spivs to the Krays. London 2005.

Thurlow (D.). THE ESSEX TRIANGLE Four Decades of Violence and Mayhem in A Sleepy Pocket of Rural England. London 1990.

Trow (M.). THE WIGWAM MURDER. London 1994.

Tullett (T.). CLUES TO MURDER Famous Forensic Cases of Professor J. M. Cameron. London 1987.

Wade (S.). SQUARE MILE BOBBIES The City Of London Police 1839–2009. Thrupp 2009.

Wallace (E.) ed. THE TRIAL OF HERBERT JOHN BENNETT (The Yarmouth Beach Murder). London 1929.

Wansell (F.). AN EVIL LOVE. London 1996.

Watson (E.) ed. TRIAL OF GEORGE JOSEPH SMITH. Edinburgh 1922.

Wensley ((F.). FORTY YEARS OF SCOTLAND YARD The Record Of A Lifetime Of Service In The Criminal Investigation Department. New York 1931.

Whittle (B.) & Ritchie (J.). HAROLD SHIPMAN Prescription for Murder. London 2004.

Wilkes (R.). BLOOD RELATIONS Jeremy Bamber and the White House Farm Murders. London 1994.

Wilson (C.). THE MAMMOTH BOOK OF TRUE CRIME. London 1988.

_____ WRITTEN IN BLOOD A History Of Forensic Detection. London 1989.

_____ THE MAMMOTH BOOK OF TRUE CRIME 2. London 1990.

_____ & Pitman (P.). ENCYCLOPAEDIA OF MURDER. London 1961.

_____ & Seaman (D.). ENCYCLOPAEDIA OF MODERN MURDER 1962–1983. London 1983.

_____ THE SERIAL KILLERS A Study Of the Psychology of Violence. London 1990.

Wilson (P.). MURDERESS A Study Of The Women Executed In Britain Since 1843. London 1971.

_____ CHILDREN WHO KILL. London 1973.

Yallop (D.). DELIVER US FROM EVIL. London 1981.

Young (F.) ed. TRIAL OF THE SEDDONS. Edinburgh 1922.

_____ TRIAL OF HERBERT ROWSE ARMSTRONG. Edinburgh 1927.

Young (W.). OBSESSIVE POISONER The Strange Story of Graham Young. London 1973.

Websites

www.murderpedia.org
www.real-crime.co.uk
www.murder-uk.com
www.britishexecutions.co.uk
www.blackkalendar.nl
www.truecrimelibrary.com
www.wikipedia.org

Newspapers

Daily Mirror
News of the World
Daily Telegraph